Financing Entrepreneurship and Innovation in Emerging Markets

Financing Entrepreneurship and Innovation in Emerging Markets

Lourdes Casanova
Director, Emerging Markets Institute
Samuel Curtis Johnson Graduate School of Management
Cornell University, Ithaca, NY, United States

Peter Klaus Cornelius
Research Fellow, Emerging Markets Institute
Samuel Curtis Johnson Graduate School of Management
Cornell University, Ithaca, NY, United States

Soumitra Dutta
Dean, Cornell SC Johnson College of Business
Cornell University, Ithaca, NY, United States

ACADEMIC PRESS
An imprint of Elsevier

Academic Press is an imprint of Elsevier
125 London Wall, London EC2Y 5AS, United Kingdom
525 B Street, Suite 1800, San Diego, CA 92101-4495, United States
50 Hampshire Street, 5th Floor, Cambridge, MA 02139, United States
The Boulevard, Langford Lane, Kidlington, Oxford OX5 1GB, United Kingdom

Library of Congress Cataloging-in-Publication Data
A catalog record for this book is available from the Library of Congress

British Library Cataloguing-in-Publication Data
A catalogue record for this book is available from the British Library

ISBN 978-0-12-804025-6

For information on all Academic Press publications
visit our website at https://www.elsevier.com/books-and-journals

Working together
to grow libraries in
developing countries

www.elsevier.com • www.bookaid.org

Publisher: Janco Candice
Acquisition Editor: J. Scott Bentley
Editorial Project Manager: Susan Ikeda
Production Project Manager: Punithavathy Govindaradjane
Cover Designer: Matthew Limbert

Typeset by SPi Global, India

In Praise of *Financing Entrepreneurship and Innovation in Emerging Markets*

"This book explores in depth the existing conditions, challenges and opportunities for driving innovation and entrepreneurship in the developing world with relevant examples of successful ventures from India and China, two of the biggest emerging economies in the world. It dexterously guides us to appreciate the nuances of the financial frameworks that are shaping the entrepreneurial ecosystems in emerging markets vis-à-vis developed economies. Expanding on the learnings from the Global Innovation Index, the book seamlessly complements its policy suggestions, and adds valuable insights and inferences to this body of work. An important read for policy makers, scholars and entrepreneurs across economies."

Chandrajit Banerjee, Director General, Confederation of Indian Industry

"Well researched and illuminating. A must read for serious investors exploring private investments outside the US."

Andrew Boyd, Head of Global Equity Capital Markets, Fidelity Investments

"The authors provide a detailed and nuanced analysis of how innovation in developing economies is shaping the global economy. While it is common knowledge that most future economic growth will happen outside the G-20, there has been little research on the details of how this will occur. *Financing Entrepreneurship and Innovation in Emerging Markets* collects what we know about entrepreneurial finance in emerging economies and combines this with a more established body of knowledge in developed economies to help the reader understand the future path of financing innovative businesses throughout the world. The authors demystify the interaction between factors of production, financing activity, and policy to provide a clear picture of how transformational entrepreneurship will drive growth in emerging economies."

Gregory W. Brown, Professor and Director, Frank H. Kenan Institute of Private Enterprise, Research Director, Institute for Private Capital, Sarah Graham Kenan Distinguished Scholar of Finance, The University of North Carolina at Chapel Hill

"*Financing Entrepreneurship and Innovation in Emerging Markets* is a must read for entrepreneurs, investors and policy makers that are looking to understand how innovation and new technologies are influencing emerging countries and how access to financing plays a fundamental role in this respect. It is a must read for any player on the emerging market tech scene."

Adalberto Flores, Co-Founder & CEO at Kueski

"Fascinating, important and necessary for policymakers, businessmen, entrepreneurs, financiers, investors, career planners, jobseekers, and anyone interested in emerging markets and economic and financial development."

Timothy Heyman, CBE, President, Franklin Templeton Asset Management, Mexico

"As entrepreneurship and innovation in China have been promoted to the national strategic level, understanding their underlying drivers has attracted more and more attention at home and abroad. This book offers unique and refreshing insights into the role of entrepreneurship and the financing of innovation in China and other emerging market countries. While the book is research-oriented, it is written in a way that makes it accessible to a broader audience. It's a book well worth reading!"

Liao Li, Professor and Executive Associate Dean,
PBC School of Finance, Tsinghua University

"In the digital economy, there are opportunities and risks for developing countries: the opportunity to use technology to leapfrog in terms of social and economic development and the risk of falling behind with wider gaps and exclusions. This book addresses a key issue to realize the opportunities for emerging countries - strengthening local innovation ecosystems to use local talent to succeed in the new economy."

Diego Molano, Former Information Technology Minister of Colombia

"This seminal work provides the most comprehensive look yet into the forces driving the pace of entrepreneurial activity and innovation in emerging economies, and importantly, the critical role efficient capital formation can play in accelerating it."

Shawn Munday, Professor of the Practice of Finance and Executive Director of the
Institute for Private Capital, The University of North Carolina at Chapel Hill

"Casanova, Cornelius and Dutta provide a comprehensive and expert account of the role that innovation and technology play in spurring growth in emerging markets, with special emphasis on India and China. The book is essential reading for anyone who wishes to understand how changes in financial markets can help promote entrepreneurship in these markets"

David T. Robinson, Professor of Finance, J. Rex Fuqua Professor of International Management, Fuqua School of Business, Duke University Faculty Research Associate, National Bureau of Economic Research

Contents

Foreword   xv
Acknowledgments   xix

1. Introduction   1

    1.1 Technological Progress and Economic Development   3
    1.2 Innovation and the Role of Transformational Entrepreneurship   5
    1.3 Entrepreneurship and the Quality of the Business Environment   7
    1.4 The Origins of Transformational Entrepreneurs   10
    1.5 Financing Entrepreneurship   13
    1.6 Structure of the Book   15
         References   26

Part I

Global Innovation Competitiveness

2. Global Innovation Competitiveness: How Emerging
    Economies Compare   31

    2.1 Measuring Innovation   32
    2.2 The Global Innovation Index   33
         2.2.1 Stability at the Top   35
         2.2.2 Innovation is Becoming More Global but Divides
                Remain   35
         2.2.3 High-Quality Innovation Continues to Matter, and
                China is Catching up   39
         2.2.4 Top Performers by Income Group   41
         2.2.5 Clustering Leaders, Innovation Achievers, and
                Underperformers   42
    2.3 Specific Characteristics of Innovation Systems in Emerging
         Countries   45
    2.4 Tailoring Innovation Policies to the Needs of Developing
         Countries   47
    2.5 Conclusion   50
         Appendix: The Global Innovation Index (GII) Conceptual
                 Framework   51
         The Rationale for the Global Innovation Index   51

An Inclusive Perspective on Innovation 51
The GII Conceptual Framework 52
The Innovation Input Subindex 52
References 67

3. **The Impact of Science and Technology Policies on Rapid Economic Development in China** 69
   3.1 Overview 69
   3.2 **Four Phases of China's S&T Policy Evolution** 70
       3.2.1 The Experimental Phase (1978–85) 70
       3.2.2 The Systemic Reform Phase (1985–95) 71
       3.2.3 The Deepening Reform Phase (1996–2006) 72
       3.2.4 Long-term Plan and Policy Optimization (2006–14) 72
   3.3 **Outcomes and Analysis of S&T Reform** 73
       3.3.1 S&T and R&D Investment 73
       3.3.2 Innovation Results: Patents, Products, and Research Publications 74
       3.3.3 Science Education 76
       3.3.4 Cultivation of an R&D Workforce 77
   3.4 **What Other Countries can Learn From China** 77
   3.5 **What China can Learn From Other Countries** 78
   3.6 **The Latest Reforms** 79
       References 80

4. **Tencent: A Giant Asserting Dominance** 81
   4.1 **Milestones** 82
       4.1.1 Finding Its Identity 82
       4.1.2 Funding Its Ambitions 83
       4.1.3 Expanding Its Potential 83
       4.1.4 Venture Capital Investments 84
   4.2 **Internationalization** 88
       4.2.1 Patent Applications—An Early Effort to go Global 89
       4.2.2 WeChat as a Tool for Internationalization 89
       4.2.3 Investment in Gaming to Expand Global Footprint 89
   4.3 **China's Innovation Ecosystem** 90
   4.4 **Tencent's Connected Universe and Unique Business Model** 93
       4.4.1 Gaming 94
       4.4.2 Messaging and Social Networking 94
   4.5 **Supporting Businesses** 95
       4.5.1 Search Engine and Email 96
       4.5.2 Software and Apps 96
       4.5.3 Online-to-Offline (O2O) Services 96
       4.5.4 Payment Platforms 96
       4.5.5 Entertainment Platforms 97
   4.6 **Unique Business Model** 97
   4.7 **Factors Contributing to Success** 100
       4.7.1 Innovation in Products and Services 100
       4.7.2 Strong Leadership 100

4.8	Chinese Market and Possibilities	**102**
	4.8.1 Growth of the Middle Class	102
	4.8.2 Young Population	104
	4.8.3 Shift to e-Commerce	104
4.9	Protected Environment	**104**
	4.9.1 Collaborative Competition	105
	4.9.2 Tencent and Baidu Against Alibaba	105
	4.9.3 Tencent and Alibaba Against Baidu	106
4.10	Challenges	**106**
	4.10.1 Challenges in Taking WeChat Global	107
	4.10.2 Challenges in the Gaming Business	108
	4.10.3 Challenges Faced in U.S. Market	108
4.11	The Future	**109**
	Appendix	**110**
	References	**114**

5. **Policies to Drive Innovation in India** **117**

5.1	The Evolving Policy Landscape and Research and Development Growth	118
5.2	Review of GII Findings and Pillars, and Their Impact on India's Ranking	119
5.3	Strengths and Weaknesses of India's Innovation Performance	121
	5.3.1 Top Indian Universities	121
	5.3.2 Publication Citations	121
	5.3.3 Mobile Networks, Information Technology, and Broadband	122
	5.3.4 Gross Capital Formation and Market Capitalization	124
	5.3.5 Small- and Medium-Sized Enterprises	124
	5.3.6 Intellectual Property Rights	125
	5.3.7 Access to Higher Education	127
5.4	Conclusions and the Way Forward	127
	References	130

6. **Flipkart and the Race to the Top of Indian e-Commerce** **133**

6.1	Flipkart Today	134
6.2	Early Years and Funding	135
6.3	Becoming a Unicorn	135
	6.3.1 Customer Focus	137
	6.3.2 Introduction of Mobile Phones and Cash on Delivery	137
	6.3.3 Introduction of Mobile Phones, Music, and Movies	138
	6.3.4 Investment in Own Supply Chain	138
	6.3.5 Branding	138
	6.3.6 Expansion into Fashion and Lifestyle Products	139
6.4	External Motivators: A Supporting Environment in India	139
	6.4.1 Availability of FDI	139
	6.4.2 Increasing Youth and Working-age Population	139
	6.4.3 Growing Economy	140

	6.4.4	Global Shift to e-Commerce	140
	6.4.5	Indians Embracing e-Commerce	141
	6.4.6	Innovation Ecosystem	142
6.5		Amazon's Entry	142
6.6		Regulation Affecting Indian e-Commerce	142
6.7		Competitive Landscape in Indian e-Commerce	143
6.8		Flipkart's Response to the Changing e-Commerce Landscape	146
	6.8.1	Change in Business Model Through Launch of Marketplace	147
	6.8.2	Acquisition of Myntra	148
	6.8.3	The Billion-Dollar Round of Funding	148
	6.8.4	First Signs of Trouble	148
	6.8.5	Misstep of Going App-Only	149
	6.8.6	Fall in Valuation	149
	6.8.7	Ownership and Management Changes	149
	6.8.8	Developing Its Own Business Model	150
6.9		The Way Forward	150
	6.9.1	Game Theory—War of Attrition	151
	6.9.2	New Entry/Consolidation	151
	6.9.3	Impact of Future Policy Changes	153
		Appendix	154
		References	155

Part II

Financing Entrepreneurship

7.		Banks, Credit Constraints, and the Financial Technology's Evolving Role	161
	7.1	Entrepreneurship and Finance	163
	7.2	Credit Constraints and the Role of Banks	166
	7.3	Microcredit	170
	7.4	Financial Technology and Marketplace Lending	173
	7.5	Conclusions	181
		References	182

8.		Technology Startups, Innovation, and the Market for Venture Capital	185
	8.1	What Do Venture Capitalists Do?	187
	8.2	Industry Focus and the Role of Venture Capital in Fostering Innovation	193
	8.3	Exporting the VC Model: The Emergence of VC Hotbeds in China and India	197
	8.4	E-Commerce and the Role of the Internet	202
	8.5	The Next Frontier	209
	8.6	Conclusions	211
		Appendix	212
		References	215

9.   **Corporate Venture Capital**   **219**
      9.1   The Size and Evolution of the CVC Market   221
            9.1.1   Market Size   221
            9.1.2   Corporate Venture Cycles   223
      9.2   Organizational Forms of Corporate Venturing   226
      9.3   How Successful is Corporate Venturing?   229
      9.4   Corporate Venturing in Emerging Markets   232
      9.5   Conclusions   236
            References   **237**

10.   **Noninstitutional Forms of Entrepreneurial Finance:
      Angel Investments, Accelerators, and Equity
      Crowdfunding**   **239**
      10.1 Early-Stage Funding and Angel Investors   240
            10.1.1 What Do Angel Investors Do?   240
            10.1.2 Size of the Market for Angel Investments   244
            10.1.3 Angel Financing's Impact   247
      10.2 Accelerators   249
            10.2.1 Basic Characteristics   249
            10.2.2 How Successful are Accelerator Programs?   251
      10.3 Crowd Investing   252
            10.3.1 The Business Model of Crowd Investing   252
            10.3.2 Market Size and the Role of Regulation   256
      10.4 Conclusions   260
            References   **261**

11.   **The Role of Government**   **263**
      11.1 Market Failures and the Rationale for Government
            Intervention   265
      11.2 Institutional Reform Aiming to Create an Active
            VC Market   267
      11.3 Public Funding of Entrepreneurship   272
            11.3.1 Government Loans and Loan Guarantees   272
            11.3.2 The Government as Venture Capitalist   274
            11.3.3 Government-Sponsored Business Accelerators and
                    Incubators   278
            11.3.4 The Role of Public Pension Funds and SWFs   280
      11.4 Entrepreneurial Finance Provided by Development Finance
            Institutions and Multilateral Organizations   282
      11.5 Conclusions   283
            Appendix   **284**
            References   **293**

Index   295

Foreword

Innovation is the key driver of long-term economic growth, increasing per capita income in both advanced and emerging economies and supporting their economic and social goals. At the OECD, our analysis clearly shows that young dynamic firms—in essence, the risk-taking entrepreneurs with high growth potential—contribute disproportionately to job creation. Across 21 OECD countries and non-OECD economies, on average, firms 5 years old or younger account for only 21% of total employment but are responsible for 47% of job creation.[1] They are also more likely to experiment with disruptive technologies and business models. Policymakers should work to provide these firms with a conducive business environment, enabling resources to flow to them and allowing them to test their ideas in the marketplace.

This is all the more important as new digital technologies take center stage in our economies and societies. The digital era is gathering pace, including in emerging economies. Between 2014 and 2020, an additional 1.1 billion individuals will acquire a mobile phone for the first time. Both China and India will soon have more internet users than the entire population of the United States and Western Europe combined. The sharing economy, enabled by smart apps, is expected to reach a global value of USD 335 billion by 2025.[2]

Successfully harnessing technological change and creating or implementing new or improved products, processes, and business models matters not only for growth but also for health, the environment, and a range of other policy objectives which underlie the well-being of citizens. Countries at all levels of development stand to gain from building the capacity and the financing models needed to make innovation and entrepreneurship drivers of inclusive growth.

Innovation can contribute to inclusive growth via more affordable products and services of higher quality, as well as new products and services that address the challenges of those facing social disadvantage. Moreover, digital technologies are offering opportunities for entrepreneurs to gain greater access to markets at relatively low cost, and even to internationalize, enabling them to grow and reach scale—with all the attendant benefits for their communities. This is

---

1. OECD (DynEmp) Database on Employment Dynamics, https://www.oecd.org/sti/ind/Policy-Note-No-Country-For-Young-Firms.pdf.
2. OECD Science, Technology and Innovation Outlook 2016 Highlights, p. 2.

particularly critical for emerging economies, where fostering entrepreneurship and small businesses will prove essential to catch up with high-income countries.

This book is an important step in that direction, providing a helpful tool for policymakers in diverse emerging economies to design, develop, and deliver the right policy settings. It asks vital questions about the dynamic process of innovation, the role of entrepreneurs, and the challenges they face, particularly in accessing effective financing.

It also comes at a crucial time when the innovation map is being redrawn. Over a third of public research carried out globally takes place in non-OECD economies.[3] China is now the second largest funder of R&D, behind the United States, but remarkably ahead of the European Union, accounting for over 20% of global gross R&D expenditure, compared to around 5% at the turn of the millennium. This increase is in contrast to the OECD's share of global gross expenditure on R&D (GERD), which has fallen from over 90% around the year 2000 to just over 70% at the last count.[4]

Nevertheless, evidence strongly suggests that insufficient access to external finance represents one of the most binding constraints for enterprises to start up and grow in emerging economies.[5] Many SMEs, especially those operating in the informal sector, are fully or partially excluded from the formal financial system. Their reliance on internal revenues and informal sources of external finance—which are usually very expensive—considerably limits their growth and innovation potential.

Innovative fast-growing ventures in particular face financing problems. Given their risk profile, external equity (rather than debt) financing is often most suited to their needs but difficult to access.[6] A lack of risk capital that constrains the growth ambitions of such dynamic firms at the micro level can translate into macroeconomic effects such as lower growth. By some estimates, the SME equity gap averages around 3% of GDP in European economies and could be much greater in developing and emerging economies,[7] which often lack an established business angel and venture capitalist community and where capital markets are relatively underdeveloped. With the contribution these firms make to jobs and R&D investments, their difficulties in attracting sufficient and appropriate sources of financing can hold back countries' efforts to catch up and turn into "knowledge-based" economies. Governments have been increasing their policy support for equity finance for SMEs. For example, in October 2016, Brazil simplified the tax regime for investors in startups and eliminated the risk for investors to be held personally liable in case of a bankruptcy. Or to provide another example, Malaysia was one of the first countries in the world to adopt a specific regulatory framework for equity investments.[8]

3. OECD Science, Technology and Innovation Outlook 2016 Highlights, p. 10.
4. OECD Science, Technology and Innovation Outlook 2016, p. 130.
5. OECD (2017), Financing SMEs and Entrepreneurs 2017: An OECD Scoreboard.
6. OECD (2015), New Approaches to SME and Entrepreneurship Financing: Broadening the Range of Instruments.
7. OECD (2018), Fostering Markets for SME Finance: Matching Business and Investor Needs, forthcoming.
8. OECD (2018), Financing SMEs and Entrepreneurs 2017: An OECD Scoreboard, forthcoming.

In this context, the digital economy offers both opportunities and challenges, especially the rise of fintech with its potential to fill financing gaps left by traditional financial firms. Digital banking, innovation in digital payments, peer-to-peer lending and investment platforms, and currency exchanges can offer financial services to the underbanked and underserviced in advanced as well as emerging economies. Such financial innovation has the potential to enhance economic productivity and ultimately foster a more inclusive and resilient financial system with positive spill-overs for economic growth. However these also come with risks and challenges that have to be anticipated. For example, such innovations introduce additional cyber resilience and digital security vulnerabilities that could undermine their benefits. There are also risks to inclusiveness: data analytics and credit scorings may result in the exclusion of the most vulnerable households.

These challenges not only need to be addressed at the level of fintech service providers but also require regulatory and other policy responses. The G20/OECD High-Level Principles on SME Financing provide a comprehensive framework for improving SME access to finance, which can be implemented by governments at all levels of development. Policymakers may play a key role in unlocking the benefits of financial innovation, while seeking to safeguard a level playing field for market participants, consumer and investor confidence and trust, and overall resilience in the financial system.[9] More broadly, the OECD's "Going Digital" project recognizes that many countries are at a pivotal moment in harnessing the digital transformation for growth and well-being. A coherent whole-of-government approach is critical if we are to maximize the benefits of our increasingly digitalized global economy. We are actively working to provide evidence-based guidance so that the digital transformation can be inclusive and foster more vibrant economies and societies.

Despite the generally accepted importance attached to entrepreneurship, finance, and innovation, the authors rightfully acknowledge that there remain formidable knowledge gaps. These are especially acute in developing countries given the often-observed paucity of reliable statistics on these crucial drivers of development. We believe that this study provides an important step forward in furthering our understanding on the linkages between SMEs and entrepreneurs, their access to finance, and their contribution to R&D and innovation. The OECD will continue to work closely with the academic community; with the private and public sectors; and with all stakeholders to help emerging and developed countries to design, develop, and deliver better innovation and entrepreneurship policies for better lives.

Angel Gurria
OECD Secretary-General

---

9. See the G20/OECD High-Level Principles on SME Financing, https://www.oecd.org/finance/G20-OECD-High-Level-%20Principles-on-SME-Financing.pdf.

Acknowledgments

There are many people to whom we owe a debt of gratitude. First and foremost, we are extremely grateful to the research team of the Global Innovation Index; their work has motivated our project and provided essential input for this study. Specifically, we would like to thank Francis Gurry, the Director General of the World Intellectual Property Organization (WIPO); the coeditors of the Global Innovation Index Report, Bruno Lanvin (INSEAD) and Sacha Wunsch-Vincent (WIPO); and key members of the team producing the research, Rafael Escalona Reynoso and Jordan Litner (Cornell University), Carsten Fink and Francesca Guadagno (WIPO), and Michaela Saisana (European Commission).

We are also indebted to many people at the Emerging Markets Institute at the SC Johnson College of Business at Cornell University. Over the past few years, we had numerous discussions with our colleagues who influenced and sharpened our thinking about innovation and the financing of entrepreneurship in emerging economies. Mentioning all of them would result in a very long list, and there is a material risk that we would miss several of those who have directly or indirectly contributed to this book. However, we wish to thank a number of Cornell University students for their outstanding research assistance, namely Devesh Verma who played an important role in preparing the case studies on Flipkart and Tencent by contributing strategic insights and qualitative analysis, as well as Yangyang Zhang, Momo Bi, Mario M. Saravia, Daryl Lwin, Maximillian A. Kaye, Steven Zhong Ren, Luna Cui, Deeksha Gupta, and Eudes Lopes. We are very grateful to all of them. Furthermore, we would like to acknowledge the very capable research support from the staff of the Management Library at the SC Johnson College of Business at Cornell University, in particular Susan F. Kendrick.

Several people have read the entire manuscript or parts of it and provided invaluable comments and suggestions. From the academy, we would like to thank especially Gregory Brown (Frank Hawkins Kenan Institute of Private Enterprise, University of North Carolina), Robert Harris (Darden School, University of Virginia), Roger Leeds (Johns Hopkins University), Stefan Morkötter (St. Gallen Institute of Management in Asia), Shawn Munday (Kenan-Flagler Business School, University of North Carolina), David Robinson (Fuqua School of Business, Duke University), and Nang Wang (Columbia Business School). We also received similarly important comments from members of the investment community, especially Erik Bosman (formerly FMO), Andrew Boyd (Fidelity), Adalberto Flores (Kueski), and Brooks Preston (formerly OPIC).

We have benefited from numerous focused discussions about specific topic areas. These include conversations with Monel Amin, Mandar Jadhav, and Heidi Thompson (Digital Vault), Dietmar Harhoff (Max Planck Institute for Innovation and Competition), Sabrina Howell (Stern School of Business, New York University), Victoria Ivashina and Josh Lerner (Harvard Business School), Steven N. Kaplan (Booth School of Business, University of Chicago), Roni Michaely and Douglas Stayman (Cornell Tech), Nuresh Sushani (RealAssets), and Eli Talmor (London Business School).

Furthermore, we had the opportunity to present some of the findings of this book at various workshops, seminars, and conferences. These provided a great opportunity for conversations with friends and colleagues, whose views are reflected in this study. In particular, we would like to note the annual conferences of the Emerging Markets Institute, presentations at Cornell Tech and at the Institute for Private Capital Winter Research Symposium in Jackson Hole in 2016.

At Elsevier, our editor, Scott Bentley, our editorial project manager, Susan Ikeda, and our production project manager, Punithavathy Govindaradjane, provided ongoing support and encouragement. We likewise thank our copyeditor Jennifer Wholey who ensured that the outcome of this project is a single book as opposed to a collection of different essays.

Finally, we would like to acknowledge financial support we received from the SC Johnson College of Business at Cornell University for which we are extremely grateful.

Chapter 1

Introduction

Most economic historians will remember the Global Financial Crisis of 2008–2009 as the deepest recession since the Great Depression. However, this period is also memorable for another reason: for the first time in history, emerging market and developing economies contributed more to global output as measured in purchasing power parity (PPP) terms than advanced economies (International Monetary Fund, 2017). Since then, emerging and developing economies have further increased their share of world Gross Domestic Product (GDP), and according to the IMF (2017), emerging economies could account for as much as 60% of world GDP by 2020. This process has been led by the four largest emerging economies—Brazil, Russia, India, and China (the BRICs)[1]—which together could overtake the combined GDP of the G7—the seven largest advanced economies—by 2035 (Goldman Sachs, 2003).

In most, but not all, emerging economies, rising living standards have accompanied the catch-up process relative to standards of advanced economies. In South Korea, for instance, real GDP per capita in 1980 amounted to only around 17% of the level in the United States (Fig. 1.1). In the subsequent decades, the per capita income gap narrowed progressively, prompting international organizations such as the IMF to reclassify South Korea as an advanced economy.[2] By 2016, South Korea's relative level of prosperity reached 67% of the United States', and IMF projections suggest that this catch-up process could continue in the future. Similarly, while China's per capita income is estimated to have amounted to just 2% relative to the United States in 1980, in 2016, the country's level of prosperity reached 27% of the U.S. benchmark.

Projections such as Goldman Sachs Group Inc's study on "Dreaming with BRICs," which received huge attention in both the investor community and policy circles, are based on the assumption that emerging economies will continue to enjoy rapid productivity growth. This growth will require continued technological progress, which, as we know from Abramowitz's (1956) and Solow's (1957) seminal contributions to the economic growth literature, explains the lion's share of economic growth. As these and subsequent studies have shown, today's advanced economies would not have been able to achieve their high

---

[1] As of 2010, BRICs has become BRICS, including South Africa as the fifth emerging country.
[2] Note, however, that South Korea was still included in the MSCI Emerging Markets Index as of June 1, 2017.

Financing Entrepreneurship and Innovation in Emerging Markets.
https://doi.org/10.1016/B978-0-12-804025-6.00001-0

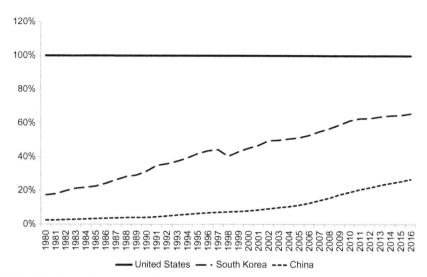

FIG. 1.1   Per-capita incomes relative to the United States. Note: Per-capita income based on purchasing power parity. *(Source: Authors, based on data from IMF WEO database, accessed 4/27/17.)*

income levels without rapid technological change.[3] Their experience suggests that today's emerging economies will be unable to narrow and eventually close their per-capita income gaps vis-à-vis richer countries unless they continuously innovate.

While it is generally accepted that countries that rely primarily on increasing the number of inputs will fail to achieve sustained economic growth, there is considerable debate about the underlying drivers of innovation (Furman et al., 2002). This debate centers around the various influences on the pace of technological change and the changing role innovation plays as developing countries catch up and achieve higher levels of economic prosperity. Similarly, while few would dispute the importance of entrepreneurship as a driver of technological progress, most of what we know in this area is based on research on developed markets. The extent to which this knowledge applies to rapidly growing emerging economies is an open question. Finally, there is substantial evidence that lack of financial resources is a significant impediment for entrepreneurship and innovation in advanced economies and to an even greater extent in emerging markets. While this evidence concentrates on traditional sources of funding, especially bank lending, research is struggling to keep pace with rapidly evolving

---

[3] In the U.S., per capita income was around $3000 in 1870 (in 2009 dollars), broadly comparable with today's per capita income levels (converted at market exchange rates) in Indonesia, Morocco and Tunisia. In 2016, the U.S.' income level per capita reached almost $52,000. During this same period, the country's population octupled to 320 million people. Source: Based on data from Johnson & Williamson. Online database. What Was the U.S. GDP then? https://www.measuringworth.com/usgdp/. Accessed 5/16/17.

forms of finance, such as angel investing, crowdfunding, accelerators and incubators, and venture capital (VC).

The main objective of this book is to shed more light on the nexus of technological change, entrepreneurship, and the finance of innovation in emerging economies. What determines the innovative process in emerging economies and hence the speed at which they can grow? What role do entrepreneurial startups play in this process, and what does the cross-country analysis tell us about the conditions under which entrepreneurship can thrive? And to what extent could new funding sources and new forms of financial intermediation alleviate the constraints startup entrepreneurs in emerging economies often fail to overcome? The answers to these questions will inform the perspectives of all players involved—innovators and entrepreneurs, financiers, and policy makers.

We are under no illusions that any discussion of these critical issues can be more than preliminary, as we are severely handicapped by the limited availability of data. Reliable data about entrepreneurial finance and its role for innovation is already hard to come by in the United States and other advanced economies, and much harder to track and analyze in emerging economies. These difficulties should not excuse neglecting one of the most profound challenges facing emerging economies as they catch up to richer countries. In fact, echoing Roger Leeds (2015), the "... formidable data gaps provide additional motivation for writing this book," which could hopefully serve "as a catalyst for better data collection and encourages others to pursue similar research."

In this sense, this book should be seen as an effort to summarize what we believe we know. As the saying goes, without data, you are just another person with an opinion. Due to the limitations of the data, many of our observations and conclusions are preliminary and remain subject to important changes as more and better data become available. As long as this book helps to shift—no matter how little—the balance from unsubstantiated opinions to a more evidence-based analysis, we feel we have succeeded.

The rest of this chapter proceeds as follows: First, we provide a brief introduction to the key issues we shall discuss in this book—the dynamic process of innovation as a function of a country's stage of economic development, the role of transformational entrepreneurs in driving innovation, and the challenges entrepreneurs face in financing innovative startups. In the latter section, we provide a brief summary of each chapter of the book.

1.1   TECHNOLOGICAL PROGRESS AND ECONOMIC DEVELOPMENT

Technological progress as it affects innovation is often associated with radically new products and production processes, a view that is largely U.S.- or OECD-centric.[4] However, as Porter (1990) argues, a broader concept of innovation is

---

[4] Organization for Economic Co-operation and Development.

needed to understand how emerging economies, which operate far away from the global technology frontier, grow and narrow their income gap against advanced economies. Porter distinguishes three development phases, each of which exhibits different competitiveness drivers. In the initial phase, economic growth is based on a country's factor endowments, primarily unskilled labor and natural resources (factor-driven stage). As wages rise in the development process, companies must begin to develop more efficient production methods and increase product quality. At this stage, sustaining economic growth increasingly hinges on a country's technological readiness, that is, the ability of firms to harness the benefits of existing technologies and innovate by adopting new technologies from abroad and improving on them (efficiency-driven stage).

In the final (technology-driven) stage of economic development, higher wages and the associated standard of living can be sustained only if companies are able to compete through innovation, producing new and different goods using the most sophisticated production processes. According to Porter (1990), successful economic development may thus be understood as a process of successive upgrading, in which businesses and their supporting environments coevolve, to foster increasingly sophisticated production and competition. Countries that fail to manage the wholesale transformation of dimensions involving both the public and private sectors usually got stuck at critical junctures of economic transition—between the factor-driven and efficiency-based stages, or between the efficiency-based and innovation-driven stages. There are several examples of countries that enjoyed significant economic progress for a period but then appeared to stall in their development. Few countries have reached the innovation-driven stage, suggesting that this transition is particularly critical.

As countries progress through the different developmental stages, their companies are likely to incorporate technical and design specifications as well as performance features into their products and services that are closer to those of the most advanced in the global market, perhaps eventually matching products that are on or near the international product technology frontier (Bell and Figueiredo, 2013). At the same time, companies within those countries improve their capability to generate and manage change in the use of technologies. This allows developing countries to move from positions of technology imitation to modest forms of innovation, potentially proceeding further to engage directly and creatively in innovation activities at the international frontier.[5] Finally, companies may employ growing innovation capabilities to create unique competitive positions in low-income markets on the basis of "new" products that are

---

[5] A well-documented example is South Korea, whose corporate sector includes a non-trivial number of firms that have emerged as global technology leaders (Joo and Lee, 2009; Kim, 1997; Lim and Lee, 2001). These firms are behind South Korea's rapid catch-up process that has narrowed the country's per-capita income gap vis-à-vis the United States to around 33% (Fig. 1.1). Another example is China, whose companies are increasingly moving from imitation to innovation (Yip and McKern, 2016).

less technologically complex than equivalent products produced by firms in advanced countries.

Reflecting the changing role of technology in different stages of development, the Organisation for Economic Co-operation and Development (2005) Oslo Manual's definition is much broader than research and development (R&D)-driven inventions. Instead, the OECD's definition of innovation encompasses the implementation of a new or significantly improved product (good or service) or process, a new marketing method, or new organizational method in business practices, workplace organization, or external relations. While all innovation must contain a degree of novelty, according to the Manual an innovation can be (i) new to the firm, (ii) new to the market, or (iii) new to the world. The first concept covers the diffusion of an existing innovation that may already have been implemented by other firms to a new firm. Innovations are new to the market when the firm is the first to introduce the innovation on its market. An innovation is new to the world when the firm is the first to introduce the innovation for all markets and industries.

The Oslo Manual's definition of innovation provides the basis for the Global Innovation Index (GII), the world's most comprehensive attempt to rank a large sample of countries according to their innovative capacity and identify particular strengths and challenges in individual economies. The GII aims to determine where countries stand in their development process relative to their peers and in which areas particular attention is required to foster innovation and the resulting economic growth. As an invaluable source for policy makers and companies alike, the GII represents the natural starting point for this book, which, combined with special case studies on individual countries and companies within these countries, provides important insights into the role of technology and innovation in economic development.

1.2   INNOVATION AND THE ROLE OF TRANSFORMATIONAL ENTREPRENEURSHIP

Innovation and creative destruction require entrepreneurs who develop new technologies, introduce more efficient production processes, and push out unproductive incumbents. Creative entrepreneurs are typically behind the most dynamic and productive companies, which innovate, expand production, and create employment opportunities at a comparatively rapid rate. To be sure, not every new small business is entrepreneurial or represents entrepreneurship according to this definition. Is a person who opens another delicatessen store or another Mexican restaurant in the American suburb an entrepreneur? Drucker argues against such a definition (Drucker, 1985). Although that business owner takes a risk, they create neither a new satisfaction nor new consumer demand. In contrast, in Drucker's assessment, McDonald's was highly entrepreneurial. While burgers had been known for a long time, McDonald's Corp. applied new management concepts and techniques, standardized the products, and designed a new process and tools, thus dramatically increasing yield from resources and creating a new market that could serve a new customer. According to Schumpeter (1911), entrepreneurship more generally encompasses the introduction of new products to the market, firm entry into new or existing markets, and organizational improvements that enable firms to enhance the quality of their products, lower their prices, or achieve more efficient modes of production.

In the more recent literature on entrepreneurship, it is increasingly common to differentiate between different types of entrepreneurs—the subsistence entrepreneur and the transformational entrepreneur (Lerner and Schoar, 2010). The former usually manages a microbusiness that does not grow beyond providing employment for the owner, or at most, for their families. Subsistence entrepreneurs are often necessity-driven as they may be unable to find employment and therefore are sometimes called reluctant entrepreneurs (Banerjee et al., 2015). The person opening yet another Mexican restaurant in Drucker's example could well fall into this category. In contrast, transformational entrepreneurs are generally opportunity-driven, and their impact is systematic, as exemplified by McDonald's process innovations (Drucker, 1985). However, as this example also illustrates, transformational entrepreneurship goes well beyond the introduction of radical technological breakthroughs at the global knowledge frontier. Instead, entrepreneurship is context-dependent, with its role varying in tandem with the innovation process as a country progresses through the different stages of economic development.

Early-stage entrepreneurship is widespread in many countries. According to the Global Entrepreneurship Monitor (GEM) (2017), which includes 60 economies, around 15% of the population ages 18–64 is involved in early-stage entrepreneurship activity. This involves entrepreneurs who have just started a business (nascent entrepreneurship) as well as owner-managers whose businesses are already up to three-and-a-half years old. There is considerable variation across regions and within regions. Latin America and the Caribbean have the highest percentage of early-stage entrepreneurship activity, averaging almost 20%. While Africa has the second highest percentage of early-stage entrepreneurs, Europe finds itself at the other end of the spectrum, with less than 8% of its working-age population involved in early-stage entrepreneurship activity. In the United States, meanwhile, around 12% of the population ages 18–64 have started a business in 2014 or in the three-and-a-half years prior. Finally, Asia-Pacific countries show significant differences. Australia and South Korea are broadly comparable with the United States, while Indonesia, the Philippines, Thailand, and Vietnam are more akin to some African and Latin American countries.

Though the data above make emerging economies appear relatively more entrepreneurial at first glance, a closer look reveals that a comparatively large share of entrepreneurs are necessity, rather than opportunity-driven. This is mirrored in the "Motivational Index," which is the ratio between the number of entrepreneurs who have started a new business in order to pursue a perceived

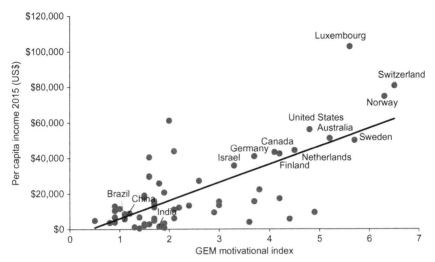

FIG. 1.2   GEM motivational index of entrepreneurial activity versus level of prosperity. *(Source: Authors' calculations, based on data from Global Entrepreneurship Monitor and IMF, WEO Database.)*

opportunity and improve their own situation and the number of entrepreneurs who become self-employed out of necessity. Fig. 1.2 depicts the GEM's Motivational Index as a function of economic prosperity measured by per capita GDP. Generally, higher levels of prosperity are associated with a greater role of opportunity-driven versus necessity-driven entrepreneurs. This suggests that it is not so much the number of startups that matter for economic prosperity, but the type of entrepreneur and their motivation.

There is, of course, no guarantee that startups founded by opportunity-driven entrepreneurs succeed, and in many cases they are just as likely to fail. And even if these startups stay in business, only a few of them are truly transformational. However, transformational entrepreneurs are much more likely to be opportunity than necessity-driven. Thus, it is possible that a country has a relatively low rank on the Motivational index—implying that the bulk of entrepreneurship is necessity-driven—and yet produces a relatively large number of high-impact transformational entrepreneurs. China and India are cases in point. Although necessity-driven entrepreneurship still plays a relatively important role, which is consistent with their overall level of development, some Chinese and Indian entrepreneurs have built game-changing businesses, including many in high-tech industries.

1.3   ENTREPRENEURSHIP AND THE QUALITY OF THE BUSINESS ENVIRONMENT

Substantial literature finds a close link between the quality of a country's legal and regulatory environment and its growth potential, based on the impact of regulations on the rate at which new (transformational) businesses are created.[6] This literature has motivated several large-scale projects that attempt to rank economies on the basis of different regulatory indicators. The World Bank's Doing Business Report, published annually, is a prime example. The World Bank's approach employs 45 variables that are grouped into 11 categories, which are then summarized into one overall index. The indicators seek to measure the complexity of business regulation, the protection of property rights, and their effects on businesses, especially small- and medium-sized enterprises. The first set of indicators track the regulatory process itself, such as the number of procedures to start a business, to register a transfer of commercial property, or to obtain a permit to construct a commercial building. Second, they document the time and cost required to achieve a regulatory goal or comply with regulations pertaining, for example, to the enforcement of a contract, bankruptcy proceedings, and cross-border trade. Third, they gauge the extent of legal protections of property, such as the protection of minority shareholders against exploitation by company directors. A fourth set of indicators focus on the tax burden on businesses, while a fifth set of indicators covers different aspects of employment regulation.

While the bulk of the existing literature employs macro data to examine the extent to which legal institutions and regulations affect investment, employment, GDP growth, and total factor productivity, Ardagna and Lusardi (2010) use micro data to study the institutional and regulatory impact on individuals' decisions to engage in new entrepreneurial activity. These data are derived from the GEM, whose dataset includes information from around 150,000 individual entrepreneurs in both advanced and emerging economies. The GEM dataset allows us to distinguish opportunity-driven entrepreneurs from those whose entrepreneurial activity is forced upon them. Additionally, the dataset provides information on a wide-ranging set of individual characteristics, such as business skills, fear of failure, and social networks. To analyze national regulatory environments, Ardagna and Lusardi (2010) rely on data from the World Bank Doing Business database, supplemented by data from the Heritage Foundation's Index of Economic Freedom, the International Country Risk Guide, and Botero et al. (2004). Overall, they found that regulation plays an important role in the individual decision to start a new business, especially for individuals who engage in an entrepreneurial activity to pursue a business opportunity. More specifically, regulation strengthens the effects of risk aversion, while curbing the effects of social networks and business skills. Finally, Ardagna's and Lusardi's results suggest that individual characteristics matter. For individuals who become entrepreneurs to pursue a business opportunity, education has a positive and statistically significant effect. However, the opposite sign is found for necessity-driven entrepreneurs.

---

[6] A list of significant contributions to this literature is provided in World Bank (2016b).

Freund (2016) suggests a fundamentally different approach to understanding entrepreneurship and the quality of a country's legal and regulatory environment. This approach focuses on the extent to which extreme personal wealth is accumulated through entrepreneurial activity as opposed to rent-seeking or heritage. More specifically, do national innovation systems foster entrepreneurship and allow exceptionally capable individuals to get rich by developing new products and services, challenging incumbent firms, and creating new markets? Well-known examples are the "Silicon Sultans," such as Bill Gates, Jeff Bezos, and Mark Zuckerberg (The Economist, January 3, 2015) whose extreme personal wealth is generally seen not only as sign of their business acumen and shrewdness but also as an indicator of America's favorable business environment.[7] Conversely, to what extent is extreme wealth based on the extraction of rent through political connections, taking advantage of government interventions such as privatization and regulation? And to what extent have large fortunes been simply transferred from one generation to the next?[8]

While the origins of extreme personal wealth have attracted considerable attention in previous studies (e.g., Acemoglu and Robinson, 2012), Freund (2016) was the first to provide systematic evidence drawn from 1645 billionaires around the world. Employing data from Forbes' list of "The World's Billionaire's," she found that almost 70% of the world's billionaires in 2014 owed their extreme wealth to their own success, up from 58.5% in 2001. With respect to self-made billionaires, almost 28% achieved superstardom (Rosen, 1981), in the sense that they accumulated their fortunes by founding companies in the nonfinance industries. Owners or executives of companies and investors represented another 31% of the global sample of billionaires, while another 11% derived their wealth from privatization or political connections.

Inherited wealth plays a significantly smaller role in emerging economies. According to Freund's (2016) study, heirs represented only around 21% of all billionaires in 2014 in these countries. Within the 79% of billionaires who were self-made in emerging economies, 24% of them were (nonfinance) company founders, representing the largest subgroup in this category. In fact,

---

[7] The "Silicon Sultans" are often compared with the entrepreneurs and businesspeople of the Gilded Age. While it is believed that there were no more than two U.S. billionaires in 1865, DeLong (1998) reported that there were 22 by 1900, the majority of them in railroads (nine) and in (railroad) finance (five). In contrast, just three billionaires inherited their fortunes. It is notable that the huge personal fortunes of the entrepreneurs of the Gilded Age (1870–1899) like Andrew Carnegie and John D. Rockefeller remain subject to considerable controversy. While these entrepreneurs are widely regarded as extremely capable businessmen, they have also been described as ruthless "robber barons." Having built enormous monopolies—Rockefeller's Standard Oil had a market share of up to 88%—their political connections shielded their firms from anti-trust legislation under the Sherman Anti-Trust Act, which the U.S. Congress approved in 1890 (Acemoglu and Robinson, 2012, pp. 322–324).

[8] While Piketty (2013) argued that the return on capital is higher than economic growth, thus favoring capital owners and leading to higher income inequality, large inheritances do not always grow, as is apparent from examples where subsequent generations destroyed old wealth.

this group is the biggest contributor to the rise of self-made billionaires in emerging markets, more than doubling their share since 2001 (11.6%). In contrast, rent-seekers and those with political connections represented 21% in 2014, up from 17.5% in 2001, i.e., a significantly smaller increase than for company founders. Overall, these findings suggest that entrepreneurship in emerging markets has gained considerable momentum, with gifted business-people amassing large fortunes, and inheritances playing a declining role in wealth generation. Although entrepreneurs who have made their fortunes by starting a company in emerging markets still make up a smaller share of the sample of billionaires than in advanced economies, the gap has shrunk in recent years.

Self-made entrepreneurs who have acquired fortunes not based on rent-seeking activities or political connections have earned their wealth in many sectors of emerging economies, including tech industries, such as software, online gaming and videos, e-commerce, and media. Arguably the most prominent entrepreneur from an emerging market economy is Jack Ma, the founder and executive chairman of China's Alibaba Group Holding Ltd., whose personal wealth was estimated at more than $20 billion in 2016. According to Forbes' List of the World's Billionaires, he was the 2nd wealthiest person in China (out of 236 billionaires) and the 33rd wealthiest person in the world.[9] Though Ma may be the best-known, the founders and chairmen or CEOs of other Chinese tech giants are not far behind, including Ma Huateng (Tencent Holdings Ltd), Robert Li (Baidu, Inc.), and Lei Jun (Xiaomi, Inc.). Other well-known Chinese tech entrepreneurs who have joined the billionaires' club are Li Quingdong (JD.com), Frank Wang (SZ DJI Technology Co.), and Wang Xing (Meituan-Dianping). Backed by venture capital, their companies have emerged as unicorns, i.e., privately held firms valued at $1 billion or more (Appendix Table A8.1 in Chapter 8).

Although China has by far the largest number of wealthy tech entrepreneurs, Forbes identifies several self-made billionaires in other emerging economies as well. Apart from the cofounders of Infosys, prominent examples in India include Azim Premji (Wipro Ltd), Shiv Nadar (HCL Technologies), and the two cofounders of Flipkart Online Services Pvt. Ltd., Binny Bansal and Sachin Bansal (unrelated).

1.4 THE ORIGINS OF TRANSFORMATIONAL ENTREPRENEURS

Where do these transformational entrepreneurs come from? Established firms often breed entrepreneurial talent. As an example, Hellmann (2007) points to the American semiconductor industry where, generation after generation, employees left their parent company to launch their own company. One of the

---

[9] Forbes, List of World's Billionaires, http://www.forbes.com/billionaires/list/#version:static; accessed February 6, 2017.

most well-known cases in the high-tech industry is the "traitorous eight," who left the Shockley Semiconductor Laboratory (founded by William Shockley, the coinventor of the transistor) to create Fairchild Semiconductor (Isaacson, 2014). Employees of Fairchild Semiconductor started, among others, National Semiconductor, Intel Corp., Advanced Micro Devices, Inc., and LSI Corp., which in turn became parent to Cypress Semiconductor Corp., Sierra Semiconductor Corp., and Zilog Inc. This lineage is not unique to the U.S. semiconductor industry. Bhidé (1994) determined that almost three-quarters of all founders replicated or modified an idea they had worked on in their previous employment.

There are numerous examples among today's universe of unicorns. For instance, the founders of Palantir Technologies Inc. are PayPal Holdings Inc. alumni, Ben Silberman, the cofounder of Pinterest Inc., comes from Google Inc., and his cofounder Evan Sharp previously worked at Facebook Inc. In China, two of the cofounders of Xiaomi worked at Google, while two other cofounders gained experience at Motorola Solutions Inc. and Microsoft Corp., respectively. Cheng Wei worked at Alipay before founding Didi Chuxing. In India, the seven founders of Infosys were software engineers at Patni Computer Systems. Binny Binsal and Sachin Binsal worked at Amazon before deciding to create Flipkart, India's version of Amazon and its main competitor. The cofounders of Ola (ANI Technologies Pvt. Ltd), India's most popular mobile app for booking a taxicab, worked at Google before becoming entrepreneurs themselves. Raphael Afaedor, a cofounder of Jumia, formerly known as Africa Internet Group and sometimes called the Amazon of Africa, was previously a product engineer at Monster.com (Monster Worldwide Inc.).

Gompers et al. (2005) focused on the creation of VC-backed entrepreneurs, a process they term "entrepreneurial spawning." Do individuals become entrepreneurs because they work in a network of entrepreneurs and venture capitalists and thus see new opportunities to pursue their ideas outside their current company? Or do they decide to become entrepreneurs because the companies they work for are large bureaucratic institutions that are reluctant to fund their entrepreneurial ideas? According to Gompers et al. (2005), the former explanation is more common. More specifically, they find that the most prolific spawning firms were public companies located in Silicon Valley and Massachusetts that were themselves once VC-backed, but there are important exceptions to the rule. A prominent example in the tech world is Tencent, one of whose cofounders, Yi Dan Chen, was employed by the Shenzhen Entry-Exit Inspection and Quarantine Branch. Another, Chen Ye Xu, came from the Shenzhen Data Telecommunications Bureau, while a third cofounder was a manager in the Shenzhen branch of China Telecom Corp. Ltd.

When individuals leave to create their own businesses, their former employers seem to lose out on the opportunities of their departing employees. However, as Hellmann (2007) points out, these departures may be the outcome of an optimal firm policy. Firms face a trade-off between providing employees with incentives for innovative ideas and focusing them on their core tasks. Thus, while some tech firms want to co-opt their employees' innovations through internal ventures or spin-offs (see Chapter 8), others want to discourage development outside their core business.

Presumably, pecuniary motives play an important role for entrepreneurial employees to leave their companies, but leaving paid employment to found a startup entails substantial risks. Wang et al. (2012) showed that "the option to accumulate wealth before entry is critical for entrepreneurship." Babina et al. (2016) found that initial public offerings (IPOs) often play an important role in an employee's decision to depart for a startup. While staff turnover tends to increase following a successful IPO, this increase was entirely driven by employees departing to startups. The authors present evidence that "following a [liquidity event] employees who received stock grants experience a positive shock to their [personal] wealth, which allows them to better tolerate the risks associated with" fundraising for their own startups or joining a startup. This suggests that IPO activity and new firm creation could be causally linked. From a structural perspective, countries with liquid exit markets are likely to see more startup (and VC) activity, an issue we return to in Chapter 8. From a cyclical perspective, startup activity may suffer if fewer firms go public.

Another group of transformational entrepreneurs includes individuals who previously worked in adjacent areas, such as consultancy or private equity firms. David Velez, founder of emerging unicorn Nubank in Brazil, is an example. Prior to Nubank, Velez was a partner at Sequoia Capital, a leading Silicon Valley venture capital firm. Before that, he gained experience in private equity at General Atlantic as well as banking at Morgan Stanley and Goldman Sachs. His cofounder Cristina Junqueira came from Itau Unibanco Holdin SA, Brazil's leading bank and the Boston Consulting Group. Similarly, Jeremy Hodara and Sacha Poignonnec, two of the cofounders of Jumia, are both McKinsey & Co. Europe alumni, with backgrounds in retail and e-commerce.

There are also many examples of transformational entrepreneurs who had not gained any meaningful experience working at established firms or other startups before founding their own firms. Some of these entrepreneurs are college dropouts, the most prominent ones being Apple Inc.'s Steve Jobs, Facebook Inc.'s Mark Zuckerberg, and Microsoft's Bill Gates. In fact, Peter Thiel, one of Silicon Valley's most well-known entrepreneurs and investors, has funded a two-year fellowship of $100,000 for those who want to skip or drop out of college to build new things. Others have created their own companies more or less straight out of college. Sergey Brin and Larry Page, the cofounders of Google, fall into this category. Other prominent examples include the cofounders of Airbnb, Brian Chersky and Joe Gebbia; Bobby Murchy and Evan Spiegel, who cofounded Snap Inc.; and Daniel Ek, the cofounder of Spotify Ltd., who founded his first company when he was 14. There are also numerous examples of transformational entrepreneurs in emerging economies who started a business very early on in their careers. Opeyemi Awoyemi from Nigeria is such a case; one of the cofounders of Jobberman, a startup that links young jobseekers to career opportunities, he founded his first company, ennovateNigeria, at the age of 16. Another prominent example is Tunde Kehinde who cofounded Jumia in 2012, one year after he had graduated from Harvard Business School.

1.5 FINANCING ENTREPRENEURSHIP

Underdeveloped financial markets are often an impediment to entrepreneurship, innovation, and private sector development in emerging economies. Consistent with the GII, there is ample research that finds that economic growth and financial development are inextricably intertwined, suggesting that emerging economies risk stagnation in their development process if they fail to continuously upgrade their financial systems. As Fig. 1.3 shows, emerging economies tend to have significantly lower penetration of bank loans, corporate bonds, and public equities. Given the lack of depth and breadth of their financial markets, many emerging economies are excluded from investable benchmarks. As far as equity markets are concerned, the family of MSCI World Indexes, widely used by global asset allocators, distinguishes three categories—MSCI World

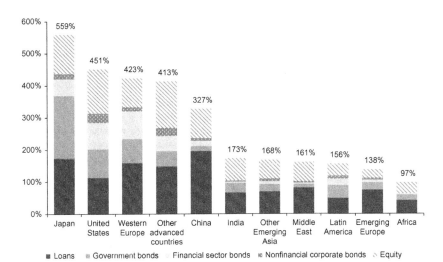

FIG. 1.3 Financial depth by region and asset class, 2015. (*Source: McKinsey Global Institute, 2016. Digital finance for all: Powering inclusive growth in emerging markets. http://www.mckinsey.com/global-themes/employment-and-growth/how-digital-finance-could-boost-growth-in-emerging-economies. Accessed January 25, 2017, and authors.*)

(Developed),[10] MSCI Emerging Markets,[11] and MSCI Frontier Markets[12]— mirroring a sliding scale of market size and liquidity. Overall, these indexes capture companies in 71 markets, implying that the majority of economies do not even have sufficiently developed equity markets to be categorized as a frontier market. The bond markets are even more limited; very few corporations in emerging markets are able to issue debt instruments, limiting the corporate bond market to a tiny fraction of funding and economic activity.

While the issuance of marketable instruments is generally available only to the most mature companies in emerging economies, our focus is on the funding of entrepreneurial firms that are in the early stages of their life cycle. Unless startups have sufficient tangible assets to pledge as collateral, bank loans are generally not available to them. Even if they have such assets, banks in emerging economies are often reluctant to lend in the absence of sufficient credit information and ill-defined legal rights pertaining to secure transactions. Not surprisingly, therefore, loan-to-GDP ratios in these economies generally fall far short of those in advanced economies, suggesting that a significant number of companies are underserved or even unserved by banks and must rely on their founders' resources or those of friends and family (Fig. 1.4). Unless external finance becomes available, startups are unable to grow and reach the stage where they become profitable due to the limited and unpredictable nature of these resources. While startups in advanced economies face the same challenge, they are more likely to be able to bridge the so-called Valley of Death by tapping into alternative funding pools, such as angel investing, venture capital, and emerging forms of financing.[13] As with their banking systems and organized financial markets, most emerging economies' alternative funding pools have yet to achieve similar penetration levels to advanced economies. However, as we discuss in this book there are signs that advancements in financial technology (fintech) could allow emerging markets to leapfrog with regard to accessing alternative funding sources, thereby fostering entrepreneurship and spurring economic growth.

---

[10] As of the end of 2016, benchmark constituents included companies from the following 23 advanced markets: Australia, Austria, Belgium, Canada, Denmark, Finland, France, Germany, Hong Kong (SAR), Ireland, Israel, Italy, Japan, the Netherlands, New Zealand, Norway, Portugal, Singapore, Spain, Sweden, Switzerland, the U.K., and the U.S.

[11] As of the end of 2016, benchmark constituents included companies from the following 23 emerging markets: Brazil, Chile, China, Colombia, Czech Republic, Egypt, Greece, Hungary, India, Indonesia, Malaysia, Mexico, Peru, Philippines, Poland, Qatar, Russia, South Africa, South Korea, Taiwan (ROC), Thailand, Turkey, and United Arab Emirates.

[12] As of the end of 2016, benchmark constituents included companies from the following 25 frontier markets: Argentina, Bahrain, Bangladesh, Burkina Faso, Cote D'Ivoire, Croatia, Estonia, Jordan, Kazakhstan, Kenya, Kuwait, Lebanon, Lithuania, Mauritius, Morocco, Nigeria, Oman, Pakistan, Romania, Senegal, Serbia, Slovenia, Sri Lanka, Tunisia, and Vietnam.

[13] This term describes the gap between funding from own resources in the initial stages of the life cycle of a company and the availability of external sources as the company matures and generates positive revenues.

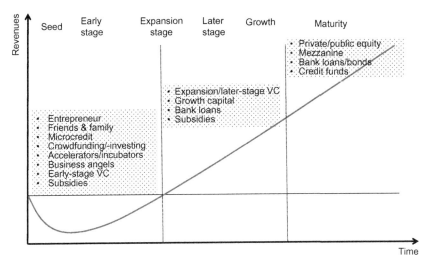

FIG. 1.4   Funding sources for companies over their life cycle. *(Source: Authors' research.)*

1.6   STRUCTURE OF THE BOOK

The book is divided into two parts, each of which contains five chapters (Fig. 1.5). The first part provides a comparative analysis of the role of innovation and technology in economic development. The second part discusses financial constraints facing entrepreneurs in emerging economies and the role evolving financial instruments and new forms of intermediation could play in alleviating these constraints.

Taking both a top-down and bottom-up perspective, the first part of the book identifies the primary factors that drive innovation and discusses appropriate economic policies as a function of a country's stage of development. Based on work presented in the GII Report, this section discusses the relative positions of economies on a global innovation scale and any recent progress in improving their innovative capacity to achieve and sustain economic growth. Of the 128 economies that are covered by the GII, we focus especially on China and India, the world's two most populous countries. Both have achieved rapid economic growth in recent decades and account for nearly 30% of world output (measured in purchasing parity terms). From a macro perspective, our interest lies particularly in the impact of economic policies on these countries' innovation capacity and their potential to catch up to more advanced economies. From a micro perspective, we look at two highly innovative companies—China's Tencent and India's Flipkart—to understand how firm strategy interacts with national innovation systems.

Chapter 2 presents the GII's framework, summarizes the overall rankings, discusses changes in the rankings over time, and, based on the lessons learnt from successful economies, identifies key areas for innovation policies. The GII

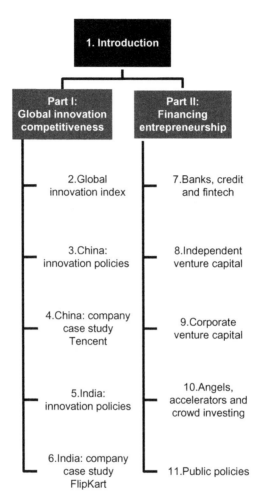

FIG. 1.5 Structure of the book.

employs the broad concept of innovation embodied in the Oslo Manual we have discussed earlier. Rather than perceiving innovation as a closed, internal, and localized process resulting in radical technological breakthroughs, the GII embraces the notion of incremental innovation and "innovation without research." Consistent with this approach, the GII goes beyond the standard metrics of innovation such as R&D expenditure and the number of utility patents registered by a country's firms. Instead, as this chapter explains, it uses a wide range of indicators grouped into two broad categories. The first one includes input variables reflecting the quality of a country's institutions, its human capital and research activities, infrastructure, market sophistication, and business sophistication. These five pillars are aggregated into the Innovation Sub-Index. On the output side, the GII focuses on two pillars, knowledge and technology outputs and creative outputs. The ratio between the Output Sub-Index and the Input Sub-Index—the Innovation Efficiency Ratio—shows how much innovation output a given economy is harvesting from its inputs.

As Chapter 2 elaborates in greater detail, the GII approach allows users to identify particular bottlenecks that may hamper a country's transition through the different phases of economic development. Emphasizing that sustained economic growth requires businesses and their supporting environments to co-evolve, the discussion focuses especially on the framework conditions for innovation that are generally found to be more challenging in emerging economies. Among those are generally less developed capital markets that undermine the financing of entrepreneurship and innovation, the subject of our discussion in Part II of this book.

However, while large sample cross-country studies provide useful benchmarks, helping identify critical bottlenecks, and design policies to remove such impediments, they leave a good part of the innovation and growth process unexplained as they are not designed to capture the idiosyncrasies of individual economies. Naturally, there is a considerable degree of variation across countries, which cannot be fully explained by the conceptual frameworks underlying the rankings. Furthermore, the country rankings are static in the sense that they measure the position of a country at a given point in time. While the comparison of rankings over time may provide important information about the progress an economy has made relative to others, this is not sufficient to fully understand the dynamic process of "creative destruction" (Schumpeter, 1942) that is essential to achieve sustained economic growth.

In Chapter 3, we drill deeper and examine the roles of science and technology policies in China's rapid economic development over the past four decades. This role has changed over time as the economy has transitioned through four distinct phases. In the experimental phase that lasted from 1978 to 1985, Chinese authorities introduced some initial policy reform, which included the partial privatization of selected parts of public research institutions. Although the number of these privatizations remained limited, they laid the foundation for some of today's most successful technology companies in China. A prominent example is Lenovo (formerly Legend computer), a spin-off from the Computing Institute of the Academy of Sciences.

Between the mid-1980s and the mid-1990s—a period that can be described as the systemic reform phase—China moved to a top-down nation-wide reform approach. The framework for this approach was provided by the Science and Technology System Reform Act, aimed at bridging the gap between research institutions and relevant industries. The newly established National Natural Science Foundation was tasked with promoting and financing basic and applied research, along with a number of other initiatives, which all sought to improve the prospects of commercialization. An integral part of these policies was the foundation of the Shenzhen Stock Exchange for small- and medium-sized enterprises. At the same time, important measures were introduced to encourage China's education system, with a special budget dedicated to support a group of leading universities.

Many of these reforms were strengthened from 1996 to 2005. The Act of Promoting Commercialization of Science and Technology Discoveries and Inventions kicked off this phase in 1996 and focused on three policy objectives—(i) shifting the drivers of innovations from public research organizations to industrial sectors; (ii) improving the R&D and innovation capacity of industrial sectors; and (iii) improving the efficiency of the commercialization of academic outputs.

The National Plan, a medium- and long-term national science and technology plan, has driven China's innovation strategy since it was issued in 2006. The plan sets goals through 2020 and emphasizes the importance of sustainable economic growth. The National Plan established guidelines for nurturing independent innovation, fostering the ability to leapfrog in key technology areas, building major infrastructure, and developing future global leadership, thus optimizing the effectiveness of innovation policies and the management of their implementation. In 2012, the 18th Communist Party National Congress established "innovation-driven growth strategy" as a national development strategy, with the goal of becoming a top innovative nation by 2020. Under this strategy, measures are envisaged to allow entrepreneurship to play a more important role, make industry the main driver behind innovation, and establish market-oriented mechanisms to facilitate collaborative technology transfer from universities and research institutes to the industrial sectors.

As Chapter 3 discusses, China's innovation strategy has achieved remarkable results, which are reflected in the country's position on the GII. However, while this strategy has played an important role in promoting economic growth, we conclude that additional reforms are needed if China is to become a leading innovative country by the end of this decade. In identifying concrete reform areas that require particular attention, we are guided by the GII approach outlined in Chapter 2.

Chapter 4 presents Tencent, one of China's most successful tech companies, founded in 1998 and initially backed by VC. Given the national context we discussed in the preceding chapter, this case study asks how Tencent has emerged as one of the world's most valuable Internet companies and achieved a degree of competitiveness that challenges global incumbents. In addressing this question, Chapter 4 argues that Tencent's interconnected ecosystem has been a critical success factor. This ecosystem originated from Tencent's instant messaging product it launched in 1999, and with mobile phones becoming increasingly popular, this service morphed into a new product that allowed a users to send messages directly to other users who could access these messages both from a computer or a mobile phone. China Mobile charged users a monthly fee, 20% of which was shared with Tencent. In an effort to make its revenue stream independent from China mobile or other partners, Tencent then launched its own online currency "Q coin," which became the de facto standard for all purchases from Tencent.

Shortly thereafter, Tencent ventured into online gaming and other enter-tainment services. In the early 2010s, it developed Weixin, a service known as WeChat in the global market. Combining the messaging features of WhatsApp, quick photo chat of Snapchat, social networking functions of Facebook, and the photo-sharing abilities of Instagram, Tencent's Wechat community has expanded to more than 800 million users worldwide by September 2016. Additionally, as Chapter 4 outlines, Tencent has entered into online to offline services, working with strategic partners in areas such as food ordering and ridesharing, and more recently into cloud computing.

China's innovation policies and the country's national innovation system have been important enablers for Tencent's remarkable success. And, as we ar-gue in Chapter 4, although the company has benefited from a protected envi-ronment, the single most important success factor has probably been Tencent's strong and visionary leadership, which has transformed a small startup into a globally operating tech giant in less than two decades. While Tencent's remark-able growth is particularly impressive, throughout this book we refer to other examples. Apart from Alibaba, our interest focuses in particular on China's growing number of unicorns, i.e., tech startups that are already valued at $1 billion or more. Importantly, several of these unicorns were funded by Tencent, indicating the company's desire to continue to expand into new areas.

In Chapter 5, we turn to India, whose innovation process provides similarly important lessons for other emerging economies. Initially, after India's indepen-dence, economic growth was thought to be best achieved through public-sector led industrialization and the development of science through the acquisition, dissemination, and discovery of scientific knowledge. In contrast, technology development played a limited role in the formulation of economic policies.

This approach began to change in the 1970s when increased emphasis was put on the promotion of competition in the domestic market coupled with technological upgrading. In the early 1980s, the government clarified that this process was to be achieved through the development of indigenous technol-ogy and the efficient absorption and adaptation of imported technology. This policy shift gained further momentum in the 1990s when economic policies gave increased weight to the collaboration between public and private institu-tions, identifying priority sectors, enhancing international collaboration, and strengthening India's human capital base. In enhancing public-private partner-ships in R&D and ensuring their funding, an important role was given to the Department of Science and Technology and the Department of Scientific and Industrial Research. This approach has been further deepened and broadened in the subsequent years and has contributed, in tandem with India's general shift toward a more outward-oriented economic policy, to a significant accel-eration in economic growth.

We assess the quality of India's national innovation system, identifying par-ticular strengths as well as remaining bottlenecks that should be removed to al-low India's economy to continue to play rapid catch-up. A key advantage—and the envy of many other economies, including those with substantially higher per-capita incomes—are India's premier universities, notably the Indian Institutes of Science, the Indian Institutes of Technology, and the Indian Institutes of Management. Their contribution to the advancement of global knowledge is widely recognized and reflected in the citation of publications originating from these institutions. Another important advantage is seen in India's relatively high market capitalization. As we discuss in Chapter 8, this factor is found to play an important role for the availability of VC as liquid stock markets may facilitate the exit of venture investments.

Equally, if not more, important for India's emergence as a global VC hotbed is the country's policy emphasis on developing mobile networks, information technology, and broadband. In the past decade, India's internet and mobile penetration has increased substantially and opened up important investment opportunities in new fields, such as e-commerce, consumer internet, and financial services. In all these areas, India has witnessed the emergence of unicorns (e.g., Flipkart in e-commerce; Ola in the consumer internet space; and One97 Communications in financial services).

Chapter 5 identifies the further development of India's small- and medium-sized enterprise (SME) sector. While this sector has a high growth potential, India's SMEs are generally severely handicapped by the lack of credit and equity, a challenge they share with virtually all other emerging economies. At the same time, India's GII scores point to the importance of further improving the country's entrepreneurial ecosystem and incentivizing innovation-driven startups and removing barriers to entry. Furthermore, although India's top universities enjoy an outstanding reputation, improving access to higher education remains a key challenge in a country with a population of more than 1.2 billion of which more than 50% is younger than 25. A final area of attention concerns the effective protection of intellectual property rights, which, if left unaddressed, could undermine the country's innovation potential.

In Chapter 6, we examine the case of Flipkart against the backdrop of India's national innovation system. Founded in 2007, Flipkart has emerged as India's most valuable tech startup, leading the country's increasing number of unicorns. Although Flipkart is sometimes viewed as a clone of Amazon—a perception that is no doubt strengthened by the fact that its founders were previously employed by America's e-commerce giant—we argue that Flipkart's success is based on its own unique business model. A differentiating factor is Flipkart's introduction of its cash-on-delivery (C.O.D) model, which recognizes India's very low credit card penetration. Another is Flipkart's investment in its own supply chain, taking into account the country's poor infrastructure and the lack of shipping capabilities of suppliers. Additionally, Flipkart's generous return policy and its strong emphasis on customer service have played important roles as well.

Flipkart's enormous growth would not have been possible without India's emphasis on developing its mobile and Internet infrastructure (Chapter 5). The increasingly deep penetration has been a factor for India's consumers to embrace e-commerce. However, as the Internet and mobile phones have been used increasingly widely, the market has become more competitive, with Amazon and Snapdeal, another Indian unicorn, having emerged as Flipkart's main competitors. These companies have been joined by new entrants such as Paytm, a startup that has originally focused on digital wallet services. In this context, Chapter 6 also discusses India's regulatory regime, which prohibits foreign direct investment in inventory-based e-commerce (with the online retailer selling directly to customers) but permits foreign investments in business-to-business (B2B) commerce.

Finally, Chapter 6 looks at Flipkart's expansion strategy through acquisitions and the funding of innovative tech startups. Like Tencent in China and several other successful tech companies in emerging economies, Flipkart has become increasingly active in corporate venturing. Alleviating the capital needs of new entrepreneurial firms, these investments provide clues as to the emerging business strategies of India's leading e-commerce company and the competitive landscape in this rapidly growing market.

The Flipkart case provides an ideal bridge to the second part of the book in which we look systematically at the financing of entrepreneurship and innovation in emerging economies. As we discuss, there are signs that entrepreneurial finance in some countries is gaining significant momentum.

In Chapter 7, we briefly review the literature on financial development and economic growth, paying particular attention to the role of banks. We then ask to what extent microcredit has helped alleviate credit constraints and fuel entrepreneurship, innovation and growth in emerging economies, and conclude that its impact has likely been limited. Although microfinance has become a global industry, randomized control trials suggest that microcredit has a sizeable impact only to the degree to which such loans fund transformational entrepreneurs. However, to the extent that loans are made available to borrowers who reluctantly become entrepreneurs in the absence of job opportunities, no lasting impact is found. While these results suggest a more targeted lending policy, we argue that this reform should be seen as a necessary, but not sufficient condition for microcredit to play a more meaningful role. First and foremost, this requires improving the efficiency of microcredit operations, which to a large extent continue to rely on manual process and cash—something microfinance institutions share with many banks in emerging economies.

Emerging financial technologies could play an important role in this reform process. Fortunately, most emerging economies have already built the necessary infrastructure that could allow digital solutions to have a transformational impact on financial services, the intermediation of capital, and the availability of entrepreneurial finance. While all countries should be able to benefit from fintech, arguably the most important beneficiaries could be emerging markets whose economic growth has been significantly impeded by underdeveloped financial economies. We argue that digital finance could help spur entrepreneurial activity and innovation not only by making existing forms of intermediation more efficient and less costly, thus enhancing the lending capacity of banks and microfinance institutions, but also by helping develop new forms of intermediation. Crowdfunding has already gained significant traction in a growing number of emerging economies, including in some African countries where credit constraints are particularly severe. These early successes suggest that there could be considerable potential for fintech to enable these economies to leapfrog to a financial system where entrepreneurship and innovation may thrive.

Fintech plays a growing role not only for entrepreneurs' access to loans but also for their ability to attract outside investors. In Chapter 8, we discuss the rising importance of VC in emerging economies, focusing on VC raised and invested by independent funds. Venture capital is an exceptional source of entrepreneurial finance very few startups have access to. Those startups that are backed by VC are usually tech companies that operate in areas of information technology (IT) and life sciences. In recent years, VC firms have also backed an increased number of fintech startups, thus contributing to financial development and indirectly helping alleviate entrepreneurial firms' credit constraints.

The fact that VC typically helps fund tech companies does not necessarily mean that VC funding spurs innovation. Conceivably, the arrival of a new technology could increase demand for VC rather than VC fostering innovation. However, our review of the literature on this important question suggests that there is a causal relationship that does run from VC to innovation, with VC found to account for a much larger share of industrial innovations than its share of corporate R&D would suggest. But VC is found to be not only a catalyst in terms of the quantity of innovations but also with regard to their importance as proxied by indicators such as the number of patent citations and litigations. Several factors are thought to explain this success—the extremely deep screening process in the VC industry; the staging of investments; and the advice entrepreneurs receive from their venture capitalists.

Much of the evidence we have on VC and its role for innovation are based on VC investments in the United States, the cradle of this form of entrepreneurial finance. For a long time, U.S. startups absorbed the lion's share of global VC, which was almost exclusively intermediated by U.S. VC firms. Although the United States remains the dominant VC market, more recently this investment model has been exported to other regions, first to Israel and Europe and then to Asia and the rest of the world. China and India have become global hotbeds, in which a growing number of startups have received substantial amounts of capital. China and India have produced the second and third largest number of unicorns. Like Tencent and Alibaba, which "graduated" in 2014 from its unicorn status in an initial public offering (IPO) raising a record amount of $25 billion, these companies have been backed by VC. While companies such as China's Xiaomi and Didi Chuxing or India's Flipkart are becoming increasingly familiar names in the West, they are just exemplary for many other VC funded tech startups in these countries.

While China and India are exceptional VC magnets, venture capitalists are taking a growing interest in other emerging economies as well. In fact, in several countries VC investing has outpaced economic growth by a significant margin, implying deeper penetration. As we discuss in Chapter 8, the rationale behind these investments is similar to backing startups in China and India—that is, the provision of entrepreneurial finance for companies that adopt business models with a proven track record in consumer-facing industries with rapid path to value realization. A critical factor is the rapidly growing proliferation of mobile phones and the internet, which helps explain why economies as diverse as Brazil, Egypt, Kenya, Nigeria, and Russia are attracting increased attention from venture capitalists.

Independent VCs (IVCs) are not the only venture capitalists who may back entrepreneurial firms. In Chapter 9, we meet companies with corporate venture programs, usually implemented as a strategic choice to complement internal R&D programs. Although corporate VC (CVC) is significantly smaller than IVC in terms of its investment volume, for a meaningful number of startups it is an important source of entrepreneurial finance. CVC programs can take various organizational forms. While some companies have decided to establish internal corporate venture groups to identify VC opportunities, others have set up external CVC funds that operate as a separate entity outside the company. Yet other programs are based on commitments to IVC partnerships, with the option to coinvest in entrepreneurial firms alongside these funds. Additionally, a growing number of corporations have set up accelerators and incubators as tools to gain access to innovative ideas.

In our discussion in Chapter 9, we stress that CVC investments are not necessarily motivated by the same objectives as IVC investments; while the latter are generally driven by financial return expectations, CVC investments are often strategic. These different motivations make it difficult to compare their relative success. However, there are several studies that find that CVCs are at least as successful as IVCs, employing proxies, such as the share of funded portfolio companies that were exited via an IPO; the number of patents generated by CVC/IVC firms; the number of citations of these patents; and the scientific publication record of startups funded by CVC/IVC.

Against this background, it may not be surprising that the number of companies with CVC programs has increased over time. In 2016, there were almost 200 corporate venture capitalists around the world, among many high-tech companies, such as Amgen, BASF, Cisco Systems, GE, Google, Intel, Microsoft, Lilly, Merck, Pfizer, and Siemens. While many of these are active VC investors in emerging economies, more recently, a growing number of emerging market companies themselves have followed their peers in advanced economies and implemented CVC programs. These include existing or former unicorns, such as Alibaba, Baidu, Flipkart, Tencent, and Xiaomi. Many of their VC investments involve—domestic as well as foreign—startups that operate in the same or adjacent industries. However, in a nontrivial number of cases CVCs have also funded startups where it is more difficult to identify a direct strategic fit between the parent companies' major line of business and the portfolio companies.

In Chapter 10, we turn to noninstitutional forms of entrepreneurial finance, specifically angel investing, incubators, and crowd investing. Traditionally, equity financing of startups has been equated with VC, with limited partnership funds intermediating capital between institutional investors and entrepreneurial firms. As VC has gained substantial traction and backed some of today's most valuable companies, it has attracted a considerable amount of academic research interest. In comparison, we know much less about angel investing, which emerged in the United States in the 1980s when the VC market was already quite mature. However, it appears that the volume of angel investing in the United States is broadly comparable with VC investing. And like VC, angel investing is increasingly a global phenomenon, with a growing number of angel groups forming in emerging economies. We discuss the degree to which angel investing and VC are substitutes or complements. Angel investors, who are often (former) entrepreneurs themselves, usually provide only seed financing, while the majority of VC investments focus on startups that have already developed beyond the initial stage of their life cycle. Additionally, angels and venture capitalists tend to have different skills and networks. Angel investors could therefore play an important role by bridging the gap between the entrepreneur's own resources and the funding by venture capitalists and other institutional investors. In other words, angel groups, after undertaking the initial financing, could "hand-off" their transactions to venture funds for subsequent financing. While the international evidence is mixed, there is some support for the complementarity hypothesis in emerging economies. In economies with less developed ecosystems for risk capital, angel investors appear to play an important role as gatekeepers, helping bridge the valley of death between an entrepreneur's own resources and debt and equity capital that could become available as the startup grows.

Another source of entrepreneurial finance that can be subsumed under noninstitutional forms are business accelerators and incubators. Although startups that are admitted to accelerator and incubator programs often receive a small amount of funding, this is generally not the most important factor in fostering entrepreneurship and innovation. What is of much greater relevance instead is the mentoring these programs provide. Additionally, they often unleash financial resources in the form of angel investments and VC. Accelerators and incubators are a relatively new phenomenon, and much of what we know about their impact is confined to the experience in the United States. As far as U.S. accelerators and incubators are concerned, it appears that regions that were "treated" with an accelerator program have been substantially more successful in attracting investments in startups than those areas that did not receive such a program. This is positive news for emerging economies where accelerators have also proliferated in recent years. While some of these programs have been set up by U.S. organizations, some countries have already seen indigenous versions of accelerators and incubators.

Finally, we return to crowdfunding, this time, however, focusing on equity crowdfunding, or crowd investing. While in the crowd lending model funders receive fixed periodic income and expect repayment of the original principal investment, in the equity-based version of crowdfunding funders receive compensation in the form of the fundraiser's equity-based revenue or profit-sharing arrangements. Crowd investing platforms are not involved in investment decisions; instead the decision to fund a startup is ultimately made by the individual crowd investor, a characteristic they have in common with angel investors.

Crowd investing has been described as the democratization of entrepreneurial funding. With online platforms being designed to reduce search frictions and improve the matching between startups and potential investors, crowd investing has been hailed as a business model that has the potential to reshape the VC landscape and early funding as a whole. While this form of entrepreneurial finance is still in an embryonic stage, it has begun to gain significant traction, following its comparatively more advanced cousin, crowd lending. China is the world's largest market for equity crowdfunding, but volumes have also increased meaningfully in some other emerging economies, especially in Asia and Latin America.

Unlike angel and VC investing, which are largely a local business, crowd investing is less geographically confined. However, while emerging online platforms may have the ability to achieve a superior match between entrepreneurs and investors, we argue that a number of important challenges remain before crowd investing can achieve the same scale as angel and VC investing. As we discuss in greater detail in Chapter 11, these challenges lie especially in informational asymmetries, inadequate due diligence, potential herding behavior, the lack of bespoke contractual arrangements, and the absence of clearly defined exits for investments.

We devote the final chapter to the government's role in promoting entrepreneurship and facilitating the funding of entrepreneurial firms. In Chapter 11, we distinguish two policy approaches. The first one aims at improving a country's entrepreneurial ecosystem. Focusing on institutional reform, these measures often include reducing regulatory barriers and developing exit markets, providing fiscal incentives, and putting in place a legal framework that is conducive to private risk-taking.

Second, many governments are directly involved in providing funding for entrepreneurial firms, in the form of grants, loans, or equity. As regards the latter, some governments act as venture capitalists by running public programs through which they invest in startups. In contrast, others commit capital to independent VC funds to help back entrepreneurial firms, with investment decisions taken by the private fund managers. Moreover, some governments sponsor accelerator or incubator programs. In several emerging economies, national efforts are amplified by VC investments by foreign development financial institutions and multilateral organizations.

In principle, government interventions in VC markets could be justified by market failures. However, as we debate in Chapter 11, actual policies have not remained undisputed. While concrete measures might have been well intended, skeptics point to numerous examples where poorly designed government initiatives have achieved little or even proved counter-productive. What interests us in particular is the question about the extent to which public VC might have displaced or crowded out private venture capitalists. With governments arguably less well positioned than private investors in picking winners, public VC investments could potentially undermine rather than foster innovation, job creation, and economic growth.

Despite the existence of enough examples of poorly designed government programs, recent empirical studies suggest that government-sponsored and private VC are complementary. When governments and private investors provide funding to back a start-up, total investment is found to be higher than in a situation where the firm receives all of its VC from private investors. However, while mixed funding is found to have the highest investment level, pure private funding comes next, with pure government funding being associated with the smallest overall investment. Although more research is required, these findings would support a strategy where governments provide more public funding for entrepreneurial firms alongside private equity funds. At the same time, it is important to note, in our view, public funding should not take place in isolation; unless governments endeavor to improve the business environment in which entrepreneurship can thrive, their role as venture capitalists is likely to be ineffective. The same can be assumed for government-sponsored accelerators. While a rising number of emerging economies have set up accelerators as part of their overall efforts to foster entrepreneurship and innovation, their impact is likely to be limited in the absence of other supporting measures, even if these accelerators are able to select the most promising startups.

REFERENCES

Abramowitz, M., 1956. Resource and output trends in the United States since 1870. Am. Econ. Rev. 46, 5–23.

Acemoglu, D., Robinson, J.A., 2012. Why Nations Fail. The Origins of Power, Prosperity, and Poverty. Crown Business, New York.

Ardagna, S., Lusardi, A., 2010. Explaining international differences in entrepreneurship. The role of individual characteristics and regulatory constraints. In: Lerner, J., Schoar, A. (Eds.), International Differences in Entrepreneurship. The University of Chicago Press, Chicago & London, pp. 17–62.

Babina, T., Quimet, P., Zarutskie, R., 2016. Going entrepreneurial? IPOs and new firm creation. Unpublished Working Paper, Federal Reserve Board. https://www.aeaweb.org/conference/2017/preliminary/paper/BiYBAstD. Accessed January 25, 2017.

Banerjee, A., Breza, E., Duflo, E., Kinnan, C., 2015. Do credit constraints limit entrepreneurship? Heterogeneity in the returns to microfinance. Unpublished Working Paper, Columbia University. https://www0.gsb.columbia.edu/faculty/ebreza/papers/BanerjeeBrezaDufloKinnan.pdf.

Bell, M., Figueiredo, P.N., 2013. Building innovative capabilities in latecomer emerging market firms: some key issues. In: Amann, E., Cantwell, J. (Eds.), Innovative Firms in Emerging Market Countries. Oxford University Press, Oxford, pp. 24–111.

Bhidé, A., 1994. How entrepreneurs craft strategies that work. Harv. Bus. Rev. 72 (2), 150–161.

Botero, J.C., Djankov, S., La Porta, R., Lopez-De-Silvances, F., Shleifer, A., 2004. The regulation of labor. Q. J. Econ. 119 (4), 1339–1381.

DeLong, J.B., 1998. Robber barons. Unpublished Working Paper. University of California at Berkeley. http://www.pitt.edu/~mitnick/EBEweb/Robber%20Barons.html.

Drucker, P., 1985. Innovation and Entrepreneurship. Harper & Row Publishers, New York.

Forbes, List of World's Billionaires. http://www.forbes.com/billionaires/list/#version:static.

Freund, C., 2016. Rich People. Poor Countries. The Rise of Emerging-Market Tycoons and their Mega Firms. Peterson Institute for International Economics, Washington, DC.

Furman, J.L., Porter, M.E., Stern, S., 2002. The determinants of national innovative capacity. Res. Policy 31 (6), 899–933.

Global Entrepreneurship Monitor, 2017. Global report 2016/17. http://www.gemconsortium.org/report/49812. Accessed May 19, 2017.

Goldman Sachs, 2003. Dreaming with BRICs: the path to 2050. Global Economics Paper No. 99. http://www.goldmansachs.com/our-thinking/archive/archive-pdfs/brics-dream.pdf. Accessed May 19, 2017.

Gompers, P., Lerner, J., Scharfstein, D., 2005. Entrepreneurial spawning: public corporations and the genesis of new ventures: 1986–1999. J. Financ. 60 (2), 577–614.

Hellmann, T., 2007. When do employees become entrepreneurs? Manag. Sci. 53 (6), 919–933.

International Monetary Fund, 2017. World Economic Outlook. International Monetary Fund, Washington, DC.

Isaacson, W., 2014. The Innovators. Simon & Schuster, New York.

Johnson & Williamson. Online database. What was the U.S. GDP then? https://www.measuringworth.com/usgdp/.

Joo, S.H., Lee, K., 2009. Samsung's catch-up with Sony: an analysis using US patent data. J. Asia Pac. Econ. 15 (3), 271–287.

Kim, L., 1997. Imitation to Innovation: The Dynamics of Korea's Technological Learning. Harvard Business School Press, Boston.

Leeds, R., 2015. Private Equity Investing in Emerging Markets. Opportunities for Value Creation. Palgrave McMillan, New York.

Lerner, J., Schoar, A. (Eds.), 2010. International Differences in Entrepreneurship. University of Chicago Press for NBER, Chicago.

Lim, C., Lee, K., 2001. Technological regimes, catching up, and leapfrogging: findings from the Korean industries. Res. Policy 30, 459–483.

McKinsey Global Institute, 2016. Digital finance for all: powering inclusive growth in emerging markets http://www.mckinsey.com/global-themes/employment-and-growth/how-digital-finance-could-boost-growth-in-emerging-economies. Accessed January 25, 2017.

Organisation for Economic Co-operation and Development, 2005. Oslo Manual: Guidelines for Collecting and Interpreting Innovation Data, third ed. Paris: OECD. http://www.oecd.org/sti/inno/oslomanualguidelinesforcollectingandinterpretinginnovationdata3rdedition.htm. Accessed May 17, 2017.

Piketty, T., 2013. Capital in the Twenty-First Century. Belknap Press, Cambridge, MA.

Porter, M.E., 1990. The Competitive Advantage of Nations. McMillan, Basingstoke.

Rosen, S., 1981. The economics of superstars. Am. Econ. Rev. 71 (5), 845–858.

Schumpeter, J., 1911. Theorie der wirtschaftlichen Entwicklung. Duncker & Humblot, Leipzig.

Schumpeter, J., 1942. Capitalism, Socialism and Democracy. Routledge, London.

Solow, R.M., 1957. Technological change and the aggregate production function. Rev. Econ. Stat. 39, 312–320.

The Economist, 2015. Robber barons and silicon sultans. January 3, 2015.

Wang, C., Wang, N., Yang, J., 2012. A unified model of entrepreneurship dynamics. J. Financ. Econ. 106 (1), 1–23.

World Bank, 2016. Doing Business in 2017. Equal Opportunity for All. The World Bank, Washington, DC.

Yip, G.S., McKern, B., 2016. China's Next Strategic Advantage. From Imitation to Innovation. MIT Press, Cambridge, MA & London.

Part I

Global Innovation
Competitiveness

Chapter 2

Global Innovation Competitiveness: How Emerging Economies Compare*

ACRONYMS

BRICS	Brazil, Russia, India, China, and South Africa
FDI	Foreign Direct Investment
GDP	Gross Domestic Product
GERD	Gross Domestic Expenditure on R&D
GII	Global Innovation Index
INSEAD	Institut Européen d'Administration des Affaires
IP	Intellectual Property
kWh	kilowatt-hour
MNEs	Multinational Enterprises
OECD	Organization for Economic Cooperation and Development
PTC	Patent Cooperation Treaty
PISA	OECD Programme for International Student Assessment
PPP	Purchasing Power Parity
R&D	Research and Development
SDG	Sustainable Development Goals
STI	Science and Technology Innovation

Innovation and entrepreneurship are high on the national strategic agenda of most economies today. Developing countries have especially increased their emphasis on fostering innovation and entrepreneurship in recent years. At the global level, leaders of economies increasingly recognize the need to spur innovation to both foster economic growth and find solutions to social challenges. Several important drivers push both public and private sector leaders to increase national innovation competitiveness and support entrepreneurship.

First and foremost, competition has become increasingly global. Organizations that emerge in different parts of the world are competing in a common global market. In order to compete effectively in such a market, firms are going global and

* The contributions of Rafael Reynoso, Jordan Litner, Bruno Lanvin, Sacha Wunsch-Vincent, and Francesca Guadagno are gratefully acknowledged.

Financing Entrepreneurship and Innovation in Emerging Markets.
https://doi.org/10.1016/B978-0-12-804025-6.00002-2
31

leveraging the comparative advantages of assets from around the world. Second, technology has become a tremendous force for transformation and change in both business and society. While technological progress continues relentlessly, consumers in both developed and emerging economies are adopting technology at rates faster than either businesses or governments. As consumer expectations evolve, both the public and private sectors face increasing pressures to continuously innovate to keep pace. Finally, the traditional engines of job creation—the government and the private sector—are unable to keep up with the growing numbers of educated youth who seek satisfying jobs, especially in emerging markets that have a younger demographic profile than their developed counterparts. In such environments, entrepreneurship is often the most desirable strategy to create jobs and provide creative opportunities for the youth.

As a result of these pressures, it is no surprise that national innovation policies and programs are flourishing in many countries around the world. Keeping true to the old adage, "what is not measured is not managed," there is also increasing emphasis on benchmarking innovation performance. Policymakers seeking ways to assess the effectiveness of their innovation systems and policies need to develop ways to measure progress. At the global level, the United Nations (U.N.) Sustainable Development Goals (SDGs), for instance, have set a new development agenda relying on innovation as a means to achieve improvements in health, environmental protection, food security, and so on, and as a goal in itself. These various U.N. fora are therefore also engaged in an ongoing process of identifying indicators that can capture innovation.

2.1 MEASURING INNOVATION

In this book, we rely on a broad definition of innovation, originally elaborated in the Oslo Manual,[1] developed by the European Communities and the Organization for Economic Cooperation and Development (OECD): "An innovation is the implementation of a new or significantly improved product (good or service), a new process, a new marketing method, or a new organizational method in business practices, workplace organization, or external relations."

This definition reflects a change in how economists and policymakers perceived and understood innovation over the last two decades. Previously experts focused on research and development (R&D)-based technological product innovation, which was largely produced in-house by companies in manufacturing industries. Typically a highly educated labor force followed a closed, internal, and localized process in an R&D-intensive company in order to achieve such innovation. Technological breakthroughs were necessarily "radical" and took place at the "global knowledge frontier." This characterization implied the existence of leading and lagging countries, with low- or middle-income economies at best catching up to higher-income economies.

---

1. http://www.oecd.org/science/inno/2367580.pdf.

Today the concept of innovation has expanded from the restrictive view articulated above to include the ability to exploit new technological combinations; it embraces the notion of incremental innovation and "innovation *without* research." Non-R&D innovative expenditure is an important component of technological innovation. Interest in understanding how innovation takes place in low- and middle-income countries is increasing, along with an appreciation for the impact that incremental forms of innovation can have on development. Furthermore, the process of innovation itself has changed significantly. Firms, countries, and global organizations have continued to increase their investment in innovation-related activity, adding new nonprofit actors and innovation actors from outside high-income economies. The structure of knowledge production is more complex and geographically dispersed than ever.

A key challenge in this context is to find metrics that capture innovation as it actually happens in the world today. Direct official measures that quantify innovation outputs remain extremely scarce. For example, there are few official statistics on the amount of innovative activity—defined as the number of new products, processes, or other innovations—for a given innovation actor or a given country. Most measures also struggle to appropriately capture the innovation outputs of a wide spectrum of innovation actors, such as the service sector or public entities.

2.2   THE GLOBAL INNOVATION INDEX

We use the results of the Global Innovation Index (GII) to understand some global trends in innovation competitiveness and to evaluate how emerging markets fare on the global stage. Professor Soumitra Dutta launched the GII at INSEAD in 2007 with the goal of determining metrics and approaches that better capture the richness of innovation in society and go beyond traditional measures of innovation, such as the number of research articles and the level of R&D expenditures. The GII framework is depicted in Fig. 2.1 and full details on the GII and its results can be found in Appendix of this chapter.

Four measures are calculated within the GII: the overall GII score, the Input and Output Subindices, and the Innovation Efficiency Ratio.

- *The overall GII score* is the simple average of the Input and Output Subindices.
- *The Innovation Input Subindex*: Five input pillars capture elements of the national economy that enable innovative activities: (1) Institutions, (2) Human capital and research, (3) Infrastructure, (4) Market sophistication, and (5) Business sophistication.
- *The Innovation Output Subindex*: Innovation outputs are the results of innovative activities within the economy. There are two additional pillars that capture output: (6) Knowledge and technology outputs and (7) Creative outputs.
- *The Innovation Efficiency Ratio* is the ratio of the Output Subindex over the Input Subindex. It shows how much innovation output a given country is getting for its inputs.

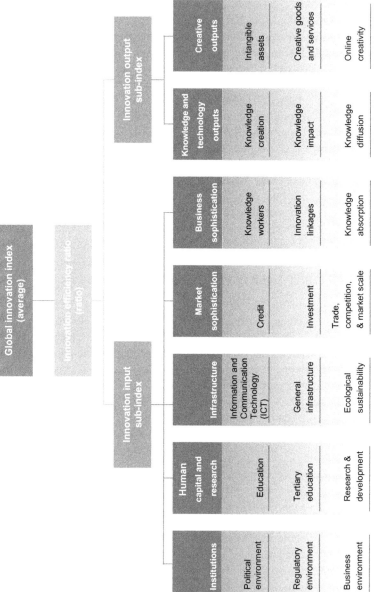

FIG. 2.1 Framework of the Global Innovation Index 2017.

Each pillar is divided into three subpillars and each subpillar is composed of individual indicators, for a total of 79 indicators.

2.2.1   Stability at the Top

In 2017, Switzerland led the rankings for the sixth consecutive year. Sweden remained at 2nd place, and the Netherlands moved up to 3rd from the 9th position in 2016. The United States remained in the 4th position and Finland dropped from the 5th in 2016 to the 8th spot. Singapore (7th), Germany (9th), and Ireland (10th) remained in the top 10.

With the benefit of several years of measurement within the GII project, one can observe a remarkable level of stability among the top-ranked (or most innovative) nations. Fig. 2.2 shows movement in the top 10 ranked economies over the last four years. This stability at the top is indicative of the significant legacy advantages of the leading nations, all of which are developed economies. These top-ranked GII countries have fine-tuned their innovation ecosystems to excel on multiple dimensions of innovation competitiveness. As outlined later in this chapter, emerging economies face significant hurdles in matching the innovation competitiveness of leading developed economies.

2.2.2   Innovation is Becoming More Global but Divides Remain

The GII rankings have also shown a remarkable level of geographic diversity among innovation leaders over the years. The top-ranked 25 nations for innovation in 2017 include economies not only from North America (such as Canada and the United States) and Europe (such as Germany, Switzerland, and the United Kingdom) but also from Southeast Asia and Oceania (such as Australia, Japan, South Korea, and Singapore) and Western Asia (Israel).

Economies that perform at least 10% higher than their peers for their level of gross domestic product (GDP) are labeled "innovation achievers" (see Fig. 2.3); the list of "innovation achievers" includes many economies from Africa (such as Kenya, Madagascar, Malawi, Rwanda, and Uganda), one from the Northern Africa and Western Asia region (Armenia), one from Southeast Asia and Oceania (Vietnam), and several from Central and Southern Asia (such as India and Tajikistan). Sub-Saharan Africa, notably, has shown consistent progress in innovation over the years and Vietnam, Kenya, Moldova, and India have continually been in the group of innovation achievers since 2011.

Despite these improvements in emerging economies, the world of research and innovation appears to be multipolar, rather than a level playing field. Most activities are concentrated in high-income economies and select middle-income economies such as Brazil, China, India, and South Africa. Among middle- income economies, only China has seen its R&D expenditures and other innovation input and output metrics advance toward rich countries such as the United States.

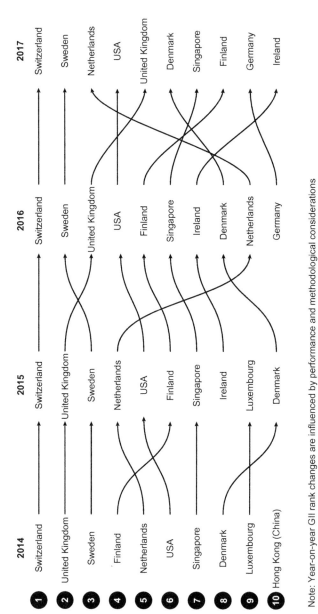

Note: Year-on-year GII rank changes are influenced by performance and methodological considerations

FIG. 2.2 Movement in the top 10 of the GII.

Economy	Income group	Years as an innovation achiever (total)
Vietnam	Lower-middle income	2017, 2016, 2015, 2014, 2013, 2012, 2011 (7)
Kenya	Lower-middle income	2017, 2016, 2015, 2014, 2013, 2012, 2011 (7)
Moldova, Rep.	Lower-middle income	2017, 2016, 2015, 2014, 2013, 2012, 2011 (7)
India	Lower-middle income	2017, 2016, 2015, 2014, 2013, 2012, 2011 (7)
Armenia	Lower-middle income	2017, 2016, 2015, 2014, 2013, 2012 (6)
Ukraine	Lower-middle income	2017, 2016, 2015, 2014, 2012 (5)
Rwanda	Low income	2017, 2016, 2015, 2014, 2012 (5)
Uganda	Low income	2017, 2016, 2015, 2014, 2013 (5)
Mozambique	Low income	2017, 2016, 2015, 2014, 2012 (5)
Malawi	Low income	2017, 2016, 2015, 2014, 2012 (5)
Senegal	Low income	2017, 2015, 2014, 2013, 2012 (5)
Tajikistan	Lower-middle income	2017, 2016, 2013 (3)
Malta	High income	2017, 2016, 2015 (3)
Madagascar	Low income	2017, 2016 (2)
Bulgaria	Upper-middle income	2017, 2015 (2)
Burundi	Low income	2017 (1)
Tanzania, United Rep.	Low income	2017 (1)

Note: World Bank Income Group Classification (July 2016): LI = low income; LM = lower-middle income; UM = upper-middle income; and HI = high income.

FIG. 2.3   Innovation achievers: Income group and years as an innovation achiever.

Innovation achievers accomplish their superior results by continuously improving their institutional framework, having a set of highly skilled workers who operate in stable innovation systems, integrating better with international markets, and displaying more solid channels of knowledge absorption. These traits result in higher economic growth rates per worker and in more sophisticated local business communities that attract foreign investment.

A total of 17 economies comprise the group of "innovation achievers" in 2017, up from 13 in 2016. Most of these economies come from the sub-Saharan region of Africa—nine in total—followed by economies in Eastern Europe, with a total of four. A stronger performance in innovation outputs in 2017 pushed the Czech Republic beyond the achiever group and into a "leader economy." Portugal moved in the opposite direction due to weaker performance in general infrastructure and knowledge absorption, performing only at par with its peers based on level of development. In turn, four new economies join this group: Burundi and United Republic of Tanzania from sub-Saharan Africa, Armenia from the Northern Africa and Western Asia region, and Bulgaria from the Eastern Europe after having been absent in 2016.

Importantly, Kenya, Rwanda, Mozambique, Uganda, Malawi, and Senegal stand out for being innovation achievers at least three times in the previous six years. Madagascar has done so in 2016 and 2017. With the exception of Senegal

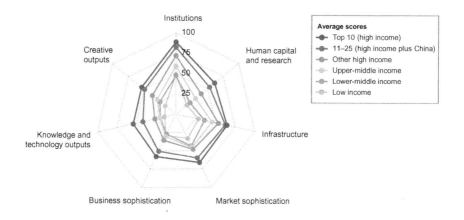

Source: GII 2017 data.

Note: Countries/economies are classified according to the World Bank Income Group Classification (July 2016).

FIG. 2.4   Distinction between the Top 10 innovation leaders and others.

and the latter two economies, all have been signaled as innovation achievers in the two most recent years. Kenya, the chief innovation achiever in the region, has made the list every year since 2011.

Fig. 2.4 shows the average scores for six groups of economies: (1) the top 10, which are all high-income economies; (2) the top 11–25, which are high-income plus China; (3) other high-income; (4) upper-middle-income (excluding China); (5) lower-middle-income; and (6) low-income economies.

The top 10 high-income economies perform above those ranked 11–25 in all pillars. This group's strengths are in Human capital and research (pillar 2), Market sophistication (pillar 4), and Knowledge and technology outputs (pillar 6). Comparing this years' results to that of five years ago shows that the gap between the two groups is currently larger in all the input-side pillars of the GII with the sole exception of the Business sophistication (pillar 5). Conversely, this comparison also shows that performance variations are narrower than they were in Knowledge and technology outputs (pillar 6) and in Creative outputs (pillar 7), both of the pillars in the output-side of the GII.

On average, the divide between middle-income and high-income economies remains large and continues to hold in Institutions (pillar 1), Human capital and research (pillar 2), Infrastructure (pillar 3), and Creative outputs (pillar 7). Relative to previous years, the divide between these groups increased in the Human capital and research (2), Business sophistication (5), and Knowledge and technology outputs (6) pillars.

Confirming a trend first spotted in the GII in 2014, on average, low-income economies continue to close the innovation divide that separates them from middle-income economies. The gap is still significant in some pillars: Human capital and research, Infrastructure, Market sophistication, Knowledge and technology outputs, and Creative outputs, but the gap between the low- and lower-middle-income clusters in two pillars—Institutions and Business sophistication—has now disappeared. In fact, low-income economies now out-perform even the lower-middle-income group on average in Business sophisti-cation. Efforts to bolster solid institutions and to enable businesses to thrive have had considerable impact, eroding the old boundaries and introducing cracks into the glass ceilings of innovation.

2.2.3   High-Quality Innovation Continues to Matter, and China is Catching up

Quality is as important an element of innovation as quantity. Since 2013, the GII has measured quality in three ways: (1) quality of universities (the aver-age rank of a nation's top three universities in QS University Rankings), (2) internationalization of local inventions (patent families filed in two offices), and (3) the number of citations that local research documents receive inter-nationally (as measured through the citable documents H index). Among the high-income group, five economies—the United States of America (USA), Japan, Switzerland, Germany, and the United Kingdom (UK)—have remained among the top five in innovation quality since the inception of this metric. In 2017 the USA moved to the first position, taking the place of Japan. The USA achieved this ranking as a result of continuous top scores in particular quality indicators and an improvement in its score in patent families. The USA takes the top position in citable papers, sharing this spot with the UK for the fifth consecutive year. In 2017 the USA also remains the world leader in the qual-ity of its universities, outranking the UK for the second consecutive year (see Fig. 2.5).

A large gap remains between high-income and middle-income economies. Without China, the difference in average scores between these two groups in both the university rankings and citable documents is expanding, while in pat-ents filed the distance is narrowing. In 2017, China moved up one spot to 16th position in innovation quality, retaining for the fifth consecutive year its posi-tion as the top middle-income economy and getting closer to high-income econ-omies. This movement can be attributed to higher scores in university rankings (4th) and citable documents (14th). Although other middle-income economies still depend greatly on their university rankings to move ahead in the quality of innovation, China—and to some extent South Africa—display a balance be-tween the three components of the quality index.

India is second in innovation quality for the second consecutive year in 2017. India's positive performance is the result of maintaining its second posi-tion in both university rankings and citable documents among middle-income economies. The country shows a small reduction in the score of patent families, which, however, does not affect its quality of innovation ranking. The Russian Federation moved to the 3rd position among the upper-middle- income econo-mies and 28th overall, positioned between India and Brazil.

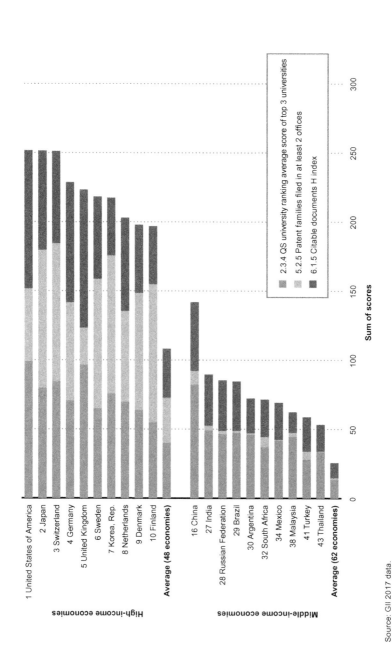

Source: GII 2017 data.

Notes: Numbers to the left of the economy name are the innovation quality rank. Economies are classified by income according to the World Bank Income Group Classification (July 2016). Upper- and lower-middle income categories are grouped together as middle-income economies.

FIG. 2.5 Metrics for quality of innovation: Top 10 high- and top 10 middle-income economies.

2.2.4   Top Performers by Income Group

Viewing economies among their income-group peers can illustrate important relative competitive advantages and help decision makers glean applicable lessons for improved performance.

Fig. 2.6 shows the 10 best-ranked economies in each innovation metric by income group. The top 24 positions in the GII are all held by high-income

	Global innovation index	Innovation input sub-index	Innovation output sub-index	Innovation efficiency ratio
High-income economies (48 in total)				
1	Switzerland (1)	Singapore (1)	Switzerland (1)	Luxembourg (1)
2	Sweden (2)	Sweden (2)	Netherlands (2)	Switzerland (2)
3	Netherlands (3)	Switzerland (3)	Sweden (3)	Netherlands (4)
4	United States of America (4)	Finland (4)	Luxembourg (4)	Iceland (5)
5	United Kingdom (5)	United States of America (5)	United States of America (5)	Ireland (6)
6	Denmark (6)	Denmark (6)	United Kingdom (6)	Germany (7)
7	Singapore (7)	United Kingdom (7)	Germany (7)	Malta (8)
8	Finland (8)	Hong Kong (China) (8)	Ireland (8)	Sweden (12)
9	Germany (9)	Netherlands (9)	Korea, Rep. (9)	Czech Republic (13)
10	Ireland (10)	Canada (10)	Iceland (10)	Korea, Rep. (14)
Upper-middle-income economies (35 in total)				
1	China (22)	China (31)	China (11)	China (3)
2	Bulgaria (36)	Malaysia (36)	Bulgaria (32)	Turkey (9)
3	Malaysia (37)	Russian Federation (43)	Turkey (36)	Bulgaria (15)
4	Romania (42)	Bulgaria (45)	Malaysia (39)	Iran, Islamic Rep. (16)
5	Turkey (43)	Mauritius (47)	Thailand (43)	Thailand (24)
6	Russian Federation (45)	South Africa (49)	Romania (44)	Panama (38)
7	Montenegro (48)	Montenegro (50)	Costa Rica (50)	Romania (39)
8	Thailand (51)	Romania (51)	Russian Federation (51)	Costa Rica (43)
9	Costa Rica (53)	Colombia (52)	Montenegro (52)	Malaysia (46)
10	South Africa (57)	TFYR of Macedonia (53)	Panama (55)	Dominican Republic (54)
Lower-middle-income economies (27 in total)				
1	Viet Nam (47)	India (66)	Viet Nam (38)	Viet Nam (10)
2	Ukraine (50)	Mongolia (67)	Ukraine (40)	Ukraine (11)
3	Mongolia (52)	Viet Nam (71)	Moldova, Rep. (42)	Armenia (17)
4	Moldova, Rep. (54)	Moldova, Rep. (73)	Armenia (47)	Moldova, Rep. (22)
5	Armenia (59)	Ukraine (77)	Mongolia (48)	Mongolia (27)
6	India (60)	Morocco (79)	India (58)	Côte d'Ivoire (40)
7	Morocco (72)	Tunisia (81)	Philippines (65)	Indonesia (42)
8	Philippines (73)	Armenia (82)	Morocco (68)	Kenya (50)
9	Tunisia (74)	Philippines (83)	Kenya (70)	India (53)
10	Kenya (80)	Kyrgyzstan (86)	Tunisia (71)	Philippines (55)
Low-income economies (17 in total)				
1	Tanzania, United Rep. (96)	Rwanda (76)	Tanzania, United Rep. (76)	Tanzania, United Rep. (29)
2	Rwanda (99)	Uganda (93)	Ethiopia (91)	Ethiopia (32)
3	Senegal (100)	Burkina Faso (101)	Madagascar (95)	Madagascar (45)
4	Uganda (102)	Senegal (102)	Senegal (98)	Mozambique (70)
5	Mozambique (107)	Nepal (108)	Mozambique (100)	Mali (78)
6	Nepal (109)	Tanzania, United Rep. (109)	Uganda (106)	Zimbabwe (89)
7	Ethiopia (110)	Benin (110)	Mali (107)	Senegal (95)
8	Madagascar (111)	Niger (111)	Malawi (112)	Malawi (98)
9	Malawi (115)	Malawi (112)	Nepal (114)	Nepal (105)
10	Benin (116)	Mozambique (114)	Zimbabwe (116)	Benin (110)

Note: Economies with top 10 positions in the GII, the Input Sub-Index, the Output Sub-Index and the Innovation Efficiency Ratio within their income group are highlighted in bold.

FIG. 2.6   Ten best-ranked economies by income group (rank).

economies. Switzerland, Sweden, and the Netherlands are among the high-income top 10 on the three main indices, and top 3 in the Innovation Output Subindex. Compared to 2016, Hungary and Estonia leave the group, making space for the Czech Republic and Korea.

Among the 10 highest-ranked upper-middle-income economies on the GII, 9 remain from 2016: China (22nd overall this year), Bulgaria (36th), Malaysia (37th), Romania (42nd), Turkey (43rd), Montenegro (48th), Thailand (51st), Costa Rica (53rd), and South Africa (57th). The newcomer to this group of the 10 best upper-middle-income performers is the Russian Federation (45th), which displaced Mauritius (64th). China, Malaysia, Bulgaria, and Romania are among the 10 best-ranked upper-middle-income economies across all three main indices and in the Innovation Efficiency Ratio.

The same analysis for lower-middle-income countries shows that 8 of the top 10 countries from 2016 remain in the top 10 in 2017. These include Vietnam (47th), Ukraine (50th), the Republic of Moldova (54th), Armenia (59th), India (60th), Morocco (72nd), the Philippines (73rd), and Kenya (80th). New to the top 10 lower-middle-income countries in 2017 are Mongolia (52nd) and Tunisia (74th), which displace Georgia (68th) and Tajikistan (94th). Seven of the top 10 lower-middle-income countries have rankings in the top 10 for each of the three indices, and the Innovation Efficiency Ratio, with the exceptions of Morocco and Tunisia.

There has also been a strong consistency among low-income countries, with 8 out of 10 economies remaining in the top 10. In 2017, the United Republic of Tanzania became the top-ranked low-income country (96th), moving up nine spots in the overall GII since 2016, and improving in the Innovation Input (109th) and Output (76th) Subindices. Following in the ranking of low-income countries are Rwanda (99th) and Senegal (100th) which displaced the now lower-middle-income economy Cambodia (101st). Ranking well across all main indices of the GII, the United Republic of Tanzania, Senegal, Mozambique, Nepal, and Malawi ascended to the top 10 low-income countries. Eight of the 10 economies in the low-income top 10 for the GII are also in the low-income top 10 in the Innovation Efficiency Ratio, with Rwanda and Uganda the only exceptions.

2.2.5 Clustering Leaders, Innovation Achievers, and Underperformers

The GII can also identify economies that over- or underperform on innovation relative to their level of development. Fig. 2.7 presents the GII scores plotted against GDP per capita in purchasing power parity (PPP) on a natural logarithmic scale. The economies that appear close to the trend line show results that are in accordance with what is expected based on their level of development. The further up and above the trend line an economy appears, the better its innovation performance is when compared with that of its peers at the same stage of development. Light-colored bubbles in the figure correspond to the efficient innovators

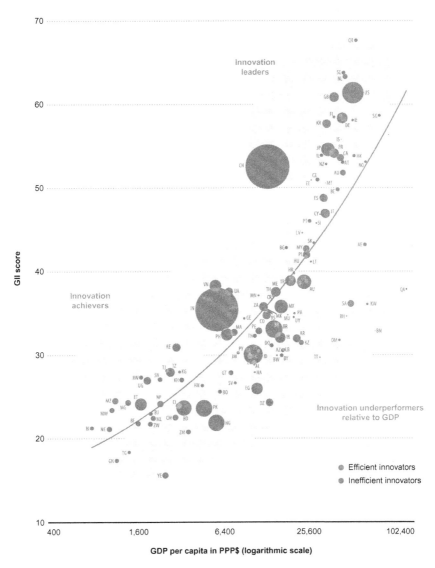

FIG. 2.7 GII scores and GDP per capita in PPP$ (bubbles sized by population): ISO-2 Country Codes.

(a majority of them are situated above the trend line), while the dark-colored bubbles represent those countries in the lower half of the Innovation Efficiency Ratio.

We find the same top 25 economies in the group of innovation leaders as in 2016, with two exceptions: the Czech Republic moved back into this group while Belgium dropped out. All of the top 25 economies are high income with

Country/ economy	Code	Country/ economy	Code	Country/ economy	Code
Albania	AL	Guatemala	GT	Oman	OM
Algeria	DZ	Guinea	GN	Pakistan	PK
Argentina	AR	Honduras	HN	Panama	PA
Armenia	AM	Hong Kong (China)	HK	Paraguay	PY
Australia	AU	Hungary	HU	Peru	PE
Austria	AT	Iceland	IS	Philippines	PH
Azerbaijan	AZ	India	IN	Poland	PL
Bahrain	BH	Indonesia	ID	Portugal	PT
Bangladesh	BD	Iran, Islamic Rep.	IR	Qatar	QA
Belarus	BY	Ireland	IE	Romania	RO
Belgium	BE	Israel	IL	Russian Federation	RU
Benin	BJ	Italy	IT	Rwanda	RW
Bolivia, Plurinational St.	BO	Jamaica	JM	Saudi Arabia	SA
Bosnia and Herzegovina.	BA	Japan	JP	Senegal	SN
Botswana	BW	Jordan	JO	Serbia	RS
Brazil	BR	Kazakhstan	KZ	Singapore	SG
Brunei Darussalam	BN	Kenya	KE	Slovakia	SK
Bulgaria	BG	Korea, Rep.	KR	Slovenia	SI
Burkina Faso	BF	Kuwait	KW	South Africa	ZA
Burundi	BI	Kyrgyzstan	KG	Spain	ES
Cambodia	KH	Latvia	LV	Sri Lanka	LK
Cameroon	CM	Lebanon	LB	Sweden	SE
Canada	CA	Lithuania	LT	Switzerland	CH
Chile	CL	Luxembourg	LU	Tajikistan	TJ
China	CN	Madagascar	MG	Tanzania, United Rep.	TZ
Colombia	CO	Malawi	MW	Thailand	TH
Costa Rica	CR	Malaysia	MY	TFYR of Macedonia	MK
Côte d'Ivoire	CI	Mali	ML	Togo	TG
Croatia	HR	Malta	MT	Trinidad and Tobago	TT
Cyprus	CY	Mauritius	MU	Tunisia	TN
Czech Republic	CZ	Mexico	MX	Turkey	TR
Denmark	DK	Moldova, Rep.	MD	Uganda	UG
Dominican Republic	DO	Mongolia	MN	Ukraine	UA
Ecuador	EC	Montenegro	ME	United Arab Emirates	AE
Egypt	EG	Morocco	MA	United Kingdom	GB
El Salvador	SV	Mozambique	MZ	United States of America	US
Estonia	EE	Namibia	NA	Uruguay	UY
Ethiopia	ET	Nepal	NP	Viet Nam	VN
Finland	FI	Netherlands	NL	Yemen	YE
France	FR	New Zealand	NZ	Zambia	ZM
Georgia	GE	Niger	NE	Zimbabwe	ZW
Germany	DE	Nigeria	NG		
Greece	GR	Norway	NO		

FIG. 2.7, CONT'D

the exception of China, which belongs to the upper-middle-income group. Most of these economies are in Southeast Asia, East Asia, Oceania, and Europe, with the rest in North America, Northern Africa, and Western Asia. All of the economies in this group have a GII score above 50. These economies host mature innovation systems, with solid institutions and high levels of market and business sophistication, allowing investment in human capital and infrastructure to translate into high-quality innovation outputs.

This analysis also allows us to identify a group of economies that perform at least 10% below their peers for their level of GDP. This underachieving cluster includes 39 countries from different regions and income groups. Mainly, 9 from the high-income group (7 of these are from the Northern Africa and Western Asia region), 17 from the upper-middle-income group, 11 from the lower-middle-income group, and 2 from the low-income group.

2.3   SPECIFIC CHARACTERISTICS OF INNOVATION SYSTEMS IN EMERGING COUNTRIES

Innovation is the result of complex interactions among various actors, including firms, education and research organizations, and the public sector. In our definition, successful innovation depends upon the coevolution of institutions and regulations as well as science, technology, and innovation policies.

One question looms large: How, if at all, can prevailing innovation policy approaches of high-income countries adapt to work for developing countries?

The starting points are so-called innovation policy mixes, which high-income economies have fine-tuned over the last couple of decades.[2] Policymakers in these countries follow an "innovation system" approach in which they treat innovation as the result of complex interactions among all innovation actors, policies, and institutions.[3] They also draw on the insight that successfully converting a scientific breakthrough or an idea into a commercialized innovation often involves a long journey without a guaranteed outcome. Bringing product, process, marketing, or organizational innovation to fruition requires additional measures beyond simply incentivizing research.

Two main policy strands form the core of contemporary innovation policy: On the one hand, there is need to improve the underlying conditions for innovation such as the business environment, access to finance, competition, and trade openness as captured in the "Innovation Input" side of the GII model.

On the other hand, nations also need dedicated innovation policies targeting both innovation actors and the linkages among them, for example, via collaborative research projects, public-private partnerships, and clusters.[4] High-income countries pursue a set of dedicated supply- and demand-side innovation policies. These policies support a strong human capital and research base (including research infrastructures), sophisticated firms and markets, innovation linkages,

2. Even in experienced innovative nations, deciding and implementing the right innovation policy mix remains al challenge as innovation parameters and objectives tend to evolve.
3. The innovation system approach aims to provide a holistic framework to analyze innovation performance (Freeman, 1987; Lundvall, 1992; Edquist, 1997). It starts from the assumption that firms do not conduct innovation in isolation, but are part of a larger system comprising multiple agents, e.g. universities, financial institutions, governments, etc. that interact with each other. The functioning and outcomes of innovation systems also depend on institutional, organizational, historic and political framework conditions.
4. OECD (2010) proposes a conceptual innovation policy framework of the sort.

knowledge absorption, and fostering innovation outputs as captured by the GII. Direct support for business R&D and innovation comes in the form of grants, subsidies, or indirect measures such as R&D tax credits. Universities and public research organizations can be funded either through across-the-board or through competitive funding mechanisms.

There is renewed interest among policymakers in demand-side measures to promote innovation, including traditional strategies such as public procurement. Some new approaches to promote innovation are aimed at overcoming key societal challenge in fields such as clean energy or health, facilitating the uptake of specific innovations (including via standards or regulations) or fostering user-led innovation.[5] Business executives in charge of innovation stress the importance of forward-thinking legislation to support future innovation and related markets (e.g., for autonomous cars), as well as the need to harmonize regulations for new technologies internationally.

Policymakers are now focused on creating an "innovation culture" with businesses, students, and society at large, intending to spur greater entrepreneurial activity and increase public appreciation for science and innovation. Governments increasingly treat the formulation and measurement of innovation policies as a science in its own right.

Notwithstanding these developments, finding the right balance between demand and supply measures, and between public and private funding for innovation, remains largely a "trial-and-error" type of endeavor. Though tempting on its face, a simple migration of policies developed in high-income countries to developing countries is unlikely to bear fruit. Innovation policies and institutions need to be context-specific and reflect the heterogeneity and varying trajectories of countries.[6]

Broadly speaking, a number of differences between developed and developing countries need to be considered[7]:

First, the structural conditions for innovation are more challenging in developing countries. This challenge often manifests itself in poorer infrastructure, weaker product, capital and labor markets, and inferior education systems, as well as regulatory systems that often do not provide sufficient or proper incentives for innovation.[8] Developing countries also disproportionately face distinct pressures from their developed counterparts, such as high-population growth and a younger population, or greater levels of inequality.

Second, for simple budgetary reasons, developing countries' capacity to finance, coordinate, and evaluate a large package of innovation policies is

5. Technopolis (2011).
6. Gault (2010), Chaminade et al. (2009) and Lundvall et al. (2009). This heterogeneity is well reflected in the eleven countries chosen as developing country outperformers this year ranging from Armenia, over China, to Uganda.
7. See Kraemer-Mbula and Wamae (2010) and WIPO (2011).
8. Maharajh and Kraemer-Mbula (2010).

constrained. Although all components of innovation policy dimensions may seem important, tough priority-setting is required. Moreover, in the context of developing countries, the innovation policy coordination between various local, regional, and national levels of government is often even more challenging.

Third, the mix of industries in most low- and middle-income countries is usually different from wealthier countries, with a greater reliance on agriculture, the extraction of raw materials, few—and mostly low-value added—manufacturing activities (e.g., in food processing or textiles), and an increasing reliance on services industries such as the creative sectors, tourism, transport, and retail activities. Micro- and small businesses play an outsized role for the broader economy and potentially innovation too. Although frequently neglected in developing countries, the informal sector often matters greatly in emerging markets.

Fourth, country- or sector-specific exceptions aside, innovation capabilities in developing countries are typically less advanced than their developed counterparts. The human resource base remains comparatively feeble and the brain drain abroad is high. Innovation actors and linkages between them are usually weaker; public research organizations are frequently the only actors engaged in research and often operate in an isolated fashion without links to the real economy, while firms tend to have a low absorptive capacity. In the formal sector, improvements in maintenance, engineering, or quality control, rather than fresh R&D investment, drive innovation. Sources of learning and innovation regularly originate from foreign direct investment (FDI) or acquisition of technologies developed abroad. Collaborating with external partners on innovation remains a significant stumbling block for many companies.

As a result of these obstacles, innovation under scarcity is a daily challenge for dynamic clusters of small, informal firms and other actors in developing countries. Their focus is usually on innovation with little investment to expand access to high-quality goods and services and improve the quality of life of poorer segments of the population.

2.4   TAILORING INNOVATION POLICIES TO THE NEEDS OF DEVELOPING COUNTRIES

A persistent, well-coordinated national innovation policy plan with clear targets and a matching institutional set-up have proved a key ingredient for success in developing countries. All too often we observe a succession of vaguely defined, uncoordinated, and inadequately implemented innovation policy plans. In addition to an effective plan, countries must be persistent. Institution-building, the development of human resources, or innovation capacities in certain fields of science or particular sectors are an expensive medium- to long-term affair which can rarely be fast-tracked.

A centralized ministry or governing body can offer the coordination and leadership required for effective deployment of innovation-supporting policies. Separating key innovation responsibilities across different ministries or agencies can be a drag on effectiveness, and the mere creation of an "innovation ministry" will rarely prove successful if it remains surrounded by a plethora of other more powerful ministries. Instead, high-performing innovation agencies or councils have reported directly to, or been chaired by, top-level government officials such as the Prime Minister.

Developing countries' innovation policies must also be coordinated with other, related policies, in particular those concerning education, skill development, and key economic policy matters such as foreign investment and international trade. A strategic coordination of intellectual property (IP) policies with innovation policy objectives is also desirable, as it can foster productive creativity, such as recognized brands and strong physical or intangible assets.

At the outset, innovation policy design requires a thorough review of the existing innovation system and its strengths and weaknesses. Key innovation actors should be involved in this process, including successful national innovators or entrepreneurs abroad. Effective implementation of these policies requires the presence of suitably skilled Science and Technology Innovation (STI) policy managers, which remains a challenge even in high-income countries.

In addition, policymakers need appropriate innovation metrics to assess their current and future state. Developing countries are increasingly adopting rich-country STI indicators and surveys, but metrics focused on R&D personnel or expenditures, or innovation surveys sent to formal firms might provide only a partial, or even distorted, measure of innovation realities in developing economies. In many of these economies, innovation is more incremental and grass-root, often taking place outside the formal business sector. Including but not limited to the GII, there is still work to be done to produce innovation metrics and survey approaches that are more appropriate for developing countries.

A few patterns regarding the substance of innovation policy emerge from countries' experiences. Despite the different nature of innovation in developing countries, policies are often framed narrowly with a focus on high-tech products, clusters, or special economic zones and formulated with an eye to the integration of local operations and products into global value chains through the facilitation of FDI and lower tariffs. These strategies often focus on the absorption of technology from foreign multinationals and the creation of national champions or strengths in particular high-tech or global value chain-related sectors. This "international specialization" approach has had some success and was central to the ascent of many technology-savvy developing countries. China, for instance, focused on telecom and electronics assembly, India on software back-office operations and software, Vietnam on

IT and automotive assembly, and Malaysia on IT assembly. Despite these successes, this type of strategy has often created enclaves of higher-productivity activities with weak links to the rest of the local economy comprising a plethora of small firms operating far from the technological frontier. Even if a country has successfully attracted FDI and become an integral part of the global value chain, there is no guarantee that such successes will automatically spur more domestic innovation.

Overall, risks associated with policies aimed at fostering national champions or pockets of excellence remain high. Many proposed high-tech clusters have remained empty shells, and strategic "national priority" sectors never took off due to such risks. Top-down approaches in designating clusters or picking champions and priority sectors might come at the expense of creating an open and truly competitive level playing field that would foster entrepreneurship and give space to potential local innovators. Additionally, an excessive attention to global opportunities sometimes comes at the expense of focusing on more domestically grown innovation addressing local challenges through technologies that may not be at the world frontier but work in the local context.

Policymakers' focus ought to be on fostering existing domestic innovation capabilities, including for traditional sectors like agriculture, food, mining, and energy. This requires a more strategic view and assessment of key strengths, followed by creative thought on how they can be built up, including through the smart use of IP.

Many countries underestimate the disruptive and impactful nature of more service-based and bottom-up innovation. Certain African countries have experienced rapid and spontaneous innovations in finance (e-banking), telecommunications, and medical technologies in recent years, such as Kenya's M-Pesa case. The developing country context and sometimes more permissive regulatory environments can provide opportunities for innovation and leapfrogging in ways rarely seen in higher-income economies. Additionally, grassroots innovations for health, education, and transportation that improve the quality of residents' daily lives have emerged in developing countries.

In sum, the potential pay-off from creating technology-neutral conditions that allow for more bottom-up innovation remains significant, pending a certain amount of luck. It may yield quicker results to introduce more labor market flexibility; allow for fair competition between private, foreign, and state-owned firms; facilitate access to finance; make it easier to start a business; and foster an efficient Information Communications Technology (ICT) infrastructure. Despite these advantages, this approach comes with a lesser degree of control, and its progress and impacts are not easily measured. Dedicated innovation policies should prioritize three opportunities: First, all our GII-related national assessments show that increasing business linkages to the science system (for example, via joint research projects), foreign subsidiaries, and scientist recruitment is often the single biggest challenge. Sadly, some developing countries produce above-par science and engineering graduates and researchers, without ever employing such talents in local business innovation, leaving these precious resources idle. Second, while significant resources are devoted to attracting foreign multinationals and investment, less attention is put on the question of how to capture and maximize positive spillovers to the local economy. Intermediate organizations such as NGOs or measuring and testing centers can play a crucial role in translating the knowledge of multinational enterprises (MNEs) to other local actors. Labor mobility is a significant driver of spillover value for the local economy, which can be promoted by incentivizing entrepreneurship among employees of MNEs. At the enterprise level, policymakers should prioritize scaling up innovative activities in small and microenterprises, whether in the formal or informal sector, and strengthening their linkages to formal institutions.[9]

Finally, it seems that too few economies have explored the potential benefits of steering innovation and research toward context-specific solutions to local challenges that may not be frontier technologies or part of existing global value chains.[10] These innovations could solve particular energy, transport, or sanitation needs; improve the processing of local produce; upgrade local artisanship; or reap greater economic rewards from a thriving creative industry. National efforts around particular national health or other developing country challenges—which remain unaddressed by innovation systems in higher-income countries—are also promising on the global scale. Other developing countries facing similar conditions and seeking similar solutions constitute a large potential set of buyers for context-specific innovation; South-South trade in tailored innovative goods and services is increasingly a reality.

2.5 CONCLUSION

The GII provides us with a quantitative measure of innovation in more than 120 economies globally. Rather than rely on anecdotal examples, the GII presents objective evidence of the progress of innovation across the world. While developed economies continue to lead in innovation, the GII shows that emerging markets, led by China, are making significant and steady progress in improving their innovation capabilities and results. Selective countries in traditionally lagging regions such as sub-Saharan Africa are also showing distinct improvements, raising the question of how to improve and leverage the innovation capabilities of emerging markets. This is the primary focus of the remainder of the book.

---

9. Fu et al. (2014) and Kraemer-Mbula and Wunsch-Vincent (2016).
10. Srinivas and Sutz (2008).

APPENDIX: THE GLOBAL INNOVATION INDEX (GII) CONCEPTUAL FRAMEWORK

The Rationale for the Global Innovation Index

Now in its 10th edition, the GII helps to create an environment in which innovation factors are under continual evaluation, and it provides a key tool for decision makers and a rich database of detailed metrics for refining innovation policies.

The GII is not meant to be the ultimate and definitive ranking of economies with respect to innovation. Measuring innovation outputs and impacts remains difficult, hence great emphasis is placed on measuring the climate and infrastructure for innovation and on assessing related outcomes.

Although the end results take the shape of several rankings, the GII is more concerned with improving the "journey" to better measure and understand innovation and with identifying targeted policies, good practices, and other levers that foster innovation. The rich metrics can be used—on the level of the index, the subindices, or the actual raw data of individual indicators—to monitor performance over time and to benchmark developments against countries in the same region or income classification.

An Inclusive Perspective on Innovation

Today, innovation capability is seen as the ability to exploit new technological combinations; it embraces the notion of incremental innovation and "innovation without research." Non-R&D innovative expenditure is an important component of reaping the rewards of technological innovation. Interest in understanding how innovation takes place in low- and middle-income countries is increasing, along with awareness that incremental forms of innovation can impact development. Furthermore, the process of innovation itself has changed significantly. Investment in innovation-related activity has consistently intensified at the firm, country, and global levels, adding both new innovation actors from outside high-income economies and nonprofit actors. The structure of knowledge production activity is more complex and geographically dispersed than ever.

The GII aims to move beyond the mere measurement of such simple innovation metrics. To do so will require the integration of new variables, with a trade-off between the quality of the variable on the one hand and achieving good country coverage on the other hand.

The timeliest possible indicators are used for the GII each year. In 2017, 38.7% of data obtained are from 2016, 38.1% from 2015, 11.3% from 2014, 5.7% from 2013, and the small remainder 6.2% from earlier years.[i]

---

i. For completeness, 2.0% of data points are from 2012, 1.2% from 2011, 1.3% from 2010, 0.7% from 2009, 0.7% from 2008, 0.3% from 2007, and 0.1% from 2006. In addition, the GII is calculated on the basis of 9225 data points (compared to 10,287 with complete series), implying that 10.3% of data points are missing.

The GII Conceptual Framework

The GII is an evolving project that builds on its previous editions while incorporating newly available data and that is inspired by the latest research on the measurement of innovation. In 2017 the GII model includes 127 countries/economies, which represent 92.5% of the world's population and 97.6% of the world's GDP (in current U.S. dollars). The GII relies on two subindices—the Innovation Input Subindex and the Innovation Output Subindex—each built around pillars. Four measures are calculated (see Fig. 2.1):

Innovation Input Subindex: Five input pillars capture elements of the national economy that enable innovative activities.

Innovation Output Subindex: Innovation outputs are the results of innovative activities within the economy. Although the Output Subindex includes only two pillars, it has the same weight in calculating the overall GII scores as the Input Subindex.

The overall GII score is the simple average of the Input and Output Subindices.

The Innovation Efficiency Ratio is the ratio of the Output Subindex to the Input Subindex. It shows how much innovation output a given country is getting for its inputs.

Each pillar is divided into three subpillars, each of which is composed of individual indicators, for a total of 81 indicators in 2017.

A table is included here for each pillar. That table provides a list of the pillar's indicators, specifying their type (composite indicators are identified with an asterisk "*," survey questions with a dagger "†," and the remaining indicators are hard data); their weight in the index (indicators with half weight are identified with the letter "a"); and the direction of their effect (indicators for which higher values imply worse outcomes are identified with the letter "b"). The table then provides each indicator's average values (in their respective units) per income group (World Bank classification) and for the whole sample of 127 economies retained in the final computation (Tables A2.1–A2.7).

The Innovation Input Subindex

The first subindex of the GII, the Innovation Input Subindex, has five enabler pillars: Institutions, Human capital and research, Infrastructure, Market sophistication, and Business sophistication. Enabler pillars define aspects of the environment conducive to innovation within an economy.

Pillar 1: Institutions

Nurturing an institutional framework that attracts business and fosters growth by providing good governance and the correct levels of protection and incentives is essential to innovation. The Institutions pillar captures the institutional framework of a country (Table A2.1).

The Political environment subpillar includes two indices: one that reflects perceptions of the likelihood that a government might be destabilized, and one that reflects the quality of public and civil services, policy formulation, and implementation.

The Regulatory environment subpillar draws on two indices tracking perceptions of the ability of the government to formulate and implement cohesive policies that promote the development of the private sector, and evaluating the extent to which the rule of law prevails (in aspects such as contract enforcement, property rights, the police, and the courts). The third indicator evaluates the cost of redundancy dismissal as the sum, in salary weeks, of the cost of advance notice requirements added to severance payments due when terminating a redundant worker.

The Business environment subpillar expands on three aspects that directly affect private entrepreneurial endeavors by using the World Bank indices on the ease of starting a business, the ease of resolving insolvency (based on the recovery rate recorded as the cents on the dollar recouped by creditors through reorganization, liquidation, or debt enforcement/foreclosure proceedings), and the ease of paying taxes.

Pillar 2: Human Capital and Research

The level and standard of education and research activity in a country are prime determinants of its innovation capacity. This pillar tries to gauge the human capital of countries (Table A2.2).

The first subpillar includes a mix of indicators aimed at capturing achievements at the elementary and secondary education levels. Education expenditure and school life expectancy are good proxies for coverage. Government expenditure per pupil gives a sense of the level of priority given to secondary education by the state. The quality of education is measured through the results to the OECD Programme for International Student Assessment (PISA), which examines 15-year-old students' performances in reading, mathematics, and science, as well as the pupil-teacher ratio.

Higher education is crucial for economies to move up the value chain beyond simple production processes and products. The subpillar on tertiary education aims at capturing coverage (tertiary enrolment); priority is given to the sectors traditionally associated with innovation (with a series on the percentage of tertiary graduates in science, engineering, manufacturing, and construction), and the mobility of tertiary students, which plays a crucial role in the exchange of ideas and skills necessary for innovation.

The last subpillar, on R&D, measures the level and quality of R&D activities, with indicators on researchers (full-time equivalence), gross expenditure, the R&D expenditures of top global R&D spenders, and the quality of scientific and research institutions as measured by the average score of the top three universities in the QS World University Ranking of 2016. The R&D expenditures of the top three firms in a given country looks at the average expenditure of these three firms that are part of the top 2500 R&D spenders worldwide. The QS university rankings indicator gives the average scores of the country's top three universities that belong to the top 700 universities worldwide. These indicators are not aimed at assessing the average level of all institutions within a particular economy.

Pillar 3: Infrastructure

The third pillar includes three subpillars: Information and communication technologies (ICTs), General infrastructure, and Ecological sustainability (Table A2.3).

Good and ecologically friendly communication, transport, and energy infrastructures facilitate the production and exchange of ideas, services, and goods and feed into the innovation system through increased productivity and efficiency, lower transaction costs, better access to markets, and sustainable growth.

The ICT subpillar includes four indices developed by international organizations on ICT access, ICT use, online service by governments, and online participation of citizens.

The subpillar on general infrastructure includes the average of electricity output in kilowatt-hours (kWh) per capita, a composite indicator on logistics performance, and gross capital formation, which consists of outlays on additions to the fixed assets and net inventories of the economy, including land improvements (fences, ditches, drains), plant, machinery, and equipment purchases, and the construction of roads, railways, and the like, including schools, offices, hospitals, private residential dwellings, and commercial and industrial buildings.

The subpillar on ecological sustainability includes three indicators: GDP per unit of energy use (a measure of efficiency in the use of energy), the Environmental Performance Index of Yale and Columbia Universities, and the number of certificates of conformity with standard ISO 14001 on environmental management systems issued.

Pillar 4: Market Sophistication

Credit availability and a supportive environment for investment, access to the international market, competition, and market scale are all critical for businesses to prosper and for innovation to occur. The Market sophistication pillar has three subpillars structured around market conditions and the total level of transactions (Table A2.4).

The Credit subpillar includes an assessment of the ease of getting credit aimed at measuring the degree to which collateral and bankruptcy laws facilitate lending by protecting the rights of borrowers and lenders, as well as the rules and practices affecting the coverage, scope, and accessibility of credit information. Transactions are given by the total value of domestic credit and, in an attempt to make the model more applicable to emerging markets, by the gross loan portfolio of microfinance institutions.

The Investment subpillar includes the ease of protecting minority investors index as well as two indicators on the level of transactions. These two indicators look at whether market size is matched by market dynamism and provide a hard data metric on venture capital deals.

The last subpillar tackles trade, competition, and market scale. The market conditions for trade are given in the first indicator measuring the average tariff rate weighted by import shares. The second indicator is a survey question that reflects the intensity of competition in local markets. Efforts made at finding hard data on competition so far remain unsuccessful. Domestic market scale, as measured by an economy's GDP, was incorporated in 2016, so the last subpillar takes into consideration the impact that the size of an economy has on its capacity to introduce and test innovations in the marketplace.

Pillar 5: Business Sophistication

The last enabler pillar tries to capture the level of business sophistication to assess how conducive firms are to innovation activity (Table A2.5). The Human capital and research pillar (pillar 2) made the case that the accumulation of human capital through education, particularly higher education and the prioritization of R&D activities, is an indispensable condition for innovation to take place. That logic is taken one step further here with the assertion that businesses foster their productivity, competitiveness, and innovation potential with the employment of highly qualified professionals and technicians.

The first subpillar includes four quantitative indicators on knowledge workers: employment in knowledge-intensive services, the availability of formal training at the firm level, gross domestic expenditure on R&D (GERD) as a percentage of GDP (i.e., GERD over GDP), and the percentage of total gross expenditure of R&D that is financed by business enterprise. In addition, the subpillar includes an indicator related to the percentage of females employed with advanced degrees. This indicator, in addition to providing a glimpse into the gender labor distributions of nations, offers more information about the degree of sophistication of the local human capital currently employed.

Innovation linkages and public/private/academic partnerships are essential to innovation. In emerging markets, pockets of wealth have developed around industrial or technological clusters and networks, in sharp contrast to the poverty that may prevail in the rest of the territory. The Innovation linkages subpillar draws on both qualitative and quantitative data regarding business/university collaboration on R&D, the prevalence of well-developed and deep clusters, the level of gross R&D expenditure financed abroad, and the number of deals on joint ventures and strategic alliances. In addition, the total number of Patent Cooperation Treaty (PCT) and national office published patent family applications filed by residents in at least two offices serves as a proxy for international linkages.

In broad terms, pillar 4 on market sophistication makes the case that well-functioning markets contribute to the innovation environment through competitive pressure, efficiency gains, and transaction economies and by allowing supply to meet demand. Markets that are open to foreign trade and investment have the additional effect of exposing domestic firms to best practices around the globe, which is critical to innovation through knowledge absorption and diffusion, which are considered in pillars 5 and 6. The rationale behind subpillars 5.3 on knowledge absorption (an enabler) and 6.3 on knowledge diffusion (a result)—two subpillars designed to be mirror images of each other—is precisely that together they will reveal how good economies are at absorbing and diffusing knowledge.

Subpillar 5.3 includes five metrics that are linked to sectors with high-tech content or are key to innovation: intellectual property payments as a percentage of total trade; high-tech net imports as a percentage of total imports; imports of communication, computer, and information services as a percentage of total trade; and net inflows of FDI as a percentage of GDP (three-year average). To strengthen the subpillar, the percentage of research talent in business was added in 2016 to provide a measurement of professionals engaged in the conception or creation of new knowledge, products, processes, methods, and systems, including business management.

The Innovation Output Subindex.

Innovation outputs are the results of innovative activities within the economy. Although the Output Subindex includes only two pillars, it has the same weight in calculating the overall GII scores as the Input Subindex. There are two output pillars: Knowledge and technology outputs and Creative outputs.

Pillar 6: Knowledge and Technology Outputs

This pillar covers all those variables that are traditionally thought to be the fruits of inventions and/or innovations (Table A2.6). The first subpillar refers to the creation of knowledge. It includes five indicators that are the result of inventive and innovative activities: patent applications filed by residents both at the national patent office and at the international level through the PCT, utility model applications filed by residents at the national office, scientific and technical published articles in peer-reviewed journals, and an economy's number of articles (H) that have received at least H citations.

The second subpillar, on knowledge impact, includes statistics representing the impact of innovation activities at the micro- and macroeconomic level or related proxies: increases in labor productivity, the entry density of new firms, spending on computer software, the number of certificates of conformity with standard ISO 9001 on quality management systems issued, and the measure of high- and medium-high-tech industrial output over total manufactured output.

The third subpillar, on knowledge diffusion, is the mirror image of the knowledge absorption subpillar of pillar 5, with the exception of indicator 5.3.5. It includes four statistics all linked to sectors with high-tech content or that are key to innovation: intellectual property receipts as a percentage of total trade, high-tech net exports as a percentage of total exports, exports of ICT services as a percentage of total trade, and net outflows of FDI as a percentage of GDP (three-year average).

Pillar 7: Creative outputs

The role of creativity in innovation is still largely underappreciated in innovation measurement and policy debates. Since its inception, the GII has always emphasized measuring creativity as part of its Innovation Output Subindex. The last pillar, on creative outputs, has three subpillars (Table A2.7).

The first subpillar on intangible assets includes statistics on trademark applications by residents at the national office, industrial designs included in applications at a regional or national office, and two survey questions regarding the use of ICTs in business and organizational models, new areas that are increasingly linked to process innovations in the literature.

The second subpillar on creative goods and services includes proxies to get at creativity and the creative outputs of an economy. In 2014, in an attempt to include broader sector coverage, we added a global entertainment and media output composite. In addition, we renamed the indicator on audio-visual and related services exports "Cultural and creative services exports" and expanded it to include information services, advertising, market research and public opinion polling, and other personal, cultural, and recreational services (as a percentage of total trade). These two indicators complement the remainder of the subpillar, which measures national feature films produced in a given country (per capita count); printing and publishing output (as a percentage of total manufactures output); and creative goods exports (as a percentage of total trade), all of which are aimed at providing an overall sense of the international reach of creative activities in the country.

The third subpillar on online creativity includes four indicators, all scaled by population aged 15- through 69-years old: generic and country-code top level domains, average yearly edits to Wikipedia, and video uploads on YouTube. Attempts made to strengthen this subpillar with indicators in areas such as Internet and machine learning, blog posting, online gaming, and the development of applications have so far proved unsuccessful.

TABLE A2.1 Institutions Pillar

Indicator		High Income	Average Value by Income Group			Mean
			Upper-Middle Income	Lower-Middle Income	Low Income	
1	Institutions					
1.1	Political environment					
1.1.1	Political stability and safety*	0.69	−0.23	−0.80	−0.66	−0.06
1.1.2	Government effectiveness*	1.21	0.04	−0.50	−0.78	0.26
1.2	Regulatory environment					
1.2.1	Regulatory quality*a	1.19	0.03	−0.45	−0.63	0.28
1.2.2	Rule of law*a	1.1.9	−0.22	−0.60	−0.64	0.18
1.2.3	Cost of redundancy dismissal, salary weeksb	14.60	17.95	26.60	16.18	18.29
1.3	Business environment					
1.3.1	Ease of starting a business*	90.29	84.76	82.13	79.87	85.64
1.3.2	Ease of resolving insolvency*	68.24	51.63	39.85	38.80	53.69
1.3.3	Ease of paying taxes*	83.83	69.51	59.52	57.51	71.19

Note: (*) index, (**) survey question, (a) half weight, (b) higher values indicate worse outcomes.

TABLE A2.2 Human Capital and Research Pillar

	Indicator	High Income	Upper-Middle Income	Lower-Middle Income	Low Income	Mean
			Average Value by Income Group			
2	Human capital and research					
2.1	Education					
2.1.1	Expenditure on education, % GDP	5.49	4.56	4.21	4.75	4.75
2.1.2	Gov't expend. on edu./pupil, secondary[1]	24.86	17.65	17.97	25.17	21.17
2.1.3	School life expectancy, years	16.56	14.31	11.86	9.67	13.95
2.1.4	PISA scales in reading, maths & science[a]	489.53	416.63	405.24	n/a	459.98
2.1.5	Pupil-teacher ratio, secondary[a,b]	11.25	15.06	20.07	27.26	16.52
2.2	Tertiary education					
2.2.1	Tertiary enrolment, % gross[a]	66.29	47.38	28.27	7.28	44.83
2.2.2	Graduates in science & engineering, %	22.76	21.04	22.06	14.44	21.32
2.2.3	Tertiary inbound mobility, %[a]	9.96	3.45	1.53	3.4.2	5.77
2.3	Research and development (R&D)					
2.3.1	Researchers, FTE/mn pop	3680.04	792.86	449.14	68.47	1938.71
2.3.2	Gross expenditure on R&D, % GDP	1.65	0.55	0.34	0.36	0.96
2.3.3	Global R&D firms, avg. exp. top 3, mn $US	1332.33	154.67	37.95	0.00	554.25
2.3.4	QS university ranking, average score top 3*	39.97	18.48	6.93	0.18	21.70

Note: (*) index, (**) survey question, (a) half weight, (b) higher values indicate worse outcomes.
1 scaled by percent of GDP per capita.

TABLE A2.3 Infrastructure Pillar

	Indicator	High Income	Upper-Middle Income	Lower-Middle Income	Low Income	Mean
			Average Value by Income Group			
3	Infrastructure					
3.1	Information and communication technologies (ICTs)					
3.1.1	ICT access*	8.08	5.98	4.41	2.68	6.01
3.1.2	ICT use*	6.86	4.36	2.30	0.86	4.41
3.1.3	Government's online service*	0.77	0.57	0.46	0.28	0.58
3.1.4	E-participation*	0.75	0.57	0.49	0.30	0.59
3.2	General infrastructure					
3.2.1	Electricity output, kWh/cap[a]	9396.97	3285.84	1135.44	221.18	5031.15
3.2.2	Logistics performance*[a]	3.60	2.83	2.64	2.56	3.04
3.2.3	Gross capital formation, % GDP	21.81	25.33	22.27	24.49	23.22
3.3	Ecological sustainability					
3.3.1	GDP/unit of energy use, 2010 PPP$/kg oil eq	10.15	9.73	8.84	4.36	9.29
3.3.2	Environmental performance*	82.18	74.11	65.77	47.86	72.08
3.3.3	ISO 14001 environ. Certificates/bn PPP$ GDP[a]	4.45	2.73	0.56	0.23	2.60

Note: (*) index, (**) survey question, (a) half weight, (b) higher values indicate worse outcomes. KwH = kilowatt hours.

TABLE A2.4 Market Sophistication Pillar

Indicator		High Income	Average Value by Income Group			Mean
			Upper-Middle Income	Lower-Middle Income	Low Income	
4	Market sophistication					
4.1	Credit					
4.1.1	Ease of getting credit*	59.79	60.29	55.74	36.76	55.98
4.1.2	Domestic credit to private sector, % GDP	99.09	59.83	41.61	23.82	66.31
4.1.3	Microfinance gross loans, % GDP	0.15	0.95	3.63	0.98	1.79
4.2	Investment					
4.2.1	Ease of protecting minority investors*	62.98	58.86	53.33	43.63	57.20
4.2.2	Market capitalization, % GDP[a]	93.18	41.80	28.10	21.82	60.25
4.2.3	Venture capital deals/bn PPP$ GDP[a]	0.11	0.02	0.02	0.03	0.06
4.3	Trade, competition, and market scale					
4.3.1	Applied tariff rate, weighted mean, %[a,b]	1.84	3.79	5.35	8.99	4.08
4.3.2	Intensity of local competition**	5.42	5.01	4.88	4.67	5.10
4.3.3	Domestic market scale, bn PPP$	1120.76	1183.87	700.32	48.06	905.18

Note: (*) index, (**) survey question, (a) half weight, (b) higher values indicate worse outcomes.

TABLE A2.5 Business Sophistication Pillar

			Average Value by Income Group			
	Indicator	High Income	Upper-Middle Income	Lower-Middle Income	Low Income	Mean
5	Business sophistication					
5.1	Knowledge workers					
5.1.1	Knowledge-intensive employment, %	38.87	23.03	17.99	3.73	27.37
5.1.2	Firms offering formal training, % firms	40.37	38.43	32.05	28.41	35.00
5.1.3	GERD performed by business, % GDP[[a	1.06	0.28	0.10	0.04	0.63
5.1.4	GERD financed by business, %[a	43.84	25.65	15.82	5.87	31.32
5.1.5	Females emp. w/adv. Degrees, % tot. Emp.[[a	18.81	13.01	10.02	2.27	14.54
5.2	Innovation linkages					
5.2.1	University/industry research collaboration**[a	4.26	3.40	3.21	3.13	3.66
5.2.2	State of cluster development**	4.37	3.64	3.48	3.29	3.85
5.2.3	GERD financed by abroad, %	14.14	9.09	8.98	30.63	13.49
5.2.4	JV-strategic alliance deals/bn PPP$ GDP[a	0.07	0.02	0.02	0.02	0.04

5.2.5	Patent families filed in 2+ offices/bn PPP$ GDP[a]	3.38	0.16	0.09	0.07	1.44
5.3	Knowledge absorption					
5.3.1	Intellectual property payments, % total trade[a]	1.90	0.69	0.44	0.13	1.00
5.3.2	High-tech imports less re-imports, % total trade	10.27	9.81	7.98	7.91	9.36
5.3.3	ICT services imports, % total trade	1.67	0.93	0.86	1.71	1.30
5.3.4	FDI net inflows, % GDP	5.32	3.94	3.18	5.32	4.49
5.3.5	Research talent, % in business enterprise	42.75	23.24	20.23	17.04	32.44

Note: (*) index, (**) survey question, (a) half weight, (b) higher values indicate worse outcomes. GERD = gross domestic expenditure on R&D.

TABLE A2.6 Knowledge and Technology Outputs Pillar

Indicator		High Income	Average Value by Income Group			Mean
			Upper-Middle Income	Lower-Middle Income	Low Income	
6	Knowledge and technology outputs					
6.1	Knowledge creation					
6.1.1	Patents by origin/bn PPP$ GDP[a]	7.65	3.02	1.27	0.25	4.10
6.1.2	PCT patent applications/bn PPP$ GDP[a]	2.50	0.23	0.10	0.06	1.17
6.1.3	Utility models by origin/bn PPP$ GDP	1.26	3.23	3.19	0.19	2.40
6.1.4	Scientific & technical articles/bn PPP$ GDP[a]	30.01	10.82	7.22	8.66	16.94
6.1.5	Citable documents H index*a	422.21	166.28	120.37	78.91	241.56
6.2	Knowledge impact					
6.2.1	Growth rate of PPP$ GDP/worker, %	0.70	0.69	1.19	2.32	0.97
6.2.2	New businesses/th pop. 15–64[a]	6.12	3.28	1.00	0.45	3.64
6.2.3	Computer software spending, % GDP[a]	0.42	0.21	0.19	0.07	0.26
6.2.4	ISO 9001 quality certificates/bn PPP$ GDP[a]	14.69	9.35	2.73	1.33	8.89

6.2.5	High- & medium-high-tech manufactures, %[a]	33.74	21.97	15.83	8.68	25.05
6.3	Knowledge diffusion					
6.3.1	Intellectual property receipts, % total trade[a]	1.20	0.08	0.11	0.05	0.51
6.3.2	High-tech exports less reexports, % total trade[a]	6.87	4.55	2.15	0.34	4.39
6.3.3	ICT services exports, % total trade[a]	2.99	1.73	2.34	2.34	2.42
6.3.4	FDI net outflows, % GDP	3.59	0.95	0.22	0.52	1.75

Note: (*) index, (**) survey question, (a) half weight, (b) higher values indicate worse outcomes.

TABLE A2.7 Creative Outputs Pillar

	Indicator		Average Value by Income Group			
		High Income	Upper-Middle Income	Lower-Middle Income	Low Income	Mean
7	Creative outputs					
7.1	Intangible assets					
7.1.1	Trademarks by origin/bn PPP$ GDP	56.96	56.80	45.97	16.72	49.60
7.1.2	Industrial designs by origin/bn PPP$ GDP[a]	5.3.5	3.09	4.48	1.26	4.10
7.1.3	ICTs & business model creation**	5.28	4.51	4.25	3.89	4.68
7.1.4	ICTs & organizational model creation**	4.93	4.04	3.87	3.40	4.28
7.2	Creative goods and services					
7.2.1	Cultural & creative services exp., % total trade[a]	0.85	0.58	0.08	0.23	0.54
7.2.2	National feature films/mn pop. 15–69[a]	9.35	3.30	2.90	1.30	5.52
7.2.3	Global ent. & media market/th pop. 15–69[a]	1.26	0.19	0.05	n/a	0.78
7.2.4	Printing & publishing manufactures, %	2.21	1.62	1.12	1.55	1.78
7.2.5	Creative goods exports, % total trade	1.90	1.70	0.86	0.07	1.39
7.3	Online creativity					
7.3.1	Generic TLDs/th pop. 15–69	33.42	5.79	1.37	0.32	14.56
7.3.2	Country-code TLDs/th pop. 15–69	31.69	6.52	0.91	0.77	14.07
7.3.3	Wikipedia yearly edits/mn pop. 15–69	60.37	46.09	33.69	9.93	44.01
7.3.4	Video uploads on YouTube/pop. 15–69	48.20	25.32	11.43	0.94	35.41

Note: (*) index, (**) survey question, (a) half weight, (b) higher values indicate worse outcomes. Scores rather than values are presented for indicators 7.3.1, 7.3.2, 7.3.3, and 7.3.4. TLDs = top-level domains.

REFERENCES

Chaminade, C., Bengt-Åke, L., Van, J., Joseph, K.J., 2009. Designing innovation policies for development: toward a systematic experimentation-based approach. In: Lundvall, B.-Å., Joseph, K.J., Chaminade, C., Vang, J. (Eds.), Handbook of Innovation Systems and Developing Countries: Building Domestic Capabilities in a Global Setting. Edward Elgar Publishing, Cheltenham.

DFID-ESRC Growth Research Programme. http://degrp.squarespace.com/.

Edquist, C., 1997. Systems of innovation approaches: their emergence and characteristics. In: Edquist, C. (Ed.), Systems of Innovation: Technologies, Institutions and Organizations. Pinter, London.

Freeman, C., 1987. Technology, Policy, and Economic Performance: Lessons from Japan. Pinter Publishers, London.

Fu, X., Zanello, B., Essegby, G., Hou, J., Mohnen, P., 2014. Innovation in low income countries. A survey report for The Diffusion of Innovation in Low Income Countries project (DILIC).

Gault, F., 2010. Innovation and development. In: Gault, F. (Ed.), Innovation Strategies for a Global Economy. Edward Elgar Publishing, Cheltenham, pp. 133–164.

GII, 2011. In: Dutta, S. (Ed.), Global Innovation Index 2011: Accelerating Growth and Development. INSEAD.

Kraemer-Mbula, E., Wamae, W., 2010. Adapting the innovation systems framework to sub-Saharan Africa. In: Kraemer-Mbula, E., Wamae, W. (Eds.), Innovation and the Development Agenda. OECD Publishing, Paris, pp. 65–90.

Kraemer-Mbula, E., Wunsch-Vincent, S., 2016. The informal economy in developing nations: hidden engine of innovation? In: New Economic Insights and Policies. Cambridge University Press, Cambridge.

Lundvall, B.-Å., 1992. National Systems of Innovation: Towards a Theory of Innovation and Interactive Learning. Pinter Publishers, London.

Lundvall, B.-Å., Vang, J., Joseph, J., Chaminade, C., 2009. Innovation system research and developing countries. In: Lundvall, B.-Å., Joseph, K.J., Chaminade, C., Vang, J. (Eds.), Handbook of Innovation Systems and Developing Countries: Building Domestic Capabilities in a Global Setting. Edward Elgar Publishing, Cheltenham.

Maharajh, R., Kraemer-Mbula, E., 2010. Innovation strategies in developing countries. In: Kraemer-Mbula, E., Wamae, W. (Eds.), Innovation and the Development Agenda. OECD Publishing, Paris, pp. 133–151.

Organisation for Economic Co-operation and Development, 2005. Oslo manual. http://www.oecd.org/sti/inno/oslomanualguidelinesforcollectingandinterpretinginnovationdata3rdedition.htm.

OECD, 2010. The innovation policy mix. Science, Technology and Industry Outlook 2010. OECD Publishing, Paris (Chapter 4).

OECD, 2013. Science, technology and industry scoreboard. Country Profile: Canada. OECD Publishing, Paris.

OECD, 2014. Science, Technology and Industry Outlook 2014. OECD Publishing, Paris.

Srinivas, S., Sutz, J., 2008. Developing countries and innovation: searching for a new analytical approach. Technol. Soc. 30, 129–140.

Technopolis, 2011. Trends and challenges in demand-side innovation policies in Europe: thematic report 2011. Report prepared for the European Commission, 26 October. Technopolis, Brighton.

WIPO, 2011. Harnessing public research for innovation: the role of intellectual property. In: World Intellectual Property Reporter 2011. WIPO, Economics and Statistics Division, Geneva (Chapter 4).

Chapter 3

The Impact of Science and Technology Policies on Rapid Economic Development in China*

ACRONYMS

BRICS	CPCI-S: Conference Proceedings Citation Index-Science
EI	Engineering Index
GDP	Gross Domestic Product
GERD	Gross Expenditure on R&D
R&D	Research and Development
S&T	Science and Technology
SCI	Science Citation Index

3.1 OVERVIEW

Policy reform and innovation are key drivers of China's remarkable economic growth.[6] Since 1978, China has implemented a series of large-scale science and

---

* This chapter is authored by Dongmin Chen,[1] Shilin Zheng,[2] and Lei Guo.[3] The chapter has been adapted from an earlier version which appeared in the "Global Innovation Index 2015: Effective Innovation Policies for Development", Chapter 6, pages 105–112 published by WIPO, Geneva, 2015. The Global Innovation Index 2015 report was co edited by Soumitra Dutta, Bruno Lanvin,[4] and Sacha Wunsch-Vincent.[5]

1. Executive Dean, School of Innovation and Entrepreneurship, Peking University.

2. Associate Researcher, Institute of Quantitative Technical Economics, Chinese Academy of Social Sciences.

3. Associate Dean, School of Innovation and Entrepreneurship, Peking University.

4. Executive Director—Global Indices, INSEAD, Fontainebleau, France.

5. Senior Economic Officer, WIPO, Geneva, Switzerland.

6. Chinese officials have long been aware of the importance of the S&T. Deng Xiaoping stated in 1988, when meeting with President Gustav Husak of Czechoslovakia, "In my opinion, science and technology is the most important productive force." Details of the speech are available at http://news.xilu.com/2009/0903/news_112_13463.html (in Chinese).

Financing Entrepreneurship and Innovation in Emerging Markets.
https://doi.org/10.1016/B978-0-12-804025-6.00003-4

technology (S&T) reforms that accelerated progress in higher education and research and development (R&D). Thirty years of ongoing economic reforms have resulted in an average annual economic growth rate of more than 9%,[7] an astonishing accomplishment for the country. In 2010, China's Gross Domestic Product (GDP) surpassed Japan's, making China the world's second-largest economy. By 2014, China's GDP reached $10 trillion: as of publication, it is one of only two countries in the world to have attained this level—the other is the United States.[8]

However, the 2008 global financial crisis disrupted the high growth rate of China's manufacturing-based economy, which adapts or imitates traditional technologies from developed economies. As a result of this crisis, China was pressed to make structural economic reforms focused on building domestic innovation infrastructure, and increasing the competitiveness of its domestic research institutions. These updated policies have greatly influenced the country's continuing economic development. In 2017, the Global Innovation Index (GII) ranked China at 22nd place worldwide. China also leads substantially in innovation among the BRICS nations (Brazil, Russia, India, China, and South Africa). China's strongest index on the GII is in the Knowledge & technology outputs pillar, in which it ranked 4th in 2017. This chapter provides an overview and analysis of the evolution of China's S&T policies and their impact over the past three decades. It also examines a new phase of policy change that could have extensive impacts in the coming decade.

3.2 FOUR PHASES OF CHINA'S S&T POLICY EVOLUTION

China's S&T policy since the late 1970s has driven progress for research itself and the economy as a whole. We consider the evolution of this policy in four phases: (i) the experimental phase, (ii) systemic reform, (iii) deepening reform, and (iv) long-term planning.

3.2.1 The Experimental Phase (1978–85)

In the early 1980s, China's economic foundation was weak, and its level of S&T research was far behind that of developed nations. It became clear that the Soviet model for S&T research, which it adopted in the 1960s, had serious drawbacks and had led to a severe disconnect between research and industry. Initial policy reform, therefore, focused on spin-offs and partial privatization of selected parts of public research institutions that were commercially viable. This separation immediately alleviated some of the financial burden of the holding institutions, and later these privatized entities became substantially valuable assets.

---

7. World Bank statistics show that since 1978, China's GDP growth rate is 9.83% on average (see the World Bank's World Development Indicators database, http://databank.shihang.org/data//reports.aspx?source=2&country=CHN&series=&period=).
8. China's GDP reached RMB 63.64 trillion ($10.36 trillion) in 2014. The data is available in the central government's 2015 work report, at http://www.guancha.cn/politics/2015_03_17_312511.shtml (in Chinese).

Some of the most successful technology companies in China today formed during this period. They include the computer products and services company Lenovo Group Ltd. (formerly Legend Computer), a spin-off from the Computing Institute of the Academy of Sciences, and the conglomerate Founder Group Co. Ltd., a spin-off from Peking University based on a digital Asian font typesetting technology. The initial phase of reform took a bottom-up approach due to the limited availability of national S&T funding at the time. At the national level, important initiatives such as the Key National Research Projects (1984) and the Key National Laboratories, among others, were launched to focus the limited available funding on better-performing research groups.[9]

3.2.2   The Systemic Reform Phase (1985–95)

The Science and Technology System Reform Act in 1985 marked the advent of top-down nationwide system reforms. The act's primary objective was to bridge the gap between research institutions and relevant industries. By emphasizing competitiveness and other connections to the market, the act aimed to gradually strengthen the economic impact of S&T funding. The most significant reforms resulting from this Act included the establishment of the National Natural Science Foundation of China, which promotes and finances basic and applied research,[10] along with a number of new initiatives supporting applied and translation research. These include the 863 Program (1986), the Spark Plan (1986), the Torch Plan (1988), and the Shenzhen Stock Exchange for small- and medium-sized enterprises (1990), which all sought to improve commercialization prospects.[11]

In 1993, the government instituted the 211 Project to improve the country's higher education system and strengthen the link between higher education and social development as part of its long-term strategies. The government allocated a special budget for leading universities selected from each province and from major cities such as Beijing. This budget was enacted in the country's 9th Five-Year National Budget Plan and was fully implemented in 1995. During this time period, the Hundred Talents Program of the Chinese Academy of Sciences, an important program which offers positions to qualified applicants with an

---

9. For more information on Chinese State Key Laboratories, see https://en.wikipedia.org/wiki/State_Key_Laboratories.
10. Details about the National Natural Science Foundation of China are available at http://www.nsfc.gov.cn/publish/portal1/.
11. Details of the Spark Plan can be found at Cao, 2006, and at http://in.china-embassy.org/eng/szyss/jm/zhongguonongye/agricultureplanning/t143140.htm, (at http://baike.baidu.com/view/57377.htm in Chinese); details of the 863 Program at https://en.wikipedia.org/wiki/863_Program (http://baike.baidu.com/view/4785616.htm in Chinese); of the Torch Plan at http://www.chinatorch.gov.cn/english/index.shtml; and of the Shenzhen Stock Exchange for small and medium-sized enterprises at http://baike.baidu.com/link?url=PpsCaaGhLeRFCF0JtxxJy3Xw1jqUugdN5Pv9vlQ1mwvJuGHe7Fr1QlCFoxeI12x2qWi1LKqFsfHTQgEwktKF9_ (in Chinese).

international doctoral degree, was introduced to encourage overseas Chinese scholars to return to China and take up key teaching and research positions.[12]

3.2.3   The Deepening Reform Phase (1996–2006)

The 9th Five-Year National Budget Plan, the Outline of the 2010 National Target, and a series of resolutions began a period of deepening systemic reform in S&T development. China established a comprehensive national strategy with the aim of "rejuvenating the nation's economy with science and education," and in 1996 the government passed the Act of Promoting Commercialization of S&T Discoveries and Inventions. These new policies focused on three areas: shifting the drivers of innovation from public research organizations to industrial sectors; improving the R&D and innovation capacity of industrial sectors; and improving the efficient commercialization of academic outputs.

During this period, four crucial changes to the national innovation infrastructure occurred. The 985 Initiative launched; this program was aimed at expanding the 211 Project to include major technology and engineering universities in the national Advanced Education Development Fund as a way to foster the development of world-class Chinese universities. The government also implemented the Knowledge Innovation Initiative in the Chinese Academy of Sciences to improve research quality at its public institutions. Finally, the government encouraged large-scale R&D funding for basic research with initiatives such as the 973 Program, and the introduction of the Yangzi River Scholars Program, which significantly increased professors' wages to attract talented researchers and professors.[13]

3.2.4   Long-term Plan and Policy Optimization (2006–14)

In 2006, the central government issued a Medium- and Long-Term National S&T Development Plan for 2006–20 (the 2006 National Plan). The 2006 National Plan outlined guidelines for S&T development: nurturing independent innovation, fostering the ability to leapfrog in key technology areas, building major infrastructure, and developing future global leadership. The plan emphasized achieving sustainable economic growth, seeking innovation-driven growth strategies, and enhancing independent innovation capacity. During this period the government focused on optimizing the policy's effectiveness and managing its implementation. Previously issued policies and regulations that had lacked coordination needed consolidation into sets of coherent policies, and adaption to foster an innovation ecosystem rather than promoting R&D. To further entice innovative talent, particularly in critical S&T fields, in 2011 the central government launched a very effective Thousand

---

12. For information on the Hundred Talents Program, see http://english.ucas.ac.cn/JoinUs/Pages/TheHundredTalentsProgram.aspx.
13. These plans have succeeded in helping Chinese colleges and universities attract many overseas talents, contributing to the progress of Chinese higher education and levels of scientific research.

Talents Recruitment Program. As of 2016, this program has drawn more than 2000 overseas scholars and leading industrial innovators back to China.

In 2012, China set the goal of becoming a "top innovative nation" by 2020. The 18th Communist Party National Congress held at the end of 2012 established "innovation-driven growth" as a national development strategic priority. The Congress called for setting clear targets, improving entrepreneurship, making industry the main driver behind innovation, and establishing market-oriented mechanisms to facilitate collaborative technology transfer from academics to the industrial sectors. Together, these changes should propel China's global competitiveness in innovation and ensure its long-term sustainable development.[14]

3.3 OUTCOMES AND ANALYSIS OF S&T REFORM

The wide range of S&T policies that China has implemented and adjusted in the past three decades has directly affected its innovation outcomes. From 2002 to 2012, China's GDP more than quadrupled, leaping from $2 trillion to $8.7 trillion. The data reveal that these policies have effectively advanced the development of an innovation ecosystem; they have also brought about a large, educated workforce, laying a solid foundation for the future development of innovation capacity in the country.

The next sections present data illustrating China's S&T development in four areas: (i) R&D investment; (ii) the results of innovation—i.e., patents, products, and research publications; (iii) science education; and (iv) the R&D talent cultivation.

3.3.1 S&T and R&D Investment

As shown in Fig. 3.1, total S&T investment in China increased from about 1% of GDP in 2002 to 2% of GDP in 2012.[15] The share of local government fiscal expenditure on S&T relative to the central government fiscal expenditure on S&T jumped from approximately 40% before 2007 to approximately 50% since 2007.[16] This increase is strongly correlated with the issuance of the 2006 National Plan. Fig. 3.2 shows that the percentage of R&D investment increased from 2002 to 2012, although investment in basic and applied research has not kept pace. Industrial sector R&D investment also increased steadily from 70% of total investment in 2002 to 80% in 2012.

14. The Reform and Opening Up of Chinese S&T in the Past 30 Years, a book by the former minister of the S&T department, Wan Gang, gives a detailed description of these policies and their influence.
15. These data are from CNKI (China National Knowledge Infrastructure), the largest Chinese database, which contains abundant data for almost every field in science and social science. CNKI is available at http://www.cnki.net/ (in Chinese).
16. Chinese R&D investment includes two parts: industrial sector funding and government funding. Government funding can be further divided into central government funding and local government funding.

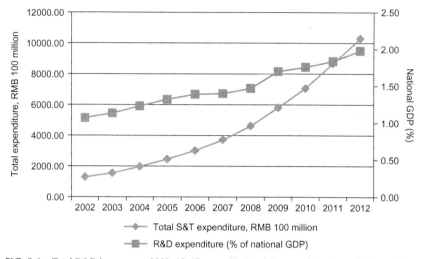

FIG. 3.1 Total R&D investment, 2002–12. *(Source: National Bureau of Statistics of China, 2013a. China Statistical Yearbook 2013. China Statistics Press, Beijing. Available at http://www.stats.gov. cn/tjsj/ndsj/2013/indexeh.htm.)*

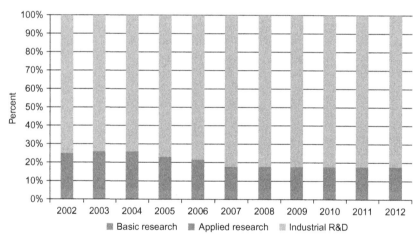

FIG. 3.2 Distribution of S&T investment, 2002–12. *(Source: National Bureau of Statistics of China, 2013b. China Statistical Yearbook on Science and Technology. China Statistics Press, Beijing.)*

3.3.2 Innovation Results: Patents, Products, and Research Publications

Domestic patent applications have grown rapidly, at an average rate of approximately 17.5% in recent years. Since 2012, China has ranked first in the GII indicator for the number of total domestic patent applications; it has also been first in the GII indicator for domestic resident utility model applications for all years from 2011 through 2017. However, based on national data, the growth of international patent applications appears to be slowing in comparison to the very rapid growth of domestic patent applications. Within domestic applications, the volume of invention patents issued grew more slowly than patents for utility models and designs (see Fig. 3.3). Between 2002 and 2012 technology product output (measured by revenue from new products, see Fig. 3.4) increased rapidly, especially after 2006. This increase demonstrates that the Chinese government's innovation policies were successful in attracting organizational investment in R&D and encouraging product output.

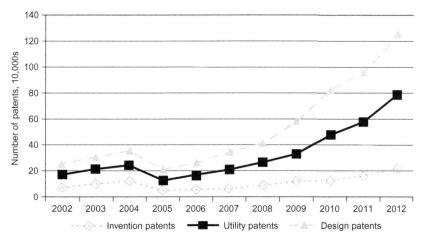

FIG. 3.3   Patents issued, 2002–12. *(Source: National Bureau of Statistics of China, 2013b. China Statistical Yearbook on Science and Technology. China Statistics Press, Beijing.)*

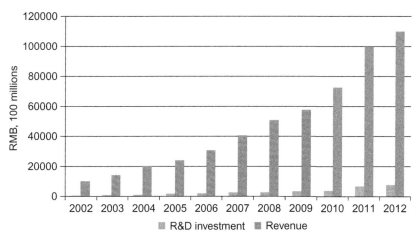

FIG. 3.4   R&D investment and revenue from new products, 2002–12. *(Source: National Bureau of Statistics of China, 2013b. China Statistical Yearbook on Science and Technology. China Statistics Press, Beijing.)*

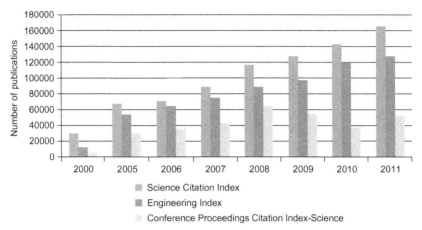

FIG. 3.5 Number of Chinese science and technology publications, 2002–12. *(Source: National Bureau of Statistics of China, 2013b. China Statistical Yearbook on Science and Technology. China Statistics Press, Beijing.)*

Fig. 3.5 shows that Chinese research publications significantly increased their reach from 2000 to 2011 according to the three key international indexes— the Science Citation Index (SCI), the Engineering Index (EI), and the Conference Proceedings Citations Index-Science (CPCI-S). The corresponding average annual growth rates are 16.6%, 22.9%, and 21.8%, respectively. In 2000, China ranked only 8th, 3rd, and 8th worldwide in the SCI, the EI, and the CPCI-S, respectively, but since 2007 has ranked in 2nd, 1st, and 2nd place, respectively. This demonstrates that both the 211 Project of 1993 and the 985 Initiative of 1998, by improving higher education, establishing the Chinese Natural Science Foundation, and launching other research institutes, have made a great impact on China's research publications.

3.3.3   Science Education

The successful development of science and technology in China has gone hand in hand with the development of education and the cultivation of a highly skilled workforce. The S&T reform focused on education and has pushed to develop top-quality education and to increase the ratio of high-school graduates who are enrolled in colleges and universities. This emphasis resulted in the number of college and university graduates in the sciences increasing from 1,337,300 students in 2002 to 6,081,600 in 2012 (Fig. 3.6)—an average annual increase of 16.4%. The number of Master and PhD graduates increased at an even higher rate from 80,800 in 2002 to 486,500 in 2012, an average annual increase of 19.7%. The growth in talent cultivated by the strong scientific education system offers an ongoing pipeline of highly skilled, educated labor for the marketplace to support the rapid build-up of China's innovation system.

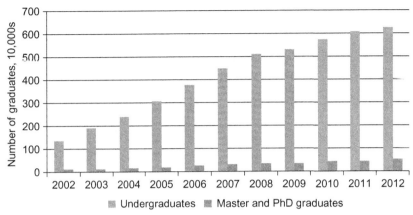

FIG. 3.6 Graduates in science, 2002–12. *(Source: National Bureau of Statistics of China, 2013b. China Statistical Yearbook on Science and Technology. China Statistics Press, Beijing.)*

3.3.4   Cultivation of an R&D Workforce

China's S&T policies place great value on attracting S&T talent. The Thousand Talents Program and a series of other talent programs have greatly increased the high-end talent pool, and a number of important breakthroughs can be attributed to those who have returned from abroad. China's focus on education has led to a rapid increase in the number of R&D personnel (the GII indicator for number of researchers per million population increased from 1.1 per million in 2009 to 1.5 per million in 2012), as well as their quality and skill. Beginning in 2004, China's R&D full-time equivalent personnel grew at an annual rate of 10% or higher every year, until by 2012 it had already reached a total of 3.3 million people.[17]

3.4   WHAT OTHER COUNTRIES CAN LEARN FROM CHINA

China's evolving S&T policies and economic reforms have had a profound effect on innovation in the country since their launch in 1980s, but especially from 2002 to 2012. We can draw the following observations from the GII: First, the shift from a bottom-up to a top-down approach has worked well for a developing economy that began with limited national resources.

Second, the increase in R&D investment that improved China's ranking in the GII indicator on gross expenditure on R&D, from 25th place in 2012 to 21st in 2013, and finally to 17th in 2017, supported a substantial increase in GDP. Following the launch of the 2006 National Plan, Chinese R&D investment increased noticeably and the rate of local government investment in R&D even

17. National Bureau of Statistics of China (2013b).

surpassed the rate he central government's investment. Moreover, the positive market response has encouraged the industrial sector to steadily increase R&D investment, as seen by improvement in the GII variable of gross expenditure on R&D (GERD) financed by business, which grew from 73.9% in 2011 to 74.6% in 2014. One cause for concern, however, is that investment in basic and applied research has not kept pace.

The third observation is that the strategy of "rejuvenating the nation's economy with science and education" has accelerated the development of China's top education system (evidenced by the GII variable QS World University Ranking, which improved from 36th in 2011 to 4th in 2017). The quantity of undergraduates and Master's graduates has clearly increased (seen by the GII variable on tertiary enrollment, which grew from 21.8% of gross enrollment in 2009 to 43% in 2015). Both the quality and quantity of researchers have greatly increased, and the increase in researchers in basic sciences has exceeded that of researchers in other areas.

The fourth observation concerns the outputs of R&D research: both patent applications and utility model applications have increased rapidly. The GII demonstrates this growth through its domestic resident patent applications indicator, which rose from 293,000 patents in 2010 to 704,000 patents in 2013, and domestic resident utility model applications, which rose from 407,000 applications in 2010 to 885,000 in 2013. In addition, science and technology publications by Chinese researchers have enjoyed a high intake worldwide by the SCI, the EI, and other international indices, although the percentage of top-quality papers remains low but is improving (seen in the GII through scientific and technical articles, in which China ranked 40th in 2011 but dropped to 54th in 2017, and citable documents H index, ranked 16th in 2014 and increased to 14th in 2017).

3.5   WHAT CHINA CAN LEARN FROM OTHER COUNTRIES

Although China has made remarkable achievements in R&D investment and S&T outputs, it still lags developed nations in investments in basic research, high-value inventions, and high-impact research, all of which are essential to sustain income growth. Indeed, the 2017 GII placed China 4th in the Knowledge and technology outputs pillar, close to or even overtaking some high-income nations. Significant progress has been made in creative outputs (ranked 59th in 2014 and 26th in 2017), and market sophistication (concerned with credit system and openness, ranked 54th in 2014 and 28th in 2017). Though China's performance in the Institutions pillar (concerned with the regulatory and legal system) has improved (ranked 114th in 2014 and 78th in 2017) this has dragged down China's overall GII competitiveness when compared with top-ranking countries.

As discussed earlier, China has set a national target of becoming a leading innovative country by 2020. This will require continued policy reform to cultivate a balanced relationship between the government and market forces;

to establish a more comprehensive innovation ecosystem; to nurture a legal and regulatory system that strengthens investment in innovation and entrepreneurship in all sectors; and to foster open and fair competition among private, state-owned, and foreign enterprises.[18] Besides boosting investment in research and commercialization activities, China can explore reforms undertaken by peer countries to address legal and regulatory systems issues, boost market forces, and foster competition among all stakeholders.

3.6   THE LATEST REFORMS

During the National Innovation Conference held in 2012, the Chinese government clearly acknowledged a need for improvement.[19] Since the ascension of the present government during the 18th Communist Party Congress, China has begun yet another round of policy reforms, five of which are noted here. First, an amendment to the National Act for Promoting Technology Transfer has been proposed; this may become China's own Bayh-Dole Act (also known as the U.S. Patent and Trademark Law Amendments Act), giving universities and public institutions the autonomous right to license the patents generated from central government R&D funding. It further ensures that inventors will share in a greater percentage of the proceeds. A pilot program to test this new law has already begun in 11 universities, and the next session of the Chinese People's Congress is likely to enact it. Second, in January 2015 the Chinese government issued the 2014–20 Action Plan on the Implementation of National Intellectual Property Strategy. The plan aims to ease market processes for transactions pertaining to intellectual property, including declassifying classified patents for civilian use and funding seed companies that specialize in intellectual property transaction services. Third, to improve efficiency in S&T funding, the Chinese government has overhauled the entire S&T funding process, increasing accountability to stakeholders in the new process. Fourth, China has launched a special stock market (the National Equity Exchange and Quotations) to allow technology startup companies, which are not yet profitable, to have more avenues to raise development capital. Furthermore, rules and regulations were simplified to encourage mergers and acquisitions. And finally, in March 2015 the Chinese government published "A Guideline for the Development of Public Incubation Space to Promote Grassroots Entrepreneurship."[20] This guide promotes the participation of multilevel capital markets, including crowdfunding.

---

18. More details are discussed in People's Publishing House (2012).

19. See speeches by General Secretary Hu Jingtao, Prime Minister Wen Jiabao, and Deputy Prime Minister Liu Yandong in the 2012 National Innovation Conference. The full content of these is not available online, but a summary is available at http://www.gov.cn/ldhd/2012-07/07/content_2178574.htm (in Chinese).

20. The Chinese government attaches great importance to entrepreneurship. Premier Li Keqiang has frequently granted interviews to representatives of successful entrepreneurs seeking to improve conditions for entrepreneurship in the country.

The new set of policies being implemented today should help to address many of the country's challenging issues in the coming years and have a positive impact on China's ranking in future GIIs.

REFERENCES

Cao, Y., 2006. The Exploration and Practice of Spark Plan for Past 20 Years. China's Agricultural Science and Technology Press, Beijing.

Lin, Y., 2014. The Miracle of China. Due Press, Shanghai.

National Bureau of Statistics of China, 2013a. China Statistical Yearbook 2013. China Statistics Press, Beijing. Available at http://www.stats.gov.cn/tjsj/ndsj/2013/indexeh.htm.

National Bureau of Statistics of China, 2013b. China Statistical Yearbook on Science and Technology. China Statistics Press, Beijing.

People's Publishing House, 2012. Speed Up the Construction of National Innovation System by Deepening the Reform of Science and Technology System. People's Publishing House, Beijing.

The People's Republic of China, 2015. A Guideline for the Development of Public Incubation Space to Promote Grassroots Entrepreneurship. Official report.

The People's Republic of China, State Council, 2006. National Outline for Medium and Long Term Science and Technology Development (2006–2020). Official report.

Wan, G., 2008. The Reform and Opening Up of Chinese S&T in the Past 30 Years. Official report.

Chapter 4

Tencent: A Giant Asserting Dominance

ACRONYMS

AI	Artificial Intelligence
API	Application Programming Interface
BAT	Baidu, Alibaba, and Tencent
CAPEX	Capital Expenditure
CBRC	China Banking Regulatory Commission
CEIBS	China Europe International Business School
GII	Global Innovation Index
IM	Instant Messenger
M&A	Mergers & Acquisitions
MAU	Monthly Average Users
MMOs	Massively Multiplayer Online Games
O2O	Online-to-Offline
PCCW	Pacific Century Cyberworks
R&D	Research & Development
VC	Venture Capital

Tencent Holdings, Ltd.,[1] a Chinese investment holding company based in Shenzhen, is the fourth most valuable Internet company in the world. With a market capitalization of $342 billion as of 2017, it is behind only Google Inc./Alphabet Inc. ($670 billion), Amazon Inc. ($474 billion), and Facebook Inc. ($442 billion), and ahead of Alibaba Group Holding ($332 billion).[2] Despite this phenomenal success, Tencent is relatively unknown outside of China.

All this is now beginning to change in light of the company's dramatic rise in the past year. Tencent provides media, entertainment, online advertising

---

1. Ticker—0700, Hong Kong Stock Exchange.
2. Source: S&P CapitalIQ, accessed August 31, 2016.

Financing Entrepreneurship and Innovation in Emerging Markets.
https://doi.org/10.1016/B978-0-12-804025-6.00004-6

services, as well as Internet and mobile phone value-added services.[3] Their share price increased by 36% between March and September 2016 at a time of slow growth in the Chinese economy and during which prices of other Internet companies grew modestly. This stellar performance has made Tencent one of the most valuable stocks in Asia (alongside Samsung Electronics Co. Ltd.) as of 2017. Tencent's stock performance is backed by consistently good financial performance. For instance, in 2015, the company's operating profit was $6.26 billion—up to 33% from the year before—and its revenue was $15.84 billion up to 30% from the corresponding values in 2014.[4]

This chapter analyzes the rise of this emerging multinational against the backdrop of China's evolving innovation ecosystem. We begin by studying Tencent's journey and probing its "interconnected" universe. In doing so, we intend to lift the mystique behind this hidden giant and uncover how it is asserting its dominance in China and beyond.[5]

4.1 MILESTONES

In this section, we provide a brief overview of Tencent's journey, which we expand in further detail in later sections.

4.1.1 Finding Its Identity

Tencent was founded in November 1998 by a group of five young men: Huateng Ma (Pony Ma), Zhidong Zhang (Tony Zhang), Chenye Xu (Daniel Xu), Yidan Chen (Charles Chen), and Liqing Zeng (Jason Zeng). At first, the company imitated successful global products for the Chinese market, with a focus on improved user experience. Tencent modeled itself after ICQ, an instant messaging service invented by three young Israelis in 1996, and launched its own instant messaging product (OICQ) in February 1999. While it soon reached a user base of 200,000, Tencent still did not have a business model for this product.

The founders knew they must raise external funding to survive. However, Chinese banks refused loans due to regulations that prohibited lending to businesses that lack paying users. Providing loans for fixed capital was not

---

3. The company was incorporated in the Cayman Islands and has 30,641 worldwide employees as of December 31, 2015. Source: Tencent's Annual Report 2015, http://www.tencent.com/en-us/content/ir/rp/2015/attachments/201502.pdf.

4. Tencent Annual Report 2015, http://www.tencent.com/en-us/content/ir/rp/2015/attachments/201502.pdf.

5. We have tried to include all major events and development up to January 2017. Due to the dynamic environment and rapid pace of developments, any events after January 2017 are beyond the scope of this report.

allowed, regardless of the Tencent's projected value. Thus, the founders were hard-pressed to look for equity funding to meet rapidly increasing investment demands.

4.1.2   Funding Its Ambitions

In 1999, IDG Capital—a San Francisco-based venture fund focused on China—and Pacific Century Cyberworks Ltd. (PCCW)—a Hong Kong-based information and communications technology company—made a conditional offer to provide $2.2 million for a 40% stake in the Tencent, shared equally between the two investors. PCCW was owned by Ricard Li, son of Li Ka-shing, who is Hong Kong's richest man as of the writing of this book.[6] Pony Ma was from the same hometown in China as Li Ka-shing and Richard Li and was able to convince them to help fund his company.

The equity funding by IDG and PCCW was contingent on a change in Tencent's business plan and on QQ[7] reaching four million registered users. As it turned out, this target was easily achieved and Tencent received the funding in April 2000. By then, the number of registered users was already close to 10 million. This funding allowed Tencent to attract more users and, more importantly, it provided Tencent's founders the necessary time and resources to discover how to generate revenue from its millions of QQ users. This initial struggle to find a viable business model was a prologue to Tencent's continued focus on reinventing its business model over the years.

4.1.3   Expanding Its Potential

Mobile phones became popular in China beginning in 2000. At the time, the state-owned telecommunication company China Mobile Communications Corp. embraced value-added services, which were contributed by providers who generated content and offered services to users. This created significant opportunities for companies such as Tencent to monetize its user base. Tencent developed Mobile QQ, a service that allowed a QQ user to send a message directly to other users who could access it both from a computer

---

6. Forbes, Hong Kong's 50 richest people, http://www.forbes.com/hong-kong-billionaires/list/, accessed June 13, 2017.

7. Two years after AOL purchased ICQ, it filed a lawsuit with the National Arbitration Forum in the U.S. accusing Tencent's OICQ of violating ICQ's intellectual property rights. The similarities between OICQ and ICQ cost Tencent the case and resulted in the shut down of OICQ's websites. In turn, Tencent shifted the OICQ service to its website and by December 2000 the company released its latest version of the software, whose name was formally changed to QQ. While these developments affected user experience, they were ultimately designed to protect Tencent from future litigation.

and a mobile phone. China Mobile charged QQ users a fee of 5 yuan ($0.85) per month and shared 20% of its revenue with Tencent. As a result, Tencent started to become profitable by 2001, thereby laying the foundation for its other blockbuster value-added services.[8]

4.1.4 Venture Capital Investments

Tencent started making venture capital (VC) investments in 1999. We analyzed 261 VC investments made by Tencent between 1999 and 2017 and found that 59% of these investments were made in China, followed by 26% in the United States, 3% in South Korea, and 2% each in Hong Kong and India. In terms of the value of these investments, we found that China's share increased to approximately 80%, followed by 13% in South Korea, 5% in the United States, and 1% in India (Fig. 4.1). While Tencent made investments in other parts of the world, we found that most investments have been within China or its natural market—i.e., neighboring countries. Figs. 4.2 and 4.3 below show the share of Tencent's VC investments in different countries by number and value of investments from 1999 to 2017.

---

8. (1) To ensure it could establish its own revenue stream independent of any partner such as China Mobile, Tencent launched its online currency "Q coin" in 2005. This virtual currency would become the de facto standard for all purchases on the Tencent ecosystem. (2) To ensure the integrativeness of its products, Tencent launched its first portal website (www.tencent.com) which ultimately became the QQ portal. (3) To boost revenues, Tencent leveraged its vast user base as a gold mine for advertisers. (4) To further diversify its revenue base, Tencent implemented the Freemium (Free and premium) model, in which all QQ users could enjoy free services, while some could choose to increase their experience with premium services. (5) To encourage further exchanges within its growing platform, Tencent created Virtual Goods, which included anything from a virtual pet to ringtones to virtual clothing and jewelry. (6) To further promote user loyalty,
Tencent launched the QQ leisure game portal. Tencent not only developed games in-house, it also purchased games elsewhere. Tencent owned the QQ portal website and messenger service and thus had the unique advantage of being able to promote at a low cost to its large user base, thereby bolstering its competitiveness.
In 2007, Tencent began licensing games and in 2013, it launched its mobile games platform with 20 titles that covered a wide range of genres and were available to its one billion users through WeChat and Mobile QQ. (7) To compete with other social media platforms, Tencent transferred the bulk of its engineers toward mobile development and created Weixin (called WeChat for the global market). Today, WeChat combines WhatsApp's messaging features, Snapchat's quick photo chat, Facebook's social networking functions, and Instagram's photo-sharing abilities. (8) To further monetize transactions between its users and its various platforms, Tencent started working with existing and prospective strategic partners in various verticals such as food ordering and ridesharing to deliver better Online-to-Offline (O2O) and transactional services to users. (9) To compete with entertainment networks, the company announced a deal with HBO that gave it exclusive rights for distribution in China, and on January 30, 2015, Tencent signed a $700 million deal with the National Basketball Association to stream American basketball games in China. (10) To compete with cloud computing providers, in 2015 Tencent announced that it would invest $1.57 billion in cloud computing over five years.

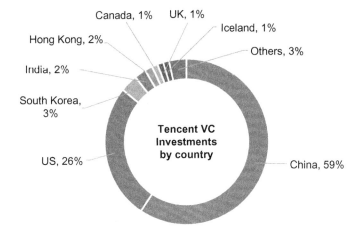

Note: Others include Israel, Japan, South Africa, France, Finland, Thailand, Argentina & Cayman Islands

FIG. 4.1   Country share (number) of 261 Tencent VC investments from 1999 to 2017. *(Source: Author analysis based on various sources.)*

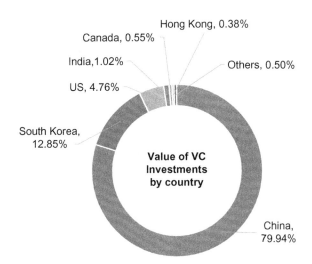

Note:Others include France, Israel, Iceland and Thailand

FIG. 4.2   Country share (value) of 261 Tencent VC investments from 1999 to 2017. *(Source: Author analysis based on various sources.)*

We compared the number and value of Tencent's VC investments by year in which the investment was made. This analysis shows that there was a significant rise in both the number (from 14 in 2013 to 62 in 2016) and value (from $114 million in 2013 to $9.4 billion in 2016) of investments. This change suggests a definite shift in company strategy to focus on VC investments for future growth.

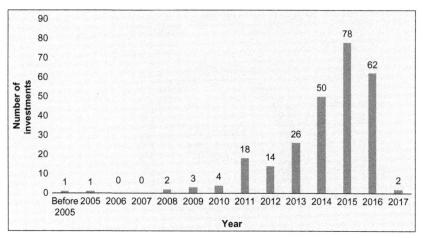

FIG. 4.3 Distribution of Tencent's VC investments by year of investment. *(Source: Author analysis based on various sources.)*

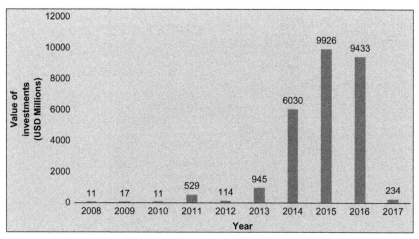

FIG. 4.4 Value of Tencent's VC investments (in $ millions) by year of investment. *(Source: Author analysis based on various sources.)*

It also suggests that the thriving innovation ecosystem in China and greater availability of funds could have played a part in the increase in investments. Figs. 4.3 and 4.4 show the yearly distribution of Tencent's investments by number and value of investments, respectively.

We also analyzed Tencent's VC investments by categorizing these investments-based size. While a majority of the 182 investments for which data was available were below the $1 billion mark, the company made five investments over $1.5 billion, as shown in Fig. 4.5.

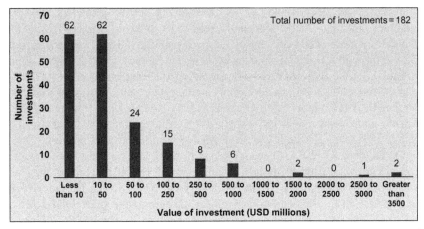

FIG. 4.5 Number of Tencent's (182) VC investments from 2005 to 2017, grouped by value in $ millions. *(Source: Author analysis based on various sources.)*

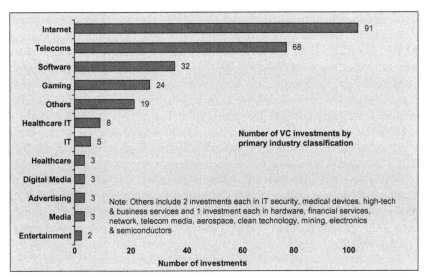

FIG. 4.6 Tencent's VC investments, industry break-up (by number of investments). *(Source: Author analysis based on various sources.)*

Lastly, we analyzed the industry break-down of Tencent's VC investments as shown in Fig. 4.6. As expected, almost 35% (91) of Tencent's 261 VC investments were in Internet companies, followed by 26% (68) and 12% (32) in telecom and software, respectively. Gaming companies received 9% (24) of investments, indicative of Tencent's intent to consolidate its leadership position in this industry, an inference reinforced by considering Tencent's biggest mergers and acquisitions (M&A) investments, such as the $8.6 billion investment by Tencent in Supercell Oy in 2016.

Tencent has since expanded its investments across industries and geographies. In June 2013, Tencent increased its stake in Kingsoft Network Technology, a subsidiary of Kingsoft Corporation Ltd., to 18% from its previous 15.68% through a $46.98 million investment. On January 15, 2014, Tencent invested HK$ 1.5 billion ($193.45 million) in logistics and warehouse firm China South City Holdings Ltd. to develop its e-commerce and logistics business; on October 16, 2014, via its wholly held subsidiary Hongze Lake Investment Ltd., Tencent announced that it had bought a 7% stake in lottery technology firm China LotSynergy Holdings Ltd. for HK$ 445.5 million ($57.4 million).

On October 23, 2014, Tencent pitched in $145 million for a 10% stake in Koudai Gouwu, a Chinese mobile shopping portal. By 2016, Tencent, together with Foxconn Technology Group and luxury-car dealer China Harmony New Energy Auto Ltd., founded Future Mobility, an automotive startup that aims to sell all-electric fully autonomous luxury cars in 2020. In August 2015, Tencent led a $90 million round of funding for Indian health-care information provider Practo, setting a new record for its investment in India. In February 2016 Tencent collaborated with Silicon Valley's Felicis Ventures to lead a $10 million "Series A" round in artificial intelligence (AI) technology startup Diffbot. Diffbot uses AI to mine the Internet and offers turnkey application programming interfaces (APIs), automatic web-crawling, and bulk data capabilities. In June 2016, Tencent teamed up with Naspers Ltd. (its own investors and Africa's largest media company) to introduce its social media app WeChat in Africa. In Hong Kong, Tencent's WeChat Wallet began to gain traction over Apple Pay, as users migrated to mobile payments. By August 2016, Tencent was the lead investor in a $175 million equity investment in Hike, a local WhatsApp rival (Techcrunch, 2016) in India, an indication of Tencent's commitment to establish itself in India's the rapidly expanding Internet ecosystem.

Ultimately, we find that VC investments were critical for Tencent to (1) broaden its ecosystem, (2) create further opportunities for monetizing its loyal user base, (3) expand its leadership position in certain business segments (e.g., gaming), and (4) foment innovation in the Chinese entrepreneurial environment.

See Table A4.1 for the top 25 VC investments by Tencent from 1999 to 2017.

4.2 INTERNATIONALIZATION

Unlike Jack Ma and his company Alibaba Group Holding Ltd., Tencent has a history of keeping a low profile domestically and internationally. However, Tencent has made bolder efforts to go global and shared more details regarding these investments. Tencent has invested $2 billion on internationalization, focusing on three key areas: international patent applications, internationalizing WeChat, and global gaming expansion (Technode, 2013). From 2008 to 2014, 51% of its investment was in the United States, 40% was in China, 5% in South Korea, 2% in India, and 2% in Russia (CBinsights, 2014).

4.2.1   Patent Applications—An Early Effort to go Global

Tencent's first worldwide patent and utility model applications were filed in 2002 and quickly grew in number from 2005 to 2007. Between 2008 and 2010, Tencent doubled its filings relative to the previous two-year period. (Most of the filings were in information technology and telecommunication, two areas at the heart of its research and development (R&D) strategy and infrastructure development) In 2014, Tencent managed the second-largest increase (year-on-year) in patent filings in the world, increasing its patent filings by 200% over the previous year (WIPO, 2015).

4.2.2   WeChat as a Tool for Internationalization

Taking WeChat global is Tencent's most public internationalization effort to date. Since 2012, this multifunction app has free text, voice, and video messaging, along with functions to post social updates (like Facebook), call cabs (like Uber), and share videos (like Snapchat), as well as other mobile payment and game functions. Tencent has allocated significant resources to consolidate its internationalization to make the app compatible with iOS, Android, Blackberry, and Windows phones. Like many Chinese companies that beginning to internationalize, Tencent has pushed WeChat to countries and users geographically close to China. Hence, WeChat was most heavily marketed and integrated in India, Malaysia, Indonesia, Thailand, and the Philippines. In 2013, Tencent opened offices in Singapore, the Philippines, Malaysia, and the United States, spending $6.4 million, $6.4 million, $8.8 million, and $5.4 million, respectively, to expand the user base of WeChat in these markets.[9]

WeChat has started to gain market share in African and Latin American countries such as South Africa, Brazil, Argentina, and Mexico. These expansions have enabled WeChat to grow at a rapid rate from 50 million users in December 2011 to around 800 million users as of 2016. In the past couple of years, Tencent has put the brakes on its aggressive expansion strategy through WeChat, deciding instead to focus on further enhancing the Tencent ecosystem in mainland China.

4.2.3   Investment in Gaming to Expand Global Footprint

While WeChat's internationalization occurred through an organic strategy, Tencent followed a different approach in the gaming industry. Tencent has invested in the gaming industry by purchasing major gaming companies, and by supporting venture capital firms to encourage startups. Since 2008, Tencent has been on a major shopping spree for popular games. In 2009, it purchased Riot Games Inc., a company that has developed some of the most profitable games

---

9. FDImarkets.com, https://app-fdimarkets-com.proxy.library.cornell.edu/library/index.cfm?fuseaction=company_profiles.profile&selected_tab=2&company_id=57721&x_col=project_year&x_val=2013&x_name=Year:%202013:%20Total, accessed January 2017.

in the industry's history. In 2012, Tencent bought 48% of Epic Games Inc., the developer of Unreal Engine, 49% of Level Up International Holdings, a Singaporean online game operator (Technode, 2012), and paid for two rounds of investment in Kamcord, a U.S. mobile game-streaming service. In 2013, Tencent made a historic purchase of a 6% stake in Activision Blizzard Inc., the developer of the legendary World of Warcraft, for an estimated $1.4 billion. At the same time, Tencent teamed up with Capstone Partners, LLC., a Korean VC firm, invested in numerous small startup South Korean games.

In 2015, Tencent made two substantial investments in San Francisco-based game developers. On April 29, Tencent paid $126 million for a 14.6% stake in Glu Mobile Inc., the developer best known for the hit app Kim Kardashian: Hollywood, then in May 13, Tencent acquired 20% of mobile developer Pocket Gems Inc. for $60 million.

It appears that Tencent's small startup and large company purchases are consistent with a broader M&A internationalization path. In 2013, Riot Games opened offices in the United States (New York City) and Australia (Sydney) at a capital expenditure (CAPEX) of $9.4 million and $25.3 million, respectively. These offices strengthened Riot Games' relationships with local customers, as well as its focus on marketing and managing local esports leagues, thereby granting Tencent better access to these markets. In line with this strategy, Riot Games is expected to open a French office in early 2017 at an expected CAPEX of $5 million.

While Riot Games is an example of Tencent acquiring a profitable game franchise in an international market and bringing it to China, Tencent's investments in startups indicate a commitment to diversification. Tencent's $8.7 billion acquisition of Supercell, the developer of "Clash of the Clans," from SoftBank Group Corp. in June 2016 appears to be motivated by this latter set of interests and is expected to further consolidate its gaming presence (Wall Street Journal, 2016). Table 4.1 shows Tencent's M&A transactions in the last two years.

4.3   CHINA'S INNOVATION ECOSYSTEM

We now describe the innovation ecosystem that led to the rise of Internet companies such as Tencent, Alibaba, and Baidu Inc. (see also, Chapter 3 above). China is the first middle-income economy to join high-income countries among the Top 25 of the Global Innovation Index (GII),[10] a group typically composed of high-income countries. In the 2017 ranking, China moved to 22nd place in the innovation index, narrowing the distance with the high-income economies.[11]

Toward the end of the 20th century, China's strong economic foundation was evidenced by a population with nearly universal primary education and high

---

10. Source: Global Innovation Index 2016 report, https://www.globalinnovationindex.org/gii-2016-report.
11. Global Innovation Index 2017 report, https://www.globalinnovationindex.org/gii-2017-report

TABLE 4.1 Tencent's M&A Investments in 2015–16

Announced Date	Role	Target	Size ($mm)
August 19, 2016	Buyer	Teambition	–
August 02, 2016	Buyer	YiXin Capital Limited	550.0
July 31, 2016	Buyer	Beijing AWcloud Software Co., Ltd.	–
July 05, 2016	Buyer	Medbanks Network Technology Co. Ltd.	30.0
June 21, 2016	Buyer	Supercell Oy	8600.0
June 06, 2016	Buyer	Bitauto Holdings Limited (NYSE:BITA)	300.0
May 31, 2016	Buyer	Beijing Zhenguanyu Science and Technology Co., Ltd.	40.0
May 27, 2016	Buyer	YG Entertainment Inc. (KOSDAQ:A122870)	–
February 11, 2016	Buyer	Mogujie	–
December 31, 2015	Buyer	Beijing Homelink Real Estate Brokerage Co., Ltd.	927.8
December 15, 2015	Buyer	Riot Games, Inc.	–
November 09, 2015	Buyer	Meta Company	50.0
November 03, 2015	Buyer	Meituan Group, Inc. (nka:China Internet Plus Group)	3300.0
October 21, 2015	Buyer	Artillery Games, Inc.	–
August 12, 2015	Buyer	sensewhere Limited	–
June 15, 2015	Buyer	iDreamSky Technology Limited	491.91
June 12, 2015	Buyer	Bona Film Group Limited	404.92
May 13, 2015	Buyer	Pocket Gems, Inc.	–
May 07, 2015	Buyer	Guangzhou Huan Company	16.11
April 29, 2015	Buyer	Glu Mobile, Inc. (NasdaqGS:GLUU)	126.0
February 18, 2015	Buyer	Miniclip Group SA	–
January 28, 2015	Buyer	Tissue Analytics, Inc.	0.75

Source: CapitalIQ.

levels of public health. Amidst a relatively stable macroeconomic environment, China invested in its transportation and energy infrastructure, increased R&D expenditure, and patent awards, and the established scientific parks and zones. While China lagged its industrial counterparts in science-based innovation such as pharmaceuticals, chemicals, or biotechnology, it made significant gains in engineering-based innovations such as communications equipment, which contributed to the robust infrastructure that Internet companies such as Tencent would leverage to grow at a rapid pace.

Several factors fueled China's innovation. First and foremost is the large domestic market with a significant proportion of working age adults.[12] The working age share of China's population has increased from 71.62% in 2004 to 73.61% in 2014,[13] providing a large customer base for companies such as Tencent. Additionally, the younger population has adopted smartphones at a rapid rate (92% in the 18–24 age group and 89% in the 25–34 age group) (eMarketer, 2014). This large customer segment stimulates innovation both through its openness to newer products and services and by enabling long-term engagement-based business models. Another important factor is China's focus on R&D investments, whose value has increased steadily and is expected to exceed that of the United States by 2019.[14] Lastly, China's extensive manufacturing ecosystem has raised productivity and accelerated innovation.

Technological influences have fueled all aspects of China's innovation process since 2000. The country has created an innovation ecosystem, wherein the stakeholders and resources necessary to achieve ongoing innovation in a modern economy are in place. While Didi Chuxing Technology Co., Qunar.com Inc., Ctrip.com (Ctrip International Ltd.), and Tuniu.com (Tunui Corp.) have changed how people travel, SouFun.com (SouFun Holdings Ltd.) and Fang.com (Fang Holdings Ltd.) have changed the way people search for homes. Similarly, Youku Inc., Meitu Inc. and WeChat have changed the entertainment and lifestyle industry while Ele.me Inc. and Meituan.com (now Meituan-Dianping) have changed the food industry.

Venture capital and a favorable policy framework have further supported China's innovation system. Angel investor funding and early-stage venture funds have risen 5.4-fold from $2.7 billion in 2009 to $17.4 billion in 2014, dominated heavily by IT and computer-related deals.[15]

In 2014, China accounted for 10% of the world's 18.5 million professional and amateur software developers, similar to India with 9.8% (ADTmag, 2014). In July of 2015, China unveiled its Internet Plus action plan. The action plan states that the government aims to deepen the Internet integration with economic and social sectors, that it will promote Internet technology infrastructure, and will also tackle the technological bottlenecks of different industries to strengthen risk control. Supported by the active policy agenda of the government, Tencent and other Internet companies like Alibaba and Baidu have increased their international presence and created their own microcosms within the broader innova-

---

12. Working age as defined by World Bank is 15–64 years.
13. Source: World Bank (Health Nutrition and Population Statistics: Population Estimates and Projections). http://databank.worldbank.org/data/reports.aspx?source=Health%20Nutrition%20and%20Population%20Statistics:%20Population%20estimates%20and%20projections, accessed June 13, 2017.
14. Source: Global Innovation Index, www.globalinnovationindex.org. Accessed by March 9th 2017.
15. Various sources including http://www.icbc.com/, http://www.zero2ipo.com.cn/en/research/ Accessed February 5th, 2017.

tion framework in China. The planned policy impetus over the next decade will give a further boost to innovation and drive Tencent's expansion.[16]

4.4   TENCENT'S CONNECTED UNIVERSE AND UNIQUE BUSINESS MODEL

Today, Tencent is more than just a company, it is an entire universe of inter-linked businesses. At the heart of this universe is Tencent's gaming business, which contributes most of the company's revenue. Tencent's instant messaging platforms—the most prominent of which are QQ messenger, WeChat (called Weixin in China), and Qzone—are crucial to Tencent's gaming business. The cohesiveness of the online search, software and apps, e-commerce platforms, web portal, omni-channel/location-based services, payment, entertainment, and social media platforms is central to users' loyalty to Tencent. This comprehensive suite of products provides a platform for brands to engage with customers through multiple touchpoints. By creating the tools, technology, and models to enable this enhanced user experience, Tencent is contributing to a "new retail model" that tech companies elsewhere are following closely.

In this section we further explore the different components of the Tencent universe (Fig. 4.7) and how they connect with each other (Wall Street Journal, 2017).

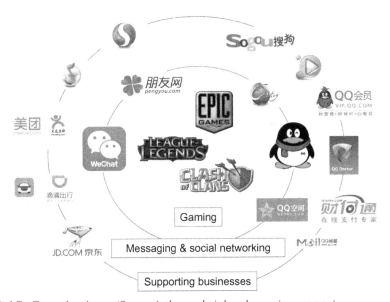

FIG. 4.7   Tencent's universe. *(Source: Author analysis based on various sources.)*

---

16. State Council, People's Republic of China, China unveils Internet Plus action plan to fuel growth, July 4, 2015. http://english.gov.cn/policies/latest_releases/2015/07/04/content_281475140165588.htm, accessed June 13, 2017.

4.4.1 Gaming

Tencent is the largest gaming company in the world and has further strengthened its position through the acquisition of Supercell. In 2015, this Finnish company made profits of €848 million ($964 million), on revenues of €2.109 billion ($2.326 billion). That compares to earnings before income tax, depreciation, and amortization of €515 million ($592 million) in 2014, on revenues of €1.545 billion ($1.777 billion) (Venturebeat, 2016b). The Supercell acquisition seems to be a win-win for both Tencent and Supercell, as it allows Tencent to expand its reach outside China and lets Supercell increase its penetration in the Chinese market.

Tencent (including Supercell) had $11.1 billion in revenue in 2015 and ranked first in global gaming ahead of Activision Blizzard and King Digital Entertainment plc (Newzoo, 2016). As of 2017, Tencent owns stakes in the most popular Massively Multiplayer Online Games (MMOs) including League of Legends, Crossfire, and Dungeon Fighter Online. These three games alone brought in $3.75 billion (Venturebeat, 2016a). League of Legends, Los Angeles-based Riot Games' only product, was the most popular online game in the world, with around 70 million monthly players. Riot Games reportedly earned $620 million in sales in 2013 as the multiplayer battle game continued to thrive.

Tencent's profitable strategy of charging premium prices on virtual goods in popular games freed the company from the risks of turning users away through other charges. Tencent was able to promote its games on WeChat and QQ, converting nongamers into casual gamers and some eventually into hardcore gamers. This approach ratcheted up customer demand and revenues for the company.

Most gamers around the world play without knowing that many of the games are actually owned by a Chinese company—Tencent. In response to fierce competition, Tencent has not only designed its own games but also made proactive acquisitions and investments in other game developers. In doing so, Tencent has reduced potential competition and generated more negotiating power. What is more, Tencent utilizes its powerful social platform to promote its games. Its access to a large base of users enhances its power both in social networking and in gaming, thereby generating cash flow and reducing its marketing costs.

4.4.2 Messaging and Social Networking

Social networks and instant messaging services have a high entry barrier due to the challenges of acquiring a large active user base. They rely on the "network effect," whereby a user joins a particular messaging service because his/her friends or family are on that service. With few major players, the social network industry is relatively concentrated and thus QQ's and WeChat's loyal and significant user base gives Tencent substantial negotiating power to generate sustainable future revenue. Tencent's messaging and social networking services are:

- *QQ messenger*: a chat messenger service in China with over 899 million monthly active users.[17] QQ provides comprehensive solutions for Internet-based instant messaging (IM) platforms that not only support basic online communication functions, including text messaging, video, and voice chat, but also allow file transmission. Additionally, QQ supports cross platform communication between computers and wireless terminals and is fully compatible with Windows XP, Vista, Linux, Mac, and other systems.
- *WeChat/Weixin*: a global messenger service in Tencent's portfolio with 806 million users worldwide. Its user base has grown 300% in little over three years from close to 200 million users in 2013.[18] The messenger is called Weixin in China and WeChat abroad. Unlike WhatsApp's single function social messaging service, WeChat offers chatting, gaming, shopping, and even banking all in one single platform through Tencent's universe, which encourages loyalty and generates substantially higher revenues.
- *Qzone*: a social network launched in May 2005 that allows users to write blogs, keep diaries, send photos, listen to music, and watch videos. Users, primarily teenagers, can set their Qzone background and select accessories based on their preferences so that every Qzone is customized to the individual member's taste. However, most Qzone accessories must be purchased. The monthly average number Qzone users was 640 million in 2015, out of which 570 million accessed the service via smart devices.
- *Pengyou*: literally, the Chinese word for "friend" is an online social market primarily for Chinese students and white collar workers. Pengyou has both a social component and is designed for corporate outreach, through which friends can become "fans" of various companies and use the platform to engage with their consumers.
- *Cityelite*: a local social networking service that connects people of different ages, occupations, hometowns, and locations who have similar interests. Users can join in online interactive entertainment activities with friends, such as calling for songs on demand, posting in the community, and taking part in hot topic discussions. Users can also participate in a wide variety of offline local activities, such as outdoor travel, attending concerts, and watching movies, among others.

4.5 SUPPORTING BUSINESSES

One of Tencent's goals is ensuring a superior user experience. The company's initial struggle for a business model was central to their later creative solutions for monetizing their large user base. Today, Tencent has supported

---

17. Source: Statista, http://www.statista.com/statistics/272014/global-social-networks-ranked-by-number-of-users/. Accessed September 2016.
18. Source: Statista, http://www.statista.com/statistics/255778/number-of-active-wechat-messenger-accounts/. Accessed September 2016.

businesses related to gaming and messaging products by not only investing in businesses such as e-commerce, search engines, ride share, food-reviews, and delivery but also engineering their own products in-house. The scale and depth of Tencent's universe cements a barrier for entry for competitors. Users are reluctant to migrate away from Tencent's broad universe of gaming and messaging products to competing companies that lack Tencent's comprehensive services.

The supporting businesses at Tencent include:

4.5.1 Search Engine and Email

- Sogou.com: A Chinese search engine that enables users to search text, images, music, and maps. Launched on August 3, 2004, Tencent bought a 40.9% stake in Sogou for $516 million in 2013, at which time Sogou's services were integrated with Tencent's popular WeChat mobile messaging platform.
- *QQ mail*: an email service similar to Hotmail and Gmail.

4.5.2 Software and Apps

- *QQ Doctor*: a free antivirus developed by Tencent for customers to protect and optimize their systems.
- *QQ Pinyin*: QQ Pinyin is a software that uses the pinyin method of transliterating Chinese to give users the flexibility to convert words from pinyin to traditional or simple Chinese.
- *QQ Software Manager*: a tool like Google Play on Android devices or the AppStore in Apple devices, which allows users to install and uninstall different Tencent products with a single click.
- *QQ Player*: a multimedia player that supports film and music files.

4.5.3 Online-to-Offline (O2O) Services

- *Didi Dache*: a ridesharing app. In April 2013, Tencent invested $15 million in this app, which was supported through WeChat as a means for users to pay cab fees. In January 2014, Tencent and venture capital firms invested another $100 million in the app, leading to a merger and then acquisition of the local subsidiary of what became a global ridesharing app (discussed in further detail in section "Cooperative Competition").

4.5.4 Payment Platforms

- *Tenpay*: a payment provider that supports business-to-business, business-to-customer, and customer-to-customer payments.
- *WeChatPay*: an in-app payment solution to transfer money between WeChat users (peer-to-peer) and to make payments online and with participating offline retailers.

- *WeBank*: an online-only bank in China, launched in 2015 when the China Banking Regulatory Commission (CBRC) approved the establishment of five private banks in China. Tencent holds 30% stake in the bank and this is the maximum percentage allowed for an online bank as per regulation in China.

4.5.5   Entertainment Platforms

- *QQShow*: An avatar-based social platform, like Korea's Cyworld. QQShow facilitates the purchase of virtual goods to outfit avatars.
- *QQMusic*: An online music streaming service similar to Spotify. In July 2016, Tencent announced the merger of QQMusic with market leader China Music Corporation in a bid valued at $2.7 billion.

4.6   UNIQUE BUSINESS MODEL

Tencent's developed its universe of products and services through efforts to monetize and improve user experience. Yet by 2015, the company recognized the importance of the internal links within its ecosystem and doubled down on this "Connection" strategy[19] (see Exhibit 4.1). Tencent's business model gave the company the means to tap and transform markets made available by the mobile Internet. In its 2015 Annual Report, the company stated its key initiatives for this "Internet-Plus" strategy were:

- Enriching products and services available within [Tencent's] platforms. For example, [Tencent] introduced personal microloan products and municipal services, such as visa applications, to Mobile QQ and Weixin.

"Connection" strategy

For merchants:
- Access to large user base
- Unified user log-in enables CRM and targeted advertising
- Online payment facilitates transactions

For users:
- Always connected
- Access to rich mix of content, services, and transactions
- Control multiple smart devices

For tencent:
- Deepen user stickiness via broadened product offering
- Increase traffic conversion through transactions and advertising
- Tap into new markets unlocked by mobile Internet

EXHIBIT 4.1   Tencent's "connection" strategy. *(Source: Tencent 2015 Annual report.)*

---

19. Source: Tencent Annual Report 2015—http://www.tencent.com/en-us/content/ir/rp/2015/attachments/201502.pdf, accessed August 2016.

- Promoting [its] online payment services through enriched payment scenarios, increasing [Monthly Average Users] (MAU) of [their] mobile payment services by over seven times year-on-year.
- Growing its mobile utility services, including security, browser, and application store, strengthening infrastructural supports to [their] mobile products.
- Investing in equity stakes in leading companies in related Internet verticals, such as Internet Plus Holdings, to provide best-in-class services to [their] users.

Tencent has more diversified revenue streams than some Internet giants. For example, advertising contributes only 17% of Tencent's revenue whereas Facebook gets 95% of its revenue from advertising and Google/Alphabet gets 92% from advertising (see Exhibit 4.2). Tencent's focus on attracting new users and encouraging interaction within communities resulted in three revenue categories:

Tencent

	Year ended 31 December			
	2015		2014	
	Amount	% of total revenues	Amount	% of total revenues
	(RMB in millions, unless specified)			
VAS[1]	80,669	78%	63,310	80%
Online advertising	17,468	17%	8,308	11%
Others[2]	4,726	5%	7,314	9%
Total revenues	102,863	100%	78,932	100%

Facebook

Revenue for the years ended December 31, 2015, 2014, and 2013 consists of the following (in millions):

| | Year Ended December 31, | | |
	2015	2014	2013
Advertising	$ 17,079	$ 11,492	$ 6,986
Payments and other fees	849	974	886
Total revenue	$ 17,928	$ 12,466	$ 7,872

Alphabet/Google

| | Year Ended December 31, | | |
	2013	2014	2015
Google segment			
Google websites	$ 37,422	$ 45,085	$ 52,357
Google Network Members' websites [1]	13,650	14,539	15,033
Google advertising revenues	51,072	59,624	67,390
Google other revenues [1]	4,435	6,050	7,151
Google segment revenues	$ 55,507	$ 65,674	$ 74,541
Other Bets			
Other Bets revenues	$ 12	$ 327	$ 448
Consolidated revenues	$ 55,519	$ 66,001	$ 74,989

EXHIBIT 4.2 Advertising revenues for Tencent, Facebook and Google. *(Source: 2015 annual reports for Tencent, Facebook, and Google/Alphabet.)*

- *Fee-based revenue*: subscription and purchase of virtual goods within games and social networks, e.g., buying a new dress for a virtual avatar or additional levels/functionality in a game.
- *Traffic-based revenue*: online advertising through cost-per-display, cost-per-thousand, cost-per-click, or cost-per-acquisition.
- *Transaction-based revenue*: includes mobile recharge or utility payments that result in a small fee charged for every transaction.

Tencent's revenue as of December 31, 2015 was approximately RMB 102.9 billion ($15.3 billion), an increase of 30% over the previous year (see Fig. 4.8 for the different revenue sources).

Value-added services contributed $12 billion (78% of Tencent's revenue) in 2015, growing 27% from the previous year due to a 30% increase in revenue from social networks and a 26% increase in online games. Online advertising contributed ~$2.6 billion (17% of Tencent's revenue) but grew an impressive 110% from the previous year due to an increase in performance-based advertising from Qzone. Other sources (including e-commerce) contributed $700 million (5% of Tencent's revenue), and this was 30% lower than the $1.09 billion from the previous year due to changes in recognition of revenue from various sources.[20]

A discussion of Tencent's business model would be incomplete without the mention of the Tencent Foundation, the first public welfare foundation established by an Internet company in China. Tencent initiated the foundation in

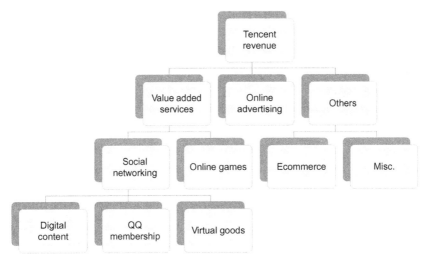

FIG. 4.8   Breakdown of Tencent's revenue sources. *(Source: Author analysis based on various sources.)*

---

20. Source: Tencent's Annual Report 2015, http://www.tencent.com/enus/content/ir/rp/2015/attachments/201502.pdf, accessed September 2016, and Using conversion 1 RMB = 0.15352 USD as of December 31, 2015.

2007 to support universally accessible technology and communication. In addition, the company runs gongyi.qq.com, "a public charity website, which focuses on youth education, assisting impoverished communities, care for the disadvantaged, and disaster relief."[21]

4.7 FACTORS CONTRIBUTING TO SUCCESS

We discussed how China's innovation ecosystem played a role in Tencent's growth. Other factors that have contributed to the success of the company include innovation in products and services, strong leadership, megatrends that fueled exponential growth, a protected economy that kept competitors at bay, and collaborative competition with companies.

4.7.1 Innovation in Products and Services

Tencent has come a long way from its beginnings, when it mostly imitated global products. Today, Tencent's innovations in products and services have earned it global recognition. It was recently ranked the 48th most innovative company in the world,[22] a testament to the rapid progress the company has made in leveraging product and business model innovation. WeChat is at the forefront of this innovation, fueling Tencent's expansion of its user base, providing a more holistic experience to its users and generating additional revenue for Tencent.

For instance, in 2014, WeChat revolutionized hongbao—the red envelopes that senior family members stuff with "lucky money" and present to junior relatives during holidays or special occasions—when it introduced a digital money-transfer feature called e-hongbao. According to China's official Xinhua News Agency, more than five million WeChat users sent e-hongbao during the first two days of 2014's New Year holiday, exchanging over 20 million e-hongbao. This number jumped in 2015 to more than one billion e-hongbao exchanges made just on New Year's Eve. In 2016, the number of e-hongbao exchanges ballooned to eight billion, with 420 million people making transfers on New Year's Eve alone.

4.7.2 Strong Leadership

As Tencent grew, each of its five young founders took a leadership role in a different segment of the company (see Table 4.2), thereby simultaneously enabling rapid growth in multiple segments.

21. Souces: Tencent website, https://www.tencent.com/en-us/abouttencent.html and Women of China, Tencent Foundation, January 23, 2014, http://www.womenofchina.cn/womenofchina/html1/source/16/9291-1.htm.
22. Forbes, The World's Biggest Companies- http://www.forbes.com/companies/tencent-holdings/, accessed in August 2016.

TABLE 4.2 Tencent Founders

Name	Education	Skill Set	Prior Industry Experience	Prior Functional Experience	Prior Global Education/ Experience	Currently in Operational role, Role
Huateng Ma (Pony Ma)	BS (Computers)	Technical	Telecom	Research & Innovation	No	Yes, CEO
Chenye Xu (Daniel Xu)	BS (Computers)	Technical	Telecom	Software system design, network administration, marketing and sales management	No	Yes, CIO
Zhidong Zhang (Tony Zhang)	BS (Computers) MS (Computers)	Technical	Info not available	Info not available	No	No
Yidan Chen (Charles Chen)	BS (Chemistry) Master (Law)	No	Government	Administration/Legal	No	No
Liqing Zeng (Jason Zeng)	BS (Computers)	Technical	Telecom	Info not available	No	No

As shown in Table 4.2, none of the founders had any global education or experience prior to Tencent. This may partially explain Tencent's initial focus on the Chinese market and reluctance to expand outside the country. Also, almost all of the founders had a technical background, while none them had a management background. This shared expertise could also explain why Tencent's products were providing great user experience despite the company's initial struggle to build a business model.

Among the founders, Charles Chen deserves to be highlighted for his prior experience working with the government; his knowledge of various aspects of the Chinese legal system likely contributed significantly to Tencent's success. As the Chief Administration Officer of Tencent since 1998, Charles oversaw administration, legal affairs, human resources, and the company's charity fund. Charles was also responsible for the Group's management system, intellectual property rights, and government relations.

Only two of the founders, Pony Ma and Daniel Xu, have active roles in the Tencent's operation. The remaining three founders have become Advisors Emeriti between 2007 and 2013. To fill the leadership positions vacated by the founders, Tencent promoted senior leaders from within its ranks to C-level roles. These included Chi Ping Lau (Martin Lau), Yuxin Ren (Mark Ren), and James Mitchell (see Table 4.3).

Table 4.3 shows that two of the nonfounder executives have studied abroad (in the United States/United Kingdom), giving them experience abroad, and the third holds an eMBA from China Europe International Business School (CEIBS) and had worked at one of the largest global telecom equipment company emerging out of China, Huawei Technologies Co. The impressive qualifications of Tencent's new leaders indicate the potential for it to maintain its momentum in the future.

4.8 CHINESE MARKET AND POSSIBILITIES

Three megatrends have bolstered Chinese internet companies in past decades: rapid growth of the affluent middle and upper classes, a young population that is not averse to spending, and a popular shift from brick-and-mortar stores to e-commerce. We examine each of these trends in detail.

4.8.1 Growth of the Middle Class

China's middle class is the biggest in the world, and growing rapidly. By 2020, this growing middle class will contribute to 13% of total middle class consumption in the world (World Bank, 2011), providing a stable customer base for companies like Tencent and creating an appetite for innovative products to meet the demands of this consumer segment. As the middle-class population grows in the coming decade, Tencent is likely to acquire/partner with other global businesses to bring global products and services to China's middle class.

TABLE 4.3 Tencent Leadership (Nonfounders)

Name	Education	Skill Set	Prior Experience	Prior Global Education/ Experience	Currently in Operational Role, Role
Chi Ping Lau (Martin Lau)	• BS (Electrical Eng.) Michigan Univ., USA • MS (Electrical Eng.,) Stanford Univ., USA • MBA, Kellogg Business School, USA	Strategy and Finance (Corporate Strategy, Investments, M&A & Investor relations	• Management Consulting (McKinsey) • Investment Banking (Goldman Sachs)	Yes	Yes, President
Yuxin Ren (Mark Ren)	• BS (Computers) • EMBA, CEIBS, China	Marketing & Sales R&D	Telecom (Huawei)	Info not available	Yes, Chief Operating Officer
James Mitchell	• Finance, Oxford, UK • Chartered Financial Analyst (CFA)	Financial Analysis, Investments	Investment Banking (Goldman Sachs, New York)	Yes	Yes, Chief Strategy Officer

4.8.2 Young Population

The millennial[23] population in China is poised to become a dominant force in the country's consumer market. The consumption of the under-35 population is growing at 14% annually, double than that of their elders. In many product categories, members of the younger generation outspend their parents and grandparents by as much as 40%. By 2020, their share of total consumption will reach 53% from its current level of 45% (Boston Consulting Group, The New China Playbook, 2015). The sheer size of this young population gives Tencent ready access to a large user base despite its limited presence outside of China. Since this demographic is not averse to spending, Tencent has the ability to further monetize its products and services.

4.8.3 Shift to e-Commerce

As of 2016, China has the largest share of e-commerce sales in the world. As much as 40% of worldwide e-commerce sales occur in China. Within China, e-commerce sales contribute close to 16% of overall retail sales, the highest percentage anywhere in the world. The share of e-commerce will exceed 33% by 2019, good news for Internet companies like Tencent.

We believe that this rapid rise in e-commerce is the reason Tencent has made venture capital investments in e-commerce businesses such as JD.com Inc. and 58.com Inc. Moreover, as customers grow accustomed to online purchasing, they can be expected to buy goods and services online more frequently. Once a customer enters the Tencent ecosystem, the company can use the "connections" within the ecosystem to sell multiple products and services, from online games to O2O services to virtual goods. Since e-commerce advertisers are most interested in targeting customers who are already "online," Tencent can leverage its vast user base to earn even more advertising revenues.[24]

4.9 PROTECTED ENVIRONMENT

China has some of the world's most restrictive policies on the dissemination of information. Chinese TV and the news media are censored; the government has censors monitoring popular social media platforms, like WeChat, and American Internet giants, like Google, Facebook, YouTube, and Twitter, have been blocked in China for years. This allows homegrown companies such as Tencent, Alibaba, and Baidu a "protective wall" against outside competition.

Tencent has managed to grow and establish its far-reaching presence in China partly because of its ability to navigate the regulatory environment and

---

23. Millennials are generally defined as those born between 1980 and the mid-2000s.
24. eMarketer, Worldwide retail e-commerce sales: eMarketer's updates estimates and forecast through 2019, http://www.emarketer.com/public_media/docs/eMarketer_eTailWest2016_Worldwide_ECommerce_Report.pdf, accessed August 2016.

its strong relationship with the government. At times, Tencent has also received criticism for giving in to government censorship requests, though these allegations are difficult to prove. The Chinese government is a key stakeholder in the Internet industry, even considering taking board seats and ownership stakes of at least 1% in operators of some Internet portals and mobile apps in exchange for granting news licenses (Bloomberg, 2016). In such a case, government representatives could monitor and block Internet providers' content, although they would not be involved in other day-to-day business decisions, according to some financial analysts.

This proposal would give authorities the ability to block news from reaching the Web, and coincides with a broad government clampdown on information distributed online. Such a move could affect Tencent and other operators and mobile apps that provide users with daily current events and news (Bloomberg, 2016). If this regulation passes, it will become even more difficult for global Internet companies like Google to compete successfully in China, as their concerns for user privacy will not allow them to operate in China.

4.9.1   Collaborative Competition

The Chinese Internet industry is dominated by three giants: Baidu, Alibaba, and Tencent, often referred to collectively as "BAT." Each of these companies is strong in one or two niches and competes with the other companies in different areas. For instance, Baidu's primary product is a search engine, Alibaba is known for its e-commerce platform and payment system, and Tencent has its strength in instant messaging and gaming.

These three Chinese companies have invested in or acquired hundreds of startups in recent years to expand their reach in mobile Internet, especially in apps that can connect online users with offline services. Some tech industry executives blame BAT for fanning price wars by pouring money into these startups (Wall Street Journal, 2015).

This three-way competition is one reason behind Tencent's desire to be the first mover in different niche areas, through organic or inorganic means. And yet, a unique aspect of the competitive landscape in the Chinese Internet industry is the tactical collaboration which occurs when two of the "big three" align against the third.

4.9.2   Tencent and Baidu Against Alibaba

In 2014, Tencent and Baidu teamed up with conglomerate Wanda Group to form an RMB 5 billion (about $814 million) e-commerce joint venture in a bid to challenge Alibaba's dominance. Wanda, a real estate and movie theater chain group, took a 70% stake, while Tencent and Baidu took 15% each (Techcrunch, 2014). The partnership promoted Tencent's online payment platforms, including TenPay and Weixin Payment, competitors to Alibaba's Alipay. TenPay and

Weixin Payment became the preferred payment method across all of Wanda's businesses, including its movie theaters. Tencent also gained access to movies, TV shows, and online dramas owned by Wanda.

4.9.3   Tencent and Alibaba Against Baidu

A primary area of competition among the Internet companies in China is in the O2O space. This refers to businesses in which consumers buy goods offline though apps online. By the end of 2015, Meituan and Dianping, two O2O companies in which Alibaba and Tencent were principal investors, agreed to merge. While the two companies were quite different, one of their core similarities was group-discounts. Meituan was an unabashed Groupon clone founded by Wang Xing, while Dianping, called the "Chinese Yelp," was actually founded before its American counterpart and often gave members discounts if they bought meals at reviewed restaurants with their friends (Fortune, 2015). Dianping and Meituan were encroached upon by a bevy of competitors, including Baidu-backed Nuomi Holdings Inc. As a result, Tencent and Alibaba agreed to join resources to compete against Nuomi.

Earlier in 2015, China's biggest taxi-hailing apps, Tencent-backed Didi Dache and Alibaba-backed Kuaidi Dache merged after a costly price war, to become Didi Chuxing. This deal helped the combined entity successfully ward off the threat from Uber Technologies Inc., which eventually sold its stake to the combined entity. In the deal announced in August 2016, Uber agreed to swap its China operations for a 20% stake in Didi Chuxing, which was valued at $28 billion in its latest fundraising round. Combined with Uber's China business valued at around $8 billion, Didi would have a valuation of around $36 billion.

These examples of "collaborative competition" show how the three Internet giants are not averse to teaming up when required—an important factor behind the accelerated growth of these three companies, particularly Tencent.

Another example of such collaboration is Tencent's partnership with JD. com, with the potential to reshape China's marketing and advertising industry. In October 2015, the two companies launched "Brand Commerce," a project intended to help companies build their brand images and improve marketing performance. By integrating Tencent's social networking data with JD.com's online shopping data, the project allowed companies to reach their target buyers while facilitating consumer.

Fig. 4.9 shows some other examples of verticals that Tencent has been able to penetrate through cooperation, investment, and M&A.

4.10   CHALLENGES

Despite its success, Tencent faces some critical challenges; the company's ability to address these challenges will play a vital role in determining its future. According to various sources, 93% of users in tier-one cities in China already

FIG. 4.9 Examples of Tencent's stake in other verticals.

use WeChat. Thus, in order to continue its rapid rate of growth, WeChat needs to expand globally, which Tencent has been reluctant to do.

4.10.1   Challenges in Taking WeChat Global

One obstacle facing Tencent is that WeChat's operations in 14 different countries require software customization for each market. Whenever WeChat releases an updated version, Tencent must create more than 10 different language versions of the software. In addition to the language issue, there are cultural differences in the way that users in different markets interact with each other while using the software. Therefore, WeChat must customize its interfaces and features for each market. This suggests that success in one market does not necessarily lead to success in other markets. WeChat's internationalization then becomes a continuous adjustment and improvement process rather than a "duplicate and distribute" process.

Another challenge that we see for WeChat pertains to users' perceptions. The perception is that because Tencent is closely linked to the Chinese government, users' privacy is at risk. This is a particularly tricky perception to address, since users' initial mistrust may undermine any potential solution. Tencent is dealing with this problem in several ways:

First, they intend to separate WeChat from Tencent both from an operations and brand perspective. Looking at the company's overall organization structure, Tencent has adopted the network center structure, having WeChat as an independent entity consisting of its own management team, its own board of directors, and its own decision-making capabilities. Tencent serves as a holding company itself and is not involved in WeChat's daily operations.

Second, Tencent is strategically teaming up with local partners to make WeChat appear more "local." For example, Google is one of Tencent's biggest local partners. In January 2014, Tencent started a marketing campaign, asking Google users to link their accounts to WeChat. Then, users of both platforms could invite their Google contacts to download and join WeChat, with the incentive to win a $25 Restaurant.com gift card. Strategies like this one are promising, as it allows WeChat to detach from the Tencent name.

4.10.2 Challenges in the Gaming Business

Apart from social networking, the other largest component of Tencent's revenue is online gaming. As discussed earlier, Tencent has spent billions of dollars to acquire global gaming business such as Supercell. Tencent must be able to take these games to China in order to recover its investments in these businesses and then create incremental value for its investors.

Tencent also faces other hurdles in its gaming businesses. One unique problem has to do with the limited presence of gameconsoles in China due to the government ban on the manufacturing and sale of game consoles until the end of 2013. The government believed that access to game consoles would make young teenagers addicted to video games, which they considered detrimental to teenagers' health and education. The result of the ban was that young gamers in China grew up playing games mostly on the PC and mobile platforms, and the general expectation of games on these two platforms is that they should be free. In this environment, Tencent faced the challenge of finding a way to make money when its gaming customers had already developed a free-to-play mindset. Tencent overcame this challenge innovating the "freemium revenue model" discussed earlier.

Another challenge for the gaming business is related to China's lack of Internet infrastructure compared to the United States. Although China has been rapidly expanding its high-speed Internet capabilities over the past decade, connection speed and stability are still far removed from that of developed countries. As a result, when players log on to the games, they often experience lags and disconnections, which are detrimental to the gaming experiences. Tencent has been tackling this issue by strategically collaborating with China's telecom giants, such as China Unicom and China Mobile, working together to push for infrastructure-building initiatives such as high-speed fiber optic lines for second- and third-tier cities.

4.10.3 Challenges Faced in U.S. Market

The United States is the largest economy in the world in terms of nominal GDP. It is also the most mature Internet business, one of the reasons that all three Internet companies ahead of Tencent in market capitalization are U.S.-based. Tencent will penetrate the U.S. market through both its products and venture capital investments, a move which has proved difficult for Tencent thus far.

Tencent's most successful U.S.-based investments have brought content back to China. It has signed agreements to stream content from the NBA, Warner Bros., and HBO for a potential audience of hundreds of millions on Tencent's video site. While WeChat is a huge success in China, it flopped when it attempted to enter the U.S. market, as few Americans could be enticed away from Facebook and Instagram. Tencent's only major successful U.S.

venture is their acquisition of Riot Games for $230 million in 2011, according to some analysts.

4.11 THE FUTURE

Tencent was named the most valuable Chinese brand and the 11th most valuable brand in the world in the 2016 in BrandZ Top 100 Most Valuable Global Brands ranking by Millward Brown and WPP.[25] It is one of the few brands capable of generating its own licensing revenue.

Competitors other than Alibaba and Baidu, with connected ecosystems of their own, will be hard-pressed to replicate Tencent's "connection strategy." As of the writing of this book, Facebook is trying to provide a more comprehensive customer experience, but we believe it is still not a match for the "one stop shop" philosophy of Tencent. This philosophy is what enabled Tencent to assert its dominance in China.

Tencent has also established a clear lead in the gaming industry, and we expect this rapidly growing segment to further accelerate the company's growth. Moreover, since Tencent continues to keep the original brand names of the games it acquires, many customers may not even realize that they are playing Tencent games. Tencent's gaming assets provide a significant opportunity for the company to keep increasing its per user revenue as it rapidly expands its portfolio of games and pushes in-game purchases.

Tencent may still have additional room to grow its online advertising revenue. Unlike Facebook and Google, in 2015, Tencent received only 17% of its revenue through online advertising. Tencent more than doubled its online advertising revenue from 2014 to 2015 and we expect this growth to continue. Tencent's revenue diversity is a key reason why rating agencies have demonstrated confidence in Tencent's ability to maintain high profitability and generate free cash flow. Rating agencies' positive outlooks also reassure investors, as can be seen by Tencent's impressive stock performance since 2015.

One of the risks that we see for Tencent is its heavy dependence on the Chinese market. This did not affect the company when the Chinese economy was expanding rapidly, but as the Chinese market could slow down, it is critical for Tencent to find innovative ways to replicate its connection strategy internationally. This will require Tencent to both leverage its gaming assets across newer geographies and expand WeChat's reach beyond China. Tencent's ability to assert its dominance within the global arena will depend on whether or not it can successfully address these challenges.

---

25. Source: Millward Brown and WPP 2016 BrandZ™ Top 100 Most Valuable Global Brands ranking and report, http://www.millwardbrown.com/brandz/top-global-brands/2016.

APPENDIX

TABLE A4.1 Top 25 Tencent venture capital investments from 1999 to 2017, by size of investment

S. No	Portfolio Company Name	Deal Date	Deal Size (USD mn)	Investors	Location	Primary Industry	Subindustries
1	Meituan-Dianping	1/19/16	3300	Baillie Gifford, Capital Today, China Development Bank Capital, CPP Investment Board, DST Global, Hillhouse Capital Management, Sequoia Capital, Temasek Holdings, Tencent, Trustbridge Partners	China	Internet	e-Commerce
2	Daum Communications	5/26/14	3300	DCM, KakaoTalk, Korea Investment Partners, Maverick Capital Ventures, Tencent, WeMade Entertainment Co., Ltd.	South Korea	Internet	Communications, Email, Media, Internet Service Providers, Network, Domain & SEO Services, Social Networking & Communication Platform, Search Engines
3	Didi Chuxing	6/15/16	2800	Alibaba Group, Ant Financial Service Group, BlackRock, Oppenheimer Alternative Investment Management, Softbank, Tencent	China	Telecoms	Taxi and Limousine Services, Mobile Applications
4	Didi Chuxing	7/7/15	2000	Alibaba Group, Capital International, China Investment Corporation, Coatue Management, Ping An Ventures, Temasek Holdings, Tencent	China	Telecoms	Taxi and Limousine Services, Mobile Applications
5	Ganji.com	4/17/15	1610	58.com, DCM, SAIF Partners, Tencent, Warburg Pincus	China	Internet	Search Engines, Advertising

#	Company	Date	Amount	Investors	Country	Sector	Description
6	Didi Chuxing	9/9/15	1000	Alibaba Group, Capital International, China Investment Corporation, Coatue Management, Ping An Ventures, Temasek Holdings, Tencent	China	Telecoms	Taxi and Limousine Services, Mobile Applications
7	17u	7/6/15	979	CITIC Capital, Dalian Wanda Group, Tencent	China	Internet	Search Engines, e-Commerce, Travel & Tourism, Consumer Services
8	Lianjia	4/7/16	928	Baidu, China Renaissance Partners, Hillhouse Capital Management, Matrix Partners, Source Code Capital, Tencent	China	Internet	Property, Analytics & Performance Software
9	DianPing	4/2/15	850	Dalian Wanda Group, Fosun International, FountainVest Partners, Temasek Holdings, Tencent, Xiaomi	China	Internet	Mobile Applications, e-Commerce, Bars & Nightclubs, Consumer Services, Search Engines, Travel & Tourism
10	Didi Dache	12/9/14	700	DST Global, Temasek Holdings, Tencent	China	Telecoms	Mobile Applications, Taxi, and Limousine Services
11	Ele.me	8/27/15	630	Beijing Hualian Group, China Media Capital, CITIC Private Equity Funds Management, Gopher Asset Management, JD.com, Sequoia Capital, Tencent	China	Internet	Food Distributors, Restaurants, e-Commerce
12	Weiying	4/27/16	462	China Media Capital, Dalian Zeus Entertainment, Everbright Financial Holding Asset Management, iDreamSky Games, Sino Ocean Land Holding Limited, Tencent	China	Internet	e-Commerce, Cinemas, Mobile Applications

Continued

TABLE A4.1 Top 25 Tencent venture capital investments from 1999 to 2017, by size of investment—cont'd

S. No	Portfolio Company Name	Deal Date	Deal Size (USD mn)	Investors	Location	Primary Industry	Subindustries
13	Sogou	9/16/13	448	Tencent	China	Internet	Search Engines
14	DianPing	2/17/14	400	Tencent	China	Internet	Mobile Applications, e-Commerce, Bars & Nightclubs, Consumer Services, Search Engines, Travel & Tourism
15	58.com	4/17/15	400	Tencent	China	Advertising	Web Applications, e-Commerce
16	We Doctor Group Limited	9/24/15	394	China Development Bank Capital, Fosun International, Goldman Sachs, Hillhouse Capital Management, Tencent	China	Healthcare IT	Internet
17	Ele.me	1/27/15	350	CITIC Private Equity Funds Management, DianPing, JD.com, Sequoia Capital, Tencent	China	Internet	Food Distributors, Restaurants, e-Commerce
18	Koudai Gouwu	10/23/14	350	Falcon Edge Capital, H Capital, Tencent, Tiger Global Management, Vy Capital	China	Internet	e-Commerce, Mobile Applications
19	Anjuke	3/1/15	267	58.com, DCM, SAIF Partners, Tencent, Warburg Pincus	China	Internet	Property, Search Engines

#	Company	Date	Amount	Investors	Country	Sector	Description
20	Weiying	11/18/15	235	Beijing Cultural Assets Chinese Film & Television Fund, Beijing Hosen Investment Management, China Southern Fund Management, CREDIT Prosperity Fund Management, GGV Capital, Gopher Asset Management, Tencent, Wanda Cinema	China	Internet	e-Commerce, Cinemas, Mobile Applications
21	Douyu TV	8/15/16	226	Nanshan Capital, Phoenix Capital Asset Management Group, Sequoia Capital, Shenzhen Capital Group, Tencent	China	Gaming	Television Broadcasting and Programming, Internet/Web Games, Social Networking & Communication Platform
22	Mobike	1/4/17	215	Ctrip/Qunar, Hanting Hotels, Hillhouse Capital Management, Sequoia Capital, Tencent, TPG, Warburg Pincus	China	Telecoms	Transportation, Mobile Applications
23	JD.com	3/10/14	214	Tencent	China	Internet	e-Commerce, Home Centres and Hardware Stores, Consumer Electronics Stores, Mobile Applications, Communications
24	Mmb.cn	3/18/14	200	MediaTek Inc., Sequoia Capital, Tencent	China	Internet	e-Commerce, Mobile Applications
25	Hike Ltd.	8/16/16	175	BSB, Foxconn Ventures, Tencent, Tiger Global Management	India	Telecoms	Mobile Applications, Mobile Messaging

REFERENCES

ADTmag, 2014. IDC study counts the world's developers: 11 millions pros, January 06, https://adtmag.com/Blogs/WatersWorks/2014/01/Worldwide-Developer-Count.aspx.

Bloomberg, 2016. http://www.bloomberg.com/news/articles/2016-05-03/china-said-to-explore-taking-stakes-in-some-news-websites-apps.

Boston Consulting Group, The New China Playbook, 2015. http://www.bcg.com.cn/en/files/publications/reports_pdf/BCG-The-New-China-Playbook-Dec-2015.pdf, Accessed August 2016.

CBinsights, 2014. Tencent's accelerated pace of private company investments, July 29, https://www.cbinsights.com/blog/tencent-private-investment/.

eMarketer, 2014. Majority of China's mobile phone users will use smart phones next year, December 22, https://www.emarketer.com/Article/Majority-of-Chinas-Mobile-Phone-Users-Will-Use-Smartphones-Next-Year/1011749, Accessed June 13, 2017.

Fortune, 2015. This $15 billion deal shows how tough times are for Chinese VC. October 8, http://fortune.com/2015/10/08/china-tencent-alibaba-vc-deal/.

Newzoo, 2016. Supercell acquisition: Tencent set to take 13% of this year's $99.6Bn global games market. June 21, https://newzoo.com/insights/articles/supercell-acquisition-tencent-set-to-take-13-percent-of-the-games-market/.

Techcrunch, 2014. Tencent, Baidu and Wanda form $814M joint venture to take on Alibaba. August 28, https://techcrunch.com/2014/08/28/tencent-baidu-and-wanda-form-814m-joint-venture-to-take-on-alibaba/.

Techcrunch, 2016. India's WhatsApp rival Hike raises $175M led by Tencent at a $1.4B valuation. August, 16, https://techcrunch.com/2016/08/16/indias-whatsapp-rival-hike-raises-175m-led-by-tencent-at-a-1-4b-valuation/.

Technode, 2012. Tencent advances in game with new acquisitions and rising revenue. August 16, http://technode.com/2012/08/16/tencent-advances-in-game-with-new-acquisition-and-rising-revenue/, Accessed June 13, 2017.

Technode, 2013. Tencent has invested $2bm in overseas markets. Here's the list. October 23, http://technode.com/2013/10/23/tencent-has-invested-2-bn-dollars-in-overseas-markets-here-is-the-list/.

Tencent's Annual Report, 2015. http://www.tencent.com/en-us/content/ir/rp/2015/attachments/201502.pdf, Accessed June 13, 2017.

Venturebeat, 2016a. League of Legends, Clash of Clans, and Crossfire drive digital games to $61.3 B in 2015. January 26, http://venturebeat.com/2016/01/26/league-of-legends-clash-of-clans-and-crossfire-drive-digital-games-to-61-3b-in-2015/.

Venturebeat, 2016b. With just 3 games, Supercell made $924M in profits on $2.3B in revenue in 2015. March 9, http://venturebeat.com/2016/03/09/with-just-3-games-supercell-made-924m-in-profits-on-2-3b-in-revenue-in-2015/.

Wall Street Journal, 2016. Tencent Seals Deal to Buy 'Clash of Clans' Developer Supercell for $8.6 Billion. June 21, http://www.wsj.com/articles/tencent-agrees-to-acquire-clash-of-clans-maker-supercell-1466493612.

Wall Street Journal, 2015. Kingmaker's of China's Internet: Baidu, Alibaba and Tencent. October 21, http://www.wsj.com/articles/kingmakers-of-chinas-internet-baidu-alibaba-and-tencent-1445451143.

Wall Street Journal, 2017. China's WeChat app applauds apple, even is unveils a challenge. January 9, http://www.wsj.com/articles/chinas-wechat-applauds-apple-even-as-it-unveils-a-challenge-1483965602.

WIPO, 2015. Telecom firms lead WIPO international patent filings. March 19, http://www.wipo.int/pressroom/en/articles/2015/article_0004.html.

Women of China, 2014. Tencent Foundation. January 23, http://www.womenofchina.cn/womenofchina/html1/source/16/9291-1.htm, Accessed June 13, 2017.

World Bank, 2011 The Emerging Middle Class in Developing Countries. June XX, http://siteresources.worldbank.org/EXTABCDE/Resources/7455676-1292528456380/7626791-1303141641402/7878676-1306699356046/Parallel-Sesssion-6-Homi-Kharas.pdf.

Chapter 5

Policies to Drive Innovation in India

ACRONYMS

BSE	Bombay Stock Exchange
BSE 30	BSE Sensex
CAGR	Compound Annual Growth Rate
CII	Confederation of Indian Industry
GDP	Gross Domestic Product
GERD	Gross Expenditure on Research & Development
GII	Global Innovation Index
GST	Goods and Services Tax
GW	Gigawatts
ICT	Information Communication Technology
IIM	Indian Institutes of Management
IISC	Indian Institutes of Science
IITs	Indian Institutes of Technology
IPR	Intellectual Property Rights
IT	Information Technology
ITeS	IT-enabled Services
MSE-CDP	The Micro & Small Enterprises Cluster Development Programme
NMCP	National Manufacturing Competitiveness Programme
NSE	National Stock Exchange
PCO	Public Call Office
R&D	Research & Development
SMEs	Small and Medium-Sized Enterprises
UNIDO	United Nations International Development Organization

This chapter is authored by Senapathy "Kris" Gopalakrishnan[1] and Jibak Dasgupta.[2] The chapter has been adapted from an earlier version which appeared in the "Global Innovation Index 2015: Effective Innovation Policies for Development," Chapter 8, pages 121–130 published by WIPO, Geneva, 2015.

---

1. Past President, Confederation of Indian Industry and Co-Founder, Infosys.
2. Deputy Director, Confederation of Indian Industry.

Financing Entrepreneurship and Innovation in Emerging Markets.
https://doi.org/10.1016/B978-0-12-804025-6.00005-8

The Global Innovation Index 2015 report was coedited by Soumitra Dutta, Bruno Lanvin,[3] and Sacha Wunsch-Vincent.[4]

India is a lower-middle-income economy in Central and Southern Asia with more than 1.2 billion people, and a Gross Domestic Product (GDP) of $2 trillion in absolute terms for 2016. According to the Global Innovation Index (GII) ranking for last six consecutive years, India has outperformed its peer group (Bhutan, Sri Lanka, Uzbekistan, and Pakistan) in innovation capacity.

5.1 THE EVOLVING POLICY LANDSCAPE AND RESEARCH AND DEVELOPMENT GROWTH

India's dominance in innovation capacity has not been mere coincidence. It is a result of the gradually increasing focus of its policy regime, a focus that has moved from science to technology and on to innovation and entrepreneurship, and supported by years of planning and implementation. After India's independence, Indian policymakers sought economic growth through industrialization and science development. Initially, policymakers planned industrial development around implementing and empowering public sector undertakings. Scientific policy focused on the acquisition, dissemination, and discovery of scientific knowledge, but stressed scientific research and development rather than focusing on technology.

The Industrial Policy Resolution of 1956 lay down policies that gave a state monopoly to all heavy industries. The Industrial Policy Statement of 1977 emphasized decentralization, and the Industrial Policy Statement of 1980 stressed the need to promote competition in the domestic market, coupled with technological upgrading.[5] The Technology Policy Statement of 1983 shifted the earlier emphasis on scientific development to technology. The 1983 statement meant to foster both the development of homegrown technology and the efficient absorption and adaptation of imported technology to cater to national priorities. During the early 1980s, the private sector expanded gradually while the performance of Indian public-sector undertakings declined. With these policy measures in place, the GDP growth rate remained sluggish (at around 3.5%) (Mohan, 2008) under an inward-looking and protectionist industrial policy regime.

In the 1990s, policy-making in the science and technology sector began to align with the country's overall economic policy framework, which favored industrial research and development (R&D), the identification of technology needs, and technology development. The focus gradually shifted toward public and private institution collaboration, identifying priority sectors and social needs, enhancing international collaborations, and strengthening human

3. Executive Director—Global Indices, INSEAD, Fontainebleau, France.
4. Senior Economic Officer, WIPO, Geneva, Switzerland.
5. The Press Information Bureau, Government of India, released a series of press notes concerning Industrial Policy Highlights. These can be found online at http://eaindustry.nic.in/handbk/chap001.pdf; subsequent versions can be found by adjusting the chapter number in the link.

capital. In a historic moment, and with the help of a reformist budget, the Indian economy opened up in 1991 by relaxing its protectionist policies.

With a more open economy and the gradual shift in R&D and industrialization policy goals, scientific departments such as the Department of Science and Technology and the Department of Scientific and Industrial Research proactively collaborated with industry in public-private partnerships. This approach incentivized R&D from private industry by sharing costs and rewards and provided a buffer against the high-risk basic research component of R&D. The government and industry now jointly funded research projects initiated at the institutes, which previously would have been funded by industry alone.

According to data released by India's Ministry of Science and Technology (updated through 2009–10 and projected for two subsequent years), gross expenditure on R&D (GERD) in the country has consistently increased over time. From 24,117.24 crore Indian rupees in 2004–05, it reached 53,041.30 crore in 2009–10, an increase of ~45%. The R&D-to-GDP ratio increased significantly, from 0.81% in 2004–05 to 0.87% in 2009–10. These data allude to the strong growth in R&D in India that has occurred over the last decade compared with its closest peers, such as Pakistan (0.68% in 2007) and Sri Lanka (0.11% in 2008).[6] GERD as a percentage of GDP from 2011 to 2014 also ranks India consistently below 50 in the GII rankings.

The next section reviews India's innovation ranking in the GII. Subsequent sections will highlight what India has done to outscore its peers in the lower-middle-income countries, the innovation policies that appear to have fostered innovation, and areas in policy that may still need improvement. The chapter concludes with lessons to learn from India's experience and that of other countries, and, finally, a proposal for policy mixes that would enable India and similar countries to improve their innovation ranking.

5.2 REVIEW OF GII FINDINGS AND PILLARS, AND THEIR IMPACT ON INDIA'S RANKING

As noted in the previous section, India's policy regime has become favorable to innovation. Since the economic slowdown in 2008 (and specifically after 2010) India's economy performed in a somewhat unstable manner until 2015, when it gained momentum. India's overall GII ranking dropped from 62nd place in 2011 to 81st in 2015 before it jumped back to the 66th position in 2016. This ranking drop can primarily be attributed to two factors: the first factor concerns the changing dynamics of the country's political, educational, and business environment, and the second concerns the GII's structural change to improve itself as an assessment tool.

According to GII data obtained prior to 2015, India consistently performed poorly in the following parameters: political stability, ease of starting a

---

6. For growth in Pakistan, see Kahn and Khattak, (2014); for growth in Sri Lanka, see Weerasinghe, (2013).

business, tertiary inbound mobility, and environmental performance. These findings also resonated with the general public's perception that the government was relatively inactive in making policy decisions during this period. Among the reasons for this inactivity was the slowdown in the overall economy, the country's high rate of inflation, and the clamor over severe corruption charges against the incumbent government. Weaknesses underscored by the GII are the ease/difficulty of starting a business, a persistent matter of contention in India, which presents regulatory hurdles to entrepreneurs through a highly complex compliance regime and heavy bureaucratic interference. Such government interference discourages entrepreneurs from effectively starting and running businesses.

Since 2014–15, proactive government measures have improved the ease of doing business and reduced bureaucratic interference, the effect of which was arguably reflected in the improved GII 2016 ranking for India. The tertiary inbound mobility indicator tracks the number of foreign students studying in Indian institutions. Although India's higher education sector ranks better than many developed economies in terms of student quality, a lack of adequate infrastructure and student support system makes Indian higher education less attractive to foreign students. Finally, as a developing nation, India still fluctuates between the procurement of expensive, eco-friendly technology and the use of traditional, low-cost technologies that have a high carbon footprint. India's dismal ranking (155th out of 176) in the 2014 Environmental Performance Index is evidence of the fact that the country lacked efficient policy measures to tackle this issue. India's ranking has improved somewhat to 141 in 2016 after the government implemented strong policy measures to lower the country's carbon footprint and increase renewable energy generation to 175 GW by 2022.

The GII model is continually updated to reflect the improved availability of statistics and a better understanding of the meaning and implications of innovation. Updated indicators have dropped India's ranking in six of the indicators that have changed. Over the years the GII has used new indicators to better capture the different elements of the model, and it has gradually stabilized. For example, the 2014 GII added indicators on global entertainment and media output and used patent applications instead of patent registrations. Changes in absolute data values have included the decrease in variables such as total value of stocks traded, market capitalization, and market access for nonagricultural exports over the 2011–14 period. Low data availability also affects India's ranking in instances where some indicators for India were not available for a more recent year, revised at the source, or simply not reported. To address these challenges, the Confederation of Indian Industry (CII) along with the GII team has worked actively with the Indian Government since 2015 to improve data availability, and to look into India-specific innovation parameters to benchmark Indian States. This exercise has resulted in a grand launch of the GII 2016 in India; for the first time, the government has formed a task force to examine existing innovation gaps.

The following section illustrates some of the areas in which India's evolving policy landscape has proven effective and other areas that need further improvement.

5.3 STRENGTHS AND WEAKNESSES OF INDIA'S INNOVATION PERFORMANCE

Since 2007, the GII has published its annual ranking of countries on their innovation capacity and analyzed the innovation input and output parameters that affect the nations' relative strengths and weaknesses. In this process, the GII has identified several key factors that have improved some nations' performance compared to their peers in a specific economic and geographical category. India has been one such "innovation achiever" among its peer group. The following section illustrates areas identified by the GII as responsible for relative strength and weaknesses of India's innovation prowess vis-à-vis its peers.

5.3.1 Top Indian Universities

India has developed a stable foundation for scientific, technological, and business education by setting up centers of excellence such as the Indian Institutes of Science (IISC), the Indian Institutes of Technology (IITs), and the Indian Institutes of Management (IIMs). Admission to these premier Indian institutions has consistently been competitive, with a 50 to 1 application to admitted student ratio for IITs (Basu, 2014), and a 150 to 1 ratio of applications to admitted students for IIMs. This competition for admission is even fiercer when compared to admission rates in the top U.S. schools such as the Massachusetts Institute of Technology (MIT), where the applicant to admitted ratio stands at around 10 to 1 (PwC, 2012). This competitive landscape and the increasing number of strong students have provided India with a natural advantage, positioning its top institutions as some of the best in the world. Average scores at top universities have been in India's favor for a superior innovation ranking, not only among its peers but also among all nations.

5.3.2 Publication Citations

Tied to higher education, India's strong scholarly publications have been a significant contributing factor to its innovation capacity. The higher education sector in India has contributed to the 66% average growth rate in the output of scientific publications as assessed over a five-year period (2006–10). Among all disciplines, engineering research made the most significant progress, and Indian scientific papers nearly quadrupled their presence in the top-ranked 1% of journals worldwide. In addition, the citation rate (measuring the impact of these papers) in engineering disciplines significantly improved, and this level of impact has grown steadily since the 1993–97 period. A government study found that Indian publications' citation impact increased from 0.35 in 1981–85 to about 0.68 in 2006–10 (Department of Science and Technology, Government of India, 2012), helping India to lead the citation index among its peers.

5.3.3   Mobile Networks, Information Technology, and Broadband

India has also distinguished itself is the category of mobile networks, information technology, and broadband. When the first National Telecom Policy launched in 1994, the world average telephone density was 10.0 per hundred persons, while in India it was a mere 0.8 per hundred persons. This density was even lower than that of other developing countries such as China (1.7 per hundred persons), Pakistan (2.0), and Malaysia (13.0) (Ministry of Communications & Information Technology, Department of Telecommunications (India), 1994). By 1999, India had approached some of the targets laid down in the 1994 policy, such offering one public call office per 522 urban residents against the target of one public call office per 500,[7] and exceeded others, such as establishing 8.7 million telephone lines—even more than the planned target of 7.5 million. In addition, the policy set targets to achieve a teledensity of 7% and 15% by 2005 and 2010, respectively, and to increase rural teledensity from 0.4% to 4% by 2010. The policy also encouraged online electronic commerce with the addition of 10 gigabytes of bandwidth on national routes (Ministry of Communications & Information Technology, Department of Telecommunications (India), 1999).

In 2004, national penetration of broadband and Internet stood at around 0.02% and 0.40%, respectively, and the government announced an exclusive broadband policy (Ministry of Communications & Information Technology, Department of Telecommunications (India), 2004). With all of these policies in place, telecommunications connectivity through mobile telephones grew rapidly in the next decade. The number of telephone connections surged from 41 million in December 2001 to more than a billion by end 2012, out of which more than 900 million were added via the cellular segment (mobile phones) alone. Increasing teledensity and sharply declining tariffs in a competitive market made India the fastest-growing telecommunications market in the world and far ahead of its peers in the Central and Southern Asian regions. The telecommunications sector was responsible for almost 3% of the country's GDP. The National Telecom Policy 2012 was conceived in this context, with the aim of transforming India into an empowered and inclusive knowledge-based society (Ministry of Communications & IT, Department of Telecommunications (India), 2012).

Information technology (IT) in India was a fledgling industry during the 1970s, and few players were active in the market. Over the years the pace of growth in this sector remained faster than in other segments; it did not require much capital to set up a business and had relatively short lead times to generate revenue. Revenue in this sector has grown from $5 billion in 1997 to around $64 billion in 2007 (Gupta, 2010), and to $108 billion in 2013 (IBEF, 2014). Fig. 5.1 illustrates the yearly growth in IT revenue from 2000 to 2013.

---

7. A public call office (PCO) is a telephone facility located in a public place in India.

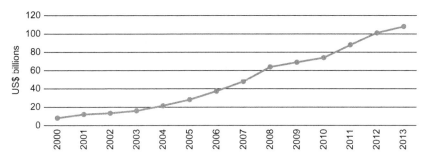

FIG. 5.1 Yearly revenue growth in IT, $ billions (2000–13). Sources: Authors' calculations, based on IBEF, 2014; NASSCOM, 2008; OECD, 2010.

Recognizing the growing potential of the IT sector, the government opened the sector up to external competition in the 1980s. In the 1990s, the government directed policies toward developing the required telecommunications infrastructure to support IT growth. As a result, during the period of 2000–13, the IT-business process management sector expanded at a compound annual growth rate (CAGR) of 25%, three to four times higher than the global average. The IT policy of 2012, looking at this trend, has put forth the ambitious target of increasing revenue to $300 billion by 2020. This policy is intended to help scale up innovation and R&D in cutting-edge technologies, provide benefits to small- and medium-sized enterprises (SMEs) and startups, create a pool of 10 million skilled workers, and make at least one individual in every household e-literate (Ministry of Communications & IT, Department of Electronics & Information Technology (DeitY), 2012). With the growth of IT, coupled with the advancement of broadband technologies, access to the Internet grew multifold from 2000 to 2013, at a CAGR of around 32.5%, as illustrated in Fig. 5.2.

This communication revolution has enabled an unprecedented pace of knowledge creation and dissemination in the helping transform innovation-driven entrepreneurship from aspiration to reality for the people of India.

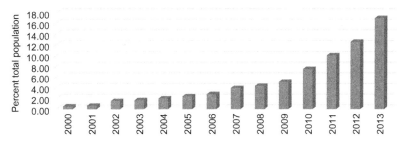

FIG. 5.2 Annual penetration: Percent of population with access to the Internet. Source: Authors' calculations, based on data available in http://www.internetlivestats.com, accessed 30 April 2015.

5.3.4   Gross Capital Formation and Market Capitalization

As one of the fastest-growing economies in the world, India has demonstrated strengths in factors such as gross capital formation, market capitalization, and total value of stocks traded. India's high GDP growth rate has complemented a strong gross capital formation consisting of outlays on fixed assets plus net changes in the level of inventories. After the country's economic liberalization in 1991, Indian industry also grew rapidly with more and more firms getting listed in the Bombay Stock Exchange (BSE) and National Stock Exchange (NSE),[8] which in turn increased the country's market capitalization over the years. As the volume of listed companies grew, so did the total value of traded stock. The BSE Sensex, also known as "BSE 30," is the most commonly used term for referring to the trading volume in India. The NSE and BSE are similar in terms of total market capitalization, but in terms of share volume, the NSE is almost twice as large as the BSE.[9] The equity market capitalization for BSE from 2011 to 12 to 2014–15 has risen from $1235.05 billion to $1626.68 billion, respectively.[10] The clear policy guidelines laid down by the Securities and Exchange Board of India for regulating the financial market have contributed greatly to this success.

Although India exhibits areas that have allowed it to outperform its peer group per the GII classification, the country also has many weaknesses. In the next part of this section we will consider three of these weak areas: SMEs, intellectual property rights, and access to higher education. In all of these areas, policies must better support innovation to advance in the GII ranking in the future.

5.3.5   Small- and Medium-Sized Enterprises

In India, the SME sector is responsible for 45% of total manufacturing output and employs around 70 million people. This sector's potential makes it critical in order to realize the policy target of achieving manufacturing output equal to 25% of GDP, an increase from its current level of 16%. Despite the SME sector's high potential, its suboptimal development can be attributed to a lack of adequate cash flow caused by low credit availability in the form of equity as well as debt.[11] This concern is magnified due to the large number of unregistered units under the

---

8. The Bombay Stock exchange is available at http://www.bseindia.com/; the National Stock Exchange is available at http://www.nse-india.com/.

9. See S&P BSE Equity Market Capitalisation, available at http://www.bseindia.com/markets/keystatics/Keystat_maktcap.aspx?expandable=0.

10. See http://www.bseindia.com/markets/keystatics/Keystat_maktcap.aspx?expandable=0, accessed 30 April 2015.

11. In India the availability and access to equity and debt for micro business is relatively low compared with that of other developed nations. The entrepreneurial sector is slowly building and gradually policies are being framed that allow creation and access to more such funds by micro businesses and startups. See 'Private sector investment for MSME' under 'Financial Resources' Working Group for the Twelfth Five Year Plan (2012–2017) of India's Planning Commission, available at http://planningcommission.gov.in/aboutus/committee/index.php?about=12strindx.htm.

purview of SMEs that struggle to obtain credit.[12] Cluster development in India has traditionally been spearheaded by the Ministry of Micro, Small, & Medium Enterprises. The ministry runs an initiative—the Micro & Small Enterprises Cluster Development Programme (MSE-CDP)—that looks at the development of industrial clusters encompassing marketing, exports, skill development, and the establishment of common facility centers as well as upgrading the technology of enterprises (Ittyerah, 2009). According to a study released by the United Nations International Development Organization (UNIDO) in 2003, around 388 SME clusters across India were affected by this initiative (UNIDO, 2003).[13]

Although this provided a good platform from which Indian SME clusters could grow, it has not been enough to bring a rapid improvement in fostering R&D-driven innovation in the sector. Recognizing this lack of competitiveness in the SME sector as a major impediment, in 2005–06, the government announced the formulation of a National Manufacturing Competitiveness Programme (NMCP) to address firm-level competitiveness. Since this development, the yearly growth of SMEs has improved marginally. Also in 2011, the National Innovation Council of the Government of India piloted a flagship initiative on innovation clusters. The overall situation of SME cluster growth in India has remained suboptimal.

5.3.6 Intellectual Property Rights

Intellectual property is a key indicator of an economy's innovation output. In India, a persistent contradiction exists between protecting intellectual rights for commercialization and profitmaking, and catering to social needs and obligations to the poor. Policy and patent laws were crafted to strike a balance between these two considerations, resulting in a relatively weaker intellectual property rights (IPR) regime than those of other developed nations. Fig. 5.3A compares patents filed to patents granted (for Indian, foreign, and total) over a 10-year period. Fig. 5.3B concerns the percentage of patents granted by the Indian patent office and indicates that this percentage has significantly declined over the years from 2008 to 2013. Fig. 5.3C compares the rate of foreign and Indian patent grants and indicates that the foreign patent grant percentage was significantly higher than the patent grant percentage in India for over a decade

---

12. For the purpose of collecting data relating to manufacturing activities through a sample survey, all manufacturing units in the country are classified into two broad sectors: registered and unregistered sectors or organized and unorganized sectors (the terms are often used interchangeably). Although the registered manufacturing sector covers the manufacturing units registered under sections 2 m (i) and 2 m (ii) of the Factories Act of 1948 or under the Bidi & Cigar Workers (Condition of Employment) Act of 1966—that is, the units employing 10 or more workers and using power or 20 or more workers but not using powerVthe unregistered manufacturing sector covers all others as well as residual manufacturing units. See Section 5, 'Industrial Statistics', from the Ministry of Statistics, available at http://mospi.nic.in/nscr/is.htm.
13. Data are taken from http://www.dcmsme.gov.in/clusters/clus/smelist.htm#clus.

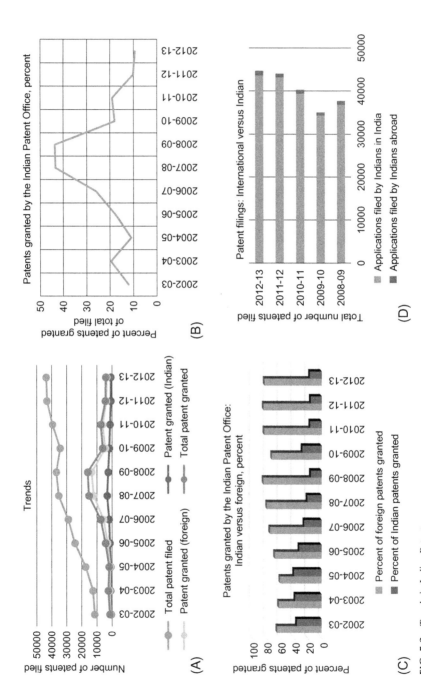

FIG. 5.3 Trends in Indian Patents

from 2002 to 2013. Fig. 5.3D contrasts international and domestic patent filings by Indians and shows that the share of international patents filed by Indians is miniscule compared with patents filed in India. This is a worrying situation for an economy like India's, which is striving to grow multifold in the near future and aspiring to become a knowledge-driven economy.

5.3.7 Access to Higher Education

Although India's top educational institutions have done relatively well over the years, India is still grappling with pressing higher education issues. With a population of more than 1.2 billion, and with 50% of that population under the age of 25, India has a huge demand for higher education. This has resulted in an enormous supply-demand gap, with an enrollment rate of only 18% in higher education institutions, leaving a large section of the population deprived of educational opportunities after high school. The government intends to increase the enrollment rate to 30% by 2020. Other issues that currently confront the higher education sector are poor teacher quality, constraints in research capacity and innovation (owing to low enrollment in PhD programs, few opportunities for interdisciplinary cooperation, a weak innovation ecosystem in academia, and low industry-university collaboration), and a large socioeconomic disparity.

5.4 CONCLUSIONS AND THE WAY FORWARD

The preceding sections have outlined how India's policy regime has influenced its economic growth. This section reiterates some of the stronger as well as weaker areas in the economy where India and other nations can learn and benefit from each other. The section also identifies key areas that need immediate and sustained policy interventions and notes some of the recent initiatives undertaken by the government and other stakeholders to improve the country's innovation capacity.

The main areas where India sets an example for the rest of the world are in the growth of its Information Communication Technology (ICT) regime (mostly mobile penetration) and in its IT and IT-enabled services (ITeS) sector. Previous sections have discussed how, with the implementation of progressive policy measures, these two sectors have become trendsetters in a span of just two decades. For countries with similar economic and demographic conditions, India's story merits consideration. Many of the lessons India has learned can be adopted to emulate a similar growth experience in a short span of time.

Although ICTs and IT together constitute a vital differentiating component that increases the pace of innovation and knowledge development in the economy, their benefit can truly be realized when areas such as higher education, IPR, the regulatory and business environment (which affect the ease of doing business), physical infrastructure (such as railways, roadways, freight transport, and son on), and institutional reforms get appropriate attention and sufficient support from the government. In these key areas India can learn from developed economies about how policy can support improvement and provide a long-term benefit. Creating entrepreneurship policy at the national and state levels to make effective use of existing resources is nearly as crucial.

In light of the above observations, we suggest the following primary areas in which government needs to carefully and deliberately formulate robust policy measures to achieve economic growth driven by innovation:

- *Access to higher education*: As noted earlier, India lacks an adequate number of higher education institutions to cater to its growing number of aspiring students. The level of university-industry collaboration in India is also miniscule compared with that of other developed nations, and there is a dearth of high-quality teachers in the education system. Government needs to consider all these aspects while devising a suitable policy for the higher education sector.
- *Industrial innovation*: SMEs are the engines of future growth in any economy; an economy is only as innovative as its SMEs. In order to infuse a culture of innovation and R&D into Indian SMEs, the government must set proper fiscal and tax guidelines so that more SMEs see the benefit in R&D and adopt this as their future business strategy.
- *Entrepreneurship*: As the world economy becomes more volatile and India faces the adverse effects of this economic instability, it is essential for the government to increasingly stimulate job creation. Building a strong entrepreneurial ecosystem and incentivizing innovation-driven startups can achieve this goal. Entrepreneurship policy is currently lacking at the national and provincial levels and needs to be formulated to stimulate this process.
- *Easing the business environment*: India ranks poorly in terms of its ease of doing business parameters. This will remain a major obstacle that India must address to expand its GDP growth from its current level of 5%–7% to 10% and above. Providing simple regulatory guidelines, moving all processes online, and reducing paperwork and bureaucratic interference are of high importance. This can be achieved only through policy-level amendments.
- *Infrastructure development*: Although IT infrastructure in the country has improved by leaps and bounds over the years, the outlook on physical infrastructure remains grim. Unless India steps up by building good roads and efficient railways (passenger and freight corridors) and modernizes its ports, it will be hard to develop industrial corridors and attract foreign investment. Clear policy guidelines and investment in these sectors will boost the economy and trigger new innovative solutions for existing bottlenecks.
- *Intellectual property rights*: The existing IPR regime in India is weak at protecting new technologies and innovations when compared with that of developed economies. The merit of strong, enforced IPR in certain sectors, such as pharmaceuticals and biotechology, may be debatable when weighing businesses' needs to protect intellectual property and to make a profit while

the needs of the country's large poor population. But India cannot afford to allow a weak IPR regime to remain a long-term barrier for its new entrepreneurs if it intends to fulfill its aspirations of becoming an innovation-driven economy. The government must find ways to study and address this important driver of innovation while restructuring its existing laws and their enforcement.

In 2014 the newly elected Indian government, as one of its first moves, established an aligned Ministry for Skill Development and Entrepreneurship. This is a step forward. With the intervention of the government and the private sector, the level of innovation in Indian industry is growing, and more and more Indian SMEs are investing in collaborative R&D. For example, public-private partnership platforms such as the Global Innovation and Technology Alliance, a not-for-profit organization, are creating opportunities for Indian companies to develop products and technology through joint R&D programs with their foreign counterparts.

To enhance PhD education in the country, in 2013 the prime minister's office launched the Prime Minister's Fellowship Scheme for Doctoral Research. According to this scheme, the government provides 50% of the total cost of a fellowship to students for performing research in a real-time industry environment. Industry provides the rest, and the student and the industry jointly own any IPR (CII, 2014, 2015).

In India's Union (central) budget presented in February 2015 (Jaitley, 2015), the government placed considerable emphasis on rapid development in the SME sector by addressing the funding issue. It has created a fund of 20,000 crore with a credit guarantee of 3000 crore for entrepreneurs in this sector.[14] In addition, it set aside 1000 crore for a Techno-Financial, Incubation, and Facilitation Programme to support all aspects of startup businesses, and other self-employment activities, particularly in technology-driven areas (Ministry of Finance (India), Press Information Bureau, 2015). The Ministry of Micro, Small, & Medium Enterprises launched Intellectual Property Facilitation Centers in different parts of the country to create an intellectual property culture within SMEs by evaluating protection, capacity building, information services, and counseling and advisory services regarding IPR.

In 2017, India is on the verge of implementing its biggest economic policy reform since1991, the rollout of the Goods and Services Tax (GST). This huge shift in policy is expected to pay a dividend to the Indian economy in the long run, which is intended to positively influence innovation-related activities driven by industry and startups.

The government also hopes to boost the development of sectors such as infrastructure, transportation, smart cities, manufacturing, and IT to supplement growth. Initiatives such as Make in India, Digital India, Skill India, and Clean

---

14. For details about MUDRA, see http://www.mudra.org.in/faq.php.

India are steps in this direction. Furthermore, reforms in India's credit delivery mechanism to its poor have been supported by credit transfer schemes such as Pradhan Mantri Jan-Dhan Yojana, which aims to increase disposable income for India's poor. The government is boosting the innovation capacity within schools by creating "tinkering labs" across the country, which will help to inculcate a culture of innovation among students from an early age.

Given the unique challenges that India faces, achieving even 40%–50% of their targets by some of these initiatives will amount to an economic revolution. The momentum is building positively and the time is favorable for India to change gears and get its innovation journey onto the fast track.

REFERENCES

Basu, S.D., 2014. Race to IITs just got tougher; number of candidates who qualified in JEE advanced 6,360 more than last year. The Economic Times, 20 June. Available at http://articles. economictimes.indiatimes.com/2014-06-20/news/50739176_1_1-26-lakh-students-joint-entrance-exam-iit-seat.

CII (Confederation of Indian Industry), 2014-2015. Prime Minister's Fellowship Scheme for Doctoral Research. Available at http://primeministerfellowshipscheme.in/Home.aspx.

Department of Science and Technology, Government of India, 2012. Bibliometric Study of India's Scientific Publication Outputs During 2001–10: Evidence for Changing Trends. Government of India, New Delhi. Available at http://dst.gov.in/whats_new/whats_new12/report.pdf.

EPI (Environmental Performance Index), 2014. India ranks 155th on the 2014 environmental performance index. Press Release. Available at http://epi.yale.edu/files/2014_epi_press_release_-_india_.pdf.

Gupta, D., 2010. Information technology industry in India growth structure and performance. Human Resource Development Practices in Information Technology Industry in India. PhD thesis, Punjab School of Economics, pp. 138–156.

Hsu, A., et al., 2016. 2016 Environmental Performance Index. Yale University, New Haven, CT. Available www.epi.yale.eduhttp://www.indiaenvironmentportal.org.in/files/file/Yale%20EPI%202016_Report.pdf.

IBEF (India Brand Equity Foundation), 2014. Indian IT and ITeS Industry Analysis. 31 August. Available at http://www.ibef.org/pages/36252.

Ittyerah, A.C., 2009. Evaluation Study of Micro & Small Enterprises Cluster Development Programme. IIPA (Indian institute of Public Administration, New Delhi. Available at http://www.dcmsme.gov.in/schemes/evaluation_study(MSME)_cluster.pdf.

Jaitley, A., 2015. Budget 2015–2016, speech of Arun Jaitley, Minister of Finance. Available at http://indiabudget.nic.in/bspeecha.asp.

Kahn, J., Kattak, N.U.R., 2014. The significance of research and development for economic growth: the case of Pakistan. MPRA Paper [No. 56006], posted 21 May. Available at http://mpra.ub.uni-muenchen.de/56005/1/MPRA_paper_56005.pdf.

Ministry of Communications & IT, Department of Electronics & Information Technology (DeitY), 2012. National Information Technology Policy 2012. Available at http://deity.gov.in/content/national-information-technology-policy-2012.

Ministry of Communications & IT, Department of Telecommunications (India), 1994. National Telecom Policy, 1994. Available at http://www.dot.gov.in/telecom-polices/national-telecom-policy-1994.

Ministry of Communications & IT, Department of Telecommunications (India), 1999. National Telecom Policy, 1999. Available at http://www.dot.gov.in/telecom-polices/new-telecom-policy-1999.

Ministry of Communications & IT, Department of Telecommunications (India), 2004. Broadband Policy, 2004. Available at http://www.dot.gov.in/telecom-polices/broadband-policy-2004.

Ministry of Communications & IT, Department of Telecommunications (India), 2012. National Telecom Policy, 2012. Available at http://www.dot.gov.in/sites/default/files/NTP-06.06.2012-final.pdf.

Ministry of Commerce & Industry, Department of Industrial Policy and Promotion (India), 2013. Intellectual Property India: Annual Report 2012–2013. Office of the Controller General of Patents, Designs, Trade Marks and Geographical Indication. Available at http://ipindia.gov.in/cgpdtm/AnnualReport_English_2012_2013.pdf.

Ministry of Finance (India), Press Information Bureau, 2015. Self-employment and talent utilisation (SETU) to be established. Press Release, 28 February. Available at http://pib.nic.in/newsite/PrintRelease.aspx?relid=116187.

Mohan, R., 2008. The growth record of the Indian economy, 1950–2008: a story of sustained savings and investment. RBI Bull. March, 373–397.

NASSCOM, 2008. Indian IT-BPO Industry: NASSCOM Analysis Factsheet. Available at http://www.almamate.in/pdf/IT_Industry_Factsheet_2008.pdf.

National Innovation Council (India), 2013. Report to the People: Third Year. National Innovation Council, New Delhi. Available at http://innovationcouncilarchive.nic.in/images/stories/report/rtp2013/Report%20to%20the%20People%202013%20-%20National%20Innovation%20Council%20(English).pdf.

National Institute for Transforming India, 2015. Report of the Expert Group on 175 GW RE by 2022. http://niti.gov.in/writereaddata/files/writereaddata/files/document_publication/report-175-GW-RE.pdf. Accessed June 2017.

OECD (Organisation for Economic Co-operation and Development), 2010. The Information and Communication Technology Sector in India: Performance, Growth and Key Challenges. Unclassified Document JT03286352. Available at http://www.oecd.org/sti/ieconomy/45576760.pdf.

PwC (PricewaterhouseCoopers), 2012. India—Higher Education Sector: Opportunities for Private Participation. Available at https://www.pwc.in/en_IN/in/assets/pdfs/industries/education-services.pdf.

The Press Information Bureau, Government of India, http://eaindustry.nic.in/handbk/chap001.pdf.

UNIDO (United Nations Industrial Development Organization), 2003. Methodology and the Action Plan for Updation on SME Industrial Clusters. Compiled by UNIDO Focal Point, CDP UNIDO, 14 November. Available at http://www.dcmsme.gov.in/clusters/unido/methcludata.htm#basic.

Weerasinhghe, M.C., 2013. R&D Country Profile: Sri Lanka. Presentation for the Consultative Expert Working Group on Research and Development: Financing and Coordination, Bangkok, Thailand, 25–26 July 2013. Available at http://www.searo.who.int/entity/intellectual_property/about/strategy/23bDrManujandDrAnton.pdf?ua=1.

Chapter 6

Flipkart and the Race to the Top of Indian e-Commerce

ACRONYMS

B2B	Business to Business
COO	Chief Operating Officer
C.O.D	cash on delivery
FDI	Foreign Direct Investment
GDP	Gross Domestic Product
GII	Global Innovation Index
GMV	Gross Merchandise Value
ICT	Information Communication Technology
NPS	Net Promoter Score
PPP	Purchasing Power Parity
R&D	Research and Development
RBI	Reserve Bank of India

In India, October and November mark the holiday season, when Hindus celebrate Dussehra, Diwali, and other festivals. In recent years, Indians have added another "celebration" to the festival season: e-commerce companies like Flipkart Online Services Pvt., Amazon India, and Snapdeal hold mega annual sales that mirror "Black Friday" in the United States or the "Single's Day" in China. In 2016, Flipkart had its annual "Big Billion Days" sale between October 2 and 6, while Amazon held its "Great Indian Festival" sale between October 1 and 5, and Snapdeal had its "Unbox Diwali" sale from October 2 to 6. During the sales period, the two home-grown e-commerce companies Flipkart and Snapdeal sold goods worth $345 million (a 10%–15% increase over a similar period in 2015) and $120 million (7% increase over a similar period in 2015), respectively, while Amazon India sold goods worth $250 million (a 41% increase over a similar period in 2015). Together these three companies achieved record-breaking sales of $2.2 billion during the entire month of October 2016 (TechinAsia, 2016). Sales during the festival season are indicative of the overall dynamics at play in the Indian e-commerce race. Flipkart maintains its top position as Amazon India makes its big push to threaten Flipkart's leadership, and Snapdeal appears to lose momentum.

Financing Entrepreneurship and Innovation in Emerging Markets.
https://doi.org/10.1016/B978-0-12-804025-6.00006-X

In this chapter, we focus on emerging multinational Flipkart's journey to market leadership, discuss the threat from Amazon India and Snapdeal, and chart the way forward in the battle for dominance for the Indian e-commerce market.

6.1 FLIPKART TODAY

Flipkart today operates through nine different companies—four in Singapore and five in India. Flipkart Pvt. Ltd. (FPL) Singapore is the ultimate holding company and registered in Singapore in October 2011. There are three other entities registered in Singapore as 100% subsidiaries of FPL: Flipkart Marketplace Pvt. Ltd., Flipkart Logistics Pvt. Ltd., and Flipkart Payments Pvt. Ltd. These companies, in turn, hold stakes in five Indian entities, two of which are: Flipkart India Pvt. Ltd., the wholesale cash-and-carry entity and Flipkart Internet Pvt. Ltd., which owns Flipkart.com and provides technology platforms to e-commerce companies. Flipkart's complicated structure may in part be attributed to Indian regulations that prohibit Foreign Direct Investment (FDI) in an inventory-based e-commerce company that directly sells to customers. For the purpose of this study, thus, we use aggregated revenue of all Flipkart companies from various sources since the complicated holding structure makes accurately estimating the revenue of individual entities a challenge.

Flipkart has shown impressive top-line growth—increasing revenue by 153% in 2014 and 249% in 2015 (see Fig. 6.1). This is a testament to the company's success in expanding its customer base and leveraging opportunities in the Indian e-commerce market. But the company is still struggling to become profitable, as its operating losses increased 83% and 182% in 2014 and 2015, respectively. While the operating margin (loss) improved from 43% in 2013 to 31% in 2014 and 25% in 2015, the progress is quite slow and at this rate, it will take the company a few years before it can show consistent profits. While investors have thus far been patient and willing to put in extensive sums of money in the promise of future returns, they are beginning to put pressure on companies

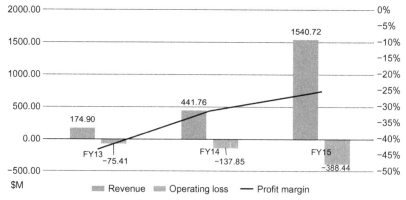

FIG. 6.1 Flipkart's financials. *(Source: Authors based on company website.)*

such as Flipkart, who will need to reduce cost and increase profits to provide successful exits to current investors and remain attractive to future ones.

6.2 EARLY YEARS AND FUNDING

Flipkart was founded in 2007 by two engineers Sachin Bansal and Binny Bansal (unrelated) both of whom grew up in the Indian city of Chandigarh, graduated from the Indian Institute of Technology Delhi, and worked for Amazon in Bangalore before Flipkart. Inspired by Amazon's online retailing model, the Bansals started Flipkart to recreate Amazon's model in the Indian context. The two founders matched seed funding of approximately $6000 with their own funds to set up the website and purchases two computers and began running the business from their Bangalore-based apartment. Over the next three years, Flipkart focused on books and then gradually added other retail categories.

Flipkart's consistent ability to receive funding is a key reason for its steady growth since inception. This has enabled the company to invest in operations and rapidly scale up. In 2009, Flipkart began a landmark year of growth, raising two rounds of angel funding of $40,000 in January and $100,000 in February By October 2009, Flipkart received its first round of venture funding—U.S.-based Accel Partners, now Accel as of publication, agreed to invest $1 million. This funding validated the business model and gave the founders the confidence to aggressively pursue their growth ambitions. Flipkart soon raised $10 million in Series B funding from U.S.-based Tiger Global Management LLC, which propelled the company to both expand its portfolio of offerings and experiment with the business model.

By 2015, Flipkart had raised $3.15 billion over 12 rounds of funding as shown in Fig. 6.2. Accel, Tiger Global Management, and Naspers Ltd., South Africa have seats on Flipkart's board. A detailed list of these investors along with the round in which they invested is shown in Table A6.1.

To date, all Flipkart's investors other than the founders are from outside India. Indian laws prohibit foreign-owned multibrand companies from directly selling to customers, creating a challenge for Flipkart to ensure it does not violate any laws. In fact, in 2014 the Indian government questioned Flipkart about its relationship with WS Retail Svcs. Pvt. Ltd. to prove that it had not violated the law during its Billion-dollar day sale (News18, 2014). To shield itself, Flipkart took advantage of loopholes in the law and planned a shift toward a marketplace.

6.3 BECOMING A UNICORN

Flipkart became a unicorn[1] in 2013, six years after its founding. We can break down its journey during this time into six internal strategic initiatives, each of which had a distinct trigger, as shown in Fig. 6.3.

---

1. A unicorn is a company that has a valuation of over $1 billion.

Date	Amount / round	Total investors	Lead investor	Other investors	Implied pre-money valuation ($B)
July 2015	$700M / Private Equity	2	None	Steadview Capital (Hong Kong) and Tiger Global Management (USA)	15
December 2014	$700M / Series H	10	Steadview Capital (Hongkong)	Baillie Gifford (UK), DST Global (Russia), GIC (Singapore), Greenoaks Capital (USA), Iconiq Capital (USA), Naspers (South Africa), Qatar Investment Authority (Qatar), T. Rowe Price (USA)	11
July 2014	$1B / Series G	8	Naspers (South Africa)	Accel Partners (USA), DST Global (Russia), GIC (Singapore), Iconiq Capital (USA), Morgan Stanley Investments (USA) and Sofina (Belgium)	6
May-14	$210M / Series F	4	Tiger Global Management (USA)	Iconiq Capital (USA), Naspers (South Africa) and Tiger Global Management (USA)	N/A
October 2013	$160M / Series E	5	DST Global (Russia)	Dragoneer Investment Group (USA), Morgan Stanley Investments (USA), Sofina (Belgium), Tiger Global Management (USA) and Vulcan Capital (USA)	N/A
July 2013	$200M / Series E	4	None	Accel Partners (USA), Iconiq Capital (USA), Naspers (South Africa) and Tiger Global Management (USA)	1.3
August 2012	$150M / Series D	4	Naspers (South Africa)	Accel Partners (USA), Iconiq Capital (USA) and Tiger Global Management (USA)	N/A
June 2011	$20M / Series C	1	Tiger Global Management	None	N/A
June 2010	$10M / Series B	1	Tiger Global Management	None	N/A
October 2009	$1M / Series A	1	Accel Partners	None	N/A
February 2009	$100k / Angel	1	Name unavailable	N/A	N/A
January 2009	$40k / Angel	1	Name unavailable	N/A	N/A

FIG. 6.2 Flipkart investors. (*Source: Crunchbase, https://www.crunchbase.com/organization/flipkart#/entity, accessed June 9, 2017.*)

Timeline	Trigger/reason	Strategic initiative/milestone	Impact
2007-08	Amazon as role model	Customer Focus; 24*7 customer helpline	Customer Loyalty
2010	Low credit card penetration	Introduction of Cash of Delivery (COD)	Expansion of customer base due to availability of alternate payment methods
2010	Desire to monetize growing customer base	Introduction of mobile phones, music and movies	Revenue growth as mobile phones is one of the largest categories by volume
2010	Challenges in third-party supply chain	Launch of own supply chain (Hub and spoke model) and delivery network	Reliability in delivery; Reinforcing customer trust
2011	Snapdeal's entry	Investments on Branding; First advertising campaign (October 2011); First TV Ad (summer 2012)	Exponential Customer growth: • Website traffic doubled to 250k • Market share ~80%
2012	Desire to monetize growing customer base	Entry into Fashion and Lifestyle	Improvement in profit margins as Fashion has one of the highest margins

FIG. 6.3   Key milestones toward becoming a unicorn. *(Source: Authors' analysis based on various public sources.)*

6.3.1   Customer Focus

Flipkart's founders not only followed Amazon's business model but also incorporated its customer-centric philosophy. In a developing country like India, in which few organizations match the service orientation and customer experiences of the developed world, Flipkart differentiated itself using a customer-focused approach. Just a year after its launch, Flipkart introduced 24/7 customer service, which strengthened Flipkart's brand name and created a strong barrier to entry for future challengers. This move enabled Flipkart to solidify customer loyalty, a critical development in an industry such as e-commerce where the cost of customer acquisition is high and where companies only recoup the cost of acquiring a customer after the customer completes three to four transactions.

6.3.2   Introduction of Mobile Phones and Cash on Delivery

Flipkart quickly understood that credit card penetration in India was very low (<1%) as of 2010. Moreover, online shopping was a new concept in the country, and customers were hesitant to trust this mode of purchase. Flipkart addressed both of these challenges by offering customers the option of cash on delivery (c.o.d.), i.e., allowing customers to pay in cash upon receipt of the product. Introduced in 2010, c.o.d. provided an alternative option for the majority of Indians who did not have a debit card, credit card, or online banking account. This move shifted the risk of service failure and/or product damage during delivery onto Flipkart, since the customer paid only if he/she was satisfied with the delivery. C.o.d. is one of the key reasons for Flipkart's dramatic early growth. As of 2017, c.o.d. is still India's most widely used payment method and is now offered by almost all e-commerce players including Amazon India.

6.3.3   Introduction of Mobile Phones, Music, and Movies

In 2010, Flipkart also diversified its offerings by introducing mobile phones, music, and movies. This was an important move, since mobile phones are one of the most popular product categories not only for Flipkart but also for almost all multicategory e-commerce companies in India.

6.3.4   Investment in Own Supply Chain

That same year, supply chain issues led to delayed, damaged, or misplaced orders that significantly harmed Flipkart's customer service. India's poor infrastructure and suppliers' lack of shipping capabilities frequently caused these issues. Moreover, sharing revenue with courier companies for logistics lowered Flipkart's profit margins, leading to significant losses. Getting cash back from partners in a reliable and secure manner presented significant challenges, given Flipkart's high percentage of c.o.d. orders. Following successful funding rounds in 2009 and 2010, Flipkart had the resources to create its own supply chain. The company set up a hub-and-spoke model with five main fulfillment centers across the country: in Delhi (North), Mumbai (West), Kolkata (East), Bangalore and Hyderabad (South). The fulfillment centers received products, completed initial sorting and packing, and sent products to different regions. Each region catered to four to five major cities and several small towns/suburban areas all within a radius of 200 kilometers. Hubs located at the center of each region carried out further sorting. These hubs were connected to >450 spokes (small storage spaces) that were the last stop in the supply chain, where goods were stored before delivery agents brought them to customers.

6.3.5   Branding

By mid-2011, Flipkart was growing at an accelerated pace. It had already created a successful business model on the back of its first-mover advantage[2] in the Indian market and three distinctive attributes: c.o.d. sales, a 30-day "No Questions Asked" return policy (something new for customers in India), and a reputation for good customer service, supported by the reliability of its own supply chain network. In June 2011, Flipkart raised its next round of funding—$10 million from an existing investor, Tiger Global Management. By September 2011, Snapdeal (a daily deal aggregator launched in 2010) changed its business model to become an online marketplace and a competitor to Flipkart.

The conditions were set for the company to make its first big push toward strengthening its brand and reaching out to the masses. The company launched

2. While there were other e-commerce players in India before Flipkart, they failed to achieve the scale, visibility, or acceptance of Flipkart.

its first advertising campaign in October 2011. This was the first such campaign by an e-commerce company in India and was strategically timed to coincide with the beginning of the festival season. Flipkart followed this success with a television advertisement that aired during Indian Premier League, a popular sports tournament in India, resulting in a huge surge in Flipkart's user base that soon reached the two million mark. The company had gained an 80% share in the market and was shipping close to 30,000 products daily (Business Standard, 2011).

6.3.6   Expansion into Fashion and Lifestyle Products

Once Flipkart had established its brand and drawn a growing user base to the website, Flipkart decided to further expand its portfolio into fashion and lifestyle products in 2012. Fashion continues to be one of the most profitable categories for e-commerce companies, with profit margins as high as 40%–45%. Over the next few years this category would become a stronghold for Flipkart, with the acquisition of online fashion players such as Myntra (in 2014) and Jabong (in 2016) helping it to gain as much as a 70% share of the market (VCCircle, 2016).

6.4   EXTERNAL MOTIVATORS: A SUPPORTING ENVIRONMENT IN INDIA

In July 2013, Flipkart raised $200 million in Series E funding from Accel, U.S.-based Iconiq Capital, Naspers, and Tiger Global Management. This funding was based on an estimated premoney valuation of $1.3 billion. In this section, we focus on five factors external to Flipkart that helped make it the first major e-commerce company in India to achieve the much-coveted unicorn status.

6.4.1   Availability of FDI

As discussed in the previous section, all Flipkart's investors were from outside India. The company benefitted from growing interest among overseas investors in the Indian economy: FDI inflows to India increased from $3.59 billion in 2000 to $27.4 billion in 2010 (an increase of 23% per annum on average) and then to $44.2 billion in 2015 (an increase of 10% per annum on average).[3]

6.4.2   Increasing Youth and Working-age Population

The youth and working-age share of the population in India has grown rapidly over the past decade. These demographic groups are also the primary customer segments served by e-commerce companies such as Flipkart. As of July 2015,

---

3. Source: Authors' analysis based on data from UNCTAD, World Investment Report (WIR) 2016. Annex Table 1, op. cit.

	Total	Work	% Working age
2004	1,126,419,321	699,432,404	62%
2014	1,295,291,543	845,811,113	65%
2020	1,388,859,000	925,489,000	67%
2030	1,461,625,000	984,742,000	67%
2040	1,527,658,000	1,033,293,000	68%
2050	1,585,350,000	1,076,151,000	68%

FIG. 6.4 The working-age population in India. *(Source: Authors' calculation based on data from the World Bank (Health Nutrition and Population Statistics: Population Estimates and Projections).)*

the share of youth under 14 years of age constituted 29% of the population while those between 15 and 24 years of age constituted 18% of the population.[4] This combined customer segment was and continues to be more amenable to purchasing products online, enabling Flipkart to establish a solid customer base. The overall percentage of the population that is of working age[5] has continued to increase from 62% in 2004 to 65% in 2014 and is expected to remain at 67%–68% until 2050 even as the total population continues to increase[6] (see Fig. 6.4).

6.4.3 Growing Economy

The Indian economy is growing rapidly, as evidenced by the growth in gross domestic product (GDP) both nominally and in terms of purchasing power parity (PPP). The nominal GDP grew from $367 billion in 1995 to $2.07 trillion in 2015, an increase of 9% per year. This growth made India the 9th-largest economy in the world in 2015 (in nominal GDP), a considerable increase from the 15th-largest a decade prior. GDP per capita in India has also grown from $382 per annum in 1995 to $1,582 per annum in 2015. (For more details on India's GDP growth and rank in the world, see Fig. 6.5.) This income expansion enabled the average person in India to increase his/her spending, a portion of which has been captured by e-commerce companies such as Flipkart. The good news for Indian e-commerce companies is that both the GDP and GDP per capita are expected to continue increasing over the next decade, sustaining the growth momentum seen over the past few years.

6.4.4 Global Shift to e-Commerce

Worldwide, consumers have consistently shifted toward online purchasing in the past decade. Global e-commerce sales increased from $695 billion in 2014 to $840 billion in 2015, an increase of 21% in a single year. This trend is likely

---

4. Source: Based on data from UNDESA (Population Division), World Population Prospects 2015 (https://esa.un.org/unpd/wpp/—accessed March 2016).
5. Working age is defined by World Bank as 15 to 64 years.
6. Source: Authors' calculation based on data from the World Bank (Health Nutrition and Population Statistics: Population Estimates and Projections).

India's nominal GDP (in $ billion)	1995	2000	2005	2010	2015
Nominal GDP	367	477	834	1708	2074
Rank in world	15				7

India's GDP in PPP ($ billion)	1995	2000	2005	2010	2015
GDP in PPP	1442	2105	3274	5312	7983
Rank in world	5				3

India's GDP per capita (in $)	1995	2000	2005	2010	2015
GDP/capita	382	452	729	1388	1582

FIG. 6.5 India's GDP growth and rank in world. *(Source: Based on data from World Bank (World Development Indicators) http://databank.worldbank.org/data/home.aspx (accessed July 1st, 2016) and Emerging Markets Institute analysis.)*

to continue, with global e-commerce sales expected to equal approximately $1.5 trillion by 2018, though growth may moderate (Kearney, 2015). This continued momentum in e-commerce has made venture capital and private investors increasingly comfortable investing in this space not only in mature markets such as the United States, the United Kingdom, and China but also in rapidly growing emerging markets such as India.

6.4.5   Indians Embracing e-Commerce

Even though India now wholeheartedly embraces e-commerce, it initially lagged some of its western and emerging markets counterparts. Interestingly, the country seems to have skipped the emergence of big box retailers in the mold of Walmart and Target in the United States. This suggests that Indian consumers had neither experienced the massive discounts that economies of scale can bring, nor witnessed the convenience of one-stop shopping as offered by big box retailers. As a result, when e-commerce companies promised customers the ability to shop in the comfort of their homes in addition to massively discounted pricing, Indian consumers were quick to welcome them. India's e-commerce sales increased from a mere $2.9 billion in 2013 to $16 billion in 2015, thus growing at an annual rate of 135% over that period. Flipkart contributed to this growth by offering a rich portfolio of products online and rapidly scaling up to establish a network across the country, and benefitted from it, by obtaining funds from venture capitalists and private equity investors at increasing valuations. The e-commerce industry in India is expected to grow 6.5 times over the next few years and cross $100 billion in revenue by 2020 (Confederation of Indian Industry and Deloitte, 2016). The promise of exponential growth in the Indian e-commerce industry continues to attract global e-commerce leaders to set up shop in the country.

6.4.6   Innovation Ecosystem

India is currently ranked a modest 66th on the Global Innovation Index (GII), but it has managed to overtake Brazil and claim the second spot, behind China, among middle-income countries. India's upward trajectory is the result of its performance in university rankings, where it is 2nd among middle-income economies and 20th overall, and of its patent families, where—due to method-ological changes—it now ranks 3rd among middle-income economies and 37th overall. India is a good example of how policy is improving the innovation en-vironment, particularly in Information and Communication Technology (ICT) services exports. The country has also shown robust growth in research and development (R&D) spending since the 2008 recession. Together, these initia-tives support an innovation ecosystem that companies such as Flipkart leverage as they expand operations across the country and look for innovative solutions to complex logistical and technological problems.[7]

6.5   AMAZON'S ENTRY

Amazon announced its plan to launch a marketplace in India in June 2013, which required a change in its business model. Unlike in the United States, where Amazon both sells products directly to customers (inventory model) and offers its platforms to third-party merchants (marketplace model), the FDI laws in India do not allow foreign companies to sell directly to customers. Thus, Amazon could not sell products to consumers directly and could only create a platform that small merchants in India could use to sell their products to online shoppers. Prior to 2013, Amazon had lobbied the Indian government to change its FDI rules as it waited on the sidelines to join the online retail market in India. Amazon's decision to conform to the marketplace-only model was an indication that Amazon was unwilling to wait any longer. Amazon's entry changed the competitive landscape in Indian e-commerce overnight. In October 2014, Jeff Bezos, Amazon's founder, announced that Amazon would invest $2 billion in its Indian subsidiary.

6.6   REGULATION AFFECTING INDIAN E-COMMERCE

In a move clearly signaling the Indian government's intent to crack down on violations, the Ministry of Commerce and Industry issued a clarifying guide-line: FDI investment in inventory-based e-commerce was illegal, though foreign investments in Business-to-Business (B2B) commerce were permitted.

Flipkart, in fact, had been using a loophole in the regulation to sell products to consumers using a different entity, called WS Retail. This company bought goods from Flipkart India Pvt. Ltd. and sold them to customers on Flipkart's site.

---

7. Source: Global Innovation Index (GII) 2016 report. Available at: https://www.globalinnovation-index.org/gii-2016-report.

Moreover, WS Retail also owned and operated e-kart that managed Flipkart's supply chain. Flipkart's cofounders Sachin Bansal and Binny Bansal also owned WS Retail and held board positions till 2012. When Indian regulatory agencies announced an investigation into Flipkart's relationship with WS Retail, the Bansals were forced to sell their stake in WS Retail to Rajeev Kuchhal, former Chief Operating Officer of OnMobile Global Ltd. in early 2013.[8]

6.7 COMPETITIVE LANDSCAPE IN INDIAN E-COMMERCE

The competitive landscape in the Indian e-commerce industry is characterized by the presence of two homegrown companies—Flipkart and Snapdeal—and a global competitor, Amazon India. To date, Flipkart has maintained its lead in terms of Gross Merchandise Value (GMV),[9] which was $4 billion in May 2016. However, Flipkart's GMV has been stagnant for some time: it reached a 12-month GMV of $3.8 billion in May 2015, but sales only amounted to a GMV of $3.7 billion by December 2015. On the other hand, Amazon India saw its GMV increase from $1 billion in May 2015 to $2.2 billion in December 2015, and then to $2.7 billion in May 2016. Snapdeal's GMV, on the other hand, fell rapidly from $2.2 billion in May 2015 to $1.8 billion in December 2015, then to $1.2 billion in May 2016 (Gadgets Now, 2016). Fig. 6.6 shows the relative growth of the three major e-commerce players in India from 2015 to 2016.

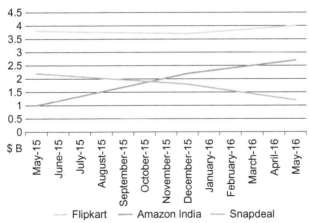

FIG. 6.6 Growth in GMV on 2015–16 for top three e-commerce companies in India. *(Source: Author's analysis based on various sources.)*

---

8. Amazon is doing something similar through Amazon Seller Services and its joint venture Cloudtail India Pvt. Ltd. (discussed in the next section). The specifics of how this is done, the different companies, holding structures and dealings are beyond the scope of this article.
9. Gross Merchandise Value (GMV) is the sum total of the value of all products sold on an e-commerce website.

	Flipkart	Amazon	Snapdeal
Revenue ($ million)—FY 2015	1541	154	141
Loss ($ million)—FY 2015	301	259	198
Market cap/implied valuation ($ billion)—March 2016	9.3	368.2*	6.5
Monthly unique visitors (millions)—May 2015	23.5	23.6	17.9
Users (millions)—September 2016	100	80	NA
Products (in million)—April 2016	40	55	35
Sellers—April 2016	90,000	85,000	300,000
Warehouses	17	21	None
GMV (in $ billion)—May 2016	4	2.7	1.2
Market share by value (GMV)—March 2015	45%	26%	12%
Market share by volume (shipments)—February 2015	37%	Unavailable	15%
Business model	Hybrid	Hybrid	Marketplace

* Valuation for Amazon Global

FIG. 6.7   The top three e-commerce companies in India (2015–16). *(Source: Author's analysis based on multiple sources.)*

Fig. 6.7 compares Flipkart, Snapdeal, Amazon India's progress in 2015–16 across a few key parameters.

For instance, Flipkart's revenue is tenfold that of Amazon India during that timeframe. This revenue differential is not expected to change in the near future, due to the investments required to build infrastructure and discount products to lure the highly price-sensitive Indian customer. The deciding factor may be determined by which company has the ability to bear losses on a sustained basis. In this respect, Flipkart (with an implied valuation of $9.3 billion) and Snapdeal (with implied valuation of $6.5 billion) may find it difficult to compete with Amazon, which has a market cap of $368.2 billion as of March 31, 2016.

One of the most important parameters to measure an e-commerce company's success is the number of unique visitors to its website. In May 2015, Amazon India managed to narrowly beat Flipkart with 23.6 million unique visitors relative to Flipkart's 23.5 million and Snapdeal's 17.9 million visitors (HuffPost India, 2015). Amazon likely achieved this feat due to its huge investment in advertising; the company spent more than $110 million on advertising during 2015 (Business Standard, 2016a). However in 2015, Amazon India declared losses of $259 million on revenue of $154 million, in part due to this large spend. In comparison, Flipkart's revenue amounted to $1.54 billion (close to tenfold Amazon's revenue), with losses of $301 million (just 15% more than Amazon's). While Flipkart charts a path toward profitability, Snapdeal seems to fall behind both in terms of revenue and operating margins; in 2015 it earned revenue of $141 million and incurred losses of $198 million.

In 2016, Flipkart and Snapdeal reduced their advertising budgets due to investor pressure to manage costs and focus on profitability (Live Mint, 2016). Amazon has several key advantages in this arena: founder Jeff Bezos' determination to succeed in the Indian market, and Amazon investors' willingness to let the company commit large sums of money to the Indian market without demanding immediate return.

Even though Amazon entered India with a marketplace model, over the past three years it has managed to replicate the combination inventory/marketplace model it uses in the U.S. Amazon's joint venture, Cloudtail India Pvt. Ltd., now allows the company to sidestep the same FDI regulations that plagued Flipkart, preventing foreign sales to consumers. In early 2016, Cloudtail sold nearly 40% of all goods purchased through the Amazon India marketplace (Live Mint, 2015). However, after additional policy guidelines (Department of Industrial Policy and Promotion, 2016) prohibited any single supplier from concentrating more than 25% of sales in one marketplace, Cloudtail moved out of mobile phones and electronic appliances, high value categories that would ensure Cloudtail sales stayed below the 25% mark. Snapdeal, on the other hand, focused on the marketplace model, which its founders publicly support. Therefore, it is no surprise that among these top three e-commerce players, Snapdeal has the largest number of sellers on its marketplace. That said, Snapdeal founders have indicated their intent to pursue an inventory-based model in the high-margin fashion industry, with plans to invest up to $100 million (Business Standard, 2016c).

Due to their business model choices, Amazon India and Flipkart both own their warehouses. Amazon owns 21 warehouses and supports 50 others owned by suppliers, while Flipkart owns 17 warehouses (because of its marketplace model, Snapdeal does not own any warehouse). Hybrid inventory and marketplace models empower both Amazon and Flipkart to have a large portfolio of products with a smaller number of sellers. Amazon has 55 million products and 85,000 sellers, whereas Flipkart has 40 million products and 90,000 sellers. Snapdeal offers 35 million products through a large network of 300,000 sellers. Moreover, Amazon India has made a huge push to increase the number of sellers on its platform. One such push was "Amazon Tatkal," an innovative program in which company executives travelled 37,000 kilometers through 50 cities, allowing potential sellers to sign up hassle-free at their studio on wheels. Programs like Amazon Tatkal allowed Amazon India to triple its number of sellers to 1.2 million in less than a year. By the end of 2015, Amazon had 45,000 sellers, which enabled the company to significantly increase its product offerings to the tune of 80 million products on offer for the festival season sale in October 2016 (Economic Times, 2016b). The additional sellers further allowed Amazon India to scale back Cloudtail's large contribution and comply more readily with FDI regulation.

Another parameter to examine is market share. Amazon increased its market share from 14% in March 2014 to 21%–24% in March 2015, whereas Flipkart's share of shipments fell from 43% to 37%. Snapdeal's market share fell from 19% to 15% during the same period. However, in terms of GMV, Flipkart's market share was 45%, Snapdeal's was 26%, and Amazon India's was 12% in February 2015. Amazon, Flipkart, and Snapdeal have each assessed the market conditions and the model that they believe best suits the Indian market. Success or failure will depend on how robust some of these assumptions are and how effectively the three companies can implement their respective strategies.

Meanwhile other contenders such as Paytm and ShopClues have emerged over the past few years. Paytm initiated a mobile recharge service in 2010 and gradually pivoted toward creating a mobile and online payment space of its own. As of December 2015, Paytm had the largest share of mobile payments in the country, with a share of 39% of users. In November 2016, the Indian government announced a massive demonetization exercise in which over 80% of the currency notes in circulation were no longer legal tender, giving a big boost to digital wallet services such as the one offered by Paytm. Paytm's transaction volume increased 700% and the amount loaded in wallets increased 1000% within a couple of days of the demonetization announcement. The total number of transactions on Paytm increased to 5 million and the average number of transactions per user increased from 3 to 18 per day (Trak.in, 2016). Following this success, Paytm set ambitious targets to increase its seller base from 125,000 to 500,000 by June 2016.

In fact, Paytm has expanded to become a full-fledged e-commerce marketplace competing directly with the likes of Flipkart, Amazon India, and Snapdeal. Chinese-based Alibaba Group Holding Ltd. has since acquired a 40% stake in Paytm, a move that may allow Alibaba to gain entry into the Indian market. ShopClues is another e-commerce contender, founded in the United States in July 2011. The company focuses on providing a platform for small- and medium-sized businesses to sell their goods online to middle-class consumers. As of June 2016 it claimed to have 500,000 sellers and achieved unicorn status in January 2016 when it raised $140 million from the Singapore-based sovereign fund GIC Pvt. Ltd. at an estimated valuation of $1.1 billion (Business Standard, 2016b). While it is difficult to see ShopClues threatening the dominance of large e-commerce players such as Flipkart, Amazon India, or Snapdeal, it could play a part in the inevitable consolidation expected in the industry, either by enabling an existing player to strengthen its position or by giving a new player the option to enter the Indian market.

Global retail giants such as Walmart from the United States and global/regional e-commerce companies such as Tencent and Baidu from China or Rakuten from Japan currently do not have a significant presence in the Indian e-commerce market. Considering the attractive growth prospects of the Indian e-commerce industry in India, some of these traditional e-commerce companies may decide to stake a claim for a share of the e-commerce pie.

6.8 FLIPKART'S RESPONSE TO THE CHANGING E-COMMERCE LANDSCAPE

As changing market dynamics in the Indian e-commerce industry threatened Flipkart's dominance, the company responded by making a few strategic moves of its own. In this section, we discuss some of these changing dynamics, and the reasoning behind Flipkart's strategic answers to these challenges. See Fig. 6.8 for these key triggers and strategic moves.

Timeline	Trigger/reason	Strategic initiative/milestone	Impact
2013	1. Amazon's entry 2. Regulations banning direct sales to customers (inventory model)	Launch of Flipkart Marketplace with 50 sellers	Expansion in product portfolio and Regulatory compliance to FDI law
May 2014	Focus on profitability, need for consolidation	Acquisition of Myntra	Gained almost 50% market share in the high margin online fashion segment
July 2014	Need to scale up fast to compete with Amazon and Snapdeal	Raised $1 billion from investors in the largest fundraise by an Indian e-commerce company	Provided cushion to invest in infrastructure, discounting and advertising—Amazon had committed investment of $ 2 billion in 2013 and then committed
July 2015	Increasing penetration and usage of smartphones	Introduced an "App only" strategy in Myntra and withdraw he desktop version	The strategy misfired, helping Amazon India to gain market share in the fashion category and the move was subsequently reversed
January 2016	Fall in valuation and challenges in managing costs	Change in Management. Binny Bansal took over as CEO and Sachin Bansal became Exec Chairman	1. Focus on cost savings and efficiency 2. Emphasis on customer service, adoption of customer focused metrics at all levels in the company
2016	1. Dilution in brand due to customer service issues 2. Change in leadership 3. Focus on profitability	Hybrid category focused model where depending on the category company decided the number of sellers	Managing to hold on to leadership position during the festival season in October 2016 selling more than Amazon

FIG. 6.8 Flipkart's response to changing e-commerce landscape.

6.8.1 Change in Business Model Through Launch of Marketplace

Amazon's successful entry into India's e-commerce landscape pushed Flipkart to shift toward the marketplace model and swiftly add sellers to its platform. Flipkart raised $200 million and $160 million for this switch in two rounds of quick-succession funding in July 2013 and October 2013. The investors included Morgan Stanley, Accel, Iconiq Capital, Naspers, and Sofina S.A. from Belgium. In these two fund-raising efforts alone, Flipkart raised twice the total funds it had raised over the previous six years, thereby reasserting its ability to entice investors and grow quickly.

While Flipkart's founders initially held Amazon (USA) as their business role model, Flipkart's shift to a marketplace model also marked a change in mindset. Instead, the company aspired to the mold of Alibaba, the Chinese marketplace-based online retailer, something that Flipkart's founders have publicly acknowledged. Around this time, Alibaba successfully completed an international IPO that may have also contributed to this change in mindset.

The shift to a marketplace model had a secondary benefit for Flipkart as well: the company could reduce WS Retail's share in its total sales, thereby steering it clear of controversy (Business Standard, 2013). On April 6, 2013, Flipkart launched its Marketplace, which comprised 50 sellers that sold books, media, and consumer electronics (YourStory, 2013). Attracted by Flipkart's burgeoning customer base of 80 million users in the 12 months prior to the Marketplace launch, 30,000 sellers participated in the Marketplace within two years of its launch.

6.8.2 Acquisition of Myntra

In May 2014, Flipkart announced that it had acquired Myntra Designs Pvt. Ltd., an online fashion retailer, in a $400 million transaction. With this one move, Flipkart controlled roughly half of the online fashion market in India. This merger was advantageous for several reasons. To compete with Amazon India, it made sense for Flipkart and Myntra to pool resources and consolidate market share, as the two companies already shared a common set of investors: Tiger Global Management, Accel, and Sofina. Furthermore, Flipkart and Myntra's product portfolios complemented each other, as Flipkart's dominant categories were electronics and books, while Myntra had the highest unit margins in fashion. Myntra was able to combine the strength of its private labels with the strength of Flipkart's logistics networks to take these labels across the country to 250 cities, whereas by itself it had only served 70. Finally, Myntra benefited from Flipkart's technological prowess in big data analysis and customer profiling, a boon to the ever-changing fashion industry retailer.

6.8.3 The Billion-Dollar Round of Funding

Almost immediately after the Myntra acquisition, Flipkart announced it had raised $210 million of equity funding from investors, led by DST Global. A stellar $1 billion equity fundraise soon followed, with eight investors led by Tiger Global Management and Naspers. This was the first time that an Indian e-commerce company raised $1 billion in equity funding, signaling the coming of age of the e-commerce industry in India.

More than a milestone, this equity funding round came at a crucial time, as e-commerce companies across India poured money into advertisements to compete with the threat of Amazon. Indian e-commerce companies spent over $100 million on advertising during the 2014 calendar year, with Flipkart, Amazon, and Snapdeal spending $20–25 million each (Economic Times, 2015). Table A6.1 details Flipkart's equity funding rounds.

6.8.4 First Signs of Trouble

As Flipkart moved to a marketplace model, the company's positive reputation for customer service and reliability began to suffer. Instead of having direct control over the quality and consistency of its products and customer service, practices like return and replacement policies varied by seller. Meanwhile, Amazon was able to implement its customer-first philosophy in India by investing in new technology and supply chains, even taking responsibility for refunds/replacements.

Flipkart's performance on October 2014's Big Billion Day sale underscored their change in service: the company announced massive discounts and sold $100 million of goods in one day, but customer traffic overwhelmed the website, crashing it. Visitors not only received "out of stock" messages for almost all products, but angry customers also complained sellers had "marked up" products so that the sale price was still more than market value. After the incident, Flipkart's founders sent a personal apology to all customers to salvage the situation (Business Standard, 2014). Unfortunately for Flipkart, poor service and seller issues would continue to damage its reputation.

6.8.5 Misstep of Going App-Only

In May 2015, Flipkart discontinued Myntra's desktop version, converting it to an app-only platform. Flipkart's leadership team believed that most customers would welcome the shift to apps and planned a similar strategy for its core platform, flipkart.com. Instead, Flipkart lost ground to Amazon in desktop purchases amid customer backlash over the switch.

6.8.6 Fall in Valuation

Over time, Flipkart increased its implied valuation at an annual growth rate of 150% through the different funding rounds.[10] In July 2015, it raised $700 million at an implied valuation of approximately $15 billion. However, in December 2015, Morgan Stanley marked down the value of the holding in Flipkart to $103.97 per share from $142.24 per share in June 2015. Many investors considered this 27% fall in just six months a confirmation that e-commerce companies such as Flipkart were overvalued. Morgan Stanley marked down Flipkart's value yet again in March 2016 to $87.90 per share—a further 15% reduction from the price on December 31, 2015, a total fall of 38% within nine months.

Soon after, Vanguard slashed share prices from $136.87 in September 2015 to $102.65 in March 2016. Vanguard also lowered the value of the shares it bought in the second tranche to $106.71 apiece from $142.23. Furthermore, other investors such as Fidelity Rutland Square Trust II, Valic Co., and T. Rowe Price have also lowered the valuation of their respective holdings in Flipkart.

Overall, Flipkart's implied valuation fell to $9.3 billion from its high of $15.2 billion. The Bansals publicly declared that they were not concerned about the markdowns because the company had no immediate plans to raise funds (Firstpost.com, 2016). However, it was clear that some changes were in the making. In November 2016, Morgan Stanley further marked down its shares in Flipkart by a massive 38.2%, pegging the implicit valuation for Flipkart at only $5.54 billion (Economic Times, 2016d).

6.8.7 Ownership and Management Changes

In January 2016, Flipkart announced that its cofounder Binny Bansal would take over as CEO and oversee day-to-day management of the business. Then-current

---

10. YS Research: Making sense of Flipkart's and Snapdeal's valuations through their GMV Available at: https://yourstory.com/2015/08/flipkart-snapdeal-valuations-and-gmv/.

CEO Sachin Bansal, who had led the company since its inception, would immediately become Executive Chairman.

Soon after the leadership reshuffle, three top management executives exited Flipkart: Mukesh Bansal, Myntra founder, and head of Flipkart's advertising and commerce platform, Chief Business Officer Ankit Nagori, and Punit Soni, a former Googler who led Flipkart's products business. The resignations continued into October 2016 with the exit of chief financial officer Sanjay Baweja (Nikkei Aisian Review, 2016).

In August 2016, Flipkart transferred control of two key business units to Kalyan Krishnamurthy, a senior executive from Tiger Global Management. Krishnamurthy initially joined Flipkart as head of its category design management unit. The shift now put the marketing, customer shopping experience, and private label business segments under the Krishnamurthy's leadership, with unit heads Samardeep Subandh, Surojit Chatterjee, and Mausam Bhatt reporting to him. The company also expanded the roles of two other executives: Ravi Garikipati, Senior Vice President, who became the Head of Engineering, and Nitin Seth, then-Chief People Officer, who became Chief Administrative Officer (Economic Times, 2016c).

In January 2017, Flipkart announced its plans to aggregate all its businesses (Myntra, Jabong, etc.) under one group. Additionally, it decided that Flipkart CEO Binny Bansal would become Group CEO, and Kalyan Krishnamurthy would be taking over as CEO of Flipkart business. It is important to note that this was the second time that Krishnamurthy had been parachuted in by Tiger Global, the first instance in 2013 when he was brought onboard as Interim CFO (Live Mint, 2017) We believe Tiger Global planned to take an active role in managing the affairs of Flipkart.com, and that this was in line with a global trend of investors taking a more active role in running their portfolio companies.

6.8.8   Developing Its Own Business Model

After trial and error, Flipkart began to understand that the Indian market required a customized model, and different approaches across product categories, rather than a model imported based on efforts in the United States or China. For some categories, Flipkart worked directly with up to 100 sellers, while for other categories Flipkart worked with a few thousand sellers who managed their own inventory. This hybrid strategy ensured product and service quality even among a wide selection of products and categories and allowed the company to retain its leadership position despite a number of setbacks.

6.9   THE WAY FORWARD

In this section, we explore possible outcomes for Flipkart, Amazon India, and Snapdeal. We use game theory concepts to examine the Indian e-commerce industry and explore how new mergers and acquisitions may change the landscape.

6.9.1 Game Theory—War of Attrition

As seen in other countries, e-commerce market leadership often boils down to which company can give customers discounts for the longest period of time. In the "war of attrition" scenario in game theory, the players lose money in each round and must decide whether to continue bearing losses, or exit the game. Likewise, an e-commerce company must decide whether to bear losses, be acquired, or shutter together. In the war of attrition, if a player exits he/she loses all the money invested until that point; the possibility of making a profit only exists if the player continues until the very end, and wins.

Flipkart and Snapdeal managed to raise funds by promising attractive returns to investors, who in turn backed these companies under the assumption of eventual profit. However, these investors cannot be expected to wait indefinitely until the e-commerce war of attrition is decided, especially with Amazon in the market.

Amazon is well situated to play the long game: it has a large capital base that it can invest, and its leadership has been extremely vocal about backing its Indian entity, committing billions of dollars to ensure that it does not lose the market, as it did to Alibaba in China. U.S.-based companies do not often publicize their investments, but in doing so, Amazon is signaling its staying power in the Indian market and suggesting that Flipkart's and Snapdeal's investors should exit sooner rather than later. These companies' fall in valuation seems to indicate that Amazon is succeeding in creating doubt in the minds of investors.

With a war of attrition at play, we believe it is only a matter of time before two players combine to successfully challenge Amazon India. Otherwise, a new global player with deep pockets may acquire either Flipkart or Snapdeal and commit to fighting the drawn-out war.

6.9.2 New Entry/Consolidation

Based on our current understanding of the players in the Indian e-commerce market, we will investigate possible scenarios and their likelihood of occurrence.

- *Scenario I: Alibaba can enter through Paytm (Likelihood: Very likely)*
  Alibaba announced its plans to enter the Indian market by early 2017, though the mode of entry was not declared. This gives rise to several possibilities. Alibaba holds 40% in Paytm. In November 2016, almost two dozen Chinese Alibaba employees camped at Paytm's office, reportedly integrating Paytm's marketplace with Alibaba's e-commerce portal (Economic Times, 2016a). Early in 2017 the Reserve Bank of India (RBI), the country's banking regulator, approved Paytm license application to become a payments bank. As of early 2017, Paytm is separating its marketplace from its wallet services, the latter of which will merge with its payments bank (Economic Times, 2016f). This move would make it easier for Alibaba to use Paytm's e-commerce business to structure its entry into India.

- *Scenario II: Alibaba can acquire ShopClues and merge it with Paytm (Likelihood: Somewhat likely)*

  In 2016, Alibaba Group discussed acquiring ShopClues and merging it with Paytm's marketplace business. Both Paytm and ShopClues have a marketplace model with a large seller base of 125,000 and 500,000 sellers, respectively. Unlike Amazon India and Flipkart, ShopClues' sellers are quite small, geographically distributed, and specialize in unstructured categories. A merger would help these companies to target price-conscious middle class customers, particularly in Tier-2 and Tier-3 cities.

- *Scenario III: Walmart can enter by investing in Flipkart (Likelihood: Possible)*

  U.S-based Wal-Mart Stores Inc. entered the Indian retail sector in 2007 by forming a joint venture with Bharti Enterprises Ltd. In 2013, the two partners split; Walmart kept the wholesale business, while Bharti retained the retail business. Walmart has been focusing on consolidation and plans to expand its footprint by 50 stores by 2020 (Financial Express, 2016).

  In September 2016, Walmart was in talks for a $1 billion investment deal with Flipkart[11]; however the consistent fall in Flipkart's valuation may complicate an agreement. A partnership would benefit both Walmart and Flipkart against the threat of Amazon India: Walmart would benefit from Flipkart's pervasive online presence, while Flipkart could benefit from Walmart's supply chain capabilities to improve efficiency and reduce costs. Flipkart is already using a complicated structure in which its Indian entity Flipkart India operates like a wholesaler to small and medium-sized retailers who in turn sell products back on the Flipkart platform. It would not be too difficult for Walmart to invest in Flipkart India and merge it with its own wholesale business in India.

- *Scenario IV: Snapdeal can acquire Paytm (Likelihood: Unlikely in near term)*

  Snapdeal and Alibaba share a common investor, SoftBank Group Corp., known for consolidating its holdings across different companies and proactively initiating mergers or acquisitions. We believe this scenario is unlikely in the near term: in April 2015, Snapdeal acquired Freecharge, Paytm's biggest competitor in the digital wallet business. Thus, acquiring Paytm creates a conflict of interest without any major gain, until Paytm can significantly scale up its marketplace business.

- *Scenario V: Flipkart can merge with Snapdeal (Likelihood: Unlikely in near term)*

  This is perhaps the only scenario that does not involve a foreign investor. We deem this scenario unlikely because of the massive fall in Flipkart's valuation over the past year and a half. The latest markdown by Morgan Stanley means that Flipkart will need to contribute a significant chunk of equity

---

11. Wal-Mart Is in Talks to Invest Up to $1 Billion in Flipkart. Available at: https://www.bloomberg.com/news/articles/2016-09-28/wal-mart-in-talks-to-invest-up-to-1-billion-in-india-s-flipkart.

to acquire a controlling stake in Snapdeal. Nevertheless, the decision may eventually be in the hands of investors. Flipkart's founders in total own about 14% of their business, while Snapdeal's founders own <6.5% of Snapdeal. As of early 2017, we believe that while such a deal may eventually happen, it is only likely to take place after one or more of the above scenarios occur.

6.9.3   Impact of Future Policy Changes

As described earlier, India's demonetization initiative resulted in a huge cash crunch across the country as more than 80% of currency in the form of 500- and 1000-rupee notes (the two highest denominations in use) ceased to be legal tender. Though most opinion polls indicate support for the policy's intent to strike down unaccounted "black" money in the economy, the sudden declaration resulted in large-scale chaos in the form of massive bank queues to withdraw cash or exchange old notes (The Wire, 2017). Moreover, India is an economy with a cash-to-GDP ratio of around 13%, much higher than major economies including the United States, the United Kingdom, and the Eurozone. Thus, demonetization will not only result in short-term logistical challenges but may also impair economic growth. In the long term, we expect the policy to move a significant proportion of the population toward the cashless economy, much to the delight of digital payment businesses such as Paytm, Freecharge, and MobiKwik. The e-commerce industry may suffer a dip in sales in the short term due to the high proportion of sales in the form of c.o.d. In the long term, we can expect growth in the cashless economy to increase online spending (helping e-commerce companies expand their customer base) and encourage digital payments (improving margins for e-commerce companies by reducing cash management costs and associated risks) (Forbes, 2016).

The Indian government appointed a 13-member committee to address the challenges of demonetization and ensure universal coverage of cashless payment options throughout the country. If successful, it will surely expand the growth of e-commerce in rural India and for those at the bottom of the pyramid.

In light of nationalistic movements worldwide, the Indian government faces pressure to use regulation to enable homegrown companies such as Flipkart and Snapdeal to win the fight against U.S.-based Amazon. In December 2016, Sachin Bansal made a direct appeal while speaking at the Carnegie Indian Global Technology Summit (Economic Times, 2016e). Despite this trend, we do not think such regulatory interventions are likely in the next three years. Not only would such regulations go against Prime Minister Modi's "open for business" image but most of Flipkart's and Snapdeal's investors are from overseas.

As India's e-commerce industry continues to grow and mature, the existing players face heavy competition and are likely to conduct additional mergers and acquisitions. Despite a promising early lead, Flipkart's dominance in the e-commerce market is not assured. A clear winner will probably not emerge before 2020.

APPENDIX

TABLE A6.1 Flipkart's Key Investors and Round of Funding Invested

Investor	Round(s)	Partner(s)
Accel Partners	Series A (Lead)	Subrata Mitra
		Sameer Gandhi
	Series D	Sameer Gandhi
		Subrata Mitra
	Series E	Subrata Mitra
		Sameer Gandhi
	Series G	Sameer Gandhi
		Subrata Mitra
Baillie Gifford	Series H	–
Dragoneer Investment Group	Series E	–
DST Global	Series F (Lead)	–
	Series G	–
	Series H	–
GIC	Series G	–
	Series H	–
Greenoaks Capital	Series H	Neil Mehta
Iconiq Capital	Series D	–
	Series E	–
	Series F	–
	Series G	–
	Series H	–
Morgan Stanley	Series E	–
Morgan Stanley Investment Management	Series G	–
Naspers	Series D (Lead)	–
	Series E	–
	Series F	–
	Series G (Lead)	–
	Series H	–

(Continued)

TABLE A6.1 Flipkart's Key Investors and Round of Funding Invested—cont'd

Investor	Round(s)	Partner(s)
Qatar Investment Authority	Series H	–
Sofina	Series E	–
	Series G	–
Steadview Capital	Series H (Lead)	–
	Private Equity	–
Tiger Global Management	Series B (Lead)	Lee Fixel
	Series C (Lead)	Lee Fixel
	Series D	Lee Fixel
	Series E	Lee Fixel
	Series E	Lee Fixel
	Series F	Lee Fixel
	Series G (Lead)	Lee Fixel
	Series H	Lee Fixel
	Private Equity	Lee Fixel
T. Rowe Price	Series H	–

Source: Crunchbase—https://www.crunchbase.com/organization/flipkart/investors, accessed June 9, 2017.

REFERENCES

Kearney, A.T., 2015. Global retail E-commerce keeps on clicking: the global retail E-commerce index. April, 2015. https://www.Atkearney.Com/Consumer-products-retail/e-commerce-index/full-report/-/asset_publisher/87xbENNHPZ3D/content/global-retail-e-commerce-keeps-on-clicking/10192. Accessed 6/6/2017.

Business Standard, 2011. Flipkart aims for 10-fold growth in revenue in FY12. December 27, 2011. http://www.business-standard.com/article/companies/flipkart-aims-for-10-fold-growth-in-revenue-in-fy12-111122700025_1.html. Accessed 6/6/2017.

Business Standard, 2013, Flipkart changes business model, launches Flipkart marketplace, April 6, 2013. http://www.business-standard.com/article/companies/flipkart-changes-business-model-launches-flipkart-marketplace-113040600051_1.html. Accessed 6/7/2017.

Business Standard, 2014. Flipkart co-founders apologise for glitches. October 8, 2014. http://www.business-standard.com/article/companies/flipkart-co-founders-apologise-for-glitches-114100701229_1.html. Accessed 6/7/2017.

Business Standard, 2016a. Amazon India reports Rs 1,724-cr loss on heavy ad spend. January 26, 2016. http://www.business-standard.com/article/companies/amazon-india-reports-rs-1-724-cr-loss-on-heavy-ad-spend-116012500826_1.html. Accessed 6/6/2017.

Business Standard, 2016b. Shopclues says it has half a million sellers. June 30, 2016. http://www.business-standard.com/article/companies/shopclues-says-it-has-half-a-million-sellers-116063000042_1.html. Accessed 6/6/2017.

Business Standard, 2016c. Snapdeal to invest $100 million in fashion portfolio. November 14, 2016. http://www.business-standard.com/article/companies/snapdeal-to-invest-100-million-in-fashion-portfolio-116111401311_1.html. Accessed 6/6/2017.

Confederation of Indian Industry and Deloitte, 2016. E-Commerce in India: A Game Changer for the Economy. https://www2.deloitte.com/content/dam/Deloitte/in/Documents/technology- media-telecommunications/in-tmt-e-commerce-in-india-noexp.pdf. Accessed 6/6/2017.

Department of Industrial Policy and Promotion, 2016. Guidelines for FDI Investment in Indian e-commerce. http://dipp.nic.in/English/acts_rules/Press_Notes/pn3_2016.pdf. Accessed 30/5/2017.

Economic Times, 2015. E-commerce firms like Flipkart Amazon and others spend mega on advertisement. April 8, 2015. http://articles.economictimes.indiatimes.com/2015-04-08/news/60943303_1_print-ads-e-commerce-sector-flipkart. Accessed 6/7/2017.

Economic Times, 2016a. Alibaba staff from China working on Paytm integration. November 3, 2016. http://economictimes.indiatimes.com/small-biz/startups/alibaba-staff-from-china-working-on-paytm-integration/articleshow/55213729.cms. Accessed 6/7/2017.

Economic Times, 2016b. Amazon India triples its seller base ahead of festive season sales. September 15, 2016. http://tech.economictimes.indiatimes.com/news/internet/amazon-india-triples-the-no-of-sellers-on-its-platform-ahead-of-festive-season/54340296. Accessed 6/6/2017.

Economic Times, 2016c. Flipkart rejigs top deck again, former Tiger global executives now in control of two key units. August 26, 2016. http://economictimes.indiatimes.com/articleshow/53872368.cms?utm_source=contentofinterest&utm_medium=text&utm_campaign=cppst. Accessed 6/6/2017.

Economic Times, 2016d. Flipkart valuation slashed to $5.54 billion by investor Morgan Stanley. November 29, 2016. http://economictimes.indiatimes.com/small-biz/flipkart-valuation-slashed-to-5-54-bln-by-investor-morgan-stanley/articleshow/55681132.cms. Accessed 6/7/2017.

Economic Times, 2016e. Flipkart's Sachin Bansal, Ola's Bhavish Aggarwal seek government's help in battle against Amazon & Uber. December 8, 2016. http://economictimes.indiatimes.com/small-biz/startups/flipkarts-sachin-bansal-olas-bhavish-aggarwal-seek-governments-help- in-battle-against-foreign-rivals/articleshow/55862027.cms. Accessed 29/5/2017.

Economic Times, 2016f. Paytm to transfer wallet business to payments bank. December 5, 2016. http://economictimes.indiatimes.com/industry/banking/finance/paytm-to-transfer-wallet-business-to-payments-bank/articleshow/55798230.cms. Accessed 6/7/2017.

Financial Express, 2016. Walmart India plans 50 more outlets by 2020. April 25, 2016. http://www.financialexpress.com/industry/walmart-india-plans-50-more-outlets-by-2020/242310/. Accessed 6/7/2017.

Firstpost.com, 2016. Flipkart's valuation marked down again signaling continuing pain in E-commerce. June 8, 2016. http://www.firstpost.com/business/after-burning-cash-flipkart-charts-strategy-to-turn-around-to-cut-costs-by-30-2866676.html. Accessed 6/7/2017.

Forbes, 2016. Demonetization will impact Amazon's growth in India. November 29, 2016. http://www.forbes.com/sites/greatspeculations/2016/11/29/demonetization-will-impact-amazons-growth-in-india/#5b4be6b1de49. Accessed 6/7/2017.

Gadgets Now, 2016. Indian e-commerce industry's growth comes to a halt, Snapdeal worst hit. July 12, 2016. http://www.gadgetsnow.com/tech-news/Indian-e-commerce-cart-hits-a-plateau/articleshow/52933341.cms. Accessed 6/6/2017.

HuffPost India, 2015. Amazon India had 23.6 million unique visitors in May, ahead of Flipkart, Snapdeal, http://www.Huffingtonpost.In/2015/06/29/amazon-india-had-23-6-million-unique-visitors-in-may-ahead-of-f/. Accessed 6/6/2017.

Live Mint, 2015. Amazon's JV Cloudtail is its biggest seller in India. October 29, 2015. http://www.livemint.com/Companies/RjEDJkA3QyBSTsMDdaXbCN/Amazons-JV-Cloudtail-is-its-biggest-seller-in-India.html. Accessed 6/6/2017.

Live Mint, 2016. Flipkart, Snapdeal, Jabong are spending less on ads. July 13, 2016. http://www.livemint.com/Companies/fCeUX3BNxjY2TqBennysMK/Flipkart-Snapdeal-Jabong-spent-less-on-ads-this-year-due-t.html. Accessed 6/6/2017.

Live Mint, 2017. Flipkart, Tiger Global's unlikely burden. January 14, 2017. http://www.livemint.com/Opinion/9jYZyiFhhTSMksYebC62WK/Flipkart-Tiger-Globals-unlikely-burden.html. Accessed 6/7/2017.

News18, 2014. ED issues notice to Flipkart for its billion-day sale, may impose Rs 1000 crore penalty. October 14, 2014. http://www.news18.com/news/business/ed-on-flipkart-arunima-720084.html. Accessed 6/6/2017.

Nikkei Aisian Review, 2016. Top-level exits at India's Flipkart continue as CFO resigns. October 27, 2016. http://asia.nikkei.com/Business/Companies/Top-level-exits-at-India-s-Flipkart-continue-as-CFO-resigns. Accessed 6/7/2017.

TechinAsia, Takeaways from the Indian online festive sales, October 21, 2016, 11:03—at1.4. https://www.techinasia.com/talk/takeaways-indian-online-festive-sales.

The Wire, 2017. What explains the popular support for Demonitizatio. February 27, 2017. https://thewire.in/112263/what-explains-the-popular-support-for-demonetisation/. Accessed 6/7/2017.

Trak.in, 2016, Paytm Introduces 'Nearby' Feature to Find Merchants Who Accept Digital Wallet; Processes 5 Mln Transactions a Day, November 14, 2016. http://trak.in/tags/business/2016/11/14/paytm-nearby-merchant-discovery/. Accessed 6/6/2017.

United Nations Conference on Trade and Development, 2016. World Investment Report 2016—Investor Nationality: Policy Challenges.

VCCircle, 2016. Flipkart to lead fashion etail with 70% market share. July 27, 2016. http://www.vccircle.com/news/technology/2016/07/26/flipkart-control-70-online-apparel-market-after-jabong-buy. Accessed 6/6/2017.

World Bank, n.d. Health Nutrition and Population Statistics: Population Estimates and Projections.

YourStory, 2013. Flipkart launches its marketplace with 50 sellers onboard. April 6, 2013. https://m.yourstory.com/2013/04/flipkart-launches-a-marketplace-platform-onboards-50-sellers/. Accessed 6/7/2017.

Part II

Financing Entrepreneurship

Chapter 7

Banks, Credit Constraints, and the Financial Technology's Evolving Role

ACRONYMS

AI	Artificial Intelligence
BRAC	Bangladesh Rehabilitation Assistance Committee
CBA	Central Bank of Africa
Fintech	Financial technology
IPO	Initial Public Offering
MFIs	Microfinance Institutions
MSMEs	Micro-, Small-, and Medium-sized Enterprises
P2P	Peer-to-Peer
TIAA-CREF	Teachers Insurance and Annuity Association of America

Financial development is a critical and inextricable part of the economic growth process. Well-functioning financial systems help mobilize savings, promote information sharing, improve resource allocation, and facilitate diversification and risk management (Levine, 2005). While recent research (as reviewed in Sahay et al., 2015) shows that the relationship between finance and growth is probably nonlinear, there is substantial evidence that financial development significantly boosts economic growth in the earlier phases of the development process following a virtuous cycle: financial development encourages savings, which in turn fosters real activity, and as real activity expands, finance grows in response to increasing demand for its services from the nonfinancial sector.

As we discussed in Part I of this book, entrepreneurship and innovation support financial development and economic growth. Economic growth is mainly driven by productivity gains. Generating these gains requires technological change, which depends upon transformational entrepreneurship. However, entrepreneurship can thrive only in an environment in which startup firms have access to external capital. Banks play a critical role in this process.

In the early phases of a country's development, banks are usually the only option for external capital; other forms of financial intermediation generally

Financing Entrepreneurship and Innovation in Emerging Markets.
https://doi.org/10.1016/B978-0-12-804025-6.00007-1

emerge in more sophisticated economies. As countries progress through the different stages of development and their financial systems deepen and broaden, companies may gain access to a wider set of external funding sources, including equity and bond markets. These sources are generally inaccessible to startups; unless they are able to obtain a bank loan, startups usually rely on informal funding from friends and family. Although these challenges also apply to startups in advanced economies, they tend to be even greater obstacles in emerging economies. While informal sources may provide affordable funding for a nascent company, funding from family and friends is often unreliable and can be associated with lower growth rates compared to countries where access to formal financing is more easily available (Chavis et al., 2012).

The lack of access to capital is one of the biggest hurdles facing entrepreneurs to start and grow a new business, which typically has few, if any, tangible assets to pledge as collateral. According to the World Bank Enterprise Surveys (2016a) of more than 130,000 companies in 135 countries, 27% of firm owners around the world report access to capital as a major constraint to growth.[1] This group includes companies in advanced economies, while in many emerging economies the share of respondents reporting a lack of external capital as a major issue is significantly higher. Furthermore, there is evidence that the lack of access to capital is particularly onerous for companies in their earliest stages of growth, i.e., during their first three years (Chavis et al., 2012).

Startups' inability to obtain traditional bank loans without tangible assets has fueled considerable interest in microcredit, a form of financing that originated in the 1970s. Since then, microcredit has become a global phenomenon, and a significant share of the 211 million individuals who have borrowed from microcredit lenders reside in advanced economies (McKinsey Global Institute, 2016, p. 25). The internationalization of microcredit mirrors the basic idea behind this funding form (to help countless millions of poor people unlock their inner entrepreneur[2]) regardless of whether the borrowers live in low-income countries or belong to marginalized groups in high-income economies. However, the extent to which microcredit has reduced poverty remains subject to debate. There are doubts about the extent to which microcredit has spurred transformational entrepreneurship rather than supporting subsistence entrepreneurs. Additionally, microcredit's potential to achieve greater scale and play a more meaningful role is under question, due to the high transaction costs microcredit organizations incur from relying primarily on manual processes and cash.

While microcredit institutions face many of the same constraints as traditional banks, an increasing number of them have changed their business model in two important ways. First, they have broadened their product range by diversifying into savings and insurance, morphing from pure microcredit lenders into

---

1. The surveys were conducted between 2009 and 2015. Database accessed January 28, 2016.
2. Quote from Muhammad Yunus, the Nobel Prize-winning founder of Grameen Bank. New York Times, Microcredit for Americans, October 28, 2013. http://www.nytimes.com/2013/10/29/business/microcredit-for-americans.html.

microfinance institutions (MFIs). Second, digital finance is gaining momentum, helping these institutions capture network effects and economies of scale, thus reducing their expense ratios. These innovations have led to cautious optimism that MFIs could narrow the financing gap startups typically face.

Advancements in digital finance affect other areas, too. For instance, entrepreneurs can more easily access capital from friends and family over longer distances, even overseas, due to technological progress in money transfer services. At the same time, new forms of financial intermediation have emerged thanks to increased investments in financial technology (fintech). While consumer lending dominates the crowdfunding market, business lending is the second largest category measured by transaction amounts. Peer-to-peer (P2P) lending has grown rapidly in recent years, both in advanced and emerging economies, with a rising number of Internet platforms serving solely as intermediaries between borrowers and lenders. In this business model, these platforms screen and analyze the creditworthiness of loan applications on the basis of "big data," assign credit ratings to loans, and allocate loan investments to the portfolios of individual and institutional investors.

This chapter discusses the nexus between entrepreneurship and finance by examining the emergence of new forms of credit intermediation and their effects on entrepreneurial funding constraints. Then, we look at the role of banks in the development process and debate policy measures to improve the availability of bank credit. Next, we turn to the role of MFIs as an alternative lending source emerging from the difficulties and inability of individuals and micro businesses to obtain bank loans. This discussion leads us to the role digital technologies could play in addressing credit constraints in traditional banking as well as in microfinance. Finally, we focus on crowdfunding as an emerging model of financial intermediation with game-changing potential.

7.1   ENTREPRENEURSHIP AND FINANCE

The relationship between financial and economic development has attracted substantial interest ever since Schumpeter's "Theory of Economic Development," which was first published in German in 1911 (Schumpeter, 1911). McKinnon (1973) and Shaw (1973) described two channels through which underdeveloped financial systems could hamper growth: the amount of savings that investors can mobilize may be limited, and there may be a lack of financial intermediaries to direct these resources into the most productive activities. Subsequent contributions to the literature on finance and growth have focused on the financial system's various functions and identified additional channels. Apart from mobilizing and pooling savings and allocating capital to productive uses, finance is believed to influence growth by producing information; monitoring investments and exerting corporate control; facilitating trade, diversification, and management of risk; and easing the exchange of goods and services (Levine, 1997).

In empirical studies, researchers have usually relied on cross-country regressions. King and Levine (1993) found that initial levels of financial depth—approximated by the size of the banking system relative to GDP—could predict subsequent economic growth rates over extended periods. Subsequent studies refined King and Levine's approach by including other proxies such as stock market depth (Levine and Zervos, 1998) and confirmed causality from finance to economic growth. However, as Ayyagari et al. (2015b) argue, pure cross-country studies can be misleading because unobserved country-specific heterogeneity is part of the error term and may bias the estimates of the included variables. Further studies have therefore employed different methods. For example, Levine et al. (2000) used an instrumental-variable approach to establish a positive relationship between financial development and economic growth.

Instead of focusing on macro variables, other researchers have used micro data at the industry and firm level to investigate causality. Rajan and Zingales (1998) suggest one approach, arguing that industries that are naturally more dependent on external capital should disproportionally benefit from more developed financial systems than industries that do not use external finance to the same degree. Using data from U.S. industries, they found that financial development substantially impacted industrial growth, both via the expansion of existing establishments and the formation of new establishments. In contrast, Demirgüç-Kunt and Maksimovic (1998) use a financial planning model to directly estimate the external financing needs of individual firms. Their model calculates how quickly firms could grow solely by using retained earnings and cash from operations. The authors show that the proportion of firms that grow faster than the rate set by the nonexternally financed firms is positively associated with stock market liquidity, the size of the banking system, and the perceived quality of the legal system.

While these and other studies suggest that financial development has a substantial impact on economic growth, this relationship is probably nonlinear. In fact, several authors have argued that the nexus between finance and growth is likely to weaken as financial systems continue to deepen and countries grow richer. As De Gregorio and Guidotti (1995) argue, high-income countries may have reached the point where financial depth no longer contributes to increasing investment efficiency. Other studies have gone even further, arguing that resources might be increasingly diverted toward the financial sector away from more productive sectors in advanced economies (Dabla-Norris et al., 2015). Furthermore, large and increasingly complex financial systems may heighten financial fragility (Rousseau and Wachtel, 2011; Gennaioli et al., 2012; Rajan, 2005), raising the risk of economic recessions. Thus, additional financial deepening could even reduce growth, suggesting that the relationship between financial development and growth follows a bell shape. In the earlier development stages, financial development increases growth, but the effects weaken at higher levels of financial development and eventually become negative (Sahay et al., 2015).

Notwithstanding the possible U-shaped relationship between finance and growth, the existing literature broadly agrees that economic development requires financial development as long as countries are still playing catch-up. This does not identify which channels affect firm and economic growth. On this point, the empirical literature is more limited, but those studies that do focus on this question (summarized in Ayyagari et al., 2015b) suggest that innovation and technological progress probably plays a key role.

Ayyagari et al. (2015a) tackle the issue of innovation directly. In their definition, innovation encompasses three types of activities: core innovation, such as the introduction of new product lines and new technology; activities that affect the firm's overall organization, such as sourcing decisions; and activities that transfer knowledge through licensing agreements or joint ventures with foreign partners. Employing data from the World Bank's Enterprise Surveys for 47 emerging economies, the authors find a positive relationship between the externally financed proportion of a firm's investment expenditures and firm innovation. Conversely, in countries where firms rely largely on internal funds, leasing arrangements, family and friends, and other informal sources, firms were less innovative.

This finding is consistent with Fig. 7.1, which shows that higher levels of economic prosperity (measured by per capita incomes) are generally associated with banks playing a greater role in financing companies' investments. In contrast, companies in countries in the early stages of economic development tend to rely more on informal finance sources to supplement retained profits. In these stages, credit constraints are usually particularly severe, and insofar as

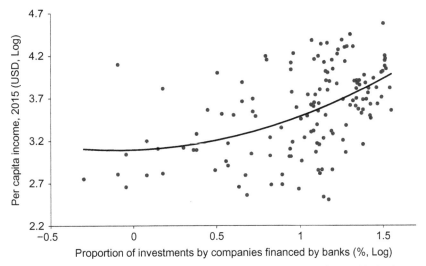

FIG. 7.1 Emerging economies: Proportion of investments by companies financed by banks as a function of per capita incomes. Note: Sample includes 139 emerging economies. *(Source: Authors' calculations, based on data from IMF WEO Database and World Bank Enterprise Surveys.)*

alternative sources are unavailable, investment activity is restricted, undermining economic growth.

There is only a loose correlation between economic prosperity and the proportion of external funding of firms' investment expenditures, suggesting that other factors also play a role. One such factor is regulation. Using data from more than three million firms across Europe, Klapper et al. (2006) found that compliance with superior accounting standards and property rights protection is associated with improved access to external finance and has a positive effect on firm entry and growth. Given startups' contribution to innovation, it is not surprising that the World Bank's "Doing Business" reports have long advocated financial sector reforms as a prerequisite for easier access to entrepreneurial finance and hence technological progress and economic growth.

7.2 CREDIT CONSTRAINTS AND THE ROLE OF BANKS

Our preceding discussion suggests that emerging economies risk developmental stagnation if they fail to continuously upgrade their financial systems. Although companies' access to bank credit generally improves as their country's economy develops, entrepreneurs in emerging economies tend to remain heavily reliant on internal sources of finance, as indicated by loan-to-GDP ratios that are generally much lower than in advanced economies, with the notable exception of China (Fig. 7.2). Based on data from the IFC Enterprise Finance Gap database and the SME Finance Forum, McKinsey (2016) estimates the gap between the amount of credit currently extended and what micro-, small-, and medium-sized enterprises (MSMEs) need at $2.2 trillion (Fig. 7.3). In total, 200 million MSMEs appear to be unserved or underserved by banks. Although this number includes micro and informal businesses, many of these companies are small- and medium-sized ones operating in the formal economy with the potential to become major job-creation and growth engines.[3] Some of these companies might have some access to short-term credit, but medium- to long-term credit, which is particularly critical for entrepreneurs, is often nonexistent.

Even if businesses have the ability to borrow from banks, other factors may restrict their access to credit. Just like in advanced countries, new firms in emerging economies are almost twice as likely as older firms to use the owner's personal assets as collateral (Chavis et al., 2012). However, the collateral required is often twice or three times as much as in advanced economies, particularly affecting young entrepreneurial firms.[4] Lending rates tend to be much higher

---

3. The sample of MSMEs includes four categories—Formal micro enterprises: less than five employees; formal small enterprises: 5–49 employees; formal medium-sized enterprises: 50–250 employees; and informal businesses of all sizes.
4. According to the World Bank Enterprise Surveys, collateral required averages 124% of the loan value in emerging economies, compared with a 50% average in advanced economies. There are significant differences with the emerging markets group, with the percentage of collateral required ranging up to 157% in sub-Saharan Africa.

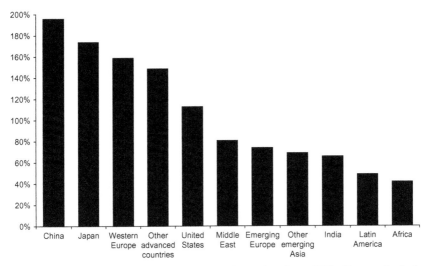

FIG. 7.2 Loan-to-GDP ratios in selected countries and regions, 2015. *(Source: Bank for International Settlements, IMF, and World Bank.)*

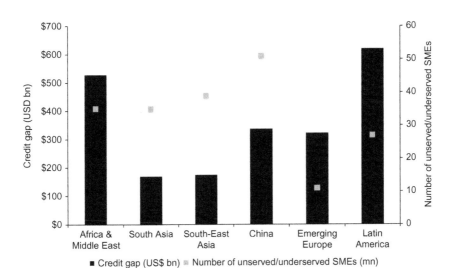

■ Credit gap (US$ bn) ■ Number of unserved/underserved SMEs (mn)

FIG. 7.3 Credit gap and number of un- and underserved small- and medium-sized enterprises in emerging economies, by region. Note: Estimates refer to 2013. *(Source: McKinsey Global Institute, 2016. Digital finance for all: Powering inclusive growth in emerging markets. http://www. mckinsey.com/global-themes/employment-and-growth/how-digital-finance-could-boost-growth-in-emerging-economies. Accessed January 25, 2017.)*

as well, making it extremely costly, if not impossible, for these companies to borrow from banks. At the same time, lending and deposit rates in emerging markets have a much wider spread than what is typically found in advanced economies, often due to different risk profiles and competitive dynamics in their respective banking systems (Dabla-Norris et al., 2015).

The total credit gap of Latin America's small- and medium-sized enterprises (SMEs) was estimated at $620 billion in 2015, wider than in any other region we consider in Fig. 7.3. Of this amount, almost 40% is due to unserved and underserved MSMEs in Brazil. Emerging Asia (South Asia, Southeast Asia, and China) has by far the highest absolute number of un- or underserved companies, with an estimated 23 million credit-constrained companies in India alone (more than two-thirds of all credit-constrained companies in South Asia). Cross-regional variations in the number of un- and underserved companies largely reflect the overall number of SMEs in individual parts of the world. In fact, there is little cross-regional variation in terms of the share of total SMEs that are un- or underserved. This percentage varies from 48% in South Asia to 53% in Africa. Within regions, the variation is more significant: in some African countries, more than 70% of MSMEs are un- or underserved.

It is not surprising that emerging economies generally show a significantly higher density of micro and small firms; their growth is impeded by credit constraints, which are generally more severe in countries with underdeveloped financial systems. Employing data from the World Bank Enterprise Surveys, Chavis et al. (2012) find that just 18% of emerging-economy firms use bank finance in their first two years, while more than 30% rely on informal finance, with the remainder using trade credit and other sources. Companies that have survived for more than 10 years tend to use informal finance less frequently. While only around 10% of the surveyed firms use trade credit, around 35%–40% rely on bank credit. Unfortunately, there is no information about how often the lack of formal external finance has caused startups to fail rather than impeded growth. Potentially, this percentage could be significant.

The relationship between firm age and funding sources is more complex than the overall numbers reported by Chavis et al. (2012) might suggest. In fact, in their study they found a significant degree of cross-country variation: younger firms had better access to bank finance relative to older firms in countries with stronger rule of law and better credit information. These findings have important policy implications, as emphasized in the World Bank's Doing Business reports. Reforms that improve credit information include establishing a new credit bureau or registry, reporting historical data, guaranteeing borrowers' right to access data by law, providing online credit information, reporting retailer and utility data, and providing credit scores.

Countries in which credit information is shared with credit reporting service providers generally show higher ratios of private credit to GDP. In these countries, more firms tend to have bank loans or lines of credit and there are usually fewer loan applications (World Bank, 2016b). However, the extent to which credit reporting service providers may spur access to bank loans depends on the comprehensiveness of the available data. In several countries where credit reporting service providers already exist, efforts are underway to cast a wider net by using data from a broad array of sources and sectors, including retail, small business, microfinance, corporate credit cards, and insurance, as well as from nontraditional sources, such as telecoms and utility companies.

Enhancing credit information not only improves MSMEs' access to bank loans but also trade credit, an area covered by credit registries in relatively few emerging markets. As emphasized in the 2017 edition of the World Bank's Doing Business Report, the use of data on trade credit—essentially an open, unsecured line of credit provided by business suppliers—can help firms without a formal loan or other credit facility develop a credit history.[5] Similarly, finance corporations and leasing companies are important finance sources for firms and could provide valuable data to credit bureaus and registries, potentially unleashing additional external funding for entrepreneurial firms, particularly beneficial in economies where weak collateral laws hinder bank lending. Leasing usually offers the advantage of not requiring collateral beyond the security of the leased asset itself and enables young firms to preserve cash for profit-generating activities.

Legal rights pertaining to secured transactions are another potential reform area. Based on recent reforms in individual emerging economies, the World Bank (2016b) advocates an approach that allows the borrower to maintain possession of the collateralized asset for use in its business operations. Equally important are reforms to ensure that secured transactions are regulated in an integrated fashion, enlarging the scope of assets that companies can use as collateral, thus expanding their access to external capital. According to the World Bank (2016a), these measures should go hand in hand with establishing a nationally centralized collateral registry that covers all types of assets (including moveable ones) and is accessible online for verifications, registrations, amendments, and renewals. Centralized collateral registries could further alleviate credit constraints faced by entrepreneurial firms by enabling secured creditors to establish their collateral priority in an efficient and transparent manner.

The impact of these and other reforms could increase to the extent that they encourage foreign banks. While foreign bank presence is generally a function of the quality of a country's legal institutions, Alfaro et al. (2015) demonstrate that foreign bank entry has a positive effect on business formation in emerging economies. More specifically, foreign banks often reduce external finance costs for bank-dependent borrowers by raising capital in one country at lower costs and redeploying that capital in countries with higher indigenous costs of capital. The effect is particularly significant in industries with a greater reliance on external finance. Interestingly, foreign entrants from other emerging economies played

---

5. Arguably, this is less relevant for startups in their early phases as they tend to serve domestic rather than international markets.

a more important role for entrepreneurship than entrants from advanced economies, with the latter generally requiring higher standards of legal protection.

Proposed legal and institutional reforms assume that identified credit gaps are supply-side driven. But what if entrepreneurs who appear unable to borrow have not even spoken to a bank? According to the Entrepreneurial Process Survey, this seems to be a real possibility (Bennett and Chatterij, 2017).[6] In fact, the vast majority (around 80%) of survey participants who cite the lack of access to capital as a barrier to entry opted out either by screening themselves out of the market or because they did not know how to approach a bank, suggesting that demand-side factors may also play a role. Thus far, the Entrepreneurial Process Survey is confined to the United States, and it is an open question to what extent its results are relevant for emerging economies.

7.3   MICROCREDIT

Credit constraints are particularly challenging in a company's early stages. This is especially true in emerging economies, which helps explain their high density of very small firms and the absence of medium and large enterprises relative to more developed countries (Banerjee and Duflo, 2005; Hsieh and Olken, 2014).

Microcredit emerged in the mid-1970s when Grameen Bank and the Bangladesh Rehabilitation Assistance Committee (BRAC) began experimenting with new lending models in response to these constraints, identified as an impediment to economic growth and a major cause of protracted poverty. Hailed as a major financial innovation by the World Economic Forum (2012), microcredit has its roots in the Irish Loan Funds of the 18th and 19th centuries (Hollis and Sweetman, 1996), and the cooperative lending banks founded by Friedrich Wilhelm Raiffeisen to support farmers in rural Germany. From its modest beginnings in the 1970s, modern microcredit has become a phenomenon with more than 200 million borrowers worldwide.

While MFIs were initially created as alternatives to moneylenders, Banerjee and Duflo (2011) note that MFIs, like traditional moneylenders, rely on their ability to keep a close check on their customers. Unlike moneylenders, however, MFIs typically maintain a close relationship with their customers by involving a group of borrowers who are liable for each other's loans and therefore are incentivized to try to make sure that the others repay. Unlike moneylenders, who are notorious for usury, MFIs' policy is never to use physical threats. Instead, MFIs rely on the power of shame and usually do not hesitate to use their connections within their social networks to put pressure on delinquent borrowers. As Banerjee et al. (2015) explain, one of their core principles in providing loans is (near-) nonselectivity. Reflecting the belief that the poor are natural entrepreneurs, who can always make good use of the loan to take advantage of a

---

6. We are grateful to David Robinson for pointing us to this research.

profitable business opportunity, almost any poor person can get a small loan from an MFI.

Since its inception, the MFI movement has evolved in different ways. First, while microcredit was primarily or even exclusively thought of as a tool to fight poverty by funding entrepreneurial activity, over time profit considerations were added to its social mission. Today, many MFIs function almost as independent banks. Globally, more than 1100 of them operate today, with an annual loan volume of around $23 billion and an estimated gross loan portfolio of $89 billion at the end of 2015. Second, as microcredit organizations have evolved from nonprofit organizations into profit-making enterprises, they have placed more emphasis on savings programs, accumulating deposits totaling $37 billion.[7] Similarly, a significant number of MFIs have diversified into insurance products, for the benefit of their customers and their own balance sheets.

Finally, MFIs' funding has changed profoundly, with microfinance investment funds assuming an important role. The universe of these funds includes a variety of vehicles, which differ significantly with regard to their missions, objectives, sources of funds, and types of shareholders, with sponsors ranging from nonprofit organizations and development agencies to commercial investors. Although the latter are mostly private individuals, institutional investors, such as pension funds, insurance companies, and mutual funds have shown interest in investing in MFIs as well (Goodman, 2007). A recent example is Bamboo's Financial Inclusion Fund II, whose investors include Teachers Insurance and Annuity Association of America (TIAA-CREF) and AXA Investment Managers.[8]

As traditional MFIs have morphed into banking institutions, offering investment products that attract yield-sensitive capital (McKinsey, 2016), mounting concerns have shifted the balance between the relative importance of social and financial returns. These concerns peaked in early 2007 with the initial public offering (IPO) of Compartamos, S.A.B. de C.V., a large Mexican MFI that raised $467 million. This offering drew attention and discontent, including from Muhammad Yunus, the founder of Grameen Bank, who received the Nobel Peace Prize for his work in popularizing microfinance. As The Economist reported (May 15, 2008), he was "shocked" by the IPO, arguing that microfinance should be about "protecting [poor people] from the moneylenders, not creating new ones." Particular sources of criticism were the extremely high interest rates, over 100% a year, that Compartamos allegedly charged—little different from what illegal loan sharks demand. Even worse, Compartamos made it deliberately difficult for poor borrowers to understand how much there were paying for their loans.

The IPO of SKS Microfinance, Ltd., India's largest MFI, was equally controversial. Raising $354 million in July 2010, the offering raised concerns that the shareholders' interests would be put ahead of the poor. Soon thereafter, SKS

---

7. All data from Mix Market. http://www.themix.org/mixmarket.
8. http://www.businesswire.com/news/home/20150416006201/en/Bamboo-Finance-Announces-Close-Financial-Inclusion-Fund.

found itself at the center of a crisis in the microfinance industry (The Economist, November 4, 2010). With an increasing number of customers holding multiple loans or taking out new loans to repay old ones, several borrower suicides were linked to the aggressive sales and collection practices by some for-profit lenders, including SKS Finance.

While the crisis has largely passed and reform efforts have resulted in a stronger, more mature sector, the fundamental question remains whether microcredit has actually boosted entrepreneurship and economic growth—and reduced poverty—by alleviating financial constraints. This question relates to our earlier discussion about transformational versus subsistence entrepreneurship. One possibility is that the poor are indeed natural entrepreneurs who can always make good use of a loan, as there are innumerable profitable business opportunities available. That these business opportunities remain unexploited is explained by credit constraints. Once the constraints are lifted, transformational entrepreneurs—or "gung-ho entrepreneurs" in the terminology used by Banerjee et al. (2015)—are likely to borrow, even at high interest rates, to expand their businesses by gaining access to high productivity technologies.

Alternatively, as Banerjee et al. (2015) argue, borrowers could mostly be subsistence, or "reluctant" entrepreneurs. Although households may use their new-found credit access to start a business, they do so because they are unable to find a job and are more likely to have access only to low-productivity business technologies. To the extent that microcredit is taken out primarily by subsistence (reluctant) entrepreneurs as opposed to transformational (gung-ho) ones, the impact of microcredit on economic growth and poverty reduction would be comparatively small.

Banerjee et al.'s (2015) findings seem to confirm this possibility. In randomized controlled trials conducted in Hyderabad, India, the authors find that increased microfinance access substantially impacted the business scale and performance of seasoned entrepreneurs who had started a business before microfinance entered. These effects persisted two years after microfinance were withdrawn from Hyderabad. However, microfinance had virtually no persistent impact on novice entrepreneurs, i.e., those without prior business experience. Overall, Banerjee et al. (2015) estimate that the marginal returns to capital for seasoned entrepreneurs are three to four times as large as for novice entrepreneurs. Thus, to the extent that the microcredit is made available indiscriminately under the assumption that the poor are natural entrepreneurs, its impact on innovation, growth, and poverty reduction could be considerably more limited than has frequently been claimed.

These results advocate a more targeted microcredit approach. However, for MFIs to play a more meaningful role in the future, other reforms are important as well. By relying primarily on manual processes and cash, microcredit organizations generally have high transaction costs that limit their ability to achieve scale and act as lenders beyond their original business model. This leads us to the potential role of digital finance to improve microcredit operations' efficiency and foster the emergence of new forms of financial intermediation.

7.4   FINANCIAL TECHNOLOGY AND MARKETPLACE LENDING

Broadly speaking, digital finance is a system in which financial services are delivered over digital infrastructure. Instead of using cash and traditional bank branches, individuals and businesses are connected to a digitalized payments infrastructure via mobile phones, computers, and point-of-sales devices. In recent years, investments in financial technology (fintech) have grown around the world (Fig. 7.4), helping develop digital solutions that could transform financial services, the intermediation of capital, and the availability of entrepreneurial finance. While all countries may benefit from fintech, its potential is arguably greatest in emerging economies, where growth has often been limited by underdeveloped financial systems. If digital finance helps these countries leapfrog with financial intermediation, the disruptive power of new technologies could unleash substantial growth.

How will digital finance benefit entrepreneurial activity and innovation? Essentially in two ways: by making existing forms of intermediation through banks and MFIs more efficient and less costly, and developing new forms of intermediation. These two mechanisms are closely intertwined.

Mobile and digital technologies that enable broad-based financial inclusion must exist for digital finance to play a meaningful role. The good news is that mobile phone penetration in emerging countries has increased dramatically. Mobile networks now reach more than 90% of people in these countries, and although phone ownership still lags behind network coverage, there are substantially more people who have a mobile subscription than those with a bank account. According

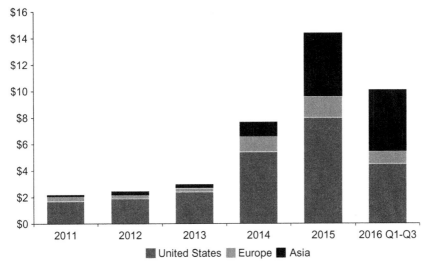

FIG. 7.4   Venture capital investments in fintech ($bn). *(Source: Authors' calculations, based on data from KPMG and CB Insights, The Pulse of Fintech, Q3 2016.)*

to McKinsey (2016), this gap is substantial: while in 2014 80% of adults in emerging economies used mobile phones, only 55% had a financial account, implying that more than two billion adults had no access to banking services. In some regions, this discrepancy is even larger. In Africa, only 1 in 4 people has a bank account, but 8 in 10 have access to a mobile phone, which explains the success of M-Pesa, a fintech phone-based payments scheme. Beck et al. (2015) document a strong positive association between the use of mobile money through M-Pesa as a method to pay suppliers and access to trade credit. Using an enterprise survey from Kenya, they find that the availability of the mobile money technology increases the macroeconomic output of the entrepreneurial sector by 0.33%–0.47%.[9]

Mobile and digital technologies facilitate payment transactions by providing easy access to digital wallets, and users, especially those in remote areas, may save considerable travel time and cost, and reduce the risk of theft. At the same time, these technologies provide access to a broader range of digitally delivered financial services. These services include savings accounts, and to the extent that households switch from cash and other forms of savings to digital bank accounts, financial intermediaries' ability to provide loans to individuals and companies increases. If M-Shwari, the savings and loan cousin of M-Pesa, is representative, this potential is huge. Launched in Kenya in November 2012, M-Shwari is based on collaboration between the Commercial Bank of Africa (CBA) and mobile network operator Safaricom Ltd. through its ubiquitous mobile money service M-Pesa, (for details, see Cook and McKay, 2015). In its first two years, 9.2 million customers opened a savings account with M-Shwari, attracting deposits of around $1.5 billion. This allowed M-Shwari to extend more than 20 million loans, with almost 2.8 million unique borrowers.

M-Pesa and M-Shwari have arguably attracted attention because their success demonstrates the huge potential of fintech to foster financial inclusion. If their services turn out to be game changers in Africa, where access to banking services is particularly challenging, fintech could also play an important role in other emerging economies. While M-Pesa has expanded to several other countries outside of Africa, other emerging market banks have developed similar services that include loans to businesses (Cheston et al., 2016). For instance, Standard Bank's mobile platform clients in Africa can already view balances, transfer money, buy electricity, purchase data, and get loan preapproval. The bank also plans to introduce full loan approval on a smartphone or the Internet. In Ghana, Fidelity Bank Ghana Ltd. has entered into a partnership with Bharti Airtel Ltd. and Tiaxa to launch a nano-loan platform that provides instant access to credit through their Airtel Money wallet. In Brazil, Itaú Unibanco S.A. offers a fully digital mortgage contract process for account holders. In Colombia, DaviPlata, Banco Davivienda S.A.'s e-money product for those without a bank

---

9. Importantly, Jack and Suri (2014) also find a positive impact on consumption. While shocks reduce consumption by 7% for nonusers, the consumption of households using M-Pesa was unaffected thanks to increases in remittances.

account, offers payment options for taxis, remittances, and phone recharges, among others. It also cross-sells insurance products and has announced plans to offer credit. In Mexico, BBVA S.A. plans to offer insurance, savings accounts, and other hybrid products via SMS to its low-income payment clients.

While phone companies or banks run most money transfer services like M-Pesa, some companies have built these businesses from scratch. One example is Zoona, a money transfer company that was founded in Zambia in 2009. Zoona operates a large network of kiosks in their home country as well as in Malawi and Mozambique and plans to expand into other countries in Africa. Agents maintain these kiosks, and Zoona ensures that they have enough float to cash large amounts. Users are sent a PIN via their phone to receive a money transfer. The sender pays about 10% on small transactions (The Economist, April 12, 2017).

The experiences of M-Pesa, M-Shwari, Zoona, and similar fintech-enabled services suggest that network effects are important to firms in the sector. These network effects also apply to traditional financial-services providers, and with more individuals and businesses using digital products, their costs will be substantially lower than using physical branches, which, interalia, should enhance their lending capacity. Additionally, individuals and businesses who use digital services and make digital payments create a data trail that helps financial service providers to improve their credit evaluation process.

While fintech revolutionizes the business models of traditional intermediaries, such as banks, MFIs, insurers, and asset managers, it has also brought about new forms of financial intermediation, for which data trails are equally critical. Crowdfunding has seen explosive growth, evolving from a mechanism limited largely to arts and creative projects to a broad-based platform for raising small amounts of capital from a large number of investors. One of the most striking features of crowdfunding is the geographic dispersion of capital suppliers and the reduced role for spatial proximity between investors and entrepreneurs.

Crowdfunding comes in various shapes and forms, involving debt and equity transactions as well as rewards and donations. Here, we are concerned with Internet-based lending transactions and rewards; in Chapter 9 we shall focus on equity crowdinvesting as a noninstitutional form of intermediation of entrepreneurial finance.

The largest form of crowdfunding by volume is P2P consumer lending, accounting for around 60% of global Internet-based debt and equity transactions.[10] Britain's *Zopa*, the first platform of its kind, pioneered P2P consumer lending in 2005.[11] In the United States, platforms, such as Prosper Marketplace, Inc.,

---

10. Based on data collected by the Cambridge Centre for Alternative Finance.
11. The business model of crowdlending has its roots in *E*-Loan, which was founded in 1997. E-Loan offers an online platform for consumers to compare loan terms across multiple lenders while slashing broker fees. Pitchbook (2016a).

LendingClub Corp., and Social Finance Inc. (SoFi), emerged shortly thereafter.[12] In recent years, similar lending platforms have also come into existence in emerging economies, including in China (e.g., CreditEase and WeLend), India (e.g., Faircent), Brazil (e.g., Lendico), Chile (e.g., Cumplo Chile S.A.), Mexico (e.g., Kueski Inc.), Poland (e.g., Kokos), and South Africa (e.g., Rainfin). Although some lending platforms are also engaged in balance-sheet lending and play a meaningful role as credit providers for consumers (e.g., Avant Inc., LendUp, and Elevate Credit Inc. in the United States), P2P lending has remained far more important, especially in Asia.

P2P lending is often likened to other forms of the "sharing economy" (Sundararajan, 2016). Like Uber Technologies Inc. with cars and Airbnb with accommodation, Internet platforms are making a commodity available that they do not provide themselves. Using an Internet-based platform, the lender and the borrower deal with each other directly, without a bank's intermediation. Hailed as the democratization of finance, these lending platforms generally do the credit-scoring and make a profit from arrangement fees,[13] but not from the spread between lending and deposit rates like a traditional bank. Lenders who provide consumer loans through P2P platforms explicitly accept that they may suffer losses. They know they will get their money back only when borrowers repay their loans. While some platforms allow potential lenders to choose their borrowers, others oblige them to lend to all those approved for credit.

The first lending platforms began operating in the mid-2000s, but consumer P2P lending started to thrive only after the global financial crisis. Banks needed to derisk their balance sheets and lend under tighter regulatory regimes, making it difficult for many consumers and businesses to obtain loans. Even those who could still borrow from conventional sources decided to turn to P2P lending platforms that offered better deals. Credit card debt was particularly susceptible because its interest rates tend to be relatively inelastic with regard to changes in policy rates and interest rates in other credit markets.

At the same time, extremely low market rates in the postcrisis period encouraged savers to provide loans to perfect strangers on the Internet. The recent increase in Internet-based consumer lending, however, has been driven by loans made by institutional investors, especially mutual funds and hedge funds, rather than by the general public. Securitizations have become increasingly common; the average size of consumer credit securitizations in the United States market

---

12. Prosper, America's first marketplace lender, was founded in 2005. Providing a platform that matches borrowers with both institutional and individual lenders, Prosper allows individuals to request loans between $2000 and $35,000, while permitting individual lenders to invest as little as $25 in each loan listing they select. LendingClub, which was founded in 2006 and is the largest online P2P lending marketplace to date, differs in two important aspects: First, LendingClub facilitates not only personal loans but also business loans, and, second, LendingClub is publicly listed since December 2014. SoFi, finally, focuses on student loan refinancing products. In addition, the company provides mortgage lending and refinancing solutions, personal and parent loans and wealth management services.

13. Public financials of LendingClub indicate that origination fees average almost 4.5% per loan, accounting for 87% of the company's revenues.

have grown to $252 million in 2016, up from $35 million in 2013 (PeerIQ, 2016).[14] At the same time, a growing number of platforms have begun to collaborate with traditional intermediaries. For instance, Citigroup Inc. announced in April 2015 that it would lend $150 million through LendingClub (The Economist, May 9, 2015). Appropriately, therefore, many Internet platforms have dropped the P2P label and describe themselves as "marketplace lenders."[15]

Several characteristics of marketplace/P2P consumer lending also apply to online business lending. In fact, marketplace/P2P lending to businesses is the second most important form of crowdfunding, and several platforms that started as pure consumer lending intermediaries have expanded into businesses lending (including LendingClub, which, according to Pitchbook (2016a), has lent almost $19 billion between 2006 and mid-2016). As with online consumer lending, some platforms have begun to collaborate with traditional banks. For instance, Santander UK plc. announced in 2014 that it would refer U.K. business loans directly to Funding Circle Ltd., a platform in which the Spanish bank has invested.[16] In 2016, Santander also announced a collaboration with Kabbage Inc., a U.S.-based lending platform.[17]

Despite many similarities, there are also important differences between marketplace/P2P consumer lending and Internet-based lending to businesses. Probably the most significant difference lies in the ability to access the creditworthiness of borrowers. Consumer lending platforms employ huge amounts of (nontraditional) data, including social media network and behavioral data, such as the way a loan applicant fills in its online application form. For instance, Kreditech Group, a German startup whose target customers are the "underbanked" with little or no credit history, has developed a credit-scoring technology that uses artificial intelligence (AI) and machine learning to process up to 20,000 data points per application in less than one minute (The Economist, May 9, 2015). However, applying fintech's "big data" approach for consumer lending to startups and other small firms is challenging as there is typically far less readily available information to help examine a business's creditworthiness, and what can be obtained from tax records, regulatory filings, and other sources is

---

14. Total securitization issuance in the U.S. amounted to $15.1 billion between the third quarter of 2013 and the end of 2016 (PeerIQ, 2016).
15. This new practice raises important regulatory issues. Recently, regulators in the U.S. acknowledged that marketplace lending helps expand access to credit to traditionally underserved segments of the economy. In late 2016, the Office of the Comptroller of the Currency announced that it would grant national bank charters to qualifying fintech firms. According to PeerIQ (2016), the charter could offer pre-emption—the ability of chartered fintech firms to export rates across state lines— and avoid the need for disparate state-by-state licensing or originating via partner-funding banks. In this context, see Bradford (2012) on the treatment of crowdfunding under U.S. federal securities laws and Hornuf and Schwienbacher (forthcoming) on the impact of securities regulation on small business finance reporting evidence from Germany.
16. https://www.fundingcircle.com/blog/2014/06/funding-circle-santander-announce-partnership-support-thousands-uk-businesses/.
17. https://www.ft.com/content/9925cc9e-f9a4-11e5-8f41-df5bda8beb40.

often out of date and of inferior quality.[18] However, given that fintech's data-driven approach is arguably less applicable to business lending, crowdfunding's primary advantage in this area may lie in a faster and more transparent application process rather than better rates.

Based on survey data collected by the Cambridge Center for Alternative Finance, marketplace/P2P and balance sheet lending totaled around $48.2 billion worldwide in 2015, an 18-fold increase from 2013 (Table 7.1). China is by far the biggest market, whose volume skyrocketed to more than $40 billion in 2015. The loans intermediated through these platforms averaged around $393,000, with each transaction involving an average of 383 lenders. In comparison with

TABLE 7.1 Market Volume of Balance Sheet and Market-Based/P2P Business Lending 2013–2015 ($M)

	2013	2014	2015
North America	837.0	2092.7	4842.6
United States	830.1	2077.6	4800.0
Canada	6.9	15.1	42.6
Latin America	11.1	38.9	54.8
Argentina	0.2	0.3	1.2
Brazil	–	–	1.3
Chile	10.5	36.9	46.5
Mexico	0.4	1.7	5.8
Europe	292.2	1091.1	2627.9
France	0.2	8.1	34.2
Germany	–	6.1	59.4
Netherlands	18.2	35.3	90.2

18. This is not to say that the big-data credit scoring models employed by marketplace/P2P consumer lending platforms are entirely reliable. In October 2016, LendingClub, the world's largest arranger of online consumer loans that had raised $1 billion in an IPO in 2014, announced several measures in response to a rise in delinquencies by borrowers. In addition to raising its interest rate by an average of 26 bps, LendingClub also said it would no longer approve loans to borrowers who meet a combination of several risk factors, including high levels of revolving debt and multiple recent installment loans. https://www.bloomberg.com/news/articles/2016-10-17/lendingclub-slumps-as-credit-deterioration-forces-higher-rates.

TABLE 7.1 Market volume of balance sheet and market-based/P2P business lending 2013–2015 ($M) — cont'd

	2013	2014	2015
Spain	2.8	13.7	26.6
Scandinavia	18.0	28.4	34.2
United Kingdom	253.0	998.0	2369.1
Other	0.4	1.5	14.2
Asia–Pacific	*1531.7*	*8328.5*	*40,671.4*
Australia	9.9	39.6	127.7
Japan	78.5	107.1	323.5
South Korea	–	–	1.3
China	1441.8	8177.5	40,195.3
India	0.6	0.4	1.0
South-East Asia[a]	0.5	1.1	9.5
Other	0.4	2.8	13.1
World	*2672.0*	*11,551.2*	*48,196.7*

[a]*Indonesia, Malaysia, Philippines, Singapore, and Thailand.*
Source: Wardrop, R., Zhang, B., Rau, R., Gray, M., 2015. Moving mainstream. The European alternative finance benchmarking report. Centre for Alternative Finance at the Judge Business School at the University of Cambridge. https://www.jbs.cam.ac.uk/fileadmin/user_upload/research/centres/alternative-finance/downloads/2015-uk-alternative-finance-benchmarking-report.pdf. Accessed April 18, 2017.
Wardrop, R., Rosenberg, R., Zhang, B., Ziegler, T., Squire, R., Burton, J., Hernandez, E., Garvey, K., 2016. Breaking new ground. The Americas alternative finance benchmarking report. Centre for Alternative Finance at the Judge Business School at the University of Cambridge and the Polsky Center for Entrepreneurship and Innovation at the Chicago Booth School of Business. Cambridge: Cambridge University. https://www.jbs.cam.ac.uk/fileadmin/user_upload/research/centres/alternative-finance/downloads/2016-americas-alternative-finance-benchmarking-report.pdf. Accessed April 18, 2017.
Zhang, B., Baeck, P. Ziegler, T., Bone, J., Garvey, K., 2016. Pushing boundaries. The 2015 UK alternative finance industry report. Centre for Alternative Finance at the Judge Business School at the University of Cambridge. https://www.jbs.cam.ac.uk/fileadmin/user_upload/research/centres/alternative-finance/downloads/2015-uk-alternative-finance-industry-report.pdf. Accessed April 18, 2017.
Zhang, B., Deer, L., Wardrop, R., Grant, A., Garvey, K., Thorp, S., Ziegler, T., Ying, K., Xinwei, Z., Huang, E., Burton, J., Chen, H.-Y., Lui, A., Gray, Y., 2016. Harnessing potential. The Asia-Pacific alternative finance benchmarking report. Centre for Alternative Finance at the Judge Business School at the University of Cambridge and The University of Sydney Business School. Cambridge: Cambridge University. https://www.jbs.cam.ac.uk/fileadmin/user_upload/research/centres/alternative-finance/downloads/harnessing-potential.pdf. Accessed April 18, 2017.
Zhang, B., Wardrop, R., Ziegler, T.; Lui, A., Burton, J., James, A., Garvey, K., 2016. Sustaining momentum. The second European alternative finance industry report. Centre for Alternative Finance at the Judge Business School at the University of Cambridge. https://www.jbs.cam.ac.uk/fileadmin/user_upload/research/centres/alternative-finance/downloads/2016-european-alternative-finance-report-sustaining-momentum.pdf. Accessed April 18, 2017.

China, crowdfunding in other emerging economies still seems insignificant, but recent developments suggest the potential for this form of entrepreneurial finance to become increasingly important. This may apply especially to emerging Southeast Asia, where transaction volumes in 2015 reached almost $10 million, a much deeper penetration than in most other countries in the region.

In Latin America, Chile has been an early adopter, accounting for almost 85% of the continent's P2P and market-based business lending volume, according to data reported by the Cambridge Center for Alternative Finance (Wardrop et al., 2015, 2016). In central and eastern Europe, this form of crowdfunding has also gained substantial momentum, albeit from a very small level. In 2015, the volume is estimated to have been around $6 million, from essentially zero in the previous year. Interestingly, Estonia, one of the smallest economies in the region, was responsible for almost 90% of this amount. There is less granular information on Africa, but according to Garvey et al. (2017) the crowdfunding volume (debt and equity) in East Africa, the largest regional crowdfunding market, totaled around $90 million in 2013–15.

Another crowdfunding model that has supported startups does not involve raising debt or equity capital. Instead, this model is based on preorders, in the sense that investors provide capital in return for a product or service. One of the most popular platforms in this area is Kickstarter PBC, which enables "project creators" to post project or product descriptions and videos in order to solicit funding. Project creators set a fundraising goal and a deadline, usually between one and three months. Importantly, Kickstarter crowdfunding campaigns are all or nothing. If the target funding goal is met within the given timeframe, the pledges are automatically collected from the donors; otherwise, no money changes hands. Although many of the projects are related to the arts, a significant number are technology related. Kickstarter operates globally, both on the funding and entrepreneurial side.

Predicting the market potential of crowdfunding in emerging economies is subject to substantial uncertainty. On the one hand, balance sheet and market-based/ P2P lending as well as reward-based crowdfunding have important advantages. These approaches may help overcome systemic biases in financial services with regard to geographies, sectors or gender; enhance the speed, customer service and convenience of providing capital; lower the cost of intermediation; widen the pool of available capital; and increase competition. On the other hand, crowdfunding comes with specific risks resulting, for example, from adverse selection, informational disadvantages, insufficient due to diligence, lack of liquidity, cyber theft, and platform failures.[19] Furthermore, in many jurisdictions there is a profound lack of regulatory clarity. In some countries, lending platforms are subject to banking regulation and hence need a banking license to operate.[20] In others, regulators have enacted specific regulations for such platforms, pertaining, for instance, to

---

19. Garvey et al. (2017) estimate that worldwide more than 4000 crowdfunding platforms (including crowd equity and reward-based platforms) have already shut down.
20. For details in individual countries, see Garvey et al. (2017).

registration requirements, business conduct, governance, and reporting requirements. These approaches are sandwiched between two extreme poles—the outright ban on debt-based activities, and the complete lack of regulation. How the regulatory regimes evolve in individual countries will have an important bearing on the role crowdfunding could play in the future.

7.5 CONCLUSIONS

In this chapter, we have focused on the debt financing of entrepreneurial firms, which has remained the dominant form of funding for startups. Our discussion began with the inextricable relationship between financial development and economic growth. As we have argued, a country's potential to achieve sustained economic growth is predicated on its ability to become more productive, which in turn is a function of technological change and transformational entrepreneurship. However, given that entrepreneurship can thrive only in an environment in which startups have access to external finance, it is imperative for countries to continuously upgrade their financial systems.

Banks play a particularly important role in this context. A large number of small- and medium-sized enterprises in emerging economies remain unserved or underserved, especially young companies that have few tangible assets and essentially no credit history. With a global credit gap estimated at $2.2 trillion, we believe that economic growth could significantly accelerate if credit constraints are alleviated. Efforts in this area thus far have focused in particular on improving the availability of credit information and introducing reforms concerning legal rights with regard to secured transactions.

The profound lack of bank loans to the poor and micro enterprises has encouraged the emergence of MFIs. As we have discussed, MFIs have become a global phenomenon, although it is not clear to what extent micro credit has achieved its fundamental objective of helping reduce poverty by fostering entrepreneurship. To the extent that MFIs support subsistence entrepreneurs rather than spurring transformational entrepreneurship, they may not contribute as much economic growth as expected. And finally, MFIs share similar constraints to traditional banks in the sense that they rely primarily on manual processes and cash, implying high transaction costs and limiting their ability to achieve greater scale.

This discussion has led us to digital finance and crowdfunding as new forms of financial intermediation and their potential impact on external finance for entrepreneurial firms. While these are early days, our assessment is generally positive. We have argued that digital finance has the potential to reach many more customers at substantially lower costs, and the lending capacity of fintech institutions and traditional banks should increase as these customers are offered a broader range of financial services, including savings accounts. Any digital transaction leaves a data trail, which allows lenders to improve their credit scoring systems. This is as important for traditional banks as it is for new Internet-based P2P platforms, which have gained substantial momentum in a growing number of emerging economies. Increasingly, banks collaborate with fintech firms, providing loans through online lenders, which could fuel financial inclusion and help reach underserved and unserved parts of the economy. However, as these collaborations deepen, resulting in larger loan volumes, it is likely that they will attract increased regulatory scrutiny (Bradford, 2012; and Hornuf and Schwienbacher, forthcoming). Thus far, the fintech revolution has been largely funded by venture capitalists and business angel investors. Instead of providing debt financing, these investors provide equity capital, a form of funding we discuss in greater detail in the following chapters.

REFERENCES

Alfaro, L., Beck, T., Calomiris, C.W., 2015. Foreign bank entry and entrepreneurship. Unpublished Working Paper. Columbia University. https://www0.gsb.columbia.edu/faculty/ccalomiris/papers/Foreign%20Bank%20Entry%20and%20Entrepreneurship.pdf. Accessed 5/2/2017.

Ayyagari, M., Demirgüç-Kunt, A., Maksimovic, V., 2015a. Firm innovation in emerging markets: the role of finance, governance, and competition. J. Financ. Quant. Anal. 46 (6), 1545–1580.

Ayyagari, M., Demirgüç-Kunt, A., & Maksimovic, V., 2015b. What determines entrepreneurial outcomes in emerging markets? The role of initial conditions. Unpublished Working Paper. The World Bank. Forthcoming Review of Financial Studies. http://documents.worldbank.org/curated/en/879001467998259448/What-determines-entrepreneurial-outcomes-in-emerging-markets-the-role-of-initial-conditions. Accessed April 17, 2017.

Banerjee, A.V., Duflo, E., 2005. Growth theory through the lens of development economics. In: P. Aghion, P., Durlauf, S.N. (Eds.), Handbook of Economic Growth, vol. 1. Elsevier, Amsterdam, pp. 473–552.

Banerjee, A., Duflo, E., 2011. Poor Economics. A Radical Rethinking of the Way to Fight Global Poverty. Public Affairs, New York.

Banerjee, A., Breza, E., Duflo, E., Kinnan, C., 2015. Do credit constraints limit entrepreneurship? Heterogeneity in the returns to microfinance. Unpublished Working Paper. Columbia University. https://www0.gsb.columbia.edu/faculty/ebreza/papers/BanerjeeBrezaDufloKinnan.pdf, Accessed 17 April, 2017.

Beck, T., Pamuk, H., Ramrattan, R., Uras, B.R., 2015. Mobile money, trade credit and economic development: theory and evidence. CentER Discussion Paper 2015-023. Tilburg University.

Bennett, V., Chatterij, A., 2017. The entrepreneurial process: evidence from a nationally representative survey. Unpublished Working Paper. Duke University http://kenaninstitute.unc.edu/kifer/wp-content/uploads/2017/03/Chatterji-KIFER.pdf. Accessed April 19, 2017.

Bradford, S.C., 2012. Crowdfunding and the federal securities laws. Columb. Bus. Law Rev. 1–150.

Chavis, L.W., Klapper, L., Love, I., 2012. International differences in entrepreneurial finance. In: Cumming, D. (Ed.), The Oxford Handbook of Entrepreneurial Finance. Oxford University Press, Oxford and New York, pp. 755–776.

Cheston, S., Conde, T., Bykere, A., Rhyne, E., 2016. The business of financial inclusion: insights from banks in emerging markets. Institute of International Finance and Center for Financial Inclusion. http://www.centerforfinancialinclusion.org/fi2020/roadmap-to-inclusion/the-business-of-financial-inclusion. Accessed January 25, 2017.

Cook, T., McKay, C., 2015. How M-Shwari works: the story so far. Consultative Group to Assist the Poor and Financial Sector Deepening Kenya. The World Bank Group, Washington, DC. https://www.cgap.org/sites/default/files/Forum-How-M-Shwari-Works-Apr-2015.pdf. Accessed January 25, 2017.

Dabla-Norris, E., Guo, S., Haksar, V., Kim, M., Kochar, K., Wiseman, K., Zdzienicka, A., 2015. The new normal: a sector-level perspective on growth and productivity trends in advanced economies. In: IMF Staff Discussion Note. International Monetary Fund, Washington, DC.

De Gregorio, J., Guidotti, P., 1995. Financial development and economic growth. World Dev. 23 (3), 433–448.

Demirgüç-Kunt, A., Maksimovic, V., 1998. Law, finance and firm growth. J. Financ. 53 (6), 2107–2137.

Financial Times, 2016. Santander UK teams up with Kabbage to offer fast loans to SMEs. https://www.ft.com/content/9925cc9e-f9a4-11e5-8f41-df5bda8beb40.

Garvey, K., Ziegler, T., Zhang, B., Wardrop, R., Rau, R., Gray, M., Ridler, S., 2017. Crowdfunding in Africa. Regulation and policy for market development. In: Centre for Alternative Finance at the Judge Business School at the University of Cambridge. Cambridge University, Cambridge. https://www.jbs.cam.ac.uk/faculty-research/centres/alternative-finance/publications/crowdfunding-in-east-africa/#.WPaem1hYpaQ. Accessed April 18, 2017.

Gennaioli, N., Shleifer, A., Vishny, R., 2012. Neglected risks, financial innovation, and financial fragility. J. Financ. Econ. 104, 452–468.

Goodman, P., 2007. Microfinance investment funds: objectives, players, potential. In: Matthäus-Maier, I., von Pischke, J.D. (Eds.), Microfinance Investment Funds. Leveraging Private Capital for Economic Growth and Poverty Reduction. Spinger Verlag, Berlin, pp. 11–45.

Hollis, A., Sweetman, A., 1996. The evolution of a microcredit institution: the Irish loan funds, 1720–1920. Unpublished Working Paper. University of Toronto. https://ideas.repec.org/p/tor/tecipa/ecpap-96-01.html. Accessed May 19, 2017.

Hornhuf, L., Schwienbacher, A., forthcoming. Should securities regulation promote equity crowdfunding? Small Bus. Econ.

Hsieh, C.-T., Olken, B.A., 2014. The missing missing middle. J. Econ. Perspect. 28 (3), 89–108.

Jack, W., Suri, T., 2014. Risk sharing and transaction costs: evidence from Kenya's mobile money revolution. Am. Econ. Rev. 104 (1), 183223.

King, R., Levine, R., 1993. Finance and growth: Schumpeter might be right. Q. J. Econ. 108, 717–737.

Klapper, L., Laeven, L., Rajan, R., 2006. Entry regulation as a barrier to entrepreneurship. J. Financ. Econ. 82 (3), 591–629.

Levine, R., 1997. Financial development and economic growth: views and agenda. J. Econ. Lit. 35, 688–726.

Levine, R., 2005. Finance and Growth: Theory and Evidence. In: Aghion, P., Durlauf, S. (Eds.), Handbook of Economic Growth. Elsevier Science, Amsterdam, pp. 866–934.

Levine, R., Loayza, N., Beck, T., 2000. Finance and the sources of economic growth. J. Financ. Econ. 58 (1/2), 261–300.

Levine, R., Zervos, S., 1998. Stock markets, banks, and economic growth. Am. Econ. Rev. 88 (3), 537–558.

McKinnon, R.I., 1973. Money and Capital in Economic Development. Brookings Institution Press, Washington, D.C.

McKinsey Global Institute, 2016. Digital finance for all: powering inclusive growth in emerging markets. http://www.mckinsey.com/global-themes/employment-and-growth/how-digital-finance-could-boost-growth-in-emerging-economies. Accessed January 25, 2017.

New York Times, Microcredit for Americans, October 28, 2013. http://www.nytimes.com/2013/10/29/business/microcredit-for-americans.html.

PeerIQ, 2016. Marketplace lending securitization tracker: 4Q2016. http://www.peeriq.com/research/. Accessed January 25, 2017.

Pitchbook, 2016a. Fintech analyst report. Part 1. Online lending. August.

Rajan, R., 2005. Has financial development made the world riskier? Proceedings – Economic Policy Symposium – Jackson Hole, Federal Reserve Bank of Kansas City, August, pp. 313–369.

Rajan, R., Zingales, L., 1998. Financial dependence and growth. Am. Econ. Rev. 88 (3), 559–586.

Rousseau, P., Wachtel, P., 2011. What is happening to the impact of financial deepening on economic growth? Econ. Inq. 49 (1), 276–288.

Sahay, R., Cihak, M., N'Diaye, P., Barajas, A., Bi, R., Ayala, D., Gao, Y., Kyobe, A., Ngyyen, L., Saborowski, C., Svirydzenka, K., Yousefi, S.R., 2015. Rethinking financial deepening: stability and growth in emerging markets. IMF Staff Discussion Note, SDN/15/08. International Monetary Fund, Washington, DC.

Schumpeter, J., 1911. Theorie der wirtschaftlichen Entwicklung. Duncker & Humblot, Leipzig.

Shaw, E.S., 1973. Financial Deepening in Economic Development. Oxford University Press, New York.

Sundararajan, A., 2016. The Sharing Economy: The End of Employment and the Rise of Crowd-Based Capitalism. MIT Press, Cambridge, MA.

The Economist, 2008. Poor people, rich returns. May 15.

The Economist, 2010. Microfinance in India. Discredited. November 4, 2010.

The Economist, 2015. The fintech revolution. May 9, 2015.

The Economist, 2017. A different approach to mobile money in Africa. April 12, 2017.

Wardrop, R., Rosenberg, R., Zhang, B., Ziegler, T., Squire, R., Burton, J., Hernandez, E., Garvey, K., 2016. Breaking new ground. The Americas alternative finance benchmarking report. Centre for Alternative Finance at the Judge Business School at the University of Cambridge and the Polsky Center for Entrepreneurship and Innovation at the Chicago Booth School of Business Cambridge University, Cambridge. https://www.jbs.cam.ac.uk/fileadmin/user_upload/research/centres/alternative-finance/downloads/2016-americas-alternative-finance-benchmarking-report.pdf. Accessed April 18, 2017.

Wardrop, R., Zhang, B., Rau, R., Gray, M., 2015. Moving mainstream. The European alternative finance benchmarking report. Centre for Alternative Finance at the Judge Business School at the University of Cambridge. https://www.jbs.cam.ac.uk/fileadmin/user_upload/research/centres/alternative-finance/downloads/2015-uk-alternative-finance-benchmarking-report.pdf. Accessed April 18, 2017.

World Bank, 2016a. Enterprise Surveys. http://www.enterprisesurveys.org/data/exploretopics/finance#--13. Accessed December 16, 2016.

World Bank, 2016b. Doing Business in 2017: Equal Opportunity for All. The World Bank, Washington, DC.

Zhang, B., Baeck, P. Ziegler, T., Bone, J., Garvey, K., 2016a. Pushing boundaries. The 2015 UK alternative finance industry report. Centre for Alternative Finance at the Judge Business School at the University of Cambridge. https://www.jbs.cam.ac.uk/fileadmin/user_upload/research/centres/alternative-finance/downloads/2015-uk-alternative-finance-industry-report.pdf. Accessed April 18, 2017.

Zhang, B., Deer, L., Wardrop, R., Grant, A., Garvey, K., Thorp, S., Ziegler, T., Ying, K., Xinwei, Z., Huang, E., Burton, J., Chen, H.-Y., Lui, A., Gray, Y., 2016b. Harnessing potential. The Asia-Pacific alternative finance benchmarking report. Centre for Alternative Finance at the Judge Business School at the University of Cambridge and The University of Sydney Business School. Cambridge University, Cambridge. https://www.jbs.cam.ac.uk/fileadmin/user_upload/research/centres/alternative-finance/downloads/harnessing-potential.pdf. Accessed April 18, 2017.

Zhang, B., Wardrop, R., Ziegler, T.; Lui, A., Burton, J., James, A., & Garvey, K., 2016c. Sustaining momentum. The second European alternative finance industry report. Centre for Alternative Finance at the Judge Business School at the University of Cambridge. https://www.jbs.cam.ac.uk/fileadmin/user_upload/research/centres/alternative-finance/downloads/2016-european-alternative-finance-report-sustaining-momentum.pdf. Accessed April 18, 2017.

Chapter 8

Technology Startups, Innovation, and the Market for Venture Capital

ACRONYMS

ARD	American Research and Development
CAGR	Compound Annual Growth Rate
CVC	Corporate Venture Capital
Fintech	Financial technology
GCR	Global Competitiveness Report
GDP	Gross Domestic Product
GII	Global Innovation Index
GP	General Partner
IPO	Initial Public Offering
IT	Information Technology
IVC	Independent Venture Capital
LP	Limited Partner
R&D	Research and Development
SWFs	Sovereign Wealth Funds
VC	Venture Capital

Entrepreneurial firms rely heavily on external debt sources. These can be personal loans from the balance sheet of the entrepreneur, who then holds levered equity claims in their firm (Robb and Robinson, 2012), resources borrowed from friends and family, or bank financing. Notwithstanding fintech's potential impact on external debt financing (Chapter 7), it generally remains challenging for entrepreneurial firms to gain access to bank credit. Banks are usually reluctant to lend to startups that have few, if any, tangible assets, little repayment history, and negative cash flows. This is true in the United States and other advanced economies; for startups in emerging economies, this challenge is often insurmountable.

As a result, the success of entrepreneurial firms often depends on whether they are able to find external investors willing to fund their projects. In this chapter, we look at the role that independent venture capital (IVC) firms can play in connecting entrepreneurs who have good ideas, but little capital, with

Financing Entrepreneurship and Innovation in Emerging Markets.
https://doi.org/10.1016/B978-0-12-804025-6.00008-3

investors who have money and are looking for good ideas. Investors in IVC funds are generally institutions, such as endowments, foundations, pension funds, and sovereign wealth funds (SWFs), whose commitments to IVC funds are motivated by expected financial returns. These investments should be distinguished from corporate venture capital groups (CVC) that invest in startups to complement their internal Research and Development (R&D) programs. As we discuss in Chapter 9, CVC is an important form of corporate venturing that is usually driven primarily by strategic considerations.

Venture capital (VC), IVC, as well as CVC are exceptional sources of entrepreneurial finance; very few startups are backed by VC funding. In the United States, the cradle of venture investing and by far the deepest VC market worldwide, only about one startup firm out of 500 receives venture capital. On the other hand, those companies that do receive VC funding make up a disproportionally large share of companies that undergo initial public offerings (IPOs). Of all the U.S. companies that made it to the public stage between 1980 and 2015, 37% were VC-backed; for technology IPOs, this ratio was 58% (Ritter, IPO database, 2016). Gornall and Strebulaev (2015) estimate that public companies in the United States that previously received VC funding account for one-fifth of the market capitalization and 44% of the R&D spending of U.S. listed companies. This set of companies includes some of the world's largest and most innovative companies, such as Adobe Systems Inc., Amazon.com Inc., Apple Inc., Cisco Systems Inc., eBay Inc., Facebook Inc., Genentech Inc., Google (Alphabet Inc.), Microsoft Corp., Skype, and Yahoo! Inc. While all these companies are publicly listed, venture capitalists have also funded today's "unicorns"—tech companies such as Uber Technologies Inc., Airbnb Inc., Palantir Technologies Inc., and Pinterest Inc. that are still privately held but whose valuations have already reached $1 billion or more. Thus, although VC funding is small, its macroeconomic impact is significant. While young firms contribute disproportionately to aggregate output growth, Haltiwanger et al. (2016) note that only a small fraction of young firms accounts for this contribution. Of these, a significant share is VC-backed.

The United States remains the world's dominant destination for VC investing. However, in recent years VC has also played an increasingly important role in backing emerging market startups. Tencent Holdings Ltd., our case study in Chapter 4, was initially funded by VC. So was Alibaba Group Holding Ltd., the Chinese e-commerce company that went public in 2014 in the largest initial public offering (IPO) in history ($25 billion). Encouraged by Tencent's and Alibaba's success, venture capitalists have backed a growing number of emerging market tech startups. Several of these companies became unicorns as well. Prominent examples include Xiaomi Inc. and Didi Chuxing (China); Flipkart Online Services Pvt. Ltd. and ANI Technologies Pvt. Ltd., known as Ola (India); Lazada Group SA (Malaysia); Avast Software (Czech Republic); Coupang (Korea); and Avito.ru (Russia). Other companies are not far behind and aspire to become the next generation of unicorns, including Jumia (Egypt/Nigeria) and Nubank (Brazil).

These unicorns exemplify the growing role of VC in financing emerging market startups. While emerging markets attracted only 13% of global VC investing in 2007, their share increased to 24% in 2016.[1] China and India absorbed most of this capital; their startups have received more VC than other entrepreneurial companies in Europe. As this form of financing has gained traction, venture capitalists have begun to look at investment opportunities in other emerging economies as well. Significant cross-country differences in VC investment flows remain, however, raising a number of important questions we address in this chapter. First, from a macroeconomic perspective, which factors determine an economy's attractiveness as a VC destination? From a structural perspective, how important are education and the quality of human resources? From a microeconomic perspective, which industries do venture capitalists favor in emerging economies? And given the nature of the industries that attract VC, what can we say about the role of VC in fostering innovation and productivity growth?

In addressing these and other questions, the rest of this chapter is organized as follows: we explain what venture capitalists do in the funding process and discuss the significance of this form of entrepreneurial finance. Next, we examine the extent to which VC has spurred innovation. These two sections draw heavily on empirical research on the U.S. market, which has by far the longest history. In the subsequent sections, we discuss the globalization of the VC industry and examine why China and India have become international VC hotbeds. Finally, we focus on the emergence of VC industries in other markets and their potential to attract more risk capital spurring entrepreneurship and innovation. In this context, we discuss key factors that help explain cross-country differences in VC investment flows.

8.1 WHAT DO VENTURE CAPITALISTS DO?

Venture capital is intermediated through an institutional market, in which VC firms form limited partnerships that raise capital to invest in startups.[2] The limited partnerships are closed-end investment vehicles in which the VC firm serves as the general partner (GP) who raises and manages a fund. As Limited Partners (LPs) in a VC partnership, investors agree to provide a certain amount of capital (capital commitments). Their liability structure allows these investors,

---

1. Authors' calculations based on data from Dow Jones VentureSource, Preqin, and Tech Crunch. Data accessed February 15, 2017.
2. We can trace the roots of this market to 1946, when American Research and Development (ARD) was formed in the U.S. Widely considered as the first true VC firm, ARD was a publicly traded closed-end fund. The first VC limited partnership—Draper, Gaither, and Anderson—formed in 1958. This legal structure is now the norm for VC investing as well as for other forms of private equity. For a discussion of the history of VC in the U.S., see Gompers and Lerner (2001a). Gompers and Lerner (2006) and Da Rin et al. (2013) also provide good surveys of the VC industry and research on this asset class.

most of whom are pension funds, insurance companies, SWFs, endowments, foundations, and family offices, to take a long-term view of their investment.

In a fund's investment phase, which usually covers the first three years, the GP acquires assets by drawing down on the capital originally committed by the fund's LPs. The fund holds its investments in portfolio companies for around four to seven years before the funds are liquidated through an IPO or a trade sale to a strategic buyer. VC funds typically have a fixed lifespan of 10 years, with possible extension periods of one or two years. During the life of the partnership, LPs have virtually no access to liquidity for their investments.[3]

The limited partnership's legal structure provides an important advantage for investors because their capital commitments expose the investors to a diversified VC portfolio. Investing in startups is inevitably prone to substantial risks, and it is not uncommon for even the most successful venture capital funds to write down or write off a nontrivial number of their investments. Instead of consistent moderate successes, fund returns are often driven by a small number of exceedingly successful investments in companies.

It is common to differentiate between four different investment stages, which are defined by the maturity of the startup company that receives funding.[4] At the seed stage, external financiers typically provide a relatively small amount of capital to an inventor or entrepreneur to prove a concept. This involves product development and market research as well as building a management team and developing a business plan, if the initial steps are successful. Early-stage financing entails investments in companies that are completing development, where products are mostly in testing or pilot production. In some cases, products may have just become commercially available. Companies may be in the process of organizing or they may have been in business for three years or less. Usually, such companies will have performed market studies, assembled the core management team, developed a business plan, and are ready to start or have already started conducting business.

At the expansion stage, financing provides working capital for a company's initial expansion; the company is already producing and shipping and has growing accounts receivables and inventories. It may or may not be showing a profit. Some of the capital's uses may include further plant expansion, marketing, working capital, or improving a product. Institutional investors are more likely to participate at this stage along with initial investors from previous rounds. The investor's role in this stage evolves from a supportive role to a more strategic role.

Finally, later-stage financing is typically for companies that have already reached a fairly stable growth rate, that is, not growing as fast as the rates attained in the expansion stages. These companies may not be profitable but are

---

3. Although a secondary market for stakes in limited partnerships has emerged, the turnover in that market is a fraction of the capital managed by GPs.
4. Definitions are from National Venture Capital Association (2016).

more likely to be than in previous stages of development. These companies' financial characteristics may include well-known product or service offerings, expansion of offerings into adjacent markets, significant revenue growth in excess of Gross Domestic Product (GDP), and positive cash flow. This also includes companies considering an IPO.

Seed financing tends to be considerably smaller than later-stage investments in startups. Furthermore, far fewer startups receive seed capital than entrepreneurial companies that are already more advanced in their life cycle. The share of startups receiving seed capital has fallen meaningfully over the past two decades. While in the second half of the 1990s about 17% of all U.S. VC-backed startups received seed capital, this ratio has fallen to around 7% in recent years as venture capitalists have become more cautious in the posttech bubble period (NVCA, 2016).

Venture capitalists providing seed financing face critical agency problems (Kaplan and Strömberg, 2004): (1) the entrepreneur may not work hard enough to maximize value after the investment is made; (2) the entrepreneur may know more about his capabilities than the venture capitalist; (3) after the investment is made, there may be circumstances in which the venture capitalist disagrees with the entrepreneur and wants the right to make decisions; and (4) the entrepreneur may "hold up" the venture capitalist by threatening to leave the venture when the entrepreneur's human capital is particularly valuable to the company.

These agency problems exacerbate the substantial risks that are already associated with investing in entrepreneurial startups that have few tangible assets (and therefore little, if any, collateral) and operate in new markets with poor or limited information. In light of these risks, venture capitalists follow a rigorous and disciplined due diligence process and structured investment approach.[5] At the market level, venture capitalists systematically examine the potential size of the market, competition, customer adoption, and technology to evaluate an investment opportunity's attractiveness and risks. At the firm level, they scrutinize the management team's quality and experience, the team's proposed strategy, and the deal terms. Once venture capitalists make an investment decision, they attempt to improve the outcomes of and add value to their portfolio companies through appropriate governance structures and monitoring. An efficiently designed VC contract ensures that the VC-backed entrepreneur is adequately incentivized. If the entrepreneur performs as expected, they do well and the venture capitalist typically does not get involved. However, if the entrepreneur fails to meet the venture capitalist's expectations, the latter will usually take control over the firm (for details on VC contracts, see, for example, Kaplan and Strömberg (2003)).

---

5. Gompers et al. (2016) provide comprehensive survey evidence on how venture capitalists actually make decisions. Based on 885 individual responses representing 681 different VC firms, the authors address a broad range of issues, including deal sourcing; deal selection; company valuation; contract design; monitoring and investor involvement in portfolio companies; exits; VC firm structure and the relationship between VC funds and their LPs.

An efficiently designed VC contract will allow for the staged infusion of capital. A potent control mechanism, staged capital infusion keeps the entrepreneur on a "tight leash" and reduces potential losses from bad decisions. This process allows venture capitalists to increase the duration of funding and reduce the frequency of reevaluation as the company becomes better established (Gompers and Lerner, 2001b). Consistent with this process, individual financing rounds are commonly classified as Round A, Round B, Round C, and so on.

Furthermore, VC transactions are usually syndicated, with the originating VC firm bringing in other VC investors to share in the investment and oversight. This syndication process has important advantages for the firm, enabling it to diversify and thus reduce the risk in any individual investment, improving the due diligence process by letting the VC firm gather additional opinions on investment opportunities (Gompers and Lerner, 2001a), and affirming the network sharing effect. Participation in a syndicated transaction is generally based on close relationships between VC firms, and as Hochberg et al. (2007) find, being well positioned in the VC network is a major factor in an investor's access to successful entrepreneurs and hence their fund performance.

Importantly, venture capitalists are not only investors backing entrepreneurial startups with capital but also act as mentors, adding value by assisting the entrepreneur with strategy, hiring other executives, and introducing management to potential customers and other partners.[6] Thus, venture capitalists generally maintain a close relationship with their portfolio companies by frequently visiting and talking to company management. Investing in startups has therefore been a regional (if not local) business. Sørenson and Stuart (2001) find that VC investments in the United States tend to be within a 500-mile radius, with portfolio companies usually clustering around leading research universities. In the United States, the most prominent examples are Silicon Valley in California, Route 128 in the Boston area, and the Research Triangle in North Carolina.

The rigorous investment process explains why only a fraction of startups receive VC funding. In the United States, roughly 600,000 new businesses (that employ others) are started each year. Between 2001 and 2015, only around 1200 businesses, or 0.2% of all startups in a given year, received their first round of funding from a VC firm (NVCA, 2016). During this period, total VC investing in the United States, including follow-on investments, averaged around $31 billion per year, or around 0.21% of GDP. However, while very few companies receive VC funding, a remarkably large fraction of the startups that eventually go public are funded with VC (Kaplan and Lerner, 2010). In fact, almost 60% of U.S. tech startups that went public in the 2000s were VC-backed (Ritter, 2016).[7]

---

6. Hellmann and Puri (2002), Kaplan and Strömberg (2004), Lerner (1995), and Gompers et al. (2016) discuss different aspects of how venture capitalists add value

7. Babina et al. (2016) find that a successful IPO has a significant effect on employee departures to startups. This effect is explained by the positive shock to employee wealth with stock grants, allowing them to better tolerate the risks associated with joining a startup. In this sense, VC funding could have an even more profound impact on entrepreneurship than usually assumed.

Investment returns vary widely among portfolio companies held by VC partnerships. Similarly, returns are highly dispersed across VC funds.[8] This dispersion of returns in VC is persistent (Harris et al., 2014; Brown et al., 2015), implying that some VC firms achieve consistently outstanding returns for their investors through a combination of superior deal sourcing, due diligence, and mentoring compared with their peers. Venture capitalists' investment decisions have an important signaling function for venture lenders who provide working capital or fund other capital expenses.[9] As Talmor et al. (2017) argue, venture lenders rely to varying degrees on VC firms' reputations, essentially piggybacking on their stringent due diligence approach and their deep postinvestment involvement. Based on a detailed dataset of transaction documents, they find a statistically significant inverse correlation between the reputation of VC firms and the credit charges VC-backed companies pay. Furthermore, they show that backing by a more reputable VC firm tends to shorten the time between equity rounds and loan issuance.

Venture capital has been subject to pronounced investment cycles. In the tech boom in the late 1990s, VC investing in the United States reached more than 1% of GDP (Fig. 8.1). However, as the tech bubble burst and the NASDAQ index fell by more than 75% from its peak in March 2000, VC investing slowed substantially and remained relatively shallow for more than a decade. More recently, however, VC investing has regained momentum driven by nontraditional investors such as mutual funds, hedge funds, and SWFs, which have provided substantial amounts of later-stage financing for nonpublic tech companies, such as Uber, Airbnb, and Palantir Technologies, whose valuations have exceeded $10 billion.[10]

A key factor behind the entry of nontraditional investors into VC investing has been the rising bar for IPOs in the posttech bubble era. When Apple went public in 1980, the company raised around $100 million. When Microsoft went public in 1986, investors acquired shares worth $65 million. Today, however, tech companies tend to wait considerably longer before they decide to go public. For instance, when Facebook went public in May 2012, it already had 845 million active users, and with an offering price set at $38 per share the company was valued at $108 billion. In its first four years as a public company, Facebook's market capitalization almost tripled to around $320 billion.

---

8. An investor who consistently committed capital to the upper-quartile VC fund in the U.S. between 1981 and 2014 would have enjoyed an average internal rate of return per vintage year of almost 24% on a capital-unweighted basis, nearly 20 percentage points higher than an investor who had picked the lower-quartile fund in each vintage year as reported by Cambridge Associates. Valuations as of September 30, 2016. Funds raised after 2014 are too young to provide meaningful return indications at the time of writing.

9. Venture lending is a type of debt financing provided to venture-backed companies by specialized banks or non-bank lenders most of which raise capital through closed-end funds. Venture lending is a relatively new phenomenon in the world of debt financing, with its roots going back to the 1980s, when it was introduced as an extension of equipment leasing (Talmor and Vasvari, 2017).

10. According to Pitchbook (2016b), unicorn deal value has accounted for around one quarter of total U.S. venture activity between mid-2014 and mid-2016.

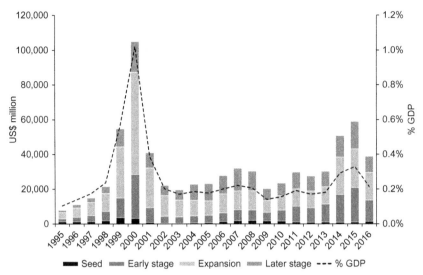

FIG. 8.1 U.S. VC investments, $M, and % of GDP. Note: Nominal GDP for 2016 based on IMF estimate. *(Source: Authors' calculations, based on data from National Venture Capital Association, 2016. Yearbook. http://nvca.org/research/stats-studies/ and International Monetary Fund, 2017. World Economic Outlook. April. Washington, DC: International Monetary Fund.)*

Facebook's success has attracted considerable investor interest in new business models whose option value could be high. An example is tech firms that fall into what has been labeled the "sharing economy," a market-based model of collaborative consumption facilitated through community-based online services.[11] Companies that exemplify this model are Uber and Airbnb, whose valuations were estimated at $62 billion and $27 billion, respectively, as of July 2016.[12] While the act of sharing between acquaintances is not new (especially in the context of giving someone a ride or hosting a guest) in the sharing economy these services are now provided to strangers for money (Sundararajan, 2016). Given the novelty of this approach, standard valuation practices may not fully capture these companies' growth potential. While the valuations of Uber, Airbnb, and similar companies are thus subject to substantial uncertainty, a number of traditional public investors such as mutual funds have decided to

---

11. Alternative terms used to describe this phenomenon include "crowd-based capitalism," "collaborative economy," peer economy," and "on-demand economy." All these terms attempt to describe a model whose key characteristics are: (1) a market-based system that enables the exchange of goods and the emergence of new services; (2) the supply of capital and labor from decentralized crowds of individuals; (3) the creation of new opportunities for everything, from assets and skills to time and money; (4) the disappearance of clear lines between the personal and the professional, with the supply of services often commercializing and scaling peer-to-peer activities; and (5) the blurring of the difference between fully-employed and casual labor.

12. TechCrunch, http://techcrunch.com/unicorn-leaderboard/. Accessed May 9, 2016.

invest in their option value by participating in pre-IPO funding rounds. In that sense, the large funding rounds for some companies in recent years could be considered as quasi-IPOs, with individual transactions having different financials, investors, and risk profiles from classic VC investments.[13]

8.2 INDUSTRY FOCUS AND THE ROLE OF VENTURE CAPITAL IN FOSTERING INNOVATION

Venture capital funds typically focus on funding tech startups in two broad industry groups—(1) information technology (IT) and (2) medical/health/life science. Investments in startups operating in these areas accounted for 88% of all VC deals in the United States in 2015, although these sectors represented less than 20% of U.S. GDP. While the majority of venture capitalists follow a specialist investment approach, some generalist firms fund startups in a range of different industries (Gompers et al., 2009). Apart from backing tech startups in IT and the medical, health, and life science sectors, a small share (12% in 2015) of VC is invested in entrepreneurial firms that are classified as "nonhigh technology" companies (NVCA, 2016). Unlike the majority of companies that are VC-backed, these startups are usually involved neither in developing cutting-edge technologies nor in bringing high-tech products to market. That does not mean that these companies are not innovative, however. What attracts venture capitalists' interest instead are their innovative corporate strategies, business models, and management practices that could allow these companies to achieve rapid growth (examples include FedEx Corp., Starbucks Corp., and Whole Foods Market Inc. (Gompers and Lerner, 2001b; Gompers et al., 2016)). As Bloom et al. (2015) argue, good management may be perceived as comparable to technology. In fact, they find that in a large sample of companies operating in 30 countries differences in management practices explain about one-quarter of cross-country productivity differences.

Startups in the IT sector have absorbed three to four times more VC funding that those operating in biotech-related sectors. There are multiple reasons for the dominance of the IT sector in VC funding. To begin with, there are substantially more startups in IT, paralleling the emergence of new technologies and their applications in areas such as mobile Internet, cloud technology, the Internet of Things, verifiable digital identity, digital payments, and fintech. Furthermore, the pay-off period tends to be considerably longer in the medical,

---

13. In this context, it is important to note that mutual funds and other non-traditional investors have usually invested in later-stage rounds. According to information reported by Pitchbook (2016b), only VC firms have backed today's U.S. unicorns at the angel and seed stage and in series A fundraisings. The earliest round in which non-traditional investors have participated were series B fundraisings. However, the majority of unicorn investments by mutual funds, hedge funds and SWFs have involved even later founding rounds. Examining mutual fund investments in unicorns, Chernenko et al. (2017) find that these investors appear to have weaker cash flow rights and to be less involved in terms of corporate governance.

health, and life science sectors. As Lo and Pisano (2016) argue, the traditional VC/entrepreneurial model, which has worked well in a wide range of technology settings such as software, computer, and the Internet, is not appropriate to deal with the costs, risks, and slow repayment of science-based industries. In biotechnology, as the authors point out, the journey from basic scientific discovery to a fully approved drug can span 10 to 20 years, significantly exceeding the typical investment period of VC funds. Additionally, the U.S. Food and Drug Administration finally approves only around 10% of drugs being developed, and the success rate in important therapeutic categories such as oncology is even lower (Hay et al., 2014).

Internet-related investments have led the investment cycles in the late 1990s and in the 2010s. At the peak of the former, almost 80% of all VC investments in the U.S. funded Internet-related startups. In the more recent cycle, this ratio approached 70%, both in value and number of VC-backed companies (Fig. 8.2). Many of the unicorns that received VC funding are consumer-Internet startups including Uber, Airbnb, Pinterest, Spotify Ltd., Lyft Inc., Vice Media LLC, Houzz Inc., and Instacart Inc. Generally, their services have a direct and immediate connection with consumers that offers extremely rapid feedback on whether investments are likely to pay off.

Does VC funding spur innovation? A priori, one would think so, given venture capitalists' focus on high-tech companies in the IT and medical, health, and life science sectors. Furthermore, VC frees innovators from the concerns of raising capital (Gompers and Lerner, 2001a) and may positively affect industrial R&D by facilitating the diffusion of technical knowledge or increasing access to

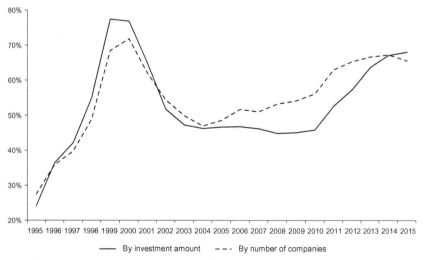

FIG. 8.2 U.S.: Share of Internet-related VC investments, by investment amount and number of companies. *(Source: National Venture Capital Association, 2016. Yearbook. http://nvca.org/research/stats-studies/.)*

potential risk capital (Gonzalez-Uribe, 2013). On the other hand, to the extent that venture capitalists are simply focused on funding existing innovation and bringing it to commercial markets, the rate of innovation itself could be unaffected by VC funding (Gompers and Lerner, 2001a, p. 74). While VC-funded companies are pure innovators in the sense that their business models are entirely predicated on commercializing new products or know-how (Bhidé, 2008), they do not normally engage in high-level research of the type conducted in labs or R&D centers. Rather, as Bhidé (2008, p.25) finds, their innovations combine or extend high-level know-how and products. Even if individual startups focus on R&D-intensive high-level innovations, the need to maintain access to continuous funding may push them to exert more effort on the development part of R&D relative to research, thus curtailing innovation (Gonzalez-Uribe, 2013).

The relatively few empirical studies that examine the nexus between VC funding and innovation provide a mixed picture. Kortum and Lerner (2000) performed the first detailed investigation, focusing on 20 industries in the U.S. manufacturing sector over the period from 1965 to 1992. Controlling for R&D spending, they found that venture disbursements are associated with a significant increase in patenting, which is used as a proxy for innovation. Finding an empirical association between VC funding and innovation does not prove causality, of course, but additional tests using instrumental variable regressions and replacing patenting with the patent-R&D ratio show that VC did spur innovation during that period.[14] Overall, Kortum and Lerner's results are robust to different measures of venture activity, subsamples of industries and representations of the relationship between patenting, R&D, and venture capital. Their findings are statistically significant and indicate an economically material effect of VC: while VC accounted for less than 3% of corporate R&D during the sample period, the authors conclude that this form of entrepreneurial finance may have been responsible for as much as 15% of U.S. industrial innovations.

But how significant are these innovations? VC-backed firms may simply patent more of their innovations in an effort to attract more capital or because they fear expropriation of their ideas by these investors. Examining a sample of 530 VC-backed and non-VC-backed companies, Kortum and Lerner (2000) find that the former do patent more. At the same time, however, their patents were more frequently cited in other patent applications and more aggressively litigated.

Gompers and Lerner (2001b) attribute VC funding's positive impact on innovation to three factors—(1) the more efficient screening process in the VC

---

14. Conceivably, the causality could run in the opposite direction, with innovations and new entrepreneurial opportunities inducing more VC funding. To investigate this possibility, Kortum and Lerner examined the impact of a major exogenous event that took place in 1979—the clarification of the "Prudent Man Clause" of the U.S. Department of Labor's Employee Retirement Income Security Act, which allowed U.S. public pension plans to invest in venture capital. This important policy shift led to a sharp increase in the amount of capital committed to the VC industry and was independent of the arrival of entrepreneurial opportunities.

industry; (2) the advice that venture firms provide to entrepreneurs as well as the postinvestment monitoring and control; and (3) the staging of investments. In their view, these factors explain why VC funding has a significantly larger impact on innovation than corporate R&D.

Kortum and Lerner's findings have not remained undisputed, however. Focusing on the U.S. manufacturing industry, Hirukawa and Ueda (2008) use both total factor productivity and patent counts as measures of innovation. They find that total factor productivity growth is often positively and significantly related with future VC investment, suggesting that the arrival of a new technology increases demand for VC rather than VC spurring the innovation.

In contrast to Hirukawa and Ueda (2008), Gonzalez-Uribe's (2013) research supports Kortum and Lerner's (2000) finding that the scale of companies' innovative activity significantly increases after VC funding. However, using firm-level data, Gonzalez-Uribe (2013) differs from Kortum and Lerner (2000) in that this study finds that VC is associated with a decrease in the quality and novelty of VC-backed companies' research output. Including company-fixed effects to control for the heterogeneity across companies, Gonzalez-Uribe (2013) found a statistically significant decline in patent citations after venture funding. This could suggest that the patents filed by VC-backed companies correspond to more marginal inventions, a result that appears consistent with Hellmann and Puri (2002) who found that VC is associated with a significant reduction in the time to bring a product to market.

Finally, Bernstein et al. (2016) focus on the role of venture capitalists in promoting innovation within portfolio companies. Even if VC-backed startups are more likely to be innovative than other entrepreneurial firms, it is not clear whether this is due to the selection of particularly innovative firms ("screening" or "selection effect") as investment targets or because the venture capitalists' on-site involvement allows portfolio companies to become more innovative ("monitoring" or "treatment effect").[15] In other words, would a startup be equally innovative if it had received funding but no mentoring?

If differences in outcomes for VC-backed companies are driven purely by selection, postinvestment involvement of VCs should have no effect. In a novel approach, Bernstein et al. (2016) look at the introduction of new airline routes that reduce the travel time between VC firms and their existing portfolio companies. New airline routes should translate into better portfolio company performance by reducing monitoring costs for VCs. This is precisely what the authors find. More specifically, they show that the reductions in travel time lead to an increase in the number of patents and the number of citations per patent of the portfolio company, as well as an increase in the likelihood of an IPO or acquisition. Overall, their results suggest that VC involvement does matter—beyond the provision of financial resources.

---

15. This important question will also play a role in the Chapter 9 where we focus on the role of corporate venturing and its impact on innovation in portfolio companies.

In Europe there is comparatively little available evidence. The few studies that exist generally find a limited impact of VC on innovation. Some studies report that European venture capitalists tend to invest in already innovative firms rather than fostering new innovations, suggesting that the selection effect dominates the treatment effect (Engel and Keilbach, 2007, for Germany; Caselli et al., 2009, for Italy). In a cross-country study using a panel of 21 European economies and 10 manufacturing industries covering the period from 1991 to 2005, Popov and Roosenboom (2012) found that contrary to Kortum and Lerner's (2000) results for the U.S. manufacturing sector, a euro invested by a VC firm has less impact on innovation than a euro spent on corporate R&D. However, this finding requires careful interpretation. Rather than proving VC has a weak impact on innovation, Popov and Roosenboom's result could reflect the more challenging regulatory environment in which Europe's VC industry operates. Their study also found that VC is relatively more successful in fostering innovation in countries with lower barriers to entry, less stringent labor regulations, more human capital, and a tax system that better attracts risk capital.

Unfortunately, there is too little history of VC investing in emerging economies to examine its impact on innovation. However, an increasing number of governments have established programs to create a VC market and hence foster innovation and economic growth. We shall return to this issue in Chapter 11.

8.3   EXPORTING THE VC MODEL: THE EMERGENCE OF VC HOTBEDS IN CHINA AND INDIA

As discussed earlier, one of the key characteristics of the VC model are the close ties between venture capitalists and entrepreneurs. While VC funding of startups has typically been a regional, if not local, business within geographically confined areas, Kogut et al. (2007) showed that VC clusters in the United States have emerged interactively. Analyzing almost 160,000 VC transactions between 1960 and 2005, they found that VC firms balance preserving ties to trusted partners against forming new ties to identify new investments through regional and sectoral diversification. Diversification into new geographies and sectors leads to forming ties with new VC firms, resulting in an increasingly integrated national market. The decision to diversify beyond a VC's original network is generally driven by the success rate of VC-backed investments in a new area (Cornelius, 2011).

Expanding across national borders is generally motivated by similar considerations. While this strategy may enhance investment opportunities, it also brings additional challenges for venture capitalists, which may help explain why the export of the VC model and the global integration of the VC market have been relatively slow. Outside the United States, VC industries emerged much later, which made it difficult for U.S. VC firms to form relationships abroad and widen their networks internationally. VC firms that spearheaded the globalization process usually chose to open foreign offices to interact more closely with potential entrepreneurs. These offices have often served as nuclei for new networks in the host countries. At the same time, the challenge of creating appropriate contractual structures required a predictable legal system ensuring contract enforceability.

In searching for new investment opportunities outside of the United States, U.S. VC firms initially focused on advanced economies in Europe. U.S. venture capitalists first ventured into Europe in the early 1980s, and the 1990s tech boom provided additional impetus to source attractive investment opportunities abroad. Although U.S. VC funds investing in Europe helped build an indigenous VC industry there, the European VC market has never reached the scale of the U.S. market.[16] Between 2010 and 2015, European startups attracted not even one-fifth of the venture capital invested in U.S. companies during this period. In most European economies, VC investment-to-GDP ratios have not exceeded 0.05%, and even in the United Kingdom and Finland, Europe's two most active VC markets, the ratio has been far lower than in the United States.

Exporting the VC model to Israel has been more successful. While Israel's VC industry also emerged in the mid-1980s, this form of entrepreneurial finance assumed a significantly more important role in fostering innovation and fueling Israel's economic growth than it did in Europe. With a close symbiosis between innovative entrepreneurs, venture capitalists, universities, the military, and a government providing substantial support for R&D, Israel today resembles Silicon Valley more than any other economy (Senor and Singer, 2011). Around 70 VC firms are headquartered in Israel or have offices there, including some of the world's most highly respected U.S. venture capitalists. In addition, more than 200 foreign funds without local offices have invested in Israeli startups, helping transform the economy into a global VC hotbed.

In the mid-1990s, there was a broad global consensus that the private sector had to be the primary catalyst for growth and development, rather than the state. At the time, many emerging economies were demonstrating encouraging progress. For this private sector strategy to succeed, the huge demand for investment capital had to be satisfied. With the financial sector still underdeveloped in most emerging markets and the financial needs of many companies exceeding what "friends and family" were able to provide, private equity looked like the logical choice (Leeds and Sunderland, 2003). At the same time, U.S. private equity and VC funds saw a large inflow of capital as they showed strong returns. Thus, several VC firms looked at opportunities in new markets that were technologically less advanced but had the potential to achieve rapid economic growth.

A key concern for foreign VC firms venturing into emerging markets has been the legal protection of their investments. Lerner and Schoar (2005) found that in structuring deals in low-enforcement countries, venture capitalists have often relied on equity and board control as opposed to convertible preferred

---

16. For details, see Cornelius (2011, p. 142). Lerner et al. (2012) provide an interesting case study about Accel Partners' venturing into Europe.

stock with covenants, a more common form in high-enforcement countries. At the same time, foreign VC firms have put significantly more emphasis on implicit relationships. Such relationships played a particular role in syndicated transactions with local venture capitalists in countries where an indigenous VC industry had already emerged (Allen and Song, 2003).

Despite this interest, the first wave of VC investing in emerging markets proved short-lived; investors were disappointed in the returns. In part, the lower-than-expected returns reflected a series of macroeconomic shocks, including the Asian Financial Crisis in 1997–98; the Russian debt default in 1998; the Brazilian balance of payment crisis in 1999; and the collapse of the Argentine currency board in 2002. Other factors contributing to the underperformance were structural, especially the poor quality of information underpinning investment decisions; underdeveloped legal systems; and the limited capacity of domestic capital markets to offer a reasonable prospect of exit through an IPO (Leeds and Sunderland, 2003).

Between the late 1990s and the mid-2000s, VC investing in emerging markets essentially disappeared. Since then, however, venture capitalists have shown renewed interest as emerging markets have become the world economy's growth engine, accounting for a rising share of global output. In 2014–15, venture capitalists deployed $81 billion in emerging markets, substantially more than the total amount of VC invested in startups in advanced economies outside the United States. As a result of this growth in VC, emerging markets absorbed more than one-quarter of global VC investing in these two years (Fig. 8.3).

The substantial rise in VC funding in emerging economies in 2014–16 was almost entirely due to higher investments in China and India, which have

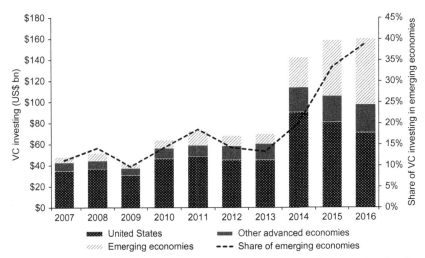

FIG. 8.3 Global VC investing by economic region. *(Source: Authors' calculations, based on data from Venture One, Dealogic, Pitchbook, and Preqin.)*

developed into global VC hotbeds. While VC funding of startups in Brazil, Russia, and several other emerging economies also rose during this period, the increase in investments outside of China and India was significantly more moderate. Chinese and Indian entrepreneurial firms absorbed around 95% of all VC investments in emerging markets in 2014–16 (Fig. 8.4). As a result, their economies are substantially more deeply penetrated than their peers at a similar stage in their development process (Fig. 8.5). In fact, Finland, Singapore, the United States, and Israel, which are classified by the Global Competitiveness Report (GCR) as innovation-driven economies, are the only countries that are similarly deeply or even more deeply penetrated than China and India.

In both economies, a vibrant VC industry has emerged, benefiting from the dynamic interplay between foreign (mainly U.S.) venture capitalists seeking investment opportunities outside their home markets and the emergence of an indigenous VC industry. A key aspect of this cross-fertilization has been deal syndication involving domestic and foreign venture capitalists. In China, there are more than 400 VC firms providing entrepreneurial finance to startups. In India's considerably smaller economy, young companies can seek funding from more than 200 VC firms. Several of the top U.S. venture capitalists who backed some of today's largest U.S. companies have opened offices in China and India and are among the most active investors. More recently, increasing amounts of VC funding have been provided by nontraditional investors, such as SWFs, hedge funds, and mutual funds, arguably for reasons that are similar to those in the United States. In addition, several Asian tech companies, such as Alibaba, Didi Chuxing, Flipkart, Snapdeal, and Tencent, have implemented in-house VC programs and become active investors in new startups as well.

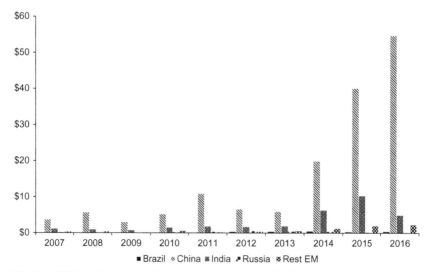

FIG. 8.4 VC investing in emerging markets by major countries ($B). *(Source: Authors' calculations, based on data from Venture Source, Dealogic, and Preqin. Accessed May 2, 2017.)*

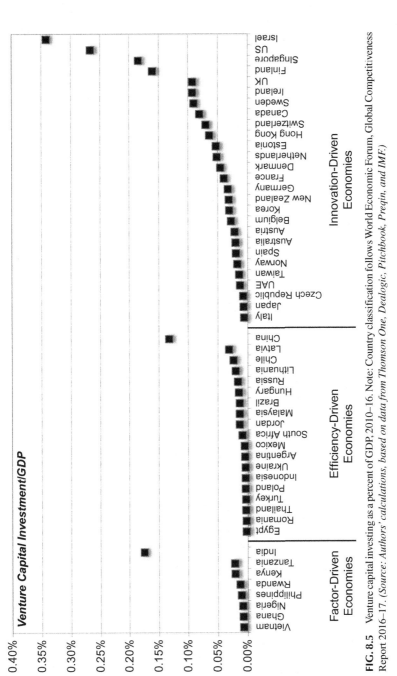

FIG. 8.5 Venture capital investing as a percent of GDP, 2010–16. Note: Country classification follows World Economic Forum, Global Competitiveness Report 2016–17. (*Source: Authors' calculations, based on data from Thomson One, Dealogic, Pitchbook, Preqin, and IMF.*)

8.4   E-COMMERCE AND THE ROLE OF THE INTERNET

What explains venture capitalists' huge interest in Chinese and Indian startups? Why have these companies been much more successful in attracting risk capital than their peers in Brazil and Russia as well as in other emerging markets? And why have China and India become even more VC-penetrated than the majority of advanced innovation-driven economies?

The literature suggests a variety of factors that may help explain cross-country differences in VC investing. Lerner et al. (2009) tested these hypotheses in a large cross section of countries. Their results were consistent with the arguments of Black and Gilson (1998) and the findings of Jeng and Wells (2000): functioning local financial markets for VC investments are important, as they provide an exit route for VC investors via IPOs. Further, Lerner, Sørensen, and Strömberg found that minority shareholder rights are important for VC (as well as growth equity) deals. This finding is consistent with the exit story, in the sense that for new minority shareholders to buy stock in an IPO, it is critical that their rights are adequately protected. However, in contrast to what might be expected, the authors find little evidence for the hypothesis that barriers to entrepreneurship undermine VC investments.

It may seem counter-intuitive that barriers to entrepreneurship have little impact on VC activity. After all, VC is generally considered to be a particularly appropriate form of entrepreneurial finance. Could it be that such barriers are incorrectly measured? In their estimations, Lerner et al. (2009) employed a measure that has become standard in similar analyses, namely the number of procedures required to start a business, which is computed by the World Bank in its "Doing Business" database. More specifically, this variable reflects all procedures that are officially required for an entrepreneur to start up and formally operate an industrial or commercial business. However, the emphasis here is on "official" and as Hallward-Driemeier and Pritchett (2015) argue, there may be a gap between rules and deals, or between de jure legal and regulatory requirements and the de facto application of such requirements.

A better measure might therefore be the actual rate of startups in a country. We are especially interested in those startups that were created by "transformational" entrepreneurs, in the sense that the companies survived for a prolonged period of time and have hired employees. There are two standard sources we employ: the Global Entrepreneurship Monitor (GEM) and the World Bank Employment Surveys.

The GEM reports a variable labeled "new business ownership rate." New businesses are defined as those managed by their owners, and which are paying wages and have existed for up to 42 months.[17] The variable, which is available for 70 advanced and emerging economies, is expressed as a percentage of individuals aged 18–64 who have created a new business relative to a country's

---

17. Companies that are older than 42 months are considered established businesses.

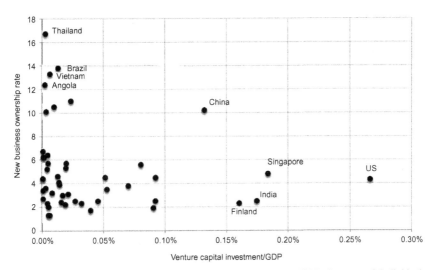

FIG. 8.6 New business ownership rate versus VC investments/GDP. Percent of individuals aged 18–64 engaged in entrepreneurial activity relative to total working age population. *(Source: Global Entrepreneurship Monitor 2016. Data for VC Investments from Capital IQ, Thomson One, Dealogic, and Preqin. GDP data from IMF (WEO Database April 2017).)*

total working age population. However, as Fig. 8.6 shows there is virtually no relationship between startups and VC investments. For instance, while India has a relatively low rate of entrepreneurship, it has one of the highest VC penetration rates. Conversely, Thailand, Vietnam, and Brazil appear significantly more entrepreneurial but have received much less VC relative to the size of their respective economies.

This finding may seem surprising as our variable refers to "transformational" entrepreneurs who have been in the business for an extended period of time and have already reached sufficient momentum to employ others. However, we obtain qualitatively similar results when we employ data from the World Bank Enterprise Surveys, which report "new business density" for a large sample of countries. This variable is defined as the number of newly created limited liability corporations per 1000 working age population. Overall, these results confirm that VC is only appropriate for a small number of startups, namely those that produce innovative goods and services and implement new business models that have the potential to disrupt incumbent firms.

China and India are clear outliers in the sense that their startups have received substantially more VC funding than the functioning of their financial markets, the protection of minority shareholder rights, and the quality of their business environment would suggest. Overall, the 2017 edition of the World Bank's Doing Business Report ranks China 78th out of 190 economies in terms of the "Ease of Doing Business." There are several emerging markets at a similar stage in their economic development which have attracted far less VC relative to the size of their economies despite easier business conditions, including, for example, Russia (40th), Mexico (47th), Chile (57th), Turkey (69th), and South Africa (74th). Furthermore, it is difficult to explain the huge increase in VC investing in China in recent years by the relatively moderate improvement in the country's ranking by 11 positions between 2010 and 2017.

Similar apparent inconsistencies apply to India, whose economy was ranked 130th on the "Ease of Doing Business" index in 2017, a small improvement by six places since 2010. While entrepreneurs in several countries at similar economic stages of development enjoy a relatively better business environment than in India (e.g., Vietnam (82nd), Indonesia (91st), Kenya (92nd), and the Philippines (99th)), their access to VC funding is generally significantly more difficult. Asked: "In your country, how easy is it for startup entrepreneurs with innovative but risky projects to obtain equity funding?" respondents to the World Economic Forum (WEF)'s Executive Opinion Survey in 2016–17 viewed VC access by Indian entrepreneurs as far easier than in most other countries, including the majority of economies that are far more advanced in their development process. Ranked 9th out of 138 countries in the WEF's Global Competitiveness Report 2016–17, India's VC market was even more vibrant than China's (ranked 14th).

So what explains the recent VC boom in China and India? One possible answer could lie in the countries' innovation potential that attracts venture capitalists. As Michael Moritz, one of Silicon Valley's most well-known venture capitalists, has recently opined: "Few markets are as ferociously competitive as the technology business in China. People there simply work a lot harder. And when you ally that with talent, creativity and a hunger to succeed, it's a formidable concoction. In China these days, there are probably four Silicon Valleys. In the U.S., there's one."[18] Moritz's view is supported by China's high ranking on the Global Innovation Index (GII). Ranked 11th on the innovation output sub-index in the 2017 edition, China's position is superior to several advanced economies, including those of Canada, France, Japan, and Italy. India's success in attracting VC is more difficult to explain. Its economy's innovation potential is considered to be significantly less than China's, and India's 58th position on the innovation output subindex puts it significantly behind China as well. However, India's ranking is relatively high in light of the country's stage of development, indicating that Indian entrepreneurs have been able to punch above their weight in terms of attracting VC funding.

In order to understand China's and India's roles as new global VC hotbeds, it is important to look at the industries in which VC-funded startups operate. The experience of unicorns is particularly revealing, as these companies have been a major driver behind the recent surge in VC investing in the two countries. According to Tech Crunch, there were 62 VC-backed unicorns in China

---

18. https://www.sequoiacap.com/people/michael-moritz/. Accessed May 5, 2016.

TABLE 8.1 Unicorns in China, India, and the United States: Percent distribution by sector (as of March 15, 2017).

	China & India		U.S.	
	Value	Number	Value	Number
E-commerce	27%	25%	4%	7%
Consumer Internet	8%	20%	34%	15%
Entertainment	3%	7%	3%	4%
Financial Services	32%	14%	8%	9%
Healthcare	2%	4%	5%	8%
Software	1%	6%	25%	29%
Hardware	16%	4%	3%	5%
Transportation	5%	10%	–	–
Real Estate	3%	6%	6%	3%
Other	3%	4%	12%	20%

Note: Tech Crunch reports 72 Chinese and Indian unicorns as of May 1, 2017. Individual unicorns in China and India and their valuations are listed in the appendix. In the United States, there were 117 unicorns as of this date.
Source: Authors' calculations based on data from Tech Crunch; accessed May 1, 2017.

and 10 in India as of May 2017 (Table 8.1 and Appendix). These companies were privately valued at $333 billion, around 17% higher than Alibaba's market capitalization of May 1, 2017. While some companies were still in their early stages and had received only one or two rounds of VC funding, much of the recent surge of VC investments involved later-stage financing of startups in follow-on rounds, frequently with the participation of nontraditional investors. Virtually all of these companies run Internet-related businesses, with e-commerce and consumer Internet-related activities representing the two dominant sectors.

Almost two-thirds of the Chinese and Indian unicorns focus on e-commerce and consumer-Internet-related services, with financial services adding another 14%. This concentration is substantially greater than the sectoral distribution in the United States, where companies operating in e-commerce and the consumer Internet account for only 22% of all unicorns as of May 1, 2017. There are several reasons why the recent VC boom in China and India has been driven primarily by investments in these areas. First, a significant number of VC-backed companies are variations of earlier startups in the United States whose business models have already shown their potential. While Baidu Inc., a Chinese version of Google, and Alibaba, a Chinese variant of eBay and Amazon, already went public, the majority of today's unicorns in China and India follow models that were invented in the United States. For example, China's Didi Chuxing offers a broad range of mobile technology-based transportation options, including taxi hailing and private car hailing, resembling Uber and Lyft in the U.S. India's version of such services is Ola, which has become the most popular mobile application for taxi bookings. Flipkart, India's most valuable unicorn (as of May 2017), is the country's version of Amazon, which may not be surprising given that the company's founders worked there. Meanwhile, Dianping, (now Meituan-Dianping) one of China's most popular restaurant-review and group-buying services, resembles a mixture of Yelp and Groupon.

However, VC-backed companies in China and India are not simply clones of U.S. startups. Instead, their business models are adapted to local circumstances and in some cases have turned out to be more successful than the original. One recent example is that of Uber, which handed over its Chinese operations to Didi Chuxing in return for a 17.7% stake in the combined company's equity (but with only 5.9% of the voting rights). This agreement was preceded by years of losses for Uber, which had launched its ride-sharing services a full year before Didi. As reported in The Economist (August 6, 2016), Didi had an 80% estimated market share of the Chinese ride-hailing market in Q4 2015, compared with Uber's share of less than 10%.

Uber's lack of success in the Chinese market was blamed on a complex set of factors. The Economist maintained that Uber waited too long before switching from Google Maps, which do not work well in China, to a local service. Furthermore, unlike Uber's chauffeur-driven business model, Didi's growth strategy started with taxi-hailing, which helped the company win over taxi drivers and local politicians. Expanding its operating platform, it then added bus-hailing, car-pooling, and other inventive offerings. These services were integrated early on via WeChat (known as Weixin in China), a hugely popular messaging app. Uber, in contrast, is said to have been repeatedly blocked from WeChat, whose owner, Tencent, is an important investor in Didi. Thus, Uber offered a credit-card-based payment system although such cards are not widely used in mainland China. In India, Flipkart has modeled its basic business model on Amazon but customized it for the local market to reflect regulatory and consumer requirements; see Chapter 6 for further information.

E-commerce and consumer Internet-related services are dominant for another reason. These services give immediate connection with consumers and venture capitalists can easily gauge whether their investments will pay off; compared with other sectors, investments in e-commerce and consumer Internet-related services generally offer a faster path to value realization.

Third, China and India are the world's two most populous nations. China's economy remains a major growth engine, despite slowing in recent years during the transition from an export- and investment-oriented growth model toward a consumption-driven one. At the same time, India's economy has expanded rapidly, and in both countries a growing middle class shows substantial demand for consumer goods and services. What's more, India boasts the world's biggest population of millennials (defined as those born between the early 1980s and 2000).

Finally, both countries have seen a rapid proliferation of the Internet and mobile phones. In China, more than 50% of the population is estimated to have used the Internet in 2015, up from 34% in 2010. In India, the share of Internet users increased to 26% from 7.5% during this period (Fig. 8.7). Given China's and India's population growth, the two countries added 253 million and 179 million Internet users, respectively, in just six years. The adoption of mobile phones has been similarly rapid. In 2015, around 1.292 billion mobile telephone subscriptions were registered in China, almost 450 million more than in 2010. In India, the number of subscriptions rose by more than 250 million during this period to more than one billion, or 77% of the population (Fig. 8.8), with a growing share of subscribers using a smartphone (McKinsey Global Institute, 2014). In 2015, VC investing amounted to around $58 per Internet user in China, a threefold increase from 2007 (Fig. 8.9). In India, the investment volume amounted to $31, a very moderate rise during this nine-year period.

The number of Internet and mobile phone users is expected to continue this rapid upward trajectory over the next decade or so. According to McKinsey Global Institute (2014), the number of mobile Internet users in India could reach 900 million by 2025, a 15-fold increase from its 2014 level. At the same time, the share of small- and medium-sized enterprises with an Internet presence could increase fivefold, reaching a penetration rate of 50% or more. As these companies enhance their visibility and increase their customer base, a substantially larger number of them are likely to use cloud technologies.

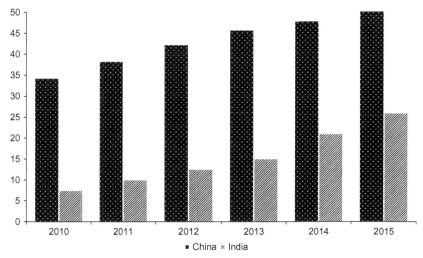

FIG. 8.7 Internet users in % of population. *(Source: International Telecommunications Union (ITC).)*

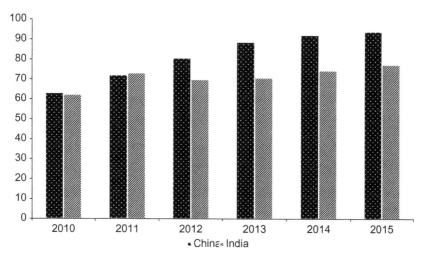

FIG. 8.8 Mobile telephone subscriptions per 100 inhabitants. *(Source: International Telecommunications Union (ITC).)*

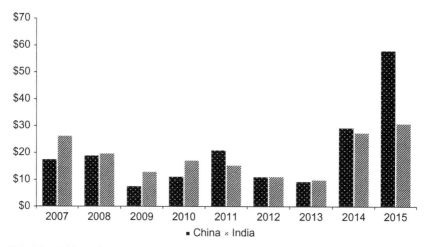

FIG. 8.9 VC investing per Internet user. *(Source: Authors' calculations, based on data from the International Telecommunications Union (ITC); Thomson One, Dealogic, and Preqin.)*

The impact of these enabling technologies could extend far beyond retailing, even effecting financial development. Given that e-commerce companies have access to online-sales data and therefore are in a privileged position to help lenders judge credit risk, they may help ease access to credit, a significant impediment for small businesses. For instance, India's Snapdeal announced in early 2016 that the State Bank of India would approve loans of up to $37,000 instantly if it was satisfied with the data that Snapdeal provided on the borrowers (The Economist, 2016a,b). Similar arrangements exist between lenders and other e-commerce companies. *E*-commerce companies can efficiently lure businesses to their sites by easing access to credit due to their business model, in which sellers pay commissions and shipping fees.

Firms that offer a broad range of services attract more shoppers. Since credit cards are less common in India, Flipkart offers the option of payment (cash) on delivery, or c.o.d. Alipay, owned by Alibaba and run by Ant Financial (Table A8.1), has more than 400 million escrow accounts. These accounts help overcome mistrust between buyers and sellers by allowing Alipay to hold on to customers' money until they have received their goods. Paytm, an Indian e-commerce shopping website, owned by One97 Communications (see Table A8.1), provides digital wallets. In early 2016, it had around 120 million accounts, nearly six times the number of credit cards in India. Amazon India has decided to follow a similar model by acquiring an online-payments service.

China is the world's biggest e-commerce market today, and the majority of its e-commerce companies are backed by venture capital. India's e-commerce market is still substantially smaller but is expected to continue growing rapidly over the next decade. The growth potential in both economies is likely to attract substantial investments from venture capitalists. While e-commerce and consumer Internet-related services are expected to absorb the lion's share of VC funding, in order to fully unleash their innovation capabilities both countries will require huge investments in a wide range of areas of science- and engineering-based industries.

8.5 THE NEXT FRONTIER

The increase in VC investing in emerging markets in recent years has outpaced economic growth by a significant margin. As a result, penetration rates have risen across the board. In Emerging Asia, excluding China and India, VC investments relative to the region's GDP increased at a compound annual growth rate (CAGR) of 35% between 2007 and 2016. In Latin America, VC investments to GDP rose at a CAGR of 32%. The sectoral focus of VC investments is similar to those in China and India, as exemplified by the few existing and emerging unicorns in these economies (Table A8.2).

Although few foreign VC firms have opened offices in these countries, several have invested in syndicated transactions alongside domestic venture capitalists. The rationale is similar to funding startups in China and India—the provision of entrepreneurial finance for companies that adopt business models with a proven track record in consumer-facing industries with rapid path to value realization. The rapid proliferation of the Internet and the use of mobile phones have fueled startups that attract venture capitalists, just as in China and India.

One obvious candidate is Brazil, a country that has attracted considerably less VC than its size would suggest. Although Brazil's economy is larger than India's and its per capita income is significantly higher than that of India or

China, the number of VC investments in recent years has been a fraction of that in the two Asian giants. While macroeconomic challenges like high real interest rates and foreign exchange rate volatility as well as political factors have probably contributed to investors' wariness,[19] there are some signs that suggest that VC could become a more important source of entrepreneurial finance in Brazil.

For starters, Brazil is more deeply Internet-penetrated than India and China. However, Brazilian startups received only around $4 per Internet user in 2015, compared with $31 and $58 per Internet user in India and China, respectively. The sectoral focus of VC transactions in Brazil has been similar to deals in India and China, concentrating on e-commerce, e-marketing, mobile apps, and fintech. Although the leading Silicon Valley firms have yet to set up shop in Brazil, some of them have already invested in Brazilian startups in cross-border transactions. Brazil's Nubank, a financial services firm that aspires to become a unicorn (Table A8.2), is one example. Originally backed by Sequoia Capital, Nubank provides a digital credit card and aims to take customers away from Brazil's highly profitable banks. Another example is PeixeUrbano. Copying Groupon's business model, the company is an online platform that enables users to find and book deals on restaurants, air tickets, beauty services, and more. Benchmark Capital, a leading Silicon Valley-based VC firm, provided early-stage funding along with others. Similarly, international CVC investors have been involved in several recent VC transactions in Brazil, an issue we return to in Chapter 9. Finally, there are a growing number of local Brazilian VC firms. As these firms gain more experience, they may serve as local partners for international VCs, increasing deal flow.

Turning to Emerging Asia, Vietnam has attracted considerable attention among local and foreign venture capitalists as a new-frontier market. The reasons are similar to those in China and India—a growing population, increasing prosperity, and a rapidly rising number of people using mobile phones and the Internet. Considered to be around 10 years behind China, prominent tech leaders have begun investing in well-positioned Vietnamese startups, especially in fast-growing digital media and entertainment sites. For instance, Tencent bought a stake in social networking and gaming startup VNG Corp., eBay bought into Vietnamese auction portal Peacesoft Solutions Corp. and Germany-based Rebate Networks formed a local social commerce site with NhomMua. vn (Fannin, 2012, p. 78).

Finally, VC has gained traction in Africa, as mobile and Internet penetration has increased. In Nigeria, the most populous African country, 77% of the population uses a mobile phone, while 43% have access to the Internet (ITC; data refer to 2015). In Kenya, penetration rates are similar, while South Africans and Egyptians have on average more than one mobile phone per person. Not surprisingly, e-commerce is increasingly popular, opening up new investment

---

19. One frequently articulated concern relates to the lack of a clear demarcation between a GP and the LPs in a fund. To the extent that LPs like pension funds are allowed to sit on the investment committee, there is concern that this could cause the fund to stray from value maximization.

opportunities. A good example is Jumia, a Cairo-based online retailer specializing in electronics, fashion, home appliances, and children's items especially for the Nigerian market. Founded in 2012 by three individuals, it now employs more than 1000 people. The firm received $211 million in three funding rounds and was valued at $555 million at the end of 2016 (Table A8.2).

Bright and Hruby (2015) argue that the term 'e-commerce' should be replaced by 'm-commerce' in Africa, as so much of local e-commerce comes from activity on mobile devices. In fact, African countries are leading the world in the development and use of mobile money. Probably the most significant innovation has been M-Pesa, a mobile phone-based money transfer and financing service that was launched in 2007 by Vodafone Group L.L.C., for Safaricom, Ltd. and Vodacom Group, Ltd., the largest mobile network operators in Kenya and Tanzania (see Chapter 7). Since its launch, M-Pesa has expanded to several other African countries, as well as Emerging Asia and Emerging Europe. Today, there are tens of millions of users who are able to transfer money to other users, pay bills, purchase goods and services, save, earn interest, and borrow, all from a basic mobile phone.

While M-Pesa has revolutionized financial services in emerging markets, there are substantial opportunities for Internet-driven growth and productivity in other sectors as well. The transformative potential of the Internet in Africa is particularly large in education, health, agriculture, government, and retail (McKinsey, 2013). Although retail may attract the greatest interest from venture capitalists, other sectors may also benefit from an emerging VC industry in Africa.

8.6   CONCLUSIONS

In this chapter, we have discussed the role of VC as a new form of entrepreneurial finance in emerging economies. In recent years, China and India have emerged as new global VC hotbeds, with indigenous and foreign VC firms providing more funding to entrepreneurial companies than in Europe, both in absolute terms and relative to the size of their economies. Much of this funding is backing startups in e-commerce and Internet-related services, resembling recent trends in the U.S. market, the cradle of venture capital. Many of these VC-backed companies are variations of earlier startups in the United States whose business models have already proved to be successful. Given the immediate connection with consumers, these industries allow venture capitalists to judge quickly whether their investments are likely to pay off, while offering a faster path to value realization. Meanwhile, the Internet and mobile phone penetration rates of both countries have increased rapidly in recent years, enabling the growing adoption of online retailing and Internet-based services.

Although VC investing in emerging markets has been concentrated on China and India, more recent VC funding of entrepreneurial startups has gained momentum in other economies. Access to the Internet and the use of mobile phones play a critical role, with some countries able to attract significantly more VC than their level of prosperity and innovation potential would seem to suggest. In these countries, like in China and India, the bulk of VC investments focus on retailing, and the next biggest impact appears to be on financial development itself. Many countries have put great emphasis on accelerating the digital transformation in order to unleash the Internet's huge transformative potential. These measures may prove more powerful than efforts to attract more VC through government-sponsored programs, an issue we return to in Chapter 11.

APPENDIX

TABLE A8.1 Chinese and Indian Unicorns (as of May 1, 2017)

Company	Post-Money Value ($B)	Founded	Country	Sector
Ant Financial (Alipay)	60.0	2004	China	Financial Services
Xiaomi	45.0	2010	China	Hardware
Didi Chuxing (Didi Kuaidi)	33.7	2012	China	E-commerce
Lufax	18.5	2011	China	Financial Services
Meituan.com	18.0	2010	China	E-commerce
Flipcart	10.0	2007	India	E-commerce
Koubei.com	8.0	2004	China	Local Business
DJI	8.0	2006	China	Hardware
ZhongAn	8.0	2013	China	Financial Services
Cainiao Logistics	7.7	2013	China	Transportation
JD Finance	7.1	1998	China	Financial Services
Snapdeal	6.5	2010	India	E-commerce
Home Link (Lianjia)	5.7	2001	China	Real Estate
One97 Communications	4.8	2000	India	Financial Services
Ola	3.5	2010	India	Consumer Internet
LeSports	3.3	2014	China	Entertainment
Ele.me	3.0	2008	China	Consumer Internet
Best Logistics Technologies	3.0	2007	China	Transportation

TABLE A8.1 Chinese and Indian Unicorns (as of May 1, 2017)—cont'd

Company	Post-Money Value ($B)	Founded	Country	Sector
Wanda e-commerce	3.0	2014	China	E-commerce
Miaopai	3.0	...	China	Consumer Internet
Kuaishou	3.0	2011	China	Consumer Internet
VANCL	3.0	2007	China	E-commerce
Ping An Good Doctor	3.0	2014	China	Healthcare
Meizu	3.0	2003	China	Entertainment
NIO	2.8	2014	China	Transportation
Bona Film Group	2.2	1999	China	Entertainment
Huimin	2.2	2012	China	E-commerce
Taobao Movie	2.1	2014	China	Entertainment
Firstp2p	2.0	2013	China	Financial Services
Trendy International Group	2.0	1999	China	Consumer Internet
Beijing Weiying Technology	2.0	2014	China	E-commerce
Lakala	1.6	2005	China	Financial Services
WeDoctor (Guahao)	1.5	2010	China	Healthcare
Qudian	1.5	2014	China	Financial Services
Hike	1.4	2012	India	Consumer Internet
Koudai	1.4	2010	China	E-commerce
58 Daojia	1.3	2014	China	Consumer Internet
Tujia	1.3	2011	China	Consumer Internet
Go-Jek	1.3	2010	India	Transportation
Dada	1.3	2014	China	Consumer Internet
Lashou.com	1.2	2010	China	E-commerce
Sogu	1.2	2004	China	Software
ShopClues	1.1	2011	India	E-commerce
Le Cloud	1.1	2004	China	Enterprise

Continued

TABLE A8.1 Chinese and Indian Unicorns (as of May 1, 2017)—cont'd

Company	Post-Money Value ($B)	Founded	Country	Sector
Zomato	1.1	2008	India	Consumer Internet
Wifi Skeleton Key	1.1	2012	China	Software
Paytm E-commerce	1.1	2016	India	E-commerce
Quikr	1.0	2008	India	Consumer Internet
UrWork	1.0	2015	China	Real Estate
Zhihu	1.0	2011	China	Consumer Internet
U51.com	1.0	2012	China	Financial Services
Panshi	1.0	2003	China	Advertising
Rong 360	1.0	2011	China	Financial Services
Ofo	1.0	2014	China	Transportation
Beibei	1.0	2014	China	E-commerce
Iwjw	1.0	2014	China	Real Estate
Fanli	1.0	2006	China	E-commerce
Huochebang	1.0	2008	China	Transportation
Mofang Gongyu	1.0	2010	China	Real Estate
Jiuxian.com	1.0	2009	China	E-commerce
Mia.com	1.0	2011	China	E-commerce
Lamabang	1.0	2013	China	Consumer Internet
iCarbonX	1.0	2015	China	Healthcare
Guazi.com	1.0	2014	China	Transportation
Womei	1.0	2008	China	E-commerce
Wandoujia	1.0	2009	China	Software
Ubtech	1.0	2012	China	Hardware
APUS Group	1.0	2014	China	Software
Douyu TV	1.0	2013	China	Entertainment
Yidao Yongche	1.0	2010	China	Consumer Internet
Xiahongshu	1.0	2013	China	E-commerce
Mogujie	1.0	2010	China	E-commerce

Source: Techcrunch, http://techcrunch.com/unicorn-leaderboard/. Accessed May 1, 2017

TABLE A8.2 Existing and Emerging Unicorns in Emerging Markets Outside of China and India (as of May 2017)

Company	Post-Money Value (US$bn)	Founded	Country	Sector
Avito.ru	1.8	2008	Russia	*E*-commerce
Lazada Group	2.5	2012	Malaysia	E-commerce
Decolar.com	1.4	1999	Brazil	Travel
Africa Internet Group	1.0	2012	Nigeria	Incubator
Careem	1.0	2012	UAE	Transportation
Sonq.com	1.0	2005	UAE	*E*-commerce
Avast Software	1.0	1988	Czech Republic	Software
Ozon.ru	0.7	1998	Russia	*E*-commerce
Hotel Urbano	0.6	2011	Brazil	Travel
Jumia	0.6	2012	Egypt	E-commerce
Nubank	0.5	2013	Brazil	Financial Services

Source: Techcrunch, http://techcrunch.com/unicorn-leaderboard/. Accessed May 1, 2017.

REFERENCES

Allen, F., Song, W.-L., 2003. Venture capital and corporate governance. In: Cornelius, P., Kogut, B. (Eds.), Corporate Governance and Capital Flows in a Global Economy. Oxford University Press, New York, pp. 133–156.

Babina, T., Quimet, P., Zarutskie, R., 2016. Going entrepreneurial? IPOs and new firm creation. Unpublished Working Paper. Federal Reserve Board. https://www.aeaweb.org/conference/2017/preliminary/paper/BiYBAstD. Accessed January 25, 2017.

Bernstein, S., Giround, X., Townsend, R.R., 2016. The impact of venture capital monitoring. J. Financ. 71 (4), 1591–1622.

Bhidé, A., 2008. The Venturesome Economy: How Innovation Sustains Prosperity in a more Connected World. Princeton University Press, Princeton and Oxford.

Black, B.S., Gilson, R.J., 1998. Venture capital and the structure of capital markets: banks versus stock markets. J. Financ. Econ. 47, 243–277.

Bloom, N., Sadun, R., Van Reenen, J., 2015. Management as a technology? Unpublished Working Paper. Harvard Business School. http://www.Hbs.Edu/faculty/publication%20Files/16-133_57bdc522-5c6f-4f26-8155-0f67b4de4f76.Pdf. Accessed April 18, 2017.

Bright, J., Hruby, A., 2015. The Next Africa: An Emerging Continent Becomes a Global Powerhouse. St. Martin's Press, New York.

Brown, G.W., Harris, R.S., Jenkinson, T., Kaplan, S.N., Robinson, D.T., 2015. What do different commercial data sets tell us about private equity performance? Unpublished Working Paper. University of North Carolina. http://uncipc.org/wp-content/uploads/2015/12/PERC_datasets_12-5-2015.pdf. Accessed April 18, 2017.

Caselli, S., Stefano, G., Perrini, F., 2009. Are venture capitalists a catalyst for innovation? Europ. Finan. Manage. 15, 92–111.

Chernenko, S., Lerner, J., Zeng, Y., 2017. Mutual funds as venture capitalists? Evidence from unicorns. Unpublished Working Paper. Harvard Business School. https://1da89346-a-62cb3a1a-ssites.googlegroups.com/site/yaozengwebsite/MutualFunds_VCs_Unicorns.pdf?attachauth=ANoY7cpCL ih9V9tbnO3JeNbz6pwgxHWJvs7E9wbJewriHBZ_CzE2NMWWAMx2OXuEldhfoYfI3il-nT-Tl08T39LgWpFDZN8vxm0zjBgcC1WIX6MeML0dIr3Qov5xSc3Ks-PDpPLSi-3haerVOiReIJv-BRFPgFQkDUYrDpmzq7D1hsWFoWJqLLnB9S8ZHFngxA-JJb4qZQGFGfNyBJjCbX3k5UH-GhuY-RqKsDasFenw2OccWMk_ha2aNo%3D&attredirects=0.

Cornelius, P., 2011. International Investments in Private Equity. Asset Allocation, Markets, and Industry Structure. Academic Press, Burlington, MA.

Engel, D., Keilbach, M., 2007. Firms-level implications of early-stage venture capital investment – an empirical investigation. J. Empir. Financ. 14, 150–167.

Fannin, R., 2012. Start-Up Asia: Top Strategies for Cashing in on Asia's Innovation Boom. Wiley, Hoboken, NJ.

Gompers, P., Gornall, W., Kaplan, S.N., Strebulaev, I.A., 2016. How do venture capitalists make decisions? Unpublished working paper. Harvard Business School. http://www.Hbs.Edu/faculty/pages/item.Aspx?Num=51659. Accessed 5/1/2017

Gompers, P., Kovner, A., Lerner, J., 2009. Specialization and success: evidence from venture capital. J. Econ. Manag. Strateg. 18 (3), 817–844.

Gompers, P., Lerner, J., 2001a. The Money of Invention. Harvard Business School Press, Boston.

Gompers, P., Lerner, J., 2001b. The venture capital revolution. J. Econ. Perspect. 15 (2), 145–168.

Gonzalez-Uribe, J., 2013. Venture capital and innovative activity (with Bruce Kogut and Morten Sorensen). Chapter 1 of venture capital and innovation. Submitted in partial fulfillment of the requirements for the degree of doctor of philosophy under the executive committee of the Graduate School of Arts and Sciences. Columbia University.

Gornall, W., Strebulaev, I.A., 2015. The economic impact of venture capital: evidence from public companies. Unpublished Working Paper. Stanford University. https://www.Gsb.Stanford.Edu/Faculty-research/working-papers/economic-impact-venture-capital-evidence-public-companies. Accessed 5/1/2017.

Hallward-Driemeier, M., Pritchett, L., 2015. How business is done in the developing world: deals versus rules. J. Econ. Perspect. 29 (3), 121–140.

Haltiwanger, J., Jarmin, R., Kulick, R., Miranda, J., 2016. High Growth Young Firms: Contribution to Job, Output and Productivity Growth. National Bureau of Economic Research. http://www.nber.org/chapters/c13492.pdf. Accessed January 25, 2017.

Harris, R., Jenkinson, T., Kaplan, S.N., Stucke, R., 2014. Has persistence persisted in private equity? Evidence from buyout and venture capital funds. Unpublished Working Paper. Said Business School. Oxford University. https://papers.ssrn.com/sol3/papers.cfm?abstract_id=2304808. Accessed May 18, 2017.

Hay, M., Thomas, D.W., Craighead, J.L., Economides, C., Rosenthal, J., 2014. Clinical development success rates for investigational drugs. Nat. Biotechnol. 32 (1), 40–51.

Hellmann, T., Puri, M., 2002. Venture capital and the professionalization of start-up firms: empirical evidence. J. Financ. 57, 169–197.

Hirukawa, M., Ueda, M., 2008. Venture capital and innovation: which is first? Pac. Econ. Rev. 16 (4), 421–465.

Hochberg, Y.V., Ljungqvist, A., Lu, Y., 2007. Whom you know matters: venture capital networks and investment performance. J. Financ. 62, 251–301.

International Monetary Fund, 2017. World Economic Outlook. April. International Monetary Fund, Washington, DC.

Jeng, L., Wells, P., 2000. The determinants of venture capital funding: evidence across countries. J. Corp. Finan. 6, 241–289.

Kaplan, S.N., Lerner, J., 2010. It ain't broke: the past, present, and future of venture capital. J. Appl. Corp. Financ. 22 (2), 1–12.

Kaplan, S.N., Strömberg, P., 2003. Financial contracting theory meets the real world: evidence from venture capital contracts. Rev. Econ. Stud. 70, 281–315.

Kaplan, S.N., Strömberg, P., 2004. Characteristics, contracts, and actions: evidence from venture capitalist analyses. J. Financ. 59, 2177–2210.

Kogut, B., Urso, P., Walker, G., 2007. Emergent properties of a new financial market: American venture capital syndication from 1960 to 2005. Manag. Sci. 53 (7), 1181–1198.

Kortum, S., Lerner, J., 2000. Assessing the contribution of venture capital to innovation. RAND J. Econ. 31 (4), 674–692.

Leeds, R., Sunderland, J., 2003. Private equity in emerging markets: rethinking the approach. J. Appl. Corp. Financ. 15 (4), 111–119.

Lerner, J., 1995. Venture capitalists and the oversight of private firms. J. Financ. 50, 4301–4318.

Lerner, J., Schoar, A., 2005. Does legal enforcement affect financial transactions? The contractional channel in private equity. Q. J. Econ. 120, 223–246.

Lerner, J., Sørensen, M., Strömberg, P., 2009. Does private equity create value globally? Working Papers. The Global Economic Impact of Private Equity Report. 2. World Economic Forum, Geneva.

Lo, A.W., Pisano, G.P., 2016. Lessons from Hollywood: a new approach to funding R&D. MIT Sloan Manag. Rev. 57 (2), 47–54.

McKinsey, 2013. Lions go digital: the internet's transformative potential in Africa. http://www.mckinsey.com/industries/high-tech/our-insights/lions-go-digital-the-internets-transformative-potential-in-africa. Accessed May 16, 2017.

McKinsey Global Institute, 2014. India's Technology Opportunity: Transforming Work. Empowering People. http://www.mckinsey.com/industries/high-tech/our-insights/indias-tech-opportunity-transforming-work-empowering-people. Accessed May 16, 2017.

National Venture Capital Association, 2016. Yearbook. http://nvca.org/research/stats-studies/.

Pitchbook, 2016. VC unicorn report.

Popov, A., Roosenboom, P., 2012. Venture capital and patented innovation: evidence from Europe. Econ. Policy 27 (71), 447–482.

Ritter, J., 2016. IPO database. https://site.warrington.ufl.edu/ritter/files/2016/01/IPOs2015Statistics.pdf.

Robb, A.M., Robinson, D.T., 2012. The capital structure decisions of new firms. Rev. Financ. Stud. 27 (1), 153–179.

Senor, D., Singer, S., 2011. Start-Up Nation. The Story of Israel's Economic Miracle. Twelve, New York.

Sequoia Capital, 2016. https://www.sequoiacap.com/people/michael-moritz/. Accessed May 5, 2016.

Sørenson, O., Stuart, T.E., 2001. Syndication networks and the spatial distribution of venture capital investments. Am. J. Sociol. 106, 1546–1588.

Sundararajan, A., 2016. The Sharing Economy: The end of Employment and the Rise of Crowd-Based Capitalism. MIT Press, Cambridge, MA.

Talmor, E., Lutz, E., Hesse, M., 2017. Venture capitalist reputation and the effect on venture lending contracts. Unpublished Working Paper. London Business School. https://www.London.Edu/Faculty-and-research/academic-research/t/the-effect-of-venture-capital-reputation-in-venture-lending-contrac#.WQdz4VhYpaQ. Accessed 5/1/2017

Talmor, E., Vasvari, F., 2017. International Private Equity, Second Edition. Wiley, Chichester.

TechCrunch.com, 2016. http://techcrunch.com/unicorn-leaderboard/. Accessed May 9, 2016.

The Economist, 2016a. Online retailing in India. The great race. March 5, 2016

The Economist, 2016b. Uber gives app. August 6, 2016

Chapter 9

Corporate Venture Capital

ACRONYMS

ARD	American Research and Development
CVC	corporate venture capital
ERISA	Employee Retirement Income Security Act
IPO	Initial Public Offering
IRR	internal rate of return
IT	Information Technology
IVC	independent venture capital
LP	Limited Partner
PARC	Xerox's Palo Alto Research Center
R&D	Research and Development
VC	Venture Capital

Entrepreneurial startups may have access not only to independent venture capital (IVC) funds but also to pools of corporate venture capital (CVC). As we will discuss in this chapter, many large and highly innovative U.S. companies run CVC programs. This diverse set includes, among others, Amgen, AT&T, Bloomberg, Chevron, Cisco Systems, eBay, Fidelity, Google, General Electric, General Motors, Hewlett-Packard, Intel, Lilly, Merck, and Pfizer, which fund new companies around the world. According to the National Venture Capital Association (2016), CVC in the United States averaged approximately $5 billion per year in 2013–15, accounting for about 12% of total VC investing. Many European companies have established similar CVC programs, including BASF, BAE Systems, Bertelsmann, BMW, BP, France Telecom, Shell, Siemens, and Unilever, to name just a few. More recently, a growing number of emerging market companies have followed their U.S. and European peers. As in advanced economies, most of these companies operate in high-tech sectors, and many of them were initially funded by VC themselves, including Alibaba, Baidu, Flipkart, Tencent, and Xiaomi.

Why do these large, successful companies provide funding for startups? Generally, a profit-seeking firm will invest in external knowledge to enhance its competitive advantage. This is the case if CVCs marginal innovative output is expected to be higher than that of internal research and development (R&D) (Dushnitsky and Lenox, 2005). However, the differential between the marginal innovative output of CVC and internal R&D may not be static. As Ma (2016)

Financing Entrepreneurship and Innovation in Emerging Markets.
https://doi.org/10.1016/B978-0-12-804025-6.00009-5

argues, firms searching for innovation use the knowledge in their portfolio companies to jumpstart internal R&D and terminate their CVC programs when the informational benefit diminishes.

Lerner (2013) identifies several reasons why CVC may achieve superior results than internal R&D alone. First, corporate venturing provides an inside look at new technological developments and a path to possible ownership or use of new ideas allowing companies to respond quickly to market transformations. Second, corporate venturing can serve as an intelligence-gathering initiative, helping a company identify emerging competitive threats. Third, by pooling its own capital with that of other venture capitalists, it is possible for a CVC program to magnify its impact, which can be particularly advantageous when technological uncertainty is high. Finally, corporations may use CVC as leverage to encourage technologies that rely on the parent company's platform.

Internal investments in innovative activities, including R&D, are generally less well suited to perform these functions. As Lerner (2013) explains, corporate R&D units tend to focus on a narrow range of projects and are not designed to identify disruptive advances that emerge outside the company. Furthermore, it requires substantial resources and may take far longer for a company to follow potentially transformative technological developments than implement a CVC program. These arguments are strengthened by research indicating that corporate R&D is often ineffective (Lerner, 2012). In a highly influential study, Jensen (1993) showed that R&D and net capital expenditures actually destroyed value in many American companies in the 1980s. Hall (1993) reported similar results, finding that a dollar of spending on R&D in the 1980s only enhanced market value a quarter as much as a dollar's investment in traditional assets.

Companies that possess corporate venturing programs generally view them as a strategic choice to complement internal R&D programs, aiming to better capture the value from waves of technology and innovation. Financial returns usually play a secondary role, which makes this form of entrepreneurial finance different from IVC funding. However, CVC comes with its own set of challenges, which depend on the specific organizational forms companies choose for their corporate venturing programs. In light of these challenges, new venturing tools have emerged over time, reflecting the specific needs and characteristics of different industries. As we shall see in this chapter, these different forms have important implications not only for the companies that provide CVC but also for the startups funded by these programs.

In the rest of this chapter, we first provide a brief history of corporate venturing and describe its different forms. We also present evidence about the volume of CVC. Next, we discuss organizational issues arising in the context of CVC programs. We then focus on the value CVC programs may provide to startups they fund and the degree to which these programs spur innovation. Finally, we look at the role of CVC in emerging economies, focusing specifically on cross-border funding by global companies and the emergence of domestic CVC programs.

9.1 THE SIZE AND EVOLUTION OF THE CVC MARKET

9.1.1 Market Size

Just like venture capital (VC) in general, CVC began in the United States. The first CVC funds emerged in the mid-1960s, around two decades after the establishment of American Research and Development (ARD), the first independent VC firm (Chapter 8). Encouraged by the success of these early funds, other companies followed suit. By the early 1970s, more than 25% of Fortune 500 firms had set up such programs (Gompers and Lerner, 2001a). Corporate venturing has gained momentum in the past 40 years. According to a recent study by the Boston Consulting Group (BCG, 2016), which focused on the 30 largest U.S. companies in seven industries,[1] 4 out of 10 had a CVC program in place in 2015. Focusing solely on the top 10 companies in each of the seven industries, 57% of the companies had such a program. The wider use of CVC programs among the largest companies mirrors the reported investment volume and the growing share of CVC in total VC investing. In 2015, U.S. CVC investments totaled almost $7.7 billion, or 13% of total U.S. VC. This was the third-largest volume and the third-highest share of CVC on record, after 2000 and 1999 (Fig. 9.1).

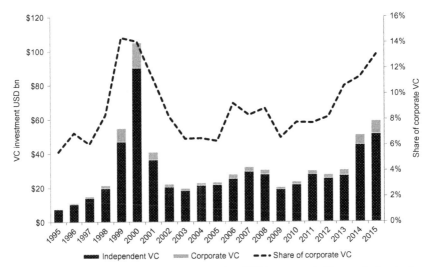

FIG. 9.1   U.S.: CVC investments ($B and share of total VC investments). *(Source: Authors' calculations, based on data from NVCA (2016).)*

---

1. The industries were automotive, chemical, consumer goods, financial services, media and publishing, technology, and telecommunications. The 30 largest companies in each of these industries are defined by their market capitalization.

Outside the United States, CVC has a shorter history and consistent activity data is harder to find. The varying definition of CVC has remained a challenge. While CVC is generally defined as the funding activity of specific, separately demarcated corporate venture arms, many corporations also make direct strategic investments in entrepreneurial firms. According to CB Insights, a VC and angel investing database, global corporate funding was almost as large as CVC funding between 2012 and the first half of 2016. Given that it is not always easy to clearly distinguish these two forms, CVC activity data must be interpreted with caution, especially in non-U.S. markets.

With this caveat in mind, it seems that non-U.S. CVC has followed a similar trajectory to CVC in the United States (Fig. 9.2). CVC has been particularly dynamic in China, amplifying IVC investments. Chinese startups absorbed almost $10 billion of CVC funds between 2012 and the first half of 2016, accounting for close to 43% of non-U.S. CVC during this period (nearly three times the share of the United Kingdom, the largest non-U.S. CVC market among advanced economies). In comparison, CVC has played a considerably smaller role in India where startups received only 6% of non-U.S. CVC. The CVC markets of other emerging markets are generally still embryonic, but some have recently shown increased activity. As in China and India, this process has been driven by foreign CVC investment, especially by venture arms of U.S. companies.

The growing amount of CVC investing around the world reflects more (and potentially larger) transactions backed by experienced CVC investors. In part, it also mirrors a significant increase in the number of corporations that provide VC to startups through their corporate venture arms. In the first quarter of 2012,

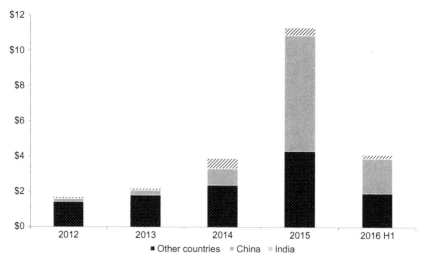

FIG. 9.2 Non-U.S.: CVC investments ($B). *(Source: Authors' calculations, based on data from CB Insights, The H1 2016 Corporate Venture Capital Report.)*

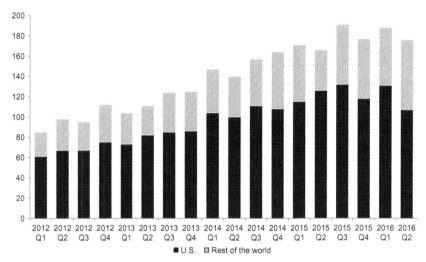

FIG. 9.3 Global venturing: Number of unique CVC investors. *(Source: Authors' calculations, based on data from CB Insights, The H1 2016 Corporate Venture Capital Report.)*

CB Insights counted 61 unique U.S. investors and 24 unique non-U.S. investors in VC deals around the globe. Four years later, these numbers more than doubled to 131 and 57, respectively (Fig. 9.3).

9.1.2   Corporate Venture Cycles

While the global CVC market has expanded substantially in recent decades, its growth has not been linear. In the United States, with the longest CVC history, we can identify several waves, which are closely linked to the different cycles in the overall VC market (Gompers and Lerner, 2001a). The first wave, which began in the second half of the 1960s, came to a halt in the early 1970s when the initial public offering (IPO) market dried up amid disappointing returns from small technology stocks. With this exit window largely shut, VC returns declined, undermining VC firms' fundraising efforts and prompting companies to scale back their CVC programs.

The VC market regained momentum in the early 1980s in response to the clarification of the "prudent-man" rule under the U.S. Department of Labor's Employee Retirement Income Security Act (ERISA), in essence allowing U.S. pension funds to invest in VC partnerships and other riskier asset classes. With capital commitments to such funds additionally fuelled by the lowering of capital-gains taxes and the reopening of the IPO window, corporate venturing also recovered meaningfully. However, the second wave of VC came to an abrupt halt when the stock market crashed in 1987, causing a substantial decline in IPO activity, discouraging new commitments to VC funds and triggering an even more dramatic adjustment in CVC programs.

The VC market remained relatively shallow until the mid-1990s when the Internet boom suddenly encouraged VC investing and fundraising, and with it, the revival of CVC programs. Corporate investors were once again attracted by the highly visible successes of VC-backed companies, this time especially in the telecommunications and Internet-related sectors. According to Cambridge Associates, the median VC fund raised in the United States in 1995 generated an internal rate of return (IRR) of almost 42% for its limited partners (LPs) (net of fees and carried interest), returning more than six times their invested capital. An LP who had invested in the upper-quartile fund (i.e., the 25th percentile of the return distribution of all funds raised in that vintage year) enjoyed an IRR of more than 80%.[2] However, some individual VC-backed companies generated even (significantly) higher returns. As institutional investors reallocated their portfolios to VC, commitments to IVC funds skyrocketed to more than $90 billion in 2000 from less than $8 billion in 1995 (Fig. 9.1). Corporate VC increased even faster, growing to almost $15 billion in 2000 with over 300 corporations investing in CVC from less than $500 million in 1995, nearly tripling their share of total VC. With over 300 corporations investing in CVC, their share in total VC investing almost tripled in the second half of the 1990s.

The substantial increase in CVC was not just a response to the surge in financial returns from the VC industry but also a reflection of a more profound reevaluation of the innovation process itself in many U.S. companies at that time. For many years, leading U.S. companies had maintained large corporate R&D laboratories that were judged on their production of patents and scientific papers. By that metric, many of these laboratories proved highly successful. Some of the most prominent examples are AT&T's Bell Labs (now known as Nokia Bell Labs), IBM Research, and Xerox Corp. In fact, no fewer than eight Nobel prizes were awarded to scientists for the work they completed at the Bell Labs, including such fundamental innovations as the transistor (Walter Brattain, John Bardeen, and William Shockley who received the Nobel Prize in 1956; for historical details see Isaacson, 2014).[3] IBMs researchers made several important scientific discoveries, especially in physics, and received six Nobel Prizes (in addition to many other prestigious awards). Xerox's Palo Alto Research Center (PARC), which was established to pave the way for the copier giant's entry into the computer industry, developed such ingenious and game-changing products as the Ethernet (the graphical user interface), the "mouse," and the laser printer. PARC's innovation capabilities culminated in 1973 with the first prototype of Alto, a very early personal computer (Gompers and Lerner, 1998).

However, while the Bell Labs and IBM Research are prime examples of the dominant role that had been given to the "R" in R&D, a growing number of companies started to look for alternative means to access new ideas,

---

2. Valuations, as of June 30, 2016. https://40926u2govf9kuqen1ndit018su-wpengine.netdna-ssl.com/wp-content/uploads/2016/11/Public-2016-Q2-USVC-Benchmark-Book.pdf.
3. In total, researchers who worked at Bell Labs received 14 Nobel Prizes.

putting more weight on the "D." The highly visible success of the VC industry influenced this shift, as CVC programs were seen as opportunities to capitalize on cooperative efforts involving, for instance, joint ventures, acquisitions, and university-based collaborations. Reflecting the shifting emphasis from research to development, in 1996 AT&T spun off Bell Laboratories, along with most of its equipment manufacturing business, into a new company named Lucent Technologies.[4] AT&T retained a small number of researchers who made up the staff of the newly created AT&T Labs. However, unlike the former Bell Labs, which focused on basic science, the new AT&T Labs were set up to support AT&T's continuous efforts to improve their network, services, and the customer experience.

In the late 1990s, a growing number of companies came to appreciate the game-changing implications of the Internet and e-commerce. As a result, many companies became interested in new forms of corporate venturing. At the same time, venture capitalists running IVC funds increasingly saw corporate investments as a potential strategic advantage (Gompers, 2002). While many had viewed corporate investors with considerable skepticism, VC firms increasingly saw important benefits from the knowledge and experience companies could provide. This shared interest led to a significant number of partnerships between venture capitalists and corporations, with the latter providing not only capital but also relevant expertise in identifying and mentoring entrepreneurial startups.

However, these happy times would prove short-lived. When the tech bubble burst, the NASDAQ lost 78% of its value between Mar. 2000 and Sep. 2002. With the IPO window shut and public valuations adjusted substantially downward, most VC funds incurred significant losses for their investors.[5] Investments in telecom startups proved particularly disastrous.[6] In light of such disappointing returns, many LPs sharply curtailed their commitments to VC funds. Whereas commitments to IVC partnerships had totaled more than $90 billion in 2000, VC funds raised just $18 billion from institutional investors in 2003. However, the decline in CVC was even more dramatic, with commitments in 2013 amounting to less than $1.3 billion, a 91% drop from their level in 2000. As a result of these changes, the share of CVC dropped by more than half to just 6% during this period.

---

4. Lucent Technologies was acquired by Alcatel in 2016. Nokia acquired Alcatel-Lucent in early 2016.

5. According to data from Cambridge Associates, the median funds raised in 1998–2000 reported negative IRRs of −0.26%, −2.86%, and −1.07%, respectively. While the upper-quartile funds in these vintage years generated IRRs in the mid-single digits, lower-quartile funds suffered losses of 6%–12%.

6. For instance, startups operating in telecom networks that received funding in 2000 are reported to have generated a negative gross IRR of almost 10%. For LPs, the loss was even more severe, taking into account management fees fund managers charge irrespective of the performance of their investments.

Researchers have posited that the sharp decline in VC returns may stem from the self-defeating dynamics of the VC industry, whose investment cycle consists of four stylized phases (Gompers and Lerner, 2000a). (1) In the first phase of the cycle, improving returns prompt investors to increase their exposure to VC as an asset class. In the second half of the 1990s CVC amplified this cyclical increase in LPs' commitments. (2) Given a finite universe of startups promising high returns commensurate with the risk investors take, too much capital chases too few deals, lowering average returns. (3) As return expectations are disappointed, investors reduce their VC exposure again. (4) In the final phase, where deals chase capital, returns become more attractive, sowing the seeds for the next cycle.

In 2012, the Ewing Marion Kauffman Foundation, a philanthropic organization aimed at fostering entrepreneurship and an important LP in many VC funds, presented a widely publicized report on its VC portfolio titled: "We Have Met the Enemy... And He is Us." In this report, the authors argued that the poor returns in the postbubble years were largely attributable to the substantial inflows to VC funds whose investments had hugely inflated valuations, leading to subsequent deflation of the bubble. The LP community generally shared this view, and for the next 10 years, most institutional investors remained skeptical as to whether VC funds could deliver attractive returns comparable with those in the 1990s.

As a result of this uncertainty, many LPs decided to stay on the sidelines and so did corporate investors. However, as less VC became available, this helped the VC market rebalance and achieve a new equilibrium between supply and demand: returns started improving. A rising number of VC-backed companies joined the unicorn club (see Chapter 8) and commitments to VC funds regained momentum, setting the stage for the fourth wave in VC investing. Unsurprisingly, CVC has helped fuel this cycle, as it did in previous waves, essentially doubling its share of total VC between 2009 and 2015.

9.2   ORGANIZATIONAL FORMS OF CORPORATE VENTURING

In complementing traditional R&D through corporate venturing, companies have chosen different organizational forms of CVC (Gompers, 2002). Some companies have established internal corporate venture groups to analyze VC opportunities and invest in startups. An important advantage for an entrepreneur seeking funding is that the sponsoring company may provide not only capital but may add substantial value thanks to its reputation, skills, and resources (including research scientists, sophisticated laboratories, and salespeople). However, while the sponsoring company may provide excellent in-depth mentoring in its area of expertise, the entrepreneur might forego the breadth of available resources they could have access to through other forms of VC. Additionally, some entrepreneurs may be particularly concerned about protecting their intellectual property and reluctant to receive CVC funding. This reluctance could ultimately undermine the effectiveness of internal corporate venture groups with insufficient deal flow.

As an alternative, other companies have set up external CVC funds as a separate entity outside the company. This structure has still not always been successful in dispelling entrepreneurs' concerns about the potential consequences of forming a close alliance with the company sponsoring the fund. Since investments by external funds are generally limited to startups that want to align themselves with the sponsoring company, their portfolios are usually as concentrated as the portfolios of internal VC funds. As a result, while the strategic insights outside the sponsoring company's direct area of expertise might be limited, the external CVC fund may be equally subject to substantial concentration risk.

Other CVC programs involve commitments to IVC funds, with the option to coinvest in entrepreneurial startups alongside these funds.[7] However, the GPs of these funds usually have little incentive to extend coinvestment invitations to early-stage startups. Instead, invitations are usually extended at a later stage at already elevated valuations, undermining financial returns. Also, as passive coinvestors in a fund, these companies have often found it difficult to achieve their strategic objectives, given the limited information flow from the portfolio companies funded by the IVCs to the LPs.

CVC funds have remained the dominant forms of corporate venturing, at least in terms of total invested capital, but many companies have employed additional tools to gain access to innovative ideas. Some corporations have formed strategic alliances with small, often startup research companies, a form that is particularly prevalent in the biotech industry. Unlike CVC, which provides firm-level capital for nascent companies, in a strategic alliance, corporations provide funding for particular projects. However, as Robinson and Stuart (2007) show, strategic alliance contracts share important commonalities with VC contracts. In addition to prescribing investment decisions in sequential stages as uncertainty diminishes to capture the associated option value, many alliances involve convertible preferred equity and sometimes contain antidilution provisions, warrants, and board seats.[8]

In recent years, accelerators and incubators have gained particular traction. Typically, accelerators and incubators do not venture alone, but form

---

7. Whether or not this form of corporate investing should be considered as CVC has remained controversial. Ma (2016) argues that commitments to an IVC fund where the corporation acts as an LP fall outside the definition of CVC. However, to the extent that corporate LPs act as co-investors, such investments should be treated as CVC, in our view.

8. Notwithstanding these similarities, Ozmel et al. (2013) find that raising firm-level capital from venture capitalists or project-level capital from strategic alliance partners differ significantly with regard to their implications for future funding and exits. As far as the latter is concerned, both VC and alliance funding increase the probability of a start-up to go public. However, while startups receiving VC are also more likely to be acquired, the link between acquisition probabilities and alliance activity is found to be less clear-cut.

partnerships with venturing operations from other corporations, or team up with an independent accelerator or incubator as we describe in Chapter 10. This allows them to gain access to a greater number of high-quality startups than they could reach on their own. By partnering with others, especially with professional accelerators and incubators, such as AngelPad, Techstars, or 500 Startups, they are able to tap into their partners' networks and connect with communities of entrepreneurs and researchers. Conversely, entrepreneurs usually prefer professional accelerators and incubators for the exposure to a broader range of companies and potentially a more diverse set of new ideas. In 2015, 44% of the top 30 companies in the seven industries covered in the aforementioned BCG study (2016) employed accelerators and incubators involving partnerships with others. As far as the top-10 companies in each of these industries are concerned, around two-thirds used this form of corporate venture. Excluding partnerships with others, the respective percentages were 29% and 39%. In 2010, accelerators and incubators had played hardly any role as a venturing tool, whether or not in partnership with other companies or professional facilitators.

While corporate accelerators and incubators focus on the specific needs of the sponsoring company, their structure follows programs that have been set up by venture capitalists (see Chapter 10). According to BCG (2016), 44% of the top-30 U.S. companies in seven industries (footnote 1 in this chapter) employed accelerators or incubators in 2015, a penetration that is broadly comparable with CVC programs. Of the 10 largest companies in these industries, two-thirds have used this form of corporate venturing.

While accelerators and incubators are the most common alternatives to CVC, some companies follow both approaches. Similarly, CVC programs are sometimes supplemented with innovation labs, which function as startups within a corporate setting. Innovation labs should not be confused with research laboratories (BCG, 2016). Typically, innovation labs are not in the R&D offices, and their projects usually do not involve the in-house R&D department. Instead, innovation labs bring together teams of in-house innovators who convene for short, intensive projects, with the aim of developing prototypes of new products and services that can be market-tested by the end of the project. Innovation labs are often motivated by the perceived existence of unmet needs, with participants taking their ideas from business units, customers, and the marketplace. In fact, it is not uncommon for customers to take part in innovation labs alongside firm employees. Of the 30 largest U.S. companies in each of the seven industries (identified in footnote 1 of this chapter), almost 20% employed this venturing tool in 2015. In 2010, only one in 20 companies had organized innovation labs. The penetration rate was even higher among the top-10 companies, with 41% of them having used innovation labs in 2015.

Which venturing tool or tools companies opt for depends, among other things, on their industries (BCG, 2016). Tech companies focusing on core-business innovation usually prefer CVC, sometimes combined with accelerators and incubators. Funding startups through internal or external CVC funds or through IVCs is regarded as the most effective tool in such fields as big-data analytics, cloud solutions, information technology (IT) security, and the Internet of Things. Similarly, telecom companies mostly use CVC on a stand-alone basis or in combination with accelerators and incubators. The same applies to media and publishing companies that search for innovative ideas in areas such as advertising technology, multiplatform distribution, and big-data analytics. Finally, CVC is the preferred venturing tool for chemical companies, investing in innovation in base chemicals, polymers, and specialty chemicals, as well as for pharmaceutical firms.

While venture capitalists have traditionally focused on funding tech startups in IT, telecoms, and life science (Chapter 8), companies in other industries often seek core-business innovation through other venturing tools. In the consumer goods industry, for example, it is much more common to employ accelerators, incubators, or a combination of both, and innovation labs. Automotive companies seeking innovation in areas such as connected cars or big data analytics more frequently use accelerators and incubators. The same is true for financial services companies, focusing on areas such as mobile payment systems, big-data analytics, and IT security.

9.3   HOW SUCCESSFUL IS CORPORATE VENTURING?

Measuring the success of CVC programs is challenging, because they may be motivated by different objectives. For some companies, the investment objective is largely, or even exclusively, financial. Chesbrough (2002) distinguishes two types of investments driven by return expectations. First, "emergent investments" in startups are defined as those that have tight links to the parent company's operating capabilities but that offer little to enhance its current strategy. Such investments may have an option-like strategic upside, in the sense that they may become strategically valuable if the business environment shifts or if the company's strategy changes. Second, in the case of "passive investments," the ventures are not connected to the parent company's own strategy and are only loosely linked to its operational capabilities. Passive investments provide little, if any, additional value for the portfolio company, beyond the financial resources the parent company provides.

By investing in startups, CVC investors expect to achieve a competitive advantage they would not be able to attain by internal R&D alone. Ma (2016) identifies a CVC life cycle that is consistent with the strategic role of CVC. More specifically, corporations tend to launch CVC programs in response to a decline in their internal innovation. Aiming to benefit from potential informational gains by connecting to highly innovative entrepreneurs, CVC programs focus on startups whose technologies can be adapted to the parent firms' needs. Corporations tend to terminate their CVC programs when the informational benefit diminishes.

In practice, strategically motivated CVC exists in two different forms. According to Chesbrough (2002), "driving investments" are investments with tight links between a startup and the parent company's operations. In this case, the VC arm plays a particularly critical role as the lynchpin between the parent company and the startup, ensuring the efficient flow of information to help the startup succeed while attaining the strategic goals of the parent company. Other CVC investments may lack tight links between the startup and parent but are undertaken to stimulate the development of the eco-system in which the parent company operates. Chesbrough (2002) calls this type of venturing "enabling investments."

While financially motivated CVC investments have a lot in common with IVC and can be judged on the basis of their returns, it is harder to assess whether a CVC program's strategic objectives have been met. There is considerable anecdotal evidence that CVC programs have helped their parent companies gain valuable insights in new technologies, allowing them to move faster, more flexibly, and more cheaply than traditional R&D. On the other hand, there is no shortage of anecdotes of spectacular failures leading companies to abandon their CVC programs, sometimes after a short while.[9] However, there is relatively little systematic evidence as to whether CVC financing enhances entrepreneurial firms' innovation productivity, and the degree to which parent companies enjoy an increase in their own innovation productivity.

To shed light on these questions, Gompers and Lerner (2001a) examined a sample of more than 32,000 investments into entrepreneurial firms in the United States between 1983 and 1994.[10] Of this sample, corporate venture investments represented around 6% of the total. To measure the success of CVC investments, they focused on the probability of a portfolio company's going public, a proxy that is commonly used in VC research. Employing this criterion, they found that 35% of the investments by corporate funds were in companies that went public by the end of the sample period. In contrast, only 31% of startups backed by IVCs went public during this period, which led Gompers and Lerner (2001) to conclude that corporate efforts were at least as successful as those funded by independent venture organizations. Importantly, their results were robust with regard to alternative success measures. Specifically, the difference

---

9. Lerner (2013) discusses two examples. A successful one is Lilly Ventures, which Eli Lilly & Co. launched in 2001. Through its CVC fund, the parent company engaged with a large number of cutting-edge biotech firms, helping the parent company to catch up with the genomics revolution that was transforming the pharmaceutical industry. A less successful example discussed by Lerner is Exxon Enterprises' venture capital effort. While the program started in 1964 as an internal effort to exploit new technologies in Exxon's corporate laboratories, it shifted to making minority investments in adjacent industries. A few years later, the program shifted course again, focusing on computing systems for office use. The initiative was abandoned in 1985, with the computer systems investments alone estimated to have generated a loss of $2 billion.
10. The number of rounds in the sample is significantly smaller (8506), implying that on average about four investors participated in each financing round.

persisted when they focused on firms that were acquired at a valuation at least three times that of the original investment, as opposed to firms that went public. Similarly, they obtained the same results when they controlled for a portfolio company's age and profitability at the time of the original investment, rejecting the possibility that their findings were driven by the concentration of CVC investments in later financing rounds.

Chemmanur et al. (2014) report results that are broadly consistent with those obtained by Gompers and Lerner. Focusing on the number of patents generated by venture-backed firms and the number of citations received by patent, they find that CVC-backed firms produced not only more patents but also patents of higher quality compared with IVC-backed startups. In principle, this finding could be attributed to CVCs' superior ability to identify and select entrepreneurial firms with higher innovation (selection effect), but the authors suggested that the outcome is more likely due to CVCs' superior ability to nurture innovation (treatment effect).

Focusing on CVC-backed biotechnology startups, Alvarez-Garrido and Dushnitsky (2016) find that these companies are more innovative than their independent VC-backed peers, as measured by the startups' scientific publication record and their patenting output. As the authors note, the superior innovation performance is not just due to CVCs selecting particularly innovative ventures but also reflects the CVCs' ability to leverage their corporate assets and nurture the investee companies. More specifically, this process entails preferential access to corporate advanced facilities, skilled R&D personnel and manufacturing and regulatory know-how, confirming the importance of the treatment effect found in other studies.

Corporate venturing's overall success rate masks important variations across individual CVC programs. To identify the underlying success factors, Gompers and Lerner (2000) classify investments based on whether there was a direct fit between one of the parent company's lines-of-business and the portfolio firm, whether there was an indirect relationship, or whether there was no apparent relationship at all. They find that CVC funds are more successful if the parent company's stated focus overlaps with the business of the VC-backed startup. More specifically, the authors show that entrepreneurial firms backed by CVC funds with well-aligned goals are more likely to go public, produce higher numbers of patents, and have better stock price performance compared with startups that are not linked with the company's objectives. At the same time, well-aligned goals make it more likely that the parent company will benefit from the flow of useful knowledge from the startup firms, facilitating the strategic objectives of its CVC program.

Apart from the alignment of goals across the CVC fund, the startups, and the parent company, there are several other factors determining the success of corporate venturing (Lerner, 2013). One important factor is the compensation of corporate venture professionals. Companies that run CVC programs can face a significant dilemma, as venture managers often expect to be compensated in a way that is comparable with what IVC fund managers earn. However, this level of compensation may be inconsistent with what comparably senior executives earn in other parts of the parent company. As Dushnitsky and Shapira (2010) show, compensation does matter. Treating venture investors like other managers can undermine a venture team's motivation, lead to a loss of talent, and makes it more difficult to achieve the parent company's long-term goals. While Dushnitsky and Shapira's research confirm the existence of a positive performance gap between CVC and IVC, they note that the difference is the largest when CVC personnel receive performance pay.

9.4 CORPORATE VENTURING IN EMERGING MARKETS

There is much less research on corporate venturing in emerging market economies and the role it plays in funding entrepreneurial startups and fostering innovation than in the United States. To help narrow this important gap, we employ a database assembled by Preqin, which focuses on transactions between 2012 and 2016. For this period, the database includes almost 59,000 deals worldwide, of which about 13,000 involve startups in emerging markets. For most of these transactions, Preqin provides information about the investee company, the stage of investment, the amount of funding per round, the total amount of capital, and the industry of the investee company. Since the database also identifies individual investors in each transaction, we are able to single out those deals that involved companies with CVC programs.

China and India account for the bulk of VC transactions in emerging economies. This is also true for deals involving corporate venturing. While CVC was involved in around 5.5% of venture capital deals in China between 2012 and 2016, in India this ratio was 8.6%. CVC played an even more active role in Brazil, whose overall VC market has remained less developed than those in China and India. In contrast, CVC in Russia has remained largely unknown, accounting for less than 1% of all VC deals during this period.

Focusing on China, it is important to note that domestic tech companies, such as Alibaba, Baidu, Tencent, and Xiaomi, have been particularly active as CVC investors. Fig. 9.4 depicts the sectoral investment focus of Alibaba's VC investments in China in 2012–16. During this period, Alibaba reportedly backed 54 entrepreneurial firms in 67 financing rounds. While Alibaba Capital Partners, the company's CVC arm, backed some of these ventures, others received financing from Alibaba itself on the basis of strategic investments. In many cases, Alibaba was the sole investor in individual rounds. In a significant number of transactions, other investors were also involved. Interestingly, Alibaba has funded startups at different stages of their life cycle. While some firms received seed or angel financing, in other cases, Alibaba has provided funding at later stages. Several of these startups have emerged as unicorns, notably Didi Chuxing, Ele.me, Meituan (later Meituan-Dianping), Wandoujia, and 58 Daojia Inc.

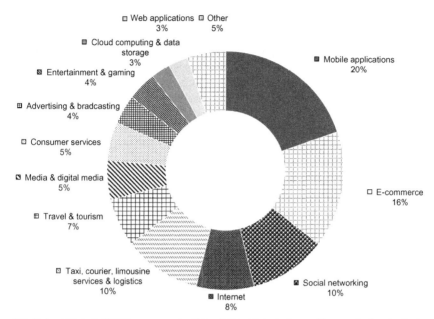

FIG. 9.4   Alibaba's CVC investments in China, 2012–16, by industry. *(Source: Authors' calculations, based on data from Preqin.)*

The bulk of Alibaba's CVC program has involved companies that operate in the same (e-commerce) or related industries (e.g., mobile applications, advertising, e-marketing, logistics, data storage). To the extent that previous research on CVC in the United States is applicable to Alibaba's case, this bodes well for the success of its strategic goals. In a nontrivial number of cases, Alibaba also funded startups where it is more difficult to identify a direct strategic fit between the parent company's major line of business and the portfolio company's. As in China, tech firms have been at the forefront of domestic corporate venturing in India, too. One example is Flipkart, India's largest unicorn.[11] While Flipkart has been involved in significantly fewer CVC deals than Alibaba,[12] it is important to note that the former is still valued at a fraction of Alibaba.[13] Flipkart's CVC investments have focused to an even greater extent on the parent company's major line of business. In fact, all of Flipkart's investments have at least indirectly been related to the company's core business, especially e-commerce, mobile and web applications, logistics software,

11. As of August 2016; based on post-money valuation. See Table 8.1 in the previous chapter. For details, see Chapter 4.
12. Between 2012 and 2016, Preqin reports 20 VC transactions in India that Flipkart was involved as an investor.
13. The latest available post-money value of Flipkart was $ 18 billion (Table 8.1) compared with Alibaba's market capitalization of around $300 billion (as of May 15, 2017).

and social networking. Furthermore, Flipkart has shown comparatively little interest in funding startups in their earlier stages.

While several other Indian tech firms (e.g., Ola, Snapdeal, and One97 Communications Ltd.) have also built CVC programs, these efforts have generally been confined to the domestic market. Outbound investments have remained limited. In contrast, inbound CVC has gained considerable momentum, with foreign CVC investors playing a significantly larger role than in China. These investors include several tech firms from China, among which Alibaba has been particularly active, backing both Snapdeal and One97 Communications, two of India's unicorns, as well as other startups. Other examples of Chinese investment in Indian startups include the activities of Baidu, Didi Chuxing, and Tencent. More recently, Alibaba and other Chinese tech firms have shown increased appetite for expanding outside Asia, notably Latin America and Central and Eastern Europe.

Many major U.S. tech firms, such as Amazon Inc., Cisco Systems Inc., eBay Inc., Google, Eli Lilly, Qualcomm Inc., and Intel Corp., have funded tech startups in emerging economies. According to CB Insights, Qualcomm, through their CVC arm Qualcomm Ventures, and Intel, through Intel Capital, have been particularly active. In fact, both firms have been involved in more VC transactions in India than domestic corporate venture capitalists. Intel invested 42% of their total emerging economy CVC in Indian startups from 2012 to 2016. This percentage was even higher than for China (Fig. 9.5). While Brazilian startups have absorbed another 11% of Intel's CVC program for emerging economies, other countries have played a very limited role.

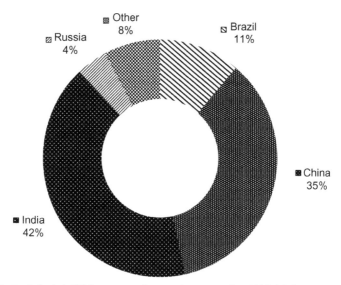

FIG. 9.5 Intel Capital: VC investments in emerging economies, 2012–16, by country. (*Source: Authors' calculations, based on data from Preqin.*)

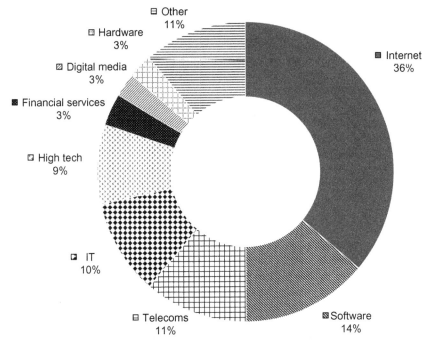

FIG. 9.6 Intel Capital: VC investments in emerging economies, 2012–16, by industry flimited their corporate venturing. *(Source: Authors' calculations, based on data from Preqin.)*

Many of Intel's CVC transactions in emerging economies fall into the category of "enabling investments," a strategy the semiconductor giant has pursued since the early 1990s (Fig. 9.6). As Chesbrough (2002) explains, this strategy is predicated on the idea that the company could benefit from nurturing start-ups making complementary products, with the demand for the complements potentially spurring increased demand for Intel's own products and services. However, not all of Intel's recent CVC investments in these economies are enabling. Some clearly are driving investments, including those in its own supply chain. Intel's sectoral focus differs across investee countries, for instance, in India it has concentrated on e-commerce, an industry that has played hardly any role for the company's investments in China.

Although the majority of foreign companies' CVC programs in India, China, and other emerging economies have focused on IT, pharmaceutical companies have become more active CVC investors, too. One example is Eli Lilly, whose Lilly Asia Ventures program has backed a significant number of biotech firms in Emerging Asia, concentrating on oncology, genetics, gene therapy, and medical diagnostics. Nor have foreign firms limited their corporate venturing in emerging economies to CVC. For example, Microsoft Ventures has established an accelerator program in Bangalore, India, focusing on areas such as smart cloud services, mobile applications, urban informatics and Big Data, the Internet of

Things, and wearable computing. This program shares many characteristics with similar programs in the United States. Running over a period of four months, it provides startups with access to business mentors, technical and design experts and other educational resources, enabling participating entrepreneurs to quickly scale up their businesses. Unlike many other programs, however, Microsoft Ventures does not make investments in these startups in exchange for equity. Another example is Target Corp., the U.S. retailer, whose Indian accelerator is also set up in Bangalore. Through this accelerator, Target aims to benefit from entrepreneurs with transformative ideas in five key areas—search, content, data, social, and mobile. As part of the nurturing process, Target offers participating startups access to mentors, business tools, resources, and operational support.

9.5   CONCLUSIONS

In this chapter, we have discussed the role of corporate venturing as an alternative funding source for startups. While corporate venturing can take different forms, in practice corporate VC, accelerators and incubators, and innovation labs dominate corporate venture programs. These programs are generally viewed as strategic tools to complement internal R&D, aiming to better capture the value from waves of technology and innovation. In the United States, CVC has accounted for around 8%–12% of total VC investing since the tech bubble, with a substantial number of large companies running their own VC funds or committing capital to IVC partnerships. Although CVC programs may face important organizational challenges, their investments overall have performed at least as well as those of IVC. The success of individual CVC programs has varied, with the probability of attaining a program's goals reflecting the fit between the parent and portfolio company's lines of business.

Corporate venturing is also increasing in emerging markets, especially in China and India. In both countries, domestic tech firms have backed a growing number of startups. At the same time, a significant number of entrepreneurial firms received funding from some of the world's leading tech firms, such as Amazon, Cisco, eBay, Eli Lilly, Google, Intel, and Microsoft, whose CVC programs have globalized, mirroring the international integration of the market for venture capital. Together, domestic and foreign CVC account for about 5%–8% of total VC investing in China and India, not far behind CVCs role in the United States.

While CVC in emerging markets is relatively recent, a review of Alibaba's and Flipkart's CVC portfolios suggests that their investments have focused on entrepreneurial firms with substantial overlap with their own major lines of business. To the extent that the evidence found in the U.S. market is applicable to emerging economies, one would expect these investments to succeed. If they do, corporate venturing by domestic and foreign companies could gain further traction, helping facilitate the funding of startups in emerging markets.

REFERENCES

Alvarez-Garrido, E., Dushnitsky, G., 2016. Are entrepreneurial venture's innovation rates sensitive to investor complementary assets? Comparing biotech ventures backed by corporate and independent VCs. Strateg. Manag. J. 37 (5), 819–834.

Boston Consulting Group, 2016. Corporate venturing shift gears. https://www.bcgperspectives.com/content/articles/innovation-growth-corporate-venturing-shifts-gears-how-largest-companies-apply-tools-innovation/. Accessed June 27, 2016.

Cambridge Associates, 2016. U.S. Venture Capital Index and Selected Benchmark Statistics. https://www.cambridgeassociates.com/wp-content/uploads/2016/11/Public-2016-Q2-USVC-Benchmark-Book.pdf.

CB Insights, 2016. The H1 2016 Corporate Venture Capital Report.

Chemmanur, T.J., Loutskina, E., Tian, X., 2014. Corporate venture capital, value creation, and innovation. Rev. Finan. Stud. 27 (8), 2438–2473.

Chesbrough, H.W., 2002. Making sense of corporate venture capital. Harv. Business Rev. March.

Dushnitsky, G., Lenox, M.J., 2005. When do firms undertake R&D by investing in new ventures? Strateg. Manag. J. 26, 947–965.

Dushnitsky, G., Shapira, Z., 2010. Entrepreneurial finance meets organizational reality: comparing investment practices and performance of corporate and independent venture capitalists. Strateg. Manag. J. 31, 990–1017.

Gompers, P.A., 2002. Corporations and the financing of innovation: the corporate venturing experience. Fed. Res. Bank Atlanta Econ. Rev. 1–17. (Fourth Quarter).

Gompers, P., Lerner, J., 1998. What drives venture capital fundraising? Brook. Pap. Econ. Act. – Microecon. 149–192.

Gompers, P., Lerner, J., 2000. The determinants of corporate venture capital success: organizational structure, incentives, and complementarities. In: Morck, R. (Ed.), Concentrated Corporate Ownership. University of Chicago Press, Chicago, pp. 17–50.

Gompers, P., Lerner, J., 2001. The Money of Invention. Harvard Business School Press, Boston.

Hall, B.H., 1993. The stock market's valuation of R&D investment during the 1980s. Am. Econ. Rev. Pap. Proc. 83, 259–264.

Isaacson, W., 2014. The Innovators. Simon & Schuster, New York.

Jensen, M.C., 1993. Presidential address: the modern industrial revolution, exit, and the failure of internal control systems. J. Financ. 48, 831–880.

Lerner, J., 2012. The Architecture of Innovation: The Economics of Creative Organizations. Oxford University Press, Oxford.

Lerner, J., 2013. Corporate venturing. Harv. Bus. Rev. 91 (10), 86–94.

Ma, S., 2016. The life cycle of corporate venture capital. https://papers.ssrn.com/sol3/papers.cfm?abstract_id=2691210 Accessed January 27, 2017.

National Venture Capital Association, 2016. Yearbook. http://nvca.org/research/stats-studies/.

Ozmel, U., Robinson, D.T., Stuart, T.E., 2013. Strategic alliances, venture capital, and exit decisions in early-stage high-tech firms. J. Financ. Econ. 107 (3), 655–670.

Robinson, D.T., Stuart, T.E., 2007. Financial contracting in bio strategic alliances. J. Law Econ. 50 (3), 559–596.

Chapter 10

Noninstitutional Forms of Entrepreneurial Finance: Angel Investments, Accelerators, and Equity Crowdfunding

Acronyms

Fintech	Financial Technology
HNWIs	High Net Worth Individuals
MSA	Metropolitan Statistical Areas
NDA	Nondisclosure Agreement
P2P	Peer-to-Peer
RDD	Regression Discontinuity Design
VC	Venture Capital

Traditionally, equity financing of entrepreneurial startups was equated with venture capital (VC). As we discussed in Chapter 8, an institutional market emerged in the United States in the 1950s, with the bulk of VC intermediated through limited partnership funds. In this chapter, we focus on noninstitutional forms of entrepreneurial finance. First, we look at the role of angel investors who are often (former) entrepreneurs themselves, investing their own money. Angel investing in the United States developed in the 1980s at a time when the VC market was already quite mature. Angel investors usually provide early-stage funding and seed capital. Now, they are often organizing groups, which allow them to see more deal flow, reduce their due diligence burden, and limit their own investment risk through diversification. While the noninstitutional nature of angel investing limits the amount of available information about the size of the angel market, evidence suggests that this form of entrepreneurial finance has gained momentum not only in the United States but also in other advanced economies and emerging markets.

What do we know about angel investors? More specifically, to what extent is angel capital a complement or a substitute for VC? How do angel investors select which startups to fund? Do angel investors focus on specific industries

Financing Entrepreneurship and Innovation in Emerging Markets.
https://doi.org/10.1016/B978-0-12-804025-6.00010-1

like venture capitalists, backing almost exclusively tech startups? What role do angel investors play for entrepreneurial startups, beyond providing seed capital? And what is the impact of angel financing on firm survival, growth, and job creation?

After exploring these questions, we turn to the role accelerators may play in fueling startup activity. While accelerators have emerged only in the mid-2000s, they have quickly proliferated, with the total number estimated at over 2000, spanning six continents (Cohen and Hochberg, 2014). Accelerator programs typically have a limited duration of around three months. During this period, the programs allow participating entrepreneurs to define and build their initial products, identify promising customer segments, and secure resources for growth. Accelerator programs themselves provide only a small amount of seed capital, if any. Instead, their main contribution lies in offering a range of networking, educational, and mentorship opportunities with both peer ventures and mentors who may also be successful entrepreneurs, program graduates, venture capitalists, or angel investors. While accelerators have become an integral part of corporate venturing (Chapter 9), such programs are increasingly in the arsenal of government-sponsored efforts to spur entrepreneurship, innovation, and growth.

Finally, we discuss crowd investing, another noninstitutional form of entrepreneurial finance. Crowd investing is a special form of crowdfunding, a concept we introduced in Chapter 7. The bulk of the crowdfunding market is for philanthropic projects (in the form of donations), consumer products (frequently for creative ventures such as music and film, in the form of prefunded orders), and lending. In contrast, crowd investing, also known as equity crowdfunding, is relatively new and represents the smallest market segment (Wilson and Testoni, 2014). The basic model for crowd investing is an online platform that posts startups' business plans and financing needs and allows potential investors to peruse the listing for investment opportunities (World Bank, 2014).

Crowd investing is still in its infancy, but recent data suggest that the market has already gained momentum, including in some emerging markets. Angel investors have contributed to this rapid growth by funding startups through online platforms. Given that crowd investors are less geographically confined, Internet-based platforms might help achieve a superior match between entrepreneurs and investors, potentially revolutionizing the VC and angel markets for startup funding. However, for this to happen, the crowd investing market requires a regulatory framework that is conducive to entrepreneurship, while adequately reflecting the risks for online investors.

10.1 EARLY-STAGE FUNDING AND ANGEL INVESTORS

10.1.1 What Do Angel Investors Do?

Angel investments are generally defined as equity investments into high-risk ventures by wealthy individuals or the family offices that manage their wealth.[1] Angel investors typically invest in companies in relatively early stages of development, with their investments usually not exceeding $1 million per startup (NVCA, 2016). For most of American economic history, angel investors (including many well-known families such as the Rockefellers, Vanderbilts, and Whitneys) provided the primary source of entrepreneurial finance to fund startup businesses (Kerr et al., 2014; Lamoreaux et al., 2004).

Since the mid-1990s, angel investors have increasingly organized as semiformal networks of high net worth individuals (HNWIs). In the United States, the Angel Capital Association lists around 260 national groups in its database. Kerr et al. (2014) identify several advantages of forming an angel group. First, the pooling of capital allows the network to make larger investments than they could otherwise. This gives angels greater economic power and influence, which enhances investment term negotiation (World Bank, 2014). Second, each angel can invest smaller amounts in individual startups, allowing more opportunities and greater diversification of investment portfolios. Third, angel investors are often (former) entrepreneurs themselves and possess relevant experience that helps them assess an investment opportunity. As a group, angel investors benefit from important informational synergies, helping them reduce their due diligence costs. In this process, new angels can learn from experienced angel investors on all aspects of investing. Fourth, angel groups may receive a superior deal flow thanks to their greater visibility to entrepreneurs.

Angel investors share a number of important features with venture capitalists. Like venture capitalists, angels fund entrepreneurial firms in their startup phases following intensive due diligence. They usually provide concrete guidance to the entrepreneur, as venture capitalists do. As mentors, angels often adopt a very hands-on role in the transactions in which they engage, offering industry-specific insights based on their own experience and knowledge, and facilitating new business connections that help startups grow.

However, as Lerner et al. (2015) stress, there are also important differences. Angel investors are less prone to the agency problems that VC funds often face. As discussed in Chapter 8, VC funds serve as financial intermediaries between institutional investors and entrepreneurial firms. Limited partners in a VC fund are charged a management fee, defined as a percentage of their individual commitments (typically 2%–2.5%). While management fees are a linear function of the fund's size, the costs of managing a fund usually flatten beyond a certain point. Thus, fee-based compensation structures could result in excessive fundraising (Metrick and Yasuda, 2010) and in suboptimal investment decisions (Gompers and Lerner, 1996). Since angels invest their own money, they are

---

1. Most angel investors in the U.S. have "accredited investor" status as defined by law. According to U.S. law, an accredited investor is any "natural person whose individual net worth, or joint net worth with that person's spouse, at the time of his investment exceeds $1 million and who has an individual income in excess of $ 200,000 in each of the two most recent years or joint income with that person's spouse in excess of $300,000 in each of those years and has a reasonable expectation of reaching the same income level in the current year. Similar definitions apply to accredited investors in Canada and the U.K.

less likely to overfund startups (Gompers and Lerner, 1998) or hold on to their investments beyond the optimal exit date.

On the other hand, angel investors might be more risk averse than venture capitalists, whose investment portfolios are generally significantly diversified. Thus, angels might be less willing to invest in truly disruptive and highly complex technologies. In fact, while the overwhelming majority of VC investments have funded high-tech startups (Chapter 8), angel investments have historically funded a broader range of industry sectors (Organisation for Economic Co-operation and Development, 2011).[2] Furthermore, entrepreneurs relying on angel investments might experience greater funding risk. Since angels are typically not professional investors, there is a worry that their opinions might change more frequently about which projects to fund. Additionally, angel investors themselves might be subject to idiosyncratic liquidity shocks (Lerner et al., 2015).

Given these important differences, are angel investments and VC funding complements or substitutes? While angel investors usually provide only seed financing, the majority of VC investments focus on startups that have developed beyond the initial stage of their life cycle. Furthermore, angels and venture capitalists have different skills and networks. If the complementarity hypothesis is correct, a well-developed VC market could make angel investing more effective. An angel's primary role would thus be to bridge the gap between the entrepreneur's own resources and the later funding by venture capitalists and other institutional investors. Angel groups, after the initial financing, could "hand off" their transactions to venture funds for subsequent financing (Lerner et al., 2015). If angels and venture capitalists are part of the same value chain, the best way for an entrepreneur to get introduced to a leading VC firm might be through the seed investors. Consistent with this logic, angel investing could be a stepping-stone for startups to obtain VC backing to fund later stage growth. Without a healthy VC market, startups may languish when they "graduate" from angel funding.

There are prominent examples that support the "stepping-stone" view. For instance, Facebook Inc. and Google (Alphabet Inc.), two of the most successful startups in recent history, both received angel financing prior to obtaining VC. Overall, however, the available evidence appears to be mixed. While angel capital and VC are more likely to be substitutes in advanced economies, in emerging economies with less-developed risk markets, angel funding and VC show signs of complementarity.[3]

---

2. While VC firms tend to geographically concentrate in a few technology and science hubs, angels live everywhere, explaining why their investments are comparatively more diversified not only in terms of industries, but also geographically (Organisation for Economic Co-operation and Development, 2011).
3. Hellmann and Thiele (2015) presented a costly search model to determine the equilibrium deal flows across the angel and VC markets. In this model, angel investors and venture capitalists are assumed to be "friends" in that they rely upon each other's investments. But they are also "foes": at the later stage the venture capitalists no longer need the angels. The venture capitalists' bargaining power depends on how competitive venture markets are, and how well angels are legally protected.

In the United States, Kerr et al. (2014) find that angel investing has essentially no effect on a startup's access to additional financing from VC funds. One possible interpretation is that risk capital in the United States is relatively abundant, enabling young entrepreneurial firms to choose between different avenues to obtain startup capital. Thus, firms might not necessarily need an angel round before receiving funding from venture capitalists.

Using a high-quality dataset from a government program in British Columbia, Canada, Hellmann et al. (2015) find that companies that obtained more angel financing in the past are less likely to subsequently obtain VC funding (and vice versa). Instead, a company that already obtained funding from one particular type of investor is likely to raise more funding from investors of the same type, albeit not necessarily through repeat investments by existing investors. Additional empirical tests support their conclusions. Conceivably, the negative dynamic between angel and VC financing could result from poorly performing companies that initially raised angel financing and then continued to rely on further angel financing because they could not graduate to the VC stage. In this case, the stepping-stone logic would only apply to the best companies, and not the potentially larger pool of struggling companies. However, when Hellmann et al. (2015) examine how the dynamic substitute pattern varied with company performance, they find little evidence for the more refined stepping-stone logic.

These findings suggest that angel investing and VC funding are substitutes rather than complements. One reason could be that investors guide their companies toward staying within their investor type. Another explanation could be that certain company attributes lend themselves to a particular type of financing. Finally, as Lerner et al. (2015) argue, Hellmann et al.'s (2015) findings could be the result of inexperienced angel investors operating in a country with a relatively developed risk-capital market. Thus, venture capitalists might not see angel funding as an accreditation and therefore not serve as a gateway for follow-on funding.

In contrast to Hellmann et al. (2015) and Kerr et al. (2014), Lerner et al. (2015) find supporting evidence of the complementarity hypothesis. Examining the record of 13 angel investment groups based in 12 countries,[4] including three emerging markets, their results suggest that angel financing enhances the ability of the funded firms to obtain follow-on financing. Thus, angel investors appear to play an important role as gatekeepers for risk capital in less-developed ecosystems. As the World Bank (2014) argues, angel investors' support may be essential for entrepreneurs to bridge the "valley of death"—the funding gap between what friends and families can offer at the initial stage and what venture capitalists, banks, and other sources are willing to contribute. Cash flows are typically negative as startups grow rapidly and traverse the valley of death, requiring the injection of capital, in the absence of which companies may fail.

---

4. Argentina, Australia, Belgium, Canada, China, Germany, Italy, Mexico, New Zealand, Switzerland, the U.K. and the U.S.

10.1.2   Size of the Market for Angel Investments

Given the informal nature of angel investing and the fact that angels tend to be private about their investments, there is relatively little systematic information about the size of the angel market. A further complication lies in the varying definitions of angel investing.[5]

To the extent that market estimates are available, they are largely confined to the United States. According to the Center for Venture Capital Research at the University of New Hampshire, U.S. angel investing has averaged around $22 billion per year in 2001–15 (Fig. 10.1). While this estimate implies that angel investing generally fell short of the volume that venture capitalists invested in U.S. startups, in most years the difference was relatively small. While angel investing and VC investing broadly displayed similar trends during this cycle, a closer look reveals important differences between these two forms of entrepreneurial finance.

First, angel investors play a much larger role than VC funds as providers of seed financing. In fact, venture capital funds invested on average only around $1 billion per year at this stage, a fraction of the $22 billion angels invested.

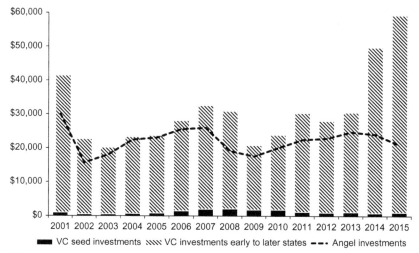

FIG. 10.1   U.S.: Angel investments versus VC investments, 2001–15 ($M). *(Source: Authors' calculations, based on data from NVCA and Center for Venture Research at Paul College, University of New Hampshire.)*

5. As the Organisation for Economic Co-operation and Development (2011) points out, the terms business angels or angel investors, informal investor, and informal venture capital are often used interchangeably. Most definitions clearly differentiate investment from founders, and family and friends from angel investors, who do not have a personal connection to the entrepreneur prior to making an investment. However, while some studies use total informal investment (founders, family and friends, plus angel investment) others use only angel investment.

Second, angels provided seed financing to a much larger number of startups than venture capitalists. On an annual average basis, almost 57,000 U.S. startups are estimated to have received angel investments in 2002–15, around 15 times as many transactions as venture capitalists were involved in (Fig. 10.2).[6] Third, angel investments tend to be much smaller. Few transactions exceed $1 million, a threshold that is typically too small for VC funds given the substantial amount of due diligence work venture capitalists usually undertake before investing. On average, angels invested less than $400,000 per deal, while VC deals had an average value of almost $7 million in 2002–15.

Finally, in 2014–15, angel investing and VC investing appeared to diverge. While the volume of angel investing and average deal size remained broadly consistent with their historical average, VC investing jumped substantially. This surge was solely driven by the rise in deal sizes rather than the number of transactions, with late-stage financings accounting for the bulk of this increase.

Outside of the United States, however, there is less systematic evidence about the evolution of angel investing and the size of the market, the available evidence suggests that angel investing has gained traction there as well. According to a survey conducted by the European Trade Association for Business Angels

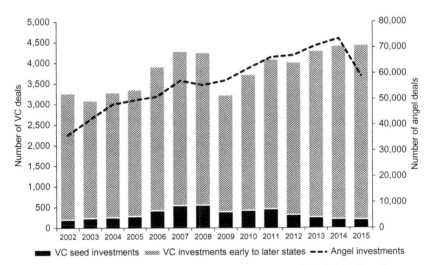

FIG. 10.2   U.S.: Angel investments versus VC investments, 2001–15 (Number of transactions). *(Source: NVCA and Center for Venture Research at Paul College, University of New Hampshire.)*

6. It is possible that the actual number of companies receiving angel investments is even larger. Shane (2008) analyzed a wide range of data sources. On this basis, he estimated the annual investment volume in the U.S. at $23 billion from 2001 to 2003. While this is more or less consistent with the data shown in Figure 10.1, he estimated that more than 50,000 U.S. startups received angel funding during this period, around one-third more than estimated by the Center for Venture Research, the source for the data shown in Figure 10.1.

(2014), there were 468 business angel networks in 2013, up from 75 in 1999. While more than 50% of these networks operated in the five largest European economies (Germany, France, the United Kingdom, Italy, and Spain), the survey also covered a significant number of organizations in Emerging Europe, including Bulgaria, Croatia, Estonia, Lithuania, Poland, Russia, Serbia, and Turkey. Business angels organized in these networks invested more than €5.5 billion ($7.4 billion) in 2013, more than twice as much as venture capitalists invested in early-stage startups.

Angel investor groups have proliferated in many emerging economies, suggesting that this form of entrepreneurial finance has gained significant traction alongside VC investing, accelerator programs, and equity crowdfunding. Preqin reported that angel groups were involved in around 2.2% of almost 13,000 VC financing rounds in emerging economies between 2012 and 2016. Specifically, their share was approximately three times higher in the seed financing stages. In India, angels were involved in 5.4% of around 3500 funding rounds during this period, with their share amounting to almost 15% of seed financing. Brazil and other Latin American economies, where angel groups are likely to have played a significantly larger role, had a higher-than-average percentage than other sources of entrepreneurial finance. In fact, anecdotal evidence suggests that in the majority of emerging economies the angel market could be approximately the same size as the VC market, with angel financing rather than VC as the primary source of external seed and early-stage equity financing (Organisation for Economic Co-operation and Development, 2011).

Who are these angel investors? As in the United States, angels in emerging economies tend to be successful entrepreneurs who want to stay engaged in the startup scene after cashing out of their own businesses (World Bank, 2014). A nontrivial percentage of them have gained meaningful experience as entrepreneurs in the United States or other advanced economies. Two of the most active angel investors in Brazil, for instance, are Fabrice Grinda, a French national, and Florian Otto from Germany. A serial angel investor, Grinda cofounded, among many others, OLX Inc., the largest classified ad website in Brazil (as well as in several other emerging economies). Otto, a vice president of ZocDoc Inc., a unicorn in the United States, is the founder of Groupon Brazil. Other angels with an entrepreneurial background are expats who want to pursue attractive investment opportunities in their home countries and give back to their home communities.

A second group of angel investors in emerging economies includes business executives, who often are wealthy professionals from large multinational companies. For instance, Rajan Anandan, an angel investor in several Indian startups, such as Sourceeasy, StepOut Solutions Pvt. Ltd., and Mobilewalla, has served as Managing Director of Google India, Microsoft India, and Dell Inc. Sharad Sharma and Vikas Taneja, two other prominent Indian angels, have held senior positions at Yahoo! India and the Boston Consulting Group, respectively. In China, a well-known angel investor is Kai-Fu Lee, a former president of Google China. Business executives represented 25% of a recent survey of 665 angel investors in networks across Latin America. Active and retired company owners made up an additional 33% and 24%, respectively, while family offices and other professionals accounted for the rest (cited in World Bank, 2014).

Angel investors in emerging markets have often been founders or cofounders of earlier startups that were funded by VC funds and angels themselves. One example is India's Kunal Bahl, the cofounder and CEO of Snapdeal, one of India's leading e-commerce platforms whose valuation has admitted the company to the global club of unicorns (Chapter 8). His investments include Tripoto, Gigstart, and Ola (Ani Technologies Pvt. Ltd.), the latter having emerged as another unicorn. Other prominent angels are Sachin Bansal, the cofounder and CEO of Flipkart Ltd., and Vijay Shekhar Sharma, the founder of One97 Communication Ltd. These companies, too, have become unicorns, with angel funding and VC fuelling their impressive growth in recent years. In China, meanwhile, Cai Wensheng, who serves as chairman of Meitu Xiuxiu, has been behind several startups as an angel investor, including 58.com, Baofengyingyin, and 4399.com. Another Chinese serial angel investor is Lei Jun, who founded Kingsoft Corp. Ltd. and was an early backer of Xiaomi,Inc.

10.1.3   Angel Financing's Impact

The available evidence suggests that VC has a positive impact on innovation and hence productivity and economic growth although the causality might be weaker than initially thought (Chapter 8). Generally, it is assumed that angel investing benefits the economy by bridging the funding gap that confronts many startups. As the Organisation for Economic Co-operation and Development (2011) argued there is a strong case for policy action to support the development of national angel markets.

Despite this presumption, there is very little research on the effects of angel investing on the success of individual startups and the broader economy, due to the private nature of such investments. Two exceptions are Kerr et al. (2014), who focused on the U.S. market only, and Lerner et al. (2015), who examined the role of angel investing in a 12-country sample. Both studies employed regression discontinuity design (RDD), a tool that is increasingly popular among economists for program evaluations.

This approach seeks to avoid the endogeneity problem in estimating the causal effects between angel investments and companies' performance. To illustrate this problem, suppose we found that companies that had received angel investor financial support grew faster and were more innovative than those that had not received angel funding. However, high-potential companies are more likely to receive angel investor funding *and* experience continued success at the same time. Comparing the outcomes of angel-funded companies and those that remained unfunded would lead to an upward bias of the estimates. Even if angel investing did not improve companies' performance at all, funded companies are likely to perform better than unfunded ones, since the funded companies had outperformed ex ante.

The intention behind the RDD approach is to compare companies with sufficiently similar exogenous characteristics, juxtaposing the outcome of funded companies with the counterfactual outcome of unfunded companies. More specifically, Kerr et al. (2014) and Lerner et al. (2015) compared companies that fall just above and just below the criteria for angel group funding. Given that firms that fall around the cut-off level have very similar exante characteristics, any difference in the expost performance should show the causal effect of angel funding.

In the U.S. market, Kerr et al. (2014) used deal flow data from Tech Coast Angels, a large angel investment group in Southern California. This database contains detailed information on the number of angels expressing interest in a given deal. Although interest does not represent a financial commitment, it expresses a belief that the group should pursue the venture further, though the final investment decision will ultimately dependent on a few angels taking the lead and championing the deal. While almost two-thirds of ventures in the sample did not receive any interest, a small number of startups received interest from at least 10% of the more than 300 angels belonging to Tech Coast Angels. Analyzing the distribution of companies that eventually did receive funding, Kerr et al. (2014) found that the investment decisions displayed break points or discontinuities where a small change in the collective interest levels of the angels led to a discrete change in the probability of funding among otherwise comparable ventures.

In the full sample, funded firms were significantly more likely to survive for at least four years. At the same time, they were more likely to show improved venture performance and growth as measured through an increase in website traffic and website rankings. Additionally, funded companies were more likely than their unfunded counterparts to raise additional financing outside the angel group. Restricting the sample to ventures just above and below the threshold, which removed the endogeneity of funding, the RDD analysis confirmed the importance of startups receiving angel investments for their continued survival and growth. In the restricted sample, however, angel investing does not seem to have an impact on accessing additional funding.

Lerner et al. (2015) extended this analysis to 13 angel groups, based in 12 countries (see footnote 3) and operating across 21 economies. Examining applicants just above and below the funding cut-off, they found that angel investors have a positive impact on the growth, performance, and survival of entrepreneurial firms. While these results are consistent with the U.S.-based study by Kerr et al. (2014), Lerner et al. (2015) also found that angel funding facilitates follow-on fundraising (supporting the stepping-stone hypothesis discussed earlier).

These findings hold across the sample of countries in which the angel groups operate, but Lerner et al. (2015) found that in less entrepreneurship-friendly economies, companies applying for angel funding tend to be older and larger. While the applicants are usually already revenue-generating, they tend to seek smaller amounts of funding than companies operating in an environment that is more conducive to entrepreneurship. The authors interpret this observation as a possible "self-censorship," meaning that the angel investors themselves are more risk-averse or less experienced in assessing very early stage investments.

10.2 ACCELERATORS

10.2.1 Basic Characteristics

Accelerator programs generally provide short- or medium-term support and resources to startups, helping them speed up their product development and time to market. Typically, these highly structured, cohort-based programs have a fixed time span, lasting no more than a few months. Offering mentorship, education, networking opportunities and usually coworking space, accelerator programs culminate in a public pitch event, often referred to as a "demo-day."[7] Many accelerator programs, but not all, provide a stipend or small seed investment of up to $150,000, with an average amount estimated at $22,000 (Cohen and Hochberg, 2014).[8] In return, the accelerator receives an equity stake in the portfolio company, typically ranging from 5 to 8%. Some accelerators offer a larger, guaranteed investment in the startup upon graduation, usually in the form of a convertible note (Fehder and Hochberg, 2014). Improved access to potential follow-on investors, including angels and venture capitalists, is an additional perk for startups participating in accelerator programs. Bernthal (2016) emphasizes the extent to which parties in many accelerator programs exchange economic value in the absence of a formal agreement. While startups share proprietary information with highly accomplished mentors, these individuals contribute their time and connections without direct compensation. Bernthal argues that the informality of accelerator programs may actually be conducive to fostering entrepreneurship and innovation by attracting a wider pool of mentor participants, including desirable professionals who would not participate as full time hires or as contributors pursuant to a contract. At the same time, an accelerator program's social integration is likely to lower the cost to mobilize group social sanctions if an individual deviates from behavioral norms. In a situation where mentors seek direct gain at the expense of a startup (or vice versa), the interconnected system allows the accelerator principals to punish such behavior through group-enforced consequences.

Most accelerator programs are generalists, though some focus on specific industries, such as healthcare, energy, digital media, or the Internet of Things. For angel investors and venture capitalists, who may decide to back the startups that have successfully graduated from an accelerator program, the accelerator

---

7. Martinez (2016) gives a lively account of a "demo-day" and the process leading up to it. Martinez' startup participated in the *Y Combinator* accelerator program.
8. Data refer to the U.S. market in 2012.

program has two important advantages. First, the accelerator application process serves as a screen to identify high-potential candidates from a larger population of startups. Second, there is an aggregation effect of bringing these candidates to a single location, significantly reducing the search costs for potential investors. These advantages also play an important role for corporate VC programs. As we discussed in Chapter 9, companies may be part of an external accelerator program's network of investors, or they may run internal accelerator programs as part of their corporate venturing initiatives.

The first accelerator, Y Combinator, formed in 2005 and quickly established itself in Silicon Valley as a tool for investors to screen startups with innovative ideas.[9] Techstars followed in 2006 when two local investors in Boulder, Colorado, decided to establish an accelerator to transform the local startup ecosystem. Today, Techstars is one of the largest programs of its kind in the United States. Since then, accelerator programs have proliferated not only in the U.S. market but worldwide, with the total number estimated at up to 2000 (Fehder and Hochberg, 2014).

Accelerators are similar to incubators, in the sense that both approaches provide the opportunity to become quickly acquainted with a broad variety of new business ideas. Thus, accelerators and incubators are sometimes considered variants of the same tool. In contrast to accelerators, incubators generally offer longer-term programs, supporting startup firms through mentoring and corporate resources for up to one year, and sometimes even longer. In many cases, startups in an incubator program already have developed a product or service but still need to design a business model in order to go to market.

Some accelerator and incubator programs operate internationally. 500 Startups, for instance, runs accelerator programs in Mexico City in addition to their programs in Mountain View and San Francisco. In fact, 500 Startups has been one of the most active foreign seed investors in Latin America in recent years. The firm has also been very active in Asia, notably in India and China. Similarly, Techstars has expanded, exporting its accelerator program to Europe, Israel, and Africa. Through its venture arm, Techstars has also made investments in Asia. At the same time, indigenous accelerator programs have emerged in several emerging markets, following a process that resembles the internationalization of venture capital. China and India have a particularly active accelerator ecosystem. Their programs generally follow the structure of their counterparts in advanced economies. ChinaAccelerator, a leading accelerator program in China, selects cohorts of participating startups twice a year and invests $30,000 in each of them in the form of convertible notes in exchange for 6% equity. These investments are made by SOSV, the $235 million VC fund behind ChinaAccelerator. A particularly active program in India is iAccelerator, launched in 2008 by the Indian Institute for Management. iAccelerator focuses

---

9. Y Combinator is no longer classified as an accelerator. Instead, it now classifies itself as a seed fund.

on startups in the Internet and mobile domains, providing seed funding of between $8000 and $16,000 per startup.

While accelerators and incubators have gained traction in other emerging economies, there is considerable cross-country variance. In some African economies, for example, individual programs face challenges on both the demand and supply sides. On the one hand, many African accelerators and incubators lack experienced mentors to guide young businesses. On the other hand, there are often not enough good entrepreneurs who would benefit from the advice of their mentors. Thus, while accelerators and incubators have thrived elsewhere, several incubators in Africa were forced to close (The Economist, April 8, 2017a).

10.2.2   How Successful are Accelerator Programs?

Research on accelerator programs remains embryonic, partly due to their novelty. The existing systematic studies of accelerator programs have largely focused on their impact on participating startups. Winston-Smith et al. (2013), who studied ventures that participated in Techstars and Y Combinator, found that these startups received their first round of follow-up financing significantly sooner than those backed by angel investors. Further, they reported that startups that Techstars and Y Combinator alumni were involved in were comparatively more likely either to be acquired or to fail. Finally, the authors find that the entrepreneurs whose startups were chosen to participate in these programs were from a relatively elite set of universities. Hallen et al. (2016) report broadly consistent results. Specifically, they find that graduating from a top accelerator program is correlated with a short time to raising VC, exit by acquisition, and achieving customer traction. Similarly, Howell (2016) reports that winning in new venture competitions, which are sponsored by governments, universities, corporations, and foundations, increases external financing and firm employment. These competitions reduce search frictions by certifying winners as high quality.

What constitutes a top accelerator program? The Seed Accelerator Rankings Project, launched by Hochberg et al. (2015), considered a broad set of criteria, including the average valuations of the portfolio companies, the percentage of graduates that raise significant venture or angel funding, the average amount of money raised by the companies, the percentage of portfolio companies that have had a significant exit event, the average valuation of the companies at exit, and the percentage of companies still operating. To ensure comparability, the outcomes were measured one, two, and three years after graduation, adjusting for differences in the stage startups are at when they enter the accelerator. Focusing exclusively on U.S.-based accelerators, data for each variable was collected directly from these programs on a confidential basis. The different variables were then aggregated to rank individual programs, and their annual rankings were reported on the project's website http://seedrankings.com. While the 2015 rankings followed a numerical approach from 1 to 20, in 2016 the top programs were classified into three categories—platinum, gold, and silver.

Instead of focusing on an accelerator's impact on participating companies, Fehder and Hochberg (2014) were interested in the broader effects such programs had on the entrepreneurial ecosystem of the regions in which they operate. Specifically, they examined the extent to which accelerators increased the availability and provision of seed and early stage VC financing for startups. They found that U.S. Metropolitan Statistical Areas (MSAs) that were "treated" with an accelerator program exhibit significant differences in seed and early-stage financing patterns relative to MSAs that did not receive such a program. Specifically, the arrival of an accelerator is associated with an annual increase in the number of seed and early-stage VC deals in the MSA of more than 100%. This was an 18-fold increase in the total dollar amount of seed and early-stage funding provided in the region, and a near doubling of the number of distinct investors investing in the region. This increase in investors came primarily from a rise in nearby investment groups, rather than from the entry of additional investors from outside the region.

Overall, Fehder and Hochberg's (2014) findings suggest that accelerator programs may foster entrepreneurship and unleash financial resources for startups. Although these results are based on accelerator programs in the United States, they may encourage local and national governments in other countries to sponsor accelerators as part of their efforts to help spur innovation and economic growth. As we discuss in more detail in Chapter 11, this is particularly relevant for emerging economies where accelerator programs may help them leapfrog in creating a VC market and building an entrepreneurial ecosystem.

10.3 CROWD INVESTING

10.3.1 The Business Model of Crowd Investing

Angel investing relies heavily on the networks of individual angels. Unless an entrepreneur knows an angel who might be interested in funding his startup, there is substantial risk that the lack of funding will prevent him from successfully traversing the "valley of death." The proliferation of angel groups in many countries has meaningfully reduced this risk, but it has not eliminated it. The same is true for accelerators. Connecting entrepreneurs who have good ideas (but no money) with investors who have money but are looking for good ideas remains an important challenge, especially at an early stage when friends and family are no longer in the position to provide the necessary funding and VC is not yet an option.

In this environment, the Internet has created new opportunities for financial intermediation of risk capital. Crowd investing, sometimes called equity crowdfunding, describes a business model that is similar to the lending-based crowdfunding approaches we discussed in Chapter 7. Under the crowd lending model funders receive fixed periodic income and expect repayment of the original principal investment, but in the equity-based version of crowdfunding funders receive compensation in the form of the fundraiser's equity-based revenue- or profit-share arrangements (Wilson and Testoni, 2014). The issuance of equity by early-stage companies to individuals is facilitated by Internet-based platforms such as AngelList and SeedInvest in the United States, Crowdcube and Seedrs in the United Kingdom, AngelCrunch and JD.com in China, and LetsVenture in India.

These online platforms are notably not financial intermediaries. Unlike venture capitalists, which raise capital from institutional investors and select start-ups they want to fund (Chapter 8), crowd investing platforms are not involved in investment decisions. Instead, the decision to back a company is ultimately made by the individual crowd investor, a characteristic she shares with angel investors. Some equity crowdfunding platforms pool the funds of the crowd into an investment vehicle and represent the crowd's interests vis-à-vis the company that receives funding. But even in this case, the platform is not engaged in portfolio management like VC fund managers (Wilson and Testoni, 2014), and therefore equity crowdfunding platforms should be considered facilitators or online marketplaces.

The fees that crowd investing platforms charge for their services can vary significantly. While companies usually pay a fee of 5–10% of the amount raised, some platforms charge an additional fixed up-front fee. Other platforms also charge fees to investors. These fees are either fixed or a percentage of the amount invested. In some cases, investors are charged a fee as a function of their profits.

Crowd investing has been described as the democratization of entrepreneurial funding. While historically investing in startups has been reserved only for venture capitalists and highly connected angel investors, these online platforms allow a broader investor community to access startup investment opportunities with minimal amounts—subject to regulatory restrictions as discussed below.[10] In practice, individual investment amounts are higher, and typically exceed commitment sizes in the peer-to-peer (P2P) business and consumer lending segments by a significant margin. At the same time, they fall far short of what angels and venture capitalists usually invest in individual startups. In the United States, for instance, crowd investing platforms raised an average amount of $965,360 per campaign in 2015. Each campaign was funded by an average of 38 investors, each of whom has invested around $25,400 (Wardrop et al., 2016).[11] In China, equity-based crowdfunding projects attracted on average 121 investors who committed on average $18,500 per company, with each crowd investing campaign attracting on average $2.24 million (Zhang et al., 2016a).

Online platforms are designed to reduce search frictions and improve matching between startups and potential investors. Startups looking for funding may

---

10. Hornuf and Schwienbacher (2017) reported that Fundsters and Companisto GmbH, two German crowd investing portals, require as little as €1 and €5, respectively.
11. AngelList reports that there were almost 3000 active investors who funded almost 400 startups in 2015.

list themselves on the platforms and post relevant information about themselves, such as the targeted amount of capital they plan to raise, the terms of funding, and their products and revenues. Potential investors (who may or may not have to be Accredited Investors, depending on the jurisdiction of the crowd investing platform) can screen their investment proposals. Investors who join these platforms may post information on their own backgrounds, their portfolio of past and current investments, and the markets and industries in which they are interested. Since Internet-based crowdfunding transactions leave data trails on entrepreneurs, companies, and investors, over time this information could be valuable for platforms to better match investors and companies (Agarwal et al., 2011).

VC funds and business angels use equity crowdfunding as a screening mechanism to identify attractive investment opportunities (Hornuf and Schmitt, 2016). While crowd investors reveal private information about a startup, equity crowdfunding also uncovers information about potential future demand for a particular product (Straucz, 2017). This screening process may occur at different stages of the investment process. Hornuf and Schmitt (2016) present an example in which venture capitalists encouraged a portfolio company to run an equity crowdfunding campaign after they had provided capital at the seed stage. In another example, a VC fund invested in a startup right after this company had successfully raised capital through a crowd investing platform.

While equity crowdfunding has been hailed as a business model with the potential to reshape the VC landscape and early stage funding as a whole (see the literature referred to in Bernstein et al., 2017), it entails risks both for entrepreneurs seeking funding and for investors attracted by potentially high returns. Entrepreneurs must understand that no investor is willing to provide funds for a startup without first assessing its potential value. When seeking funding from venture capitalists and angel investors, the entrepreneur usually provides detailed information about the business idea on the basis of a legally binding nondisclosure agreement (NDA) to be signed by the potential investor. However, the basic idea of crowd investing excludes individual NDAs, requiring entrepreneurs to publicly disclose their business ideas and strategy. This early disclosure might harm startups with an innovative business model that can easily be copied (Agarwal et al., 2011; Hornuf and Schwienbacher, 2017). Thus, as Wilson and Testoni (2014) argue, seeking equity funding through online platforms might be less appropriate for startups whose business is particularly innovative, unless there are other ways to protect their intellectual capital. Other things being equal, one would therefore expect equity crowdfunding to be more industry-diverse than VC, which is strongly focused on tech startups. Unfortunately, there is not enough consistent information to substantiate this hypothesis.[12]

---

12. Several existing U.S. unicorns we mentioned in Chapter 7 raised seed capital through crowd investing platforms, including Uber (Bernstein et al., 2017).

As far as crowd investors are concerned, their incentive to perform detailed due diligence may be limited because their investments are relatively small (Agarwal et al., 2011). Furthermore, the crowd often includes nonprofessional investors who do not have the skills or expertise to perform adequate due diligence and properly assess the value of a company. Similarly, crowd investors may lack the necessary resources to perform postinvestment monitoring, making it more difficult for crowd investors to detect fraud. Even for those startups run by well-intentioned entrepreneurs, information asymmetry renders investments riskier as the competence of the entrepreneur and the quality of the business plan are more difficult to assess (Wilson and Testoni, 2014).

Given their lack of necessary resources to undertake proper due diligence and postinvestment monitoring, individual crowd investors may decide to free-ride on the investment decisions of others. However, this raises the risk of herd behavior and the risk of selecting underperforming entrepreneurial projects. In order to mitigate this risk, some platforms, such as AngelList, offer the opportunity for investors to form syndicates. These syndicates usually include experienced angels and venture capitalists.[13] Less experienced investors may coinvest with a syndicate, in exchange for a share in the profit (carry), a model that could help reduce the information asymmetry problems that arise due to the lack of appropriate due diligence by the majority of investors (Wilson and Testoni, 2014).

Another important investment risk for crowd investors is the lack of customized contractual arrangements that are customary for startups financed by venture capitalists and angel investors. While venture capitalists and business angels typically use various covenants in the contracts they negotiate with entrepreneurs, crowd investing is usually based on standard contracts that are provided by the crowd investing platforms. Furthermore, an important risk management tool of venture investing (and sometimes angel investing) is the staged provision of capital. Employing this tool requires contractual arrangements with strong monitoring and oversight of the entrepreneurial firm, which are difficult to implement with a large number of crowd investors in individual deals. Furthermore, to the extent that crowd investors are unable to participate in follow-on investment rounds, their shares get diluted and so does their participation in the potential success of the startup they have helped to fund.

Finally, in order for the crowd investors to get their investment back and reap a return that is commensurate with the risks they take, an exit must occur, generally through either an IPO or an acquisition by another company through a trade sale, for instance, to a VC fund or a business angel. As we have discussed in

---

13. In fact, some platforms, such as AngelList have been used by high-profile venture capitalists and entrepreneurs themselves, such as Marc Andreessen and Ben Horowitz (of the venture capital firm Andreessen Horowitz), Dave McClure (of the accelerator 500 Startups), Reid Hoffman (co-founder of LinkedIn), Marissa Mayer (former president and CEO of Yahoo! Inc.), and Othman Laraki (co-founder of Color Genomics).

Chapter 8, while the legal structure of VC funds forces venture capitalists to develop a clear exit strategy as part of their investment decision, this is less true for crowd investors and angels (Hornuf and Schwienbacher, 2017). As a result, it might take even longer for crowd investors to receive their invested capital, plus a positive return, subjecting their investments to a greater degree of illiquidity.[14]

Given that the crowd investing market is a relatively new phenomenon, there have been a limited number of exits.[15] As a result, there is no empirical evidence yet about the investment returns achieved by crowd investors and the degree to which they are adequately compensated for the risks they take. Efforts are underway, however, to create a secondary market for crowd investments, where buyers and sellers can exchange shares. Seedrs, for instance, has already announced plans to add a mechanism through which sellers can convert investments into returns and rebalance their portfolios by selling their shares to other investors. To the extent that investors make a profit on a sale, Seedrs takes a cut of the gains. At the same time, this platform will allow current investors in a firm to invest in businesses outside of funding rounds without paying fees when making an investment (The Economist, May 20, 2017b).

10.3.2 Market Size and the Role of Regulation

While equity crowdfunding is still in an embryonic stage, data collected by the Centre for Alternative Finance at the University of Cambridge (2015 and 2016), in partnership with other organizations, suggest that this form of fundraising has gained traction.[16] According to benchmarking reports for the Americas, Asia-Pacific, and Europe, the global volume increased to around $2 billion in 2015, a near-10-fold increase from 2013 (Table 10.1). Although this amount represents less than 1% of VC and angel investing during that year and is still far smaller than P2P business and consumer lending, crowd investing is attracting attention as a new form of entrepreneurial finance that could play a larger role in the future.

---

14. As Hornuf and Schwienbacher (2017) posit, venture capitalists and angel investors may themselves provide an exit opportunity for the crowd by providing follow-on funding.

15. Zhang et al. (2016a) report that there were two exits in the U.K. in 2015.

16. The data reported in Table 10.1 are based on surveys conducted by the Cambridge Centre for Alternative Finance at the Judge Business School at Cambridge University in collaboration with the Tsinghua University Graduate School (China) and the University of Sydney Business School (Australia) in the Asia-Pacific region, and the Polsky Center for Entrepreneurship and Innovation at the Chicago Booth School of Business in the U.S. For the 2016 Asia-Pacific Benchmarking Report, survey data were collected from 503 leading alternative finance platforms operating in 17 countries. Of these platforms, 376 were from mainland China. In the Americas, survey data were collected from 257 online alternative platforms, of which 178 were from the U.S. and Canada. In Europe, finally, the Centre for Alternative Finance partnered with 14 leading national and regional industry associations to collect industry data directly from 255 leading platforms in Europe. Of these, 96 platforms operated in the U.K. Wardrop et al. (2015); Wardrop et al. (2016); Zhang et al. (2016a); Zhang et al. (2016b).

TABLE 10.1 Market Volume of Equity-Based Crowdfunding, 2013–15 ($M)

	2013	2014	2015
North America	86.3	271.8	595.6
The United States	86.3	271.7	590.5
Canada	–	0.1	5.1
Latin America	–	0.2	2.1
Brazil	–	0.2	1.7
Mexico	–	–	0.4
Other	–	–	–
Europe	112.4	257.4	668.0
France	12.6	25.1	83.3
Germany	23.0	39.6	26.3
The Netherlands	8.2	14.9	18.4
Spain	8.2	14.0	5.8
Scandinavia	3.9	4.9	14.1
The United Kingdom	49.2	147.6	507.5
Other	7.2	11.3	12.6
Asia-Pacific	12.1	55.9	1022.5
Australia	5.5	8.2	26.0
Japan	5.9	10.2	8.6
New Zealand	–	1.4	11.9
China	0.3	26.1	950.0
India	0.4	6.3	18.5
South-East Asia[a]	–	3.7	7.5
World	210.8	585.3	2288.2

[a]*Indonesia, Malaysia, Philippines, Singapore, and Thailand.*

Source: Wardrop, R., Zhang, B., Rau, R., Gray, M., 2015. Moving mainstream. The European alternative finance benchmarking report. Centre for Alternative Finance at the Judge Business School at the University of Cambridge. https://www.jbs.cam.ac.uk/fileadmin/user_upload/research/centres/alternative-finance/downloads/2015-uk-alternative-finance-benchmarking-report.pdf. Accessed April 18, 2017.
Wardrop, R., Rosenberg, R., Zhang, B., Ziegler, T., Squire, R., Burton, J., Hernandez, E., Garvey, K., 2016. Breaking new ground. The Americas alternative finance benchmarking report. Centre for Alternative Finance at the Judge Business School at the University of Cambridge and the Polsky Center for Entrepreneurship and Innovation at the Chicago Booth School of Business. Cambridge: Cambridge University. https://www.jbs.cam.ac.uk/fileadmin/user_upload/research/centres/alternative-finance/downloads/2016-americas-alternative-finance-benchmarking-report.pdf. Accessed April 18, 2017.
Zhang, B., Deer, L., Wardrop, R., Grant, A., Garvey, K., Thorp, S., Ziegler, T., Ying, K., Xinwei, Z., Huang, E., Burton, J., Chen, H.-Y., Lui, A., Gray, Y., 2016. Harnessing potential. The Asia-Pacific alternative finance benchmarking report. Centre for Alternative Finance at the Judge Business School at the University of Cambridge and The University of Sydney Business School. Cambridge: Cambridge University. https://www.jbs.cam.ac.uk/fileadmin/user_upload/research/centres/alternative-finance/downloads/harnessing-potential.pdf. Accessed April 18, 2017.
Zhang, B., Wardrop, R., Ziegler, T.; Lui, A., Burton, J., James, A., and Garvey, K., 2016. Sustaining momentum. The second European alternative finance industry report. Centre for Alternative Finance at the Judge Business School at the University of Cambridge. https://www.jbs.cam.ac.uk/fileadmin/user_upload/research/centres/alternative-finance/downloads/2016-european-alternative-finance-report-sustaining-momentum.pdf. Accessed April 18, 2017.

China has become the world's largest market for equity crowdfunding, followed by the United States and the United Kingdom. These three markets had a combined market share of more than 90% in 2015. Although crowd investing in India is still small compared with China, it is the second largest emerging market for this form of fundraising. What's more, crowd investing has been the second most active form of India's crowdfunding market, second only to P2P consumer lending. This is in stark contrast to most other emerging economies, where crowdfunding platforms have generally been more active in raising debt for businesses and consumers.

While angel investing is largely a local business, evidence from the United States suggests that crowd investors are less geographically confined (Agarwal et al., 2011), a potential indicator of online platforms' ability to better match entrepreneurs and investors. Hornuf and Schmitt (2016) examine a sample of more than 20,000 equity crowdfunding transactions from two Internet platforms in Germany. Their data allow them to distinguish between different investor types. Friends, family, and business angels exhibit a significant local bias, perhaps because of local market knowledge, helping them resolve information asymmetries. In contrast, diversified investors are often less home-biased, but cross-border transactions remain very limited. Eighty six percentage of the U.S. platforms surveyed in 2015 by the Centre of Alternative Finance (Wardrop et al., 2016) had no cross-border outflows, while 69% reported no cross-border inflows.

As the number of Internet and mobile phone users continues to increase, the potential exists for crowd investing (just like other forms of crowdfunding) to grow, depending on how the diverse and rapidly changing regulatory environment in individual economies evolves.[17] While some countries have begun to draft new regulations governing crowdfunding, others have already implemented important new policies in response to the rapid progress in financial technology (fintech). Generally, these efforts are motivated by the dual objective of supporting entrepreneurial activity while protecting investors. In pursuing this objective, some countries have opted to regulate crowdfunding within preexisting regulatory frameworks, while others have customized regulation to

---

17. Some observers believe that new Regulation A + —also known as Title IV under the U.S. "Jumpstart Our Business Startups" (JOBS) Act—could provide an impetus for regulatory reforms in other markets. The JOBS Act was voted into law by Congress and signed by President Barack Obama in April 2012. The first portion of equity crowdfunding laws was implemented in September 2013, when Title II allowed for public advertising of fundraising. However, under Title II, crowd investing was still restricted to Accredited Investors. Title IV of the JOBS Act, which came into effect in May 2015, broadens the definition of "qualified investors" to include non-accredited investors. Given that non-accredited investors are typically less experienced, their investments are limited to 10% of their income/net worth per year. This regulatory shift allows for investor self-certification and pre-empts state-level requirements (Wardrop et al., 2016). At the same time, the total amount of capital companies may try to raise through crowd investing Internet platforms was split into two tiers of up to $20 million and $50 million. It is widely expected that this new regulation will significantly increase the number of platforms, thus providing a boost to funding startups and small and medium-sized enterprises, potentially serving as a blueprint for other markets.

govern debt- and equity-based alternative finance activities. Policies differ with respect to (i) restrictions on the type of investors who are permitted to invest in entrepreneurial startups through online platforms; (ii) the amount of capital each investor is allowed to invest; and (iii) the amount of equity a business can raise from the crowd per year and in total.

In Asia-Pacific, most countries have no regulatory framework that allows for retail investor participation through general solicitation and advertising. In China, for instance, the draft regulation on equity crowdfunding issued in 2015 restricts participation to only accredited investors who possess net assets of RMB 10 million (around $1.5 million) or who possess financial assets of RMB 3 million (around $450,000) and have had an annual income of at least RMB 500,000 (around $75000) for the past three years. If implemented, these rules would essentially prevent retail investors from participating in crowd investing, turning Internet platforms into vehicles for small online private placements for early-stage VC or angel investing.

Notable exceptions in Asia-Pacific are Malaysia and South Korea. In Malaysia, Section 34 of the Capital Markets and Services Act of 2015 stipulates that retail investors may engage in online equity crowdfunding up to a maximum of RM 5000 (around $1200) per issuer with a total amount of investment not exceeding RM 50,000 ($12,000). At the same time, companies are permitted to raise up to RM 3 million (around $715,000) within a 12-month period, up to a maximum of RM 5 million (around $1.2 million). In South Korea, the regulatory authorities distinguish between three types of investors for the purpose of equity crowdfunding—professional investors, investors that meet certain income requirements, and general (retail investors). For each group, different restrictions apply to the amount that can be invested in each project and overall per year.

In Latin America, regulations governing crowd investing are equally diverse. In Brazil, equity transactions are open to all investors, and there are currently no limits on how much individuals can invest. Companies may raise up to $690,000 per year. In contrast, equity crowdfunding in Mexico is permitted only for accredited investors who earn at least the equivalent of $160,000 per year.

Meanwhile, the European alternative finance market has remained substantially fragmented, and although there is no consistent data on cross-border flows, survey evidence suggests that such flows have been very limited. This observation applies to flows between member countries of the euro area and between member countries and other European countries, notably the United Kingdom. While important efforts have been made to ensure financial integration within the euro area and the European Union, regulations remain highly fragmented in the crowdfunding market. This arguably explains why there are significant differences in equity raised through Internet platforms across Europe. As in other regions, the national regulatory environment for crowd investing is likely to change as technological opportunities evolve and market participants and regulators learn more about the benefits and risks in this form of entrepreneurial finance.

10.4   CONCLUSIONS

In this chapter, we have focused on three noninstitutional forms of equity financing of entrepreneurial startups: angel investing, accelerators, and equity crowdfunding. In emerging economies, angel investing is already believed to be at least as important as VC as a funding source. Accelerator programs have gained momentum in several countries, but crowd investing remains at an embryonic stage, growing in countries where the rapid proliferation of the Internet has fuelled the creation of online platforms to match entrepreneurs with investors.

Given the noninstitutional character of angel investing, accelerators, and equity crowdfunding, relatively little is known about their significance as a source of startup funding and their impact on the companies that they fund. We can draw a few early conclusions based on recent research. First, angel investing appears to be a greater complement to VC than substitute, at least in countries with less developed risk capital markets. In these countries, angel investors seem to play a gatekeeping role, enhancing the funded firms' ability to obtain follow-on financing. Thus, angel investing may bridge the funding gap between what friends and families can provide at the initial stage and what venture capitalists, banks, and other sources are willing to contribute as the company gains traction.

Second, angel investing is less focused on high-tech startups than VC. While it remains unclear to what extent angel investing has fostered innovation, the available evidence suggests that angel funding has a positive impact on the survival, growth, and job creation of funded companies. Additionally, it appears that in economies that are less entrepreneurship friendly, companies applying for angel funding tend to be older, larger, and usually already revenue-generating. At the same time, they tend to seek smaller amounts of funding than companies in a more conducive entrepreneurial environment, suggesting that their owners could be self-censoring amid greater perceived (or actual) risk aversion of angel investors.

Third, while accelerator programs themselves provide only moderate amounts of funding, their educational and networking effects are significant. Accelerators not only improve the success rate of participating startups but also foster the development of an entrepreneurial ecosystem and help unleash follow-on funding from angels and venture capitalists. Thus, accelerators have become an integral corporate venturing tool for a growing number of companies (Chapter 9) as well as a focal point for governments aiming to spur innovation and economic growth (Chapter 11).

Fourth, equity crowdfunding could play a larger role in bringing together startups seeking financing and investors looking for good ideas. Unlike angel investors, accelerator programs, and venture capitalists, crowd investors are less geographically confined, enabling online platforms to ensure a superior match over significant distances. However, most crowd investors are relatively inexperienced, and given the significantly smaller amount of capital invested, they are less likely to undertake the thorough due diligence usually conducted by venture capitalists and angel investors. Instead, they may decide to follow more experienced investors who lead investment syndicates. In this case, crowd investing and angel investing would be complements rather than substitutes, with the former helping to fill funding gaps at the lower end of the market. At the same time, however, coinvesting with experienced angels could significantly increase the risk of herd behavior.

Finally, many countries still lack a regulatory framework that allows for retail investor participation in crowd investing through general solicitation and advertising. Regulatory initiatives are underway in several countries, aiming to balance the goals of supporting entrepreneurship while limiting the risks for investors. However, the specific regulations that each country enacts will determine whether or not equity crowdfunding will reshape the venture capital landscape and early-stage funding.

REFERENCES

Agarwal, A.K., Catalini, C., Goldfab, A., 2011. The geography of crowdfunding. NBER Working-Paper 16820. National Bureau of Economic Research.

Bernstein, S., Korteweg, A., Laws, K., 2017. Attracting early stage investors: evidence from a randomized field experiment. J. Financ. 72 (2), 509–538.

Bernthal, B., 2016. Investment accelerators. Unpublished Working Paper. University of Colorado. https://lawweb.colorado.edu/profiles/pubpdfs/bernthal/Investment%20Accelerators(SJLBF%202016).pdf. Accessed April 4, 2017.

Cohen, S.G., Hochberg, Y.V., 2014. Accelerating startups: the seed accelerator phenomenon. http://papers.ssrn.com/sol3/papers.cfm?abstract_id=2418000. Accessed August 24, 2016.

European Trade Association for Business Angels, Seed Funds, and Other Early Stage Market Players, 2014. Statistics compendium 2014. http://www.eban.org/wp-content/uploads/2014/09/13.-Statistics-Compendium-2014.pdf. Accessed May 20, 2016.

Fehder, D.C., Hochberg, Y.V., 2014. Accelerators and the regional supply of venture capital investment. http://papers.ssrn.com/sol3/papers.cfm?abstract_id=2518668. Accessed August 24, 2016.

Gompers, P., Lerner, J., 1996. Grandstanding in the venture capital industry. J. Financ. Econ. 42, 133–156.

Gompers, P., Lerner, J., 1998. What drives venture capital fundraising? Brook. Pap. Econ. Act. – Microecon. 149–192.

Hallen, B., Bingham, C., Cohen, S.L., 2016. Do accelerators accelerate? The role of indirect learning in new venture development. http://papers.ssrn.Com/sol3/papers.Cfm?abstract_id=2719810. Accessed May, 18, 2017.

Hellmann, T., Schure, P., Vo, D., 2015. Angels and venture capitalists: substitutes or complements? Unpublished Working Paper. Said Business School, Oxford University. https://papers.ssrn.com/sol3/papers.cfm?abstract_id=2602739. Accessed May 19, 2017.

Hellmann, T., Thiele, V., 2015. Friends or foes? The interrelationship between angel and venture capital markets. J. Financ. Econ. 115 (3), 639–653.

Hochberg, Y. V., Cohen, S., Fehder, D., 2015. The top 20 start-up accelerators in the U.S. Harvard Business Review. March 31, 2015. https://hbr.org/2015/03/the-top-20-start-up-accelerators-in-the-u-s. Accessed August 26, 2016.

Hornuf, L., Schmitt, M., 2016. Success and failure in equity crowdfunding. CESifo DICE report. 2/2016.

Hornuf, L., Schwienbacher, A., 2017. Should securities regulation promote equity crowdfunding? Small Bus. Econ. 49 (3), 579–593.

Howell, S., 2016. Very early venture finance: how competitions reduce financial frictions. Unpublished Working Paper. New York University.

Kerr, W.R., Lerner, J., Schoar, A., 2014. The consequences of entrepreneurial finance: a regression discontinuity analysis. Rev. Financ. Stud. 21 (1), 20–55.

Lamoreaux, N.R., Levenstein, M., Sokoloff, K.L., 2004. Financing invention during the second industrial revolution: Cleveland, Ohio 1870–1920. NBER Working Paper 10923. National Bureau of Economic Research, Cambridge, MA.

Lerner, J., Schoar, A., Sokolinski, S., Wilson, K., 2015. The globalization of angel investments: evidence across countries. Unpublished Working Paper 16-072. Harvard Business School.

Martinez, A.G., 2016. Chaos Monkeys: Obscene Fortune and Random Failure in Silicon Valley. Harper Collins, New York.

Metrick, A., Yasuda, A., 2010. The economics of private equity funds. Rev. Financ. Stud. 23, 2303–2341.

National Venture Capital Association, 2016. Yearbook. http://nvca.org/research/stats-studies/.

Organisation for Economic Co-operation and Development, 2011a. Financing High-Growth Firms: The Role of Angel Investors. OECD, Paris.

Shane, S., 2008. The importance of angel investing in financing the growth of entrepreneurial ventures. Unpublished Working Paper. Small Business Administration, Office of Advocacy.

Strauez, R., 2017. Crowdfunding, demand uncertainty, and moral hazard – a mechanism design approach. Am. Econ. Rev. 107 (6), 1430–1476.

The Economist, 2017a. A different approach to mobile money in Africa . April 12, 2017.

The Economist, 2017b. A different approach to mobile money in Africa . May 20, 2017.

Wardrop, R., Rosenberg, R., Zhang, B., Ziegler, T., Squire, R., Burton, J., Hernandez, E., Garvey, K., 2016. Breaking new ground. The Americas alternative finance benchmarking report. Centre for Alternative Finance at the Judge Business School at the University of Cambridge and the Polsky Center for Entrepreneurship and Innovation at the Chicago Booth School of Business Cambridge University, Cambridge. https://www.jbs.cam.ac.uk/fileadmin/user_upload/research/centres/alternative-finance/downloads/2016-americas-alternative-finance-benchmarking-report.pdf. Accessed April 18, 2017.

Wardrop, R., Zhang, B., Rau, R., Gray, M., 2015. Moving mainstream. The European alternative finance benchmarking report. Centre for Alternative Finance at the Judge Business School at the University of Cambridge. https://www.jbs.cam.ac.uk/fileadmin/user_upload/research/centres/alternative-finance/downloads/2015-uk-alternative-finance-benchmarking-report.pdf. Accessed April 18, 2017.

Wilson, K.E., Testoni, M., 2014. Improving the role of equity crowdfunding in Europe's capital markets. Bruegel Policy Contribution. Issue 2014/9. August.

Winston-Smith, C., Hannigan, T.J., Gasiorowski, L., 2013. Accelerators and crowdfunding: complementarity, competition, or convergence in the earliest stages of financing new ventures? http://papers.ssrn.com/sol3/papers.cfm?abstract_id=2298875. Accessed August 27, 2016.

World Bank, 2014. Creating your own Angel Investor Group: A Guide for Emerging and Frontier Markets. The World Bank, Washington, DC.

Zhang, B., Deer, L., Wardrop, R., Grant, A., Garvey, K., Thorp, S., Ziegler, T., Ying, K., Xinwei, Z., Huang, E., Burton, J., Chen, H.-Y., Lui, A., Gray, Y., 2016a. Harnessing potential. The Asia-Pacific alternative finance benchmarking report. Centre for Alternative Finance at the Judge Business School at the University of Cambridge and The University of Sydney Business School. Cambridge University, Cambridge. https://www.jbs.cam.ac.uk/fileadmin/user_upload/research/centres/alternative-finance/downloads/harnessing-potential.pdf. Accessed April 18, 2017.

Zhang, B., Wardrop, R., Ziegler, T.; Lui, A., Burton, J., James, A., Garvey, K., 2016b. Sustaining momentum. The second European alternative finance industry report. Centre for Alternative Finance at the Judge Business School at the University of Cambridge. https://www.jbs.cam.ac.uk/fileadmin/user_upload/research/centres/alternative-finance/downloads/2016-european-alternative-finance-report-sustaining-momentum.pdf. Accessed April 18, 2017.

Chapter 11

The Role of Government

ACRONYMS

ADB	Asian Development Bank
AfDB	African Development Bank
BITS	Building on Information Technology Strengths
CAF	Development Bank of Latin America
DEG	Deutsche Investitions- und Entwicklungsgesellschaft
DFIs	Development Financial Institutions
DIF	Direct Investment Facility
EAF	European Angels Fund
EBRD	European Bank for Reconstruction and Development
EDF	Estonian Development Fund
EIB	European Investment Bank
EIF	European Investment Fund
ENCTI	Estratégia Nacional de Ciência, Tecnologia e Inovação
FMF	Federal Ministry of Finance
FMO	Netherlands Development Finance Company
FSU	Former Soviet Union
GOVC	Government-Owned Venture Capital
GP	General Partner
GSVC	Government-Supported Venture Capital
GVC	Government Venture Capital
GVFL	Gujarat Venture Finance Limited
ICT	Information and Communication Technology
IDB	Inter-American Development Bank
IFC	International Finance Corporation
IPO	Initial Public Offering
IVC	Independent Venture Capital
IVCI	Istanbul Venture Capital Initiative
IVF	Tatarstan Investment and Venture Fund
KFC	Kerala Financial Corporation
KITVEN	Karnataka Information Technology Venture Capital Fund
KSIDC	Kerala State Industrial Development Corporation
KPERS	Kansas Public Employees Retirement System
LPs	Limited Partners
MAVCAP	Venture Capital management Berhad
MCTI	Ministério da Ciência, Tecnologia e Inovação

Financing Entrepreneurship and Innovation in Emerging Markets.
https://doi.org/10.1016/B978-0-12-804025-6.00011-3

MIF	Multilateral Investment Fund
MSIP	Ministry of Science, ICT, and Future Planning
NCF	National Capital Fund
NSIA	Nigeria Sovereign Investment Authority
NTI	National Technology Initiative
NVCA	National Venture Capital Association
OPIC	Overseas Private Investment Corporation
R&D	Research & Development
RVCF	Rajasthan Venture Capital Fund
RVCJCS	Russia's VC Fund
SBA	Small Business Association
SBIR	Small Business Innovation Research
SCAF	Seed Capital Assistance Facility
SEIS	Seed Enterprise Investment Scheme
SIDBI	Small Industries Development Bank of India
SITRA	Finnish National Fund for Research and Development
SME	Small or Medium Enterprise
SWF	Sovereign Wealth Fund
VC	Venture Capital
VCFC	Venture Capital Finance Companies
VCTF	Venture Capital Trust Fund

In the preceding chapters, we have discussed the role of private sources of entrepreneurial finance. In this chapter, we look at the roles governments play in promoting entrepreneurship and facilitating the funding of tech startups as important drivers of innovation, job creation, and economic growth. These efforts generally are intended to improve a country's entrepreneurial ecosystem, for example, by reducing regulatory barriers and developing exit markets; providing fiscal incentives; licensing technology derived from government-sponsored research; and implementing a legal environment conducive to private risk-taking.

In addition to measures focusing on institutional reform, many governments around the world provide funding to entrepreneurial firms. In a large number of countries, startups have access to government grants or debt financing. Furthermore, in an effort to develop national venture capital (VC) markets, many governments have become venture capitalists themselves. While some have enacted public programs through which they may invest directly in entrepreneurial firms, others commit capital to independent VC funds to help fund startups, with the General Partner (GP) handling investment decisions. Some also sponsor accelerator or incubator programs. National efforts in emerging economies to foster entrepreneurship and innovation by backing technology startups are in many cases amplified by foreign development financial institutions (DFIs), such as the Overseas Private Investment Corporation (OPIC) in the United States or Britain's CDC Group, as well as regional (e.g., the European Investment Fund (EIF)) and international organizations (especially the International Finance Corporation (IFC)).

While market failures might create a reasonable rationale for government intervention in VC markets (Brander et al., 2015), the effects of specific policies have been subject to dispute. Lerner (2009) cites numerous examples from around the world where well-intended, but poorly designed government initiatives have achieved little or even proved counter-productive, resulting in substantial losses of taxpayer money. The provision of government-sponsored VC has received the greatest amount of skepticism. More specifically, public VC may displace or crowd out private venture capitalists rather than provide additional entrepreneurial finance. If governments are less well positioned than private investors to pick winning investments, there is a risk that government-sponsored VC could undermine innovation, job creation, and economic growth.

This chapter discusses the rationale for government public interventions. In the following section, we focus on measures aimed at improving the institutional framework for entrepreneurship and encouraging private investors to finance technology startups. Next, we assess governments' role as venture capitalists backing entrepreneurial firms directly or indirectly as limited partners (LPs) in independent VC funds. Specifically, we are interested in the question whether public VC is additive to private VC or, in contrast, crowds out private financing of startups. Additionally, we look at the evidence about the efficacy of government-sponsored accelerators and incubators, which in a growing number of countries complement governmental VC investments. We then analyze the role of public pension funds and sovereign wealth funds (SWFs) and the extent to which their investment strategies may be guided not only by return objectives but also by long-term economic development goals. To complete the picture, we finally turn to DFIs and international organizations as important foreign public sources backing entrepreneurial firms in emerging countries.

11.1 MARKET FAILURES AND THE RATIONALE FOR GOVERNMENT INTERVENTION

Government initiatives aimed at spurring innovation by providing debt and equity funding have generally been justified on the basis of the following considerations. First, while economic growth is driven by technological progress, the innovation process is prone to market failures. One market failure may arise from the imperfect degree to which research & development (R&D) returns accrue to the innovator as opposed to other market participants. This appropriability problem (Arrow, 1962) can arise from knowledge spill-overs, which may undermine firms' incentives to invest in R&D (Hall, 2002). Lerner (2009, p. 71) cites the portable digital music player as an example. While the key technology was developed by SaeHan Information Systems, which introduced its first device in 1998, the Korean manufacturer's ultimate sales were tiny compared with Apple's iPod.

Patent laws protecting intellectual property rights are intended to address the free-rider problem of innovation and the resulting under-supply of R&D

and technological progress. While patents are meant to promote innovation, in practice they may hinder technological progress by blocking related innovation by other firms (Jaffe and Lerner, 2004). To the extent that knowledge spill-overs take place, rendering innovation a public good, they create positive externalities which may cause the private and social values of innovation to differ (Boadway and Tremblay, 2005). While it is challenging to calculate the gap between the private and social rate of return from innovations, estimates by Griliches (1992) suggest that the gap between the private and social rate of return from innovation could be between 50% and 100%. In other words, society would earn 15%–20% on an investment in R&D from which an individual firm earned a 10% rate of return.

The risk that companies do less research than desirable, and the potentially large gap between private and social returns on R&D create a powerful argument for governments to provide research subsidies. In the United States, Mazzucato (2015) argues that many highly innovative firms have directly benefited from early-stage government funding and were able to build their products on top of government-funded technologies. Apple's iPhone is a good example: As Mazzucato points out, every technology that makes the iPhone "smart" was government-funded—the Internet, GPS, touch-screen display, and SIRI—while Apple applied its remarkable design skills to these technologies to develop a highly successful commercial product. There are many examples in biotechnology as well, for which the National Institutes of Health have played a crucial role in fostering the research of small innovative companies.

The second argument for government intervention follows from the empirical observation that innovation is largely driven by young entrepreneurial firms, rather than large, mature companies (Chapter 8). Good examples are biotechnology and the Internet, arguably the most revolutionary technological innovations in recent decades. As Lerner (2009) points out, neither established drug companies nor computer software manufacturers pioneered these technologies. The enabling technologies were developed with government funds at academic institutions and research laboratories (Chapter 9), and it was the small entrants who first seized upon the commercial opportunities. However, as we know from Chapter 7, startups generally face significantly tighter credit constraints than mature companies, as they possess few, if any, tangible assets that they can pledge as collateral. In an effort to mitigate such constraints, many governments provide loans or loan guarantees to such firms (see Section 11.3.1).

Finally, a significant number of technology startups are VC-backed, and as our literature review in Chapter 8 suggests, there appears to be a causal relationship between VC and innovation. The fact that VC has played a disproportionately large role in funding high-tech companies is generally attributed to the particular risk profile of these startups and the expertise of venture capitalists who are seen as having superior screening abilities to banks (Boadway and Tremblay, 2005). The inherent risks of funding tech startups stem from informational asymmetries between the entrepreneur and outside investors, with the former invariably knowing much more about the central technology that determines the market potential of his product. Since investors cannot uncritically accept the claims that entrepreneurs make, great ideas may go unfunded (Lerner, 2009), another potentially important market failure in the innovation process (Brander et al., 2015). The ways that venture capitalists screen and monitor high-tech investments and craft their contracts puts them in a privileged position to address this market failure effectively. In addition to providing funding themselves, venture capitalists' approval may act as a catalyst for entrepreneurs to unlock funding from other investors.

Given the important role VC may play for innovation and economic growth, it is understandable that many governments want to establish vibrant VC markets. One set of measures has focused on improving the institutional framework for government financing. In many countries, such measures are underpinned by public investments in startups and/or commitments of public money to independent VC funds. These investments have generally been justified on the grounds that venture capitalists may be subject to herding (Lerner, 2009, p. 70), i.e., their investments tend to focus narrowly on a small set of industries. Entrepreneurial firms that fall outside of these industries may get ignored by independent venture capitalists, despite their technological potential and their ability to grow rapidly and create new jobs. To the extent that governments invest in VC, they might provide certification just like independent VCs, overcoming problems of asymmetric information and allowing high-quality startups to receive additional private funding more easily (Boadway and Tremblay, 2005).

11.2 INSTITUTIONAL REFORM AIMING TO CREATE AN ACTIVE VC MARKET

Our preceding discussion suggests that there are compelling reasons for governments to play an active role in fostering VC. For high-tech startups, VC is an important form of funding due to venture capitalists' screening abilities and the catalyst function that venture funding can have for other investors. Many governments aim to boost economic growth and job creation by developing a vibrant VC market to support the young technology firms that drive innovation and productivity.

Macroeconomic stability is a necessary precondition for VC to flourish. High real interest rates that are often associated with significant macroeconomic imbalances and expectations of high inflation usually serve as a substantial disincentive for private investors to invest in VC. In such environments, investors tend to prefer government bonds that are perceived to offer high returns with low risk. Fortunately, many emerging economies have made significant progress over the past few decades in addressing macroeconomic disequilibria and stabilizing expectations. As such progress has materialized, the focus of national policies has shifted to institutional and regulatory reforms that look to increase the supply of, and the demand for, VC. There are large cross-country differences with regard to the role VC plays in financing entrepreneurship, and as we have discussed in Chapter 8, these differences are largely explained by the quality of their institutions and their regulatory regime. Four areas of potential reform and policy seem to be particularly important (Lerner and Tag, 2013).

First, a well-functioning VC market is generally predicated on a legal environment that allows venture capitalists and entrepreneurs to write efficient and enforceable contracts. The quality of legal institutions determines venture capitalists' ability to screen and monitor their portfolio companies as well as the way entrepreneurs are compensated. From our literature review in Chapter 8 (especially Lerner and Schoar, 2005), we know that VC contract complexity tends to be a function of the quality of the legal environment. In countries where the legal environment is weak and contracts are hard to enforce, private equity firms usually rely more on direct ownership stakes in companies. In contrast, in countries with strong and predictable legal institutions, the contractual use of convertible preferred stock with covenants is more common.

The quality of the legal environment affects not only the choice of the form of investments in entrepreneurial firms but also the speed at which deals are screened (Cumming et al., 2010). In countries whose legal institutions are weak, it is harder to write enforceable contracts, and bureaucratic procedures are slow. In such an environment, boards tend to be less well-informed, limiting the value of board presentation.

While VC tends to play a lesser role in countries with less developed legal institutions and cumbersome judicial processes, the relationship between VC activity and the quality of the legal framework does not seem to be linear. Small differences in the legal environment may not matter much, and as Lerner and Tag (2013) noted, may be dwarfed by differences in VC firms' experience. This hypothesis is consistent with the picture we obtain by focusing more specifically on the protection of minority shareholder rights (Fig. 11.1). Although countries that rank higher on such protection tend to attract more VC relative to the size of their economies, this relationship is not particularly tight. Studying VC contracts in Europe, Kaplan et al. (2007) found that venture capitalists generally use contract terms similar to those used in their home countries. However, more experienced VC firms tend to use U.S.-style contracts regardless of the specific legal environment in their home countries. This is not to say that the quality of the legal environment is of secondary importance. Larger differences, which are usually found in emerging markets, do matter (Lerner and Schoar, 2005), and governments seeking to improve the availability of entrepreneurial finance from VC activity will need to cultivate an appropriate legal framework. Encouragingly, the World Bank (2016b) reports and documents 166 reforms that were implemented in 100 economies between 2005 and mid-2016, aimed at improving shareholder empowerment.

Public policies concerning financial market development are the second area the literature identifies as particularly important, and specifically the establishment of well-functioning stock markets. As we have discussed in Chapter 8,

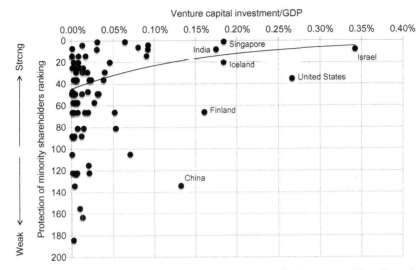

FIG. 11.1 Protection of minority shareholders and venture capital investments. Note: Protection of minority shareholder rankings refer to 2016; VC investment/GDP ratios refer to average 2012–15. https://doi.org/10.1016/B978-0-12-804025-6.00011-3. *(Source: Authors' calculations, based on data from World Bank, 2016a. Enterprise surveys. Available from: http://www.enterprisesurveys. org/data/exploretopics/finance#--13, accessed 16 December 2016, and Thomson One.)*

exits are crucial for venture capitalists. Limited partnership funds, the dominant form of VC investing, have a limited lifetime—usually 10 years—with companies typically held in the fund portfolios for 5–7 years. Venture capitalists generally have the greatest impact in the initial phases of the life cycle of a company, and as the company matures, the skills and capital that VC firms provide can be better deployed elsewhere (Lerner and Tag, 2013; Black and Gilson, 1998). At the same time, it becomes easier for VC-backed companies to attract equity financing from other investors or from banks. For LPs in a VC fund, exits are critical to realize returns from their investments and free up funding for future investments in entrepreneurial firms. Unless investors are able to capitalize their returns, they will not have the funds to recycle into new commitments (Michelacci and Suarez, 2004; Wilson, 2015). Additionally, successful liquidity events provide important signals to LPs in selecting fund managers, thus helping GPs raise a new fund.

The preferred exit route for VC investors is usually an initial public offering (IPO). While startups exited through an IPO often generate comparatively higher returns, a public listing may also be beneficial for the entrepreneur. The IPO allows the entrepreneurs to regain control of the firm as the control rights awarded to the VC firm that backed the start-up expires. Moreover, as Babina et al. (2016) argue, IPOs may foster the creation of new firms as employees benefiting from stock allocations tend to show increased risk appetite and are more likely to become entrepreneurs. As mentioned in Chapter 8, many of today's most valuable publicly listed companies were backed by VC, including Apple Inc., Facebook Inc., Google (Alphabet Inc.), and Microsoft Corp. However, China's Alibaba dwarfed their IPOs: its public listing on the New York Stock Exchange on September 19, 2014 raised $21.8 billion, becoming the world's largest IPO as of the end of 2016.

IPOs of VC-backed companies are relatively rare events, even in countries with well-functioning stock markets. Trade sales to strategic buyers are far more common as a way for a VC fund to liquidate an investment. According to the National Venture Capital Association (2016), strategic buyers acquired 7515 VC-backed companies in the United States between 1995 and 2015, compared with 2010 VC-backed IPOs. In emerging economies, whose VC markets have evolved only recently, there is much less evidence on exits. However, to the extent that liquidity events have occurred in these economies, trade sales have generally accounted for an even higher share than in the United States. A notable exception is China, whose IPO market has seen substantial activity involving both VC and private equity-backed companies. The share of IPOs has declined in recent years as Chinese companies, such as Tencent Holdings Ltd., Baidu Inc., and Didi Chuxing (Chapter 8), acquired a growing number of tech startups through trade sales, but public listings continue to play a key role for venture capitalists to exit their investments. According to PWC (2017), of the 680 exits recorded in China between 2013 and 2015, 268 involved an IPO.[1] Presumably, the substantial overall number of exits and the significant percentage of IPOs of VC-backed startups have been an important driver for fundraising and investing in the Chinese VC market.

Labor market regulations also affect the attractiveness of a VC market (Jeng and Wells, 2000; Bozkaya and Kerr, 2011). Countries whose labor market flexibility is impeded by strong employment protection laws generally attract less VC investments because of two factors: First, if companies find it hard to lay off workers, they are more likely to be reluctant to hire workers in the first place. Second, strong employment protection laws provide a high level of income security, which raises the opportunity costs for potential entrepreneurs to leave their workplace. Additionally, social insurance systems may impose significant wage costs for companies, potentially undermining the desire of would-be entrepreneurs to set up their own firms in light of the social security benefits they have access to as employees (Lerner and Tag, 2013).

Labor mobility is particularly critical in sectors subject to high information asymmetry and investment risk. This includes information technology (IT), life sciences, and other high-tech sectors that attract a substantial share of VC. Job-hopping in Silicon Valley is extremely common (Fallick et al., 2006), and as Bozkaya and Kerr (2011) reported for the European market, labor volatility

---

1. Most VC and private equity-backed companies were listed on the Hong Kong Stock Exchange (98), followed by Shenzhen (93) and Shanghai A (54). The remaining companies were listed abroad, the bulk (18) on the New York Stock Exchange, including Alibaba.

tends to be higher in VC-backed firms than in similar non-VC-backed companies. In designing labor market policies that are conducive to VC activity, it is important to note that it is not just the level of regulation that matters, but the type of regulation is even more important. In a cross-country sample, Bozkaya and Kerr (2011) showed that VC markets are generally more developed in countries that rely on unemployment insurance as opposed to those that put greater emphasis on employment protection schemes.

A final lever for governments to ensure a business environment in which VC can thrive is that of the tax system. Higher capital gains tax rates reduce the number of VC-backed companies (Achleitner et al., 2012) through both demand and supply effects. On the demand side, higher capital gains taxes reduce the returns that entrepreneurs earn if their startups are successful, lowering incentives for them to exert effort and build new businesses that require VC. On the supply side, venture capitalists are less likely to invest in startups whose owners are disincentivized by high corporate gains taxes. As investment activity is curtailed, less VC is raised from LPs (Gompers and Lerner, 1998).

Some countries have applied tax incentives to spur entrepreneurial activity. The United Kingdom, for instance, introduced the Seed Enterprise Investment Scheme (SEIS) in 2012, which offers tax reliefs for equity investments in young firms with less than £200,000 in assets. These reliefs effectively double the realized returns for equity investors in the average eligible firm. Based on the experience with SEIS, Gonzales-Uribe and Paravisini (2016) find a relatively high elasticity of investment activity with respect to the cost of outside capital. According to their estimates, investment increases 1.6% in response to a 10% decline in the cost of outside capital. While only around 1% of eligible firms issued new equity in response to the tax subsidy, firms that did issue new equity increased their investments by a factor of eight, suggesting a high degree of complementarity between outside equity and other nonequity funding sources, especially bank loans.[2]

Income taxes can also affect VC and entrepreneurship, as progressive taxation is generally associated with less entrepreneurial entry. However, this effect also depends on the capital gains tax rate. If the latter is relatively low and if income from entrepreneurship is largely capital gains income, high wage taxes may discourage employment and encourage entrepreneurship (Keuschnigg and Nielsen, 2004, 2005). In this context, Gordon (1998) and Boadway and Tremblay (2005) noted that there are incentives for entrepreneurs to reclassify earnings as corporate rather than personal. For instance, startup employees may receive part of their compensation as stock options. However, the extent to which this is possible depends on the design of tax policies, and several countries maintain restrictions in their tax laws about equity compensation and various nontax costs, rendering income shifting more difficult for corporate employees (as opposed to the owners of a startup).

---

2. These findings are broadly consistent with the results reported by Robb and Robinson (2012) who examined capital structure decisions of young firms in the U.S. See also our discussion in Chapter 7.

While income and corporate gains taxes affect the business environment generally, several countries provide fiscal incentives with the goal of supporting young entrepreneurial firms. These incentives may take different forms, including tax credits for investment, reduced capital gains taxes for investors in startups, and provisions for rollover or carry forward of capital gains or losses. These and other incentives have grown in popularity, although there is little evidence about their impact on startup activity and the availability of private VC funding (Wilson, 2015).

11.3 PUBLIC FUNDING OF ENTREPRENEURSHIP

The preceding discussion has focused on key areas in which governments may implement policy reforms to create more hospitable conditions for entrepreneurship and investing. In fact, in a large number of emerging economies these reforms have allowed the private sector to play a growing role (World Bank, 2016a), although substantial cross-country differences persist. At the same time, many governments in emerging economies have provided debt and/or equity financing through various channels to address market failures in the innovation process. In some cases, these channels have involved public pension funds and SWFs, although market failures generally fall outside of their mandate. Domestic funding efforts in emerging economies have often been accompanied by equity investments in entrepreneurial firms by DFIs and international organizations. Fig. 11.2 presents a schematic overview of the different initiatives. However, such measures have caused controversy as in some cases they have brought about unintended consequences.

11.3.1 Government Loans and Loan Guarantees

In Chapter 7, we saw that debt financing is the most common source of external financing for startups. For entrepreneurs who are confident that their startups will generate high returns loans may be the more attractive funding source. While entrepreneurs whose startups are funded entirely with loans obtain all returns above the loan repayment, entrepreneurs who took equity investments will retain only a share. Additionally, as we discussed in Chapter 8, in situations where entrepreneurs do get funded by VC, venture debt could help delay the next equity round. For young tech firms, however, access to credit may be particularly difficult due to their risk profile and lack of tangible assets that could serve as collateral. Since lenders are not easily able to identify businesses that turn out to be successful enough to service and repay a loan—a challenge that is particularly pertinent in the case of technology startups—they may provide less funding than the company needs and demand a high interest rate. This in turn can raise the risk to the borrower and result in a greater share of higher-risk firms in the pool of borrowers.

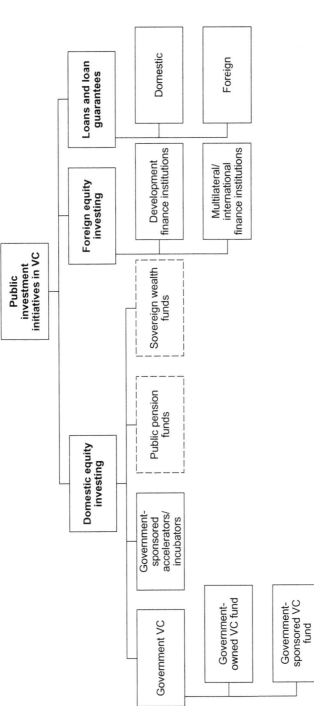

FIG. 11.2 Public equity investments in VC. (*Source: Authors' research.*)

Banks are not the only lenders from which entrepreneurial firms may obtain loans. For instance, startups may also receive funding from venture debt funds to finance their capital expenses and working capital. These providers typically combine their loans with warrants to compensate for the higher risk of default. However, venture debt funds usually provide funding to startups that are backed by equity VC. Furthermore, the amount available is small—between 2010 and 2016 venture debt funds raised less than $1 billion per year worldwide.

Against this background, governments around the world have established programs that provide debt financing to technology-based firms. Generally, this lending is additive, as it provides financing to firms that would not be available from other sources. To the extent that entrepreneurial firms do have access to private sector credit, government loans may be offered on more attractive terms. This may include preferential rates of interest, extended duration loans, or non-refundable debt in case of borrower failure.

Many countries offer some form of government-backed guarantee covering loans to entrepreneurial firms. Under such programs, the government guarantees a share of a qualified loan made by a financial institution. By providing a floor on how much a lender can lose, government loan guarantees serve as a substitute for collateral. To compensate for expected losses from loan guarantee programs, some governments charge an interest rate premium, which typically rises with the percentage of the loan the guarantee covers.

11.3.2   The Government as Venture Capitalist

Governments in many advanced economies have also set up public programs to provide early-stage equity financing to entrepreneurial firms to try to address the risk of market failures. Many of these programs specifically target tech startups whose risk profiles prompt them to seek equity financing more often than other types of small firms (Wilson, 2015). One of the oldest government initiatives is the Small Business Innovation Research (SBIR) program in the United States. Established in 1982, the SBIR remains the largest U.S. public VC initiative, investing seed capital in high-technology startups to foster R&D. But the SBIR is not the only program, as many states have set up their own initiatives. In New York, for example, the State Innovation Venture Capital Fund is a seed and early-stage VC fund with $100 million to support and attract new high-growth businesses.

Governments in a large number of other advanced economies have followed the U.S. example and have enacted similar programs, such as Australia's Industry Investment Fund, Germany's High-Tech Gründerfonds, Israel's Yozma program, and New Zealand's Venture Investment Fund. Governments usually use two different channels when providing VC. Some governments have set up their own government-owned VC funds that invest directly in startups (GOVCs). Instead of trying to pick winners themselves, others commit capital to privately managed VC funds that also rely on private investors (GSVCs).

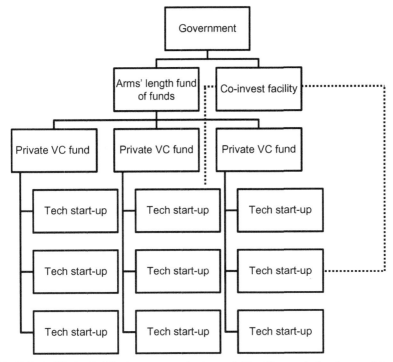

FIG. 11.3   Public fund-of-funds structure and coinvest facility. *(Source: Authors' research.)*

In the latter case, the government typically provides funds to an arm's-length, independently managed quasi-government organization (Fig. 11.3). This organization acts as a fund of funds, screening privately managed VC partnerships and committing capital to those funds believed to be best positioned to deliver on the government's objectives. In addition, the overarching fund may decide to coinvest alongside an independent VC fund in individual portfolio companies.

In some economies, public VC programs play a substantial role as a source of equity capital for startups. In Europe, government agencies, which include national institutions as well as multilateral organizations (EIF and European Bank for Reconstruction and Development (EBRD)), invested almost €10 billion between 2007 and 2015. With a total amount of committed VC of €45.1 billion, government agencies were by far the most important investors in the European VC market, dwarfing the aggregate value of commitments from pension funds, insurance companies, endowments, and family offices (Fig. 11.4).

In emerging economies, public VC programs have also become increasingly common. As in advanced economies, some countries have chosen to follow the GOVC model, while others prefer the GSVC approach, serving as LPs in private VC funds and investing alongside private investors. Both forms are found at the federal government level as well as at the level of individual states. Table A11.1 provides select examples from several emerging economies.

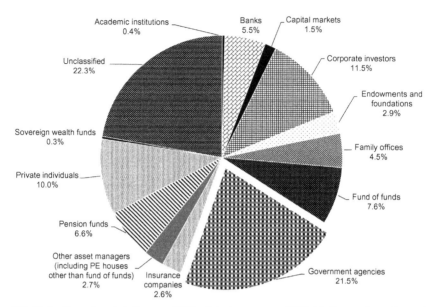

FIG. 11.4 Commitments to European VC funds by investor type, 2007–15. *(Source: InvestEurope.)*

While many governments have provided startup financing to entrepreneurial firms through the intermediate channels of public VC funds or private partnerships, much of what we know about the impact of such programs is based on anecdotal evidence. Lerner (2009) cited a significant number of examples in which governments have attempted to spur innovation, growth, and employment through various policy measures—often with limited, if any success. Among others, these examples include the Kansas Investment Fund in the 1980s; Canada's Labor Fund Program in the 1990s; Finland's efforts to promote entrepreneurship and VC by establishing the Finnish Industry Investment Ltd. and the Finnish National Fund for Research and Development (SITRA) in the mid-1990s; Australia's Building on Information Technology Strengths (BITS) program in the late 1990s; and Malaysia's ill-conceived BioValley project of the 2000s. However, not all public initiatives have been wasteful: juxtaposing successful cases with those that proved wasteful allowed Lerner (2009) to identify important takeaways.

Notwithstanding these early observations, few systematic studies exist that employ large samples to examine the success of public VC initiatives. One exception is Brander et al. (2015) who focused on two major questions: First, to what extent have government-sponsored venture capitalists provided additional startup capital as opposed to displacing or crowding out private venture capitalists? Second, to what extent have startups that have received GVC been successful?

As far as the quantitative impact of GVC funding is concerned, Brander et al. (2015) focused on both the enterprise and the market levels. Government-sponsored programs may have a positive impact on the overall availability of VC either by providing more funding per enterprise or by backing more startups with a given amount of capital. While one would usually assume that enterprise-level additionality would result in market-level additionality, this does not have to be the case. For example, as the authors emphasized, it is possible that even if GVC funding in a given startup displaces private funding in that firm, the displaced capital might be invested in other startups in that market—with markets defined as the firms in a particular industry in a particular country. To answer the second question, Brander et al. (2015) focused mainly on the enterprise level by examining the number of successful exits of startups that have received GVC funding.

The authors employed a dataset that combined deal-level data from Thomson One and the Asian Venture Capital Journal to examine the impact of government-sponsored VC. In total, their sample included almost 20,500 enterprises that received VC funding between 2000 and 2008. Around 89% of these startups were located in 21 advanced economies, with U.S. startups alone accounting for around 50% of the sample. Within emerging economies, the sample includes VC-backed companies from Brazil, China, India, and Malaysia, with China accounting for more than 6% of the total sample.[3] Since Thomson One and the Asian Venture Capital Journal generally lack information on investors and LPs in a VC fund, the authors relied on Capital IQ to identify the sources of capital. Supplementing data from Capital IQ with information obtained from VC websites, they found that on average 29% of all enterprises in the sample received government VC, with country-specific percentages ranging from 6% in Malaysia to 62% in South Korea. In the overwhelming majority of cases in the sample (86%), government funding was provided through government-supported VC partnerships as opposed to government-owned VC funds. These shares do not include funding from pension funds or SWFs, which may also have committed capital to private VC partnerships, but are typically motivated solely by return considerations (see Section 11.4).

Brander et al. (2015) main findings were as follows: First, government-sponsored and private VC appear to be complementary. When governments and private investors provide funding (mixed funding) to back a startup, total investment tends to be higher than when the enterprise receives all of its VC from private investors or all of its funding from government VC. While mixed funding had the highest investment level, pure private funding came next, with pure government funding associated with the smallest overall investment. At the market level, the conclusions are similar: Markets that receive more government funding also receive more funding overall and, importantly, receive more private VC.

Second, the authors found that when government and private VC are present in the same startup, that company is more likely to have a successful exit than when only private VC funds provide funding or the company is backed only by government VC. The positive impact of mixed funding appears to be related to

---

3. In total, Thomson One and the Asian Venture Capital Journal datasets include enterprise data from 56 countries. However, given that 96% of VC investments occurred in the top-25 countries, Brander et al. (2015) decided to concentrate their study on these economies.

the additionality of government VC: Once exits are controlled for the amount of investment, mixed funding no longer has a statistically significant effect on exit performance.

Grilli and Murtinu (2014) focused more narrowly on the impact of government-sponsored VC programs on high-tech entrepreneurial firms in Europe, defining success for a firm in terms of sales and employee growth rather than exit activity. Using a European Union-sponsored firm-level longitudinal dataset, they found that while independent venture capital (IVC) has a statistically significant and positive effect on firm sales growth, the impact of government venture capital (GVC) alone appears to be negligible. Syndicated investments involving both IVC and GVC also show a positive impact on firm sales growth, but this is only the case when IVC investors lead investments. Overall, Grilli and Murtinu's (2014) findings cast doubt on governments' ability to support high-tech entrepreneurial firms through direct and active involvement in VC markets.

While these studies appear to be broadly consistent with the available anecdotal evidence, their results should be interpreted with caution. The econometric tests conducted by Brander et al. (2015) and Grilli and Murtinu (2014) potentially omitted variables. Although the authors used various control variables to deal with omitted variables and employ instrumental variables to correct for any remaining endogeneity, it is possible that there were unobservable characteristics related to enterprise quality. Those characteristics could explain why some companies attract VC funding from governments, or determine how much funding they receive. Thus, more research is needed to determine the extent to which government VC programs actually "cause" entrepreneurship and innovation.

11.3.3 Government-Sponsored Business Accelerators and Incubators

While government-owned VC funds or government-sponsored investments remain the main channels through which governments attempt to foster entrepreneurship and innovation, a growing number of countries have launched government-sponsored business accelerators and incubators. In the United States, for instance, the Startup America Initiative includes a Mentorship Program for Clean Tech Startups that the Small Business Administration (SBA) and the Department of Energy jointly launched. This program funds four private business accelerators to support an additional 100 clean energy startups across the United States. Another Startup America program aims to help veterans launch high-growth businesses through new incubators supported by the Department of Veterans. Another example is Australia's Incubator Support Initiative. Initially funded with AUS$ 5 million and subsequently increased by another AUS$ 15 million, this initiative seeks to support entrepreneurial activity, contribute to the development of Australia's innovation ecosystem and improve the prospects of Australian startups achieving commercial success in international markets.

One of the most recent initiatives is Korea's K-Startup Grand Challenge program, launched in early 2016. Organized by Korea's Ministry of Science, ICT, and Future Planning (MSIP), this program was developed in partnership with Seoul-based accelerators SparkLabs, DEV Korea, ActnerLab, and Shift. Unlike previous initiatives, K-Startup can directly support foreign startups, a program feature that aims to make Korea's tech industry more diverse. Under the three-month program, 40 startups will be selected to receive mentoring from 15 leading Korean tech companies, including Samsung Electronics, LG Electronics, Kakao, and Naver. The 20 most promising startups that are selected on demo day receive $33,000 in funding from the government, with the top four getting an additional $6000–$100,000.[4]

Several governments in emerging markets have also set up accelerators and incubators to foster entrepreneurship and innovation. These instruments have proved particularly popular in Latin America. Brazil's National Startup Acceleration Program, Start-Up Brazil, began as an initiative of the Brazilian Federal Government and was created by the Ministry of Science, Technology, and Innovation (Ministério da Ciência, Tecnologia e Inovação, or MCTI). It is managed by Softex and partners with accelerators to support new technology-based companies. Start-Up Brazil is part of TI Maior, a strategic program of software and IT services, which is one of the initiatives of the National Strategy of Science, Technology, and Innovation (Estratégia Nacional de Ciência, Tecnologia e Inovação, or ENCTI), which selects the best TIC's among priority programs to boost the Brazilian economy.

Start-Up Chile is probably Latin America's best-known government-sponsored accelerator program, which seeks to attract early-stage, high-potential entrepreneurs to bootstrap their startups using Chile as a platform from which to go global. Founded in 2010, the end goal of this program is to position Chile as the innovation and entrepreneurship hub of Latin America. Chile's accelerator program is open to both Chilean and non-Chilean startups. Those that are selected receive a grant of $40,000 (without giving up any equity), a one-year work visa (if required), and shared office space for six months in Santiago de Chile. Furthermore, participating startups may be selected into the Highway program, the mentoring arm of the program where participants are given additional access to top mentors. Start-Up Chile offers around 100 coveted spots every 4 months, for which approximately 650 startups compete. In selecting participants, Start-Up Chile follows a rules-based approach, with external judges scoring and ranking applicants after each round of the process. The rankings are based on three criteria—(i) the quality of the founding team, (ii) the merits of the project, and (iii) the expected impact of the project on Chile's entrepreneurial environment.

---

4. https://techcrunch.com/2016/05/12/south-koreas-government-launches-its-first-accelerator-program-for-international-startups/

Start-Up Chile sponsors three distinct programs based on the stage of the startup. The S Factory is a pre-acceleration program for startups in early concept stage focusing on female founders. Selected companies receive CLP10 million (around $14,000) equity-free and 3 months' acceleration. There are two rounds a year of 20–30 companies each. The Seed Program is an accelerator program for startups with a functional product and early validation. Selected companies receive CLP20 million (around $30,000) equity-free and 6 months' acceleration. There are two rounds a year of 80–100 companies each. Finally, the Scale Program is a follow-on fund for top performing startups that are incorporated in Chile, have traction, and are looking to scale in Latin America and globally. Selected companies receive CLP60 million (around $86,000) equity-free with the condition that they incorporate and open operations in Chile. The Scale Program is run twice a year, with 20–30 companies participating in each program.

Start-Up Chile's success has encouraged several other governments in Latin America to set up similar programs to establish regional tech hubs in their countries. In 2012, the Government of Colombia formed iNNpulsa in order to address the country's lack of VC funding and to promote entrepreneurship and innovation. Housed under the Ministry of Commerce, Industry, and Tourism, iNNpulsa issues government-funded grants to promising entrepreneurs in a wide range of industries. Apps.co is another, more tech-specific government initiative, providing funding to accelerators and university partnership programs as well as training and mentorship to aspiring entrepreneurs. Similar programs have recently been set up in Peru (Start-Up Peru) and Argentina (Incubar).

Most of these initiatives are too new to allow a meaningful assessment of their impact. Gonzales-Uribe and Leatherbee (2016) employ a regression discontinuity approach to examine the impact of Start-Up Chile, comparing the performance of startups that rank marginally above and marginally below the 100th company threshold for the sample period from 2010 to 2013. Their findings do not provide statistically significant evidence that startups admitted to the accelerator program are more successful than those that are rejected. However, those companies that subsequently apply to the Highway and are selected to receive mentoring (approximately 20% of the applicants) are found to significantly outperform their peers in the accelerator program. Gonzales-Uribe and Leatherbee (2016a) suggest that government-sponsored programs possess selection skills and add significant value through mentoring for startups.

11.3.4   The Role of Public Pension Funds and SWFs

So far, we have focused our discussion on public investment initiatives that intend to foster an entrepreneurial ecosystem, innovation, and economic growth. Arguably, financial returns are of second-order importance for these investment decisions. Their objective function distinguishes them from public pension funds and SWFs whose asset allocations are generally assumed to be driven by investment returns. According to the Organisation of Economic Co-operation and Development (2016), pension funds in emerging markets managed around $1.5 trillion in 2015, with funds in Brazil, South Africa, Mexico, and Chile representing the largest (absolute) pools of capital.[5] Pension funds are dwarfed by SWFs, whose assets are estimated at more than $5.1 trillion at the middle of 2016 (see Table A11.2 in the appendix for a list of SWFs in emerging markets). In fact, some countries have established multiple institutions that pursue different investment strategies, thus diversifying investment portfolios and managing risk.

However, recent research casts some doubt on whether investments by pension funds and SWFs are purely motivated by return considerations. A well-documented case that dates back to the 1980s concerns the Kansas Public Employees Retirement System (KPERS). In this case, the state legislature mandated the public pension plan to loan money to local businesses and Kansas real estate developers in an effort to boost economic development (Lerner, 2009, p. 78). By the mid-1980s, KPERS had earmarked a full 20% of the pension plan for these homegrown investments. However, a significant number of these investments led to substantial losses as the two local investment firms handling the Kansas Investment Fund's investment activities were instructed to accelerate their investment pace by expanding the universe of permissible investments to riskier projects.

KPERS is not the only case in which investment strategies seem to have been influenced by considerations other than risk-adjusted returns. Examining investment decisions of U.S. public pension funds, Hochberg and Rauh (2013) find a substantial home-state bias, which is particularly pronounced in VC (and real estate). While other institutional investors, such as endowments, foundations, and corporate pension funds also tend to over-allocate assets in their home states, the authors show this over-allocation to in-state managers is substantially larger for public pension funds. This over-allocation could be justified if public pension funds possessed important informational advantages that could play a particularly critical role in private markets, such as VC, which are typically characterized by asymmetric information. However, this does not appear to be the case. According to Hochberg and Rauh's analysis, U.S. public pension funds significantly underperformed on their in-state VC investments relative to other investments in the same state and vintage, and achieved worse performance than both their own out-of-state investments and investments by out-of-state LPs in their state.

Poor managerial talent or potential mismanagement are two possible reasons for over-allocation. Another possibility suggested by Lerner et al. (2007) could be political pressures on public pension funds to support the local economy. In fact, Andonov et al. (2016) find that funds whose boards have high proportions of members who either sit on the board by virtue of their position

5. Relative to GDP, South Africa has the largest pool of pension assets, accounting for 94%. The next largest pension systems are Namibia (77%) and Chile (68%), Organisation of Economic Co-operation and Development (2016).

in state government (ex officio) or were appointed by a state official underperformed the most, followed by funds whose boards have a high share of members elected by participants. Whatever the exact causes, the hypothetical costs are huge. If each public pension LP had performed as well on its in-state investments as out-of-state public pension LPs performed on investments in the same state, Andonov, Hochberg, and Rauh estimate that the public pension LPs would have reaped $1.25 billion annual in additional returns. It is important to note, however, that these hypothetical costs do not capture the positive welfare implications of home-state investments by public pension funds. While political pressures to invest in in-state funds may result in lower returns on investment, Mollica and Zingales (2007) noted that these investments could have positive externalities for state residents or taxpayers.

Irrespective of whether pension investing in VC is welfare-destroying or welfare-enhancing, from our vantage point it is important to keep in mind that governments may attempt to promote entrepreneurship and innovation not only through GOVCs, GSVCs, and accelerators but also via public pension plans. The same seems to be true in the case of SWFs. Examining the direct private equity investment strategies across SWFs and their relationship to the funds' organizational structures, Bernstein et al. (2013) showed that when political leaders are more involved in fund management, the SWFs' investment strategies seem to favor short-term economic policy goals in their respective countries at the expense of longer-term maximization of returns. Again, the point here is not so much whether or not this strategy results in net welfare losses. Rather, the authors' findings suggest that governments may play a significantly larger role as venture capitalists than their investments through GOVC or GSVC-focused strategies suggest.

11.4   ENTREPRENEURIAL FINANCE PROVIDED BY DEVELOPMENT FINANCE INSTITUTIONS AND MULTILATERAL ORGANIZATIONS

Entrepreneurs in emerging markets may also benefit from VC investments undertaken by foreign public institutions. Several governments in advanced economies have set up DFIs that invest directly in startups or commit capital to VC funds that operate in emerging economies. Prominent examples (see summary in Table A11.3) are Britain's CDC Group; Germany's Deutsche Investitions- und Entwicklungsgesellschaft (DEG); the Dutch Development Finance Company (FMO) and U.S.OPIC in the United States. Their investments are primarily motivated by considerations similar to those of domestic government institutions. Although expected returns may play a role, the primary objective is generally to develop the private sector in the host country. As a result, DFIs often invest in geographies that may be considered to be too risky by private investors. A good example is Afghanistan's Renewal Fund, the country's first VC fund, which is managed by Acap Partners. The fund's LPs are mainly government agencies, including CDC and OPIC. Funding from DFIs is usually reduced and eventually terminated as private sources become available, allowing countries to "gradu-ate" from VC programs run by these organizations.

In emerging economies, DFIs often collaborate closely with regional institu-tions, such as the African Development Bank (AfDB), the Asian Development Bank (ADB), the Multilateral Investment Fund, the Development Bank of Latin America (CAF), and the EBRD. These institutions also run VC and private eq-uity programs funded by their member countries (for details, see Table A11.4). By far the most active investor among regional institutions is the EIF, whose multibillion euro portfolio includes a substantial number of investments in Emerging Europe. This approach to investments is largely similar to that of the IFC, which operates on a global scale.

The potential crowding-out effect we have discussed in the context of VC in-vestments by national GOVCs and GSVCs is probably less relevant in the con-text of DFIs and multilateral institutions, as the latter often invest in countries whose VC industry is still at an embryonic stage. In fact, the risk of crowding out private investments is one reason why these organizations withdraw as soon as private funding gets sufficient momentum. One exception is the EIF, whose abundant resources are substantially invested in VC funds that target assets in advanced member countries of the EU. Not surprisingly, therefore, the EIF has repeatedly received criticism for unfair competition, and inducing private inves-tors with stricter financial criteria to leave the European VC industry altogether (Borgdorff, 2004).

11.5 CONCLUSIONS

Governmental involvement may be justifiable due to the varied market fail-ures that potentially impede innovation, but in practice such interventions take differing forms. Broadly speaking, there are two different approaches. One approach focuses on policy reforms that render the business environment more conducive to entrepreneurship and VC investing. Key areas we have discussed in this context are the legal system, financial sector development, labor market reform, and the tax system. A second approach aims to increase the supply of debt and equity capital. Governments around the globe have set up different schemes, either investing directly in entrepreneurial firms or via commitments to independent VC funds. It is not clear whether concerns about government funding are justified, as there is precious little systematic research on this topic. The research that does exist suggests that government funding has been largely additive. Generally, it is reasonable to assume that the risk of crowding-out effects increases as VC markets mature, validating the approach taken by DFIs, regional, and international organizations that exit the market when private VC funding gains sufficient momentum. Public in-stitutions may play an important role as VC providers; their impact on entre-preneurship and innovation depends on the specific design and governance of their funding vehicles.

APPENDIX

TABLE A11.1 Select Government-Owned and Government-Sponsored Venture Capital Funds in Emerging Markets

Country	Fund	Activity
Brazil	Brazilian Development Bank (BNDES)	Investing in a significant number of VC partnerships, the Brazilian Development Bank is one of the country's largest LPs.[a]
China	To be announced	In 2016, the Chinese government decided to launch a new VC fund to invest in seed-stage tech startups. The fund is expected to be as large as $30 billion. Owned by the government, this initiative will be part of a broader plan to wean the economy off its dependence on fixed asset investment in infrastructure and property, while fostering new opportunities for private sector companies.[b] This new VC fund was preceded by the government's decision to allow insurance companies to invest in VC funds, and its capital is expected to come from both such private investors and the government.
Estonia	Estonian Development Fund (EDF)	The Estonian Development Fund (EDF) was set up as a state-run public institution that invests in young and growth-oriented technology companies together with the private sector. More specifically, the EDF aims to invest into knowledge-intensive and high-tech Estonian companies that are in launching stage, offering management-related support to the relevant operators. In providing investment support, the EDF can invest in small and medium-sized enterprises (SMEs) registered in Estonia. The Fund's objective is to identify and encourage venture capitalists and business angels to coinvest into knowledge-based company startups.
Ghana	Venture Capital Trust Fund (VCTF)	Ghana's VCTF was established in 2005 to help create an active VC industry with investments in various sectors. The VCTF provides capital to eligible Venture Capital Finance Companies (VCFCs) to support SMEs as well as financial resources to foster other activities and programs for the promotion of venture capital financing.

Country	Fund	Description
India	Karnataka Information Technology Venture Capital Fund (KITVEN Fund)	The Karnataka Information Technology Venture Capital Fund is a venture capital fund backed by institutions of the State of Karnataka and the Indian Central Government. Operating since 1999 in the IT and biotech sectors, the fund invests in emerging companies with a long-term investment approach, focusing on investments in seed/rapid growth opportunities within the State of Karnataka. Frequently, the fund is the founding/first investor.
	Rajasthan Venture Capital (RVCF)	Rajasthan Venture Capital, which is supported by the Rajasthan State Industrial Development and Investment Corporation the Small Industries Development Bank of India (SIDBI), focuses on investments in startups and mid-stage companies that operate in high-growth sectors with a sustainable revenue model.
	Gujarat Venture Finance Limited (GVFL)	Gujarat Venture Finance Limited (GVFL), which is jointly owned by the government and the private sector, was founded in 1990 at the initiative of the World Bank. GVFL is an independent venture finance company. Since its inception, GVFL has set up seven investment vehicles, providing VC to tech startups.
	Kerala State Industrial Development Corporation (KSIDC)	The Kerala State Industrial Development Corporation (KSIDC) has recently established an INR 10 billion angel fund to support startups in the state of Kerala. However, instead of investing this capital directly in entrepreneurial firms, KSIDC partners with Kerala Financial Corporation (KFC) to commit capital to and help launch private VC funds.
Malaysia	Venture Capital Management Berhad (MAVCAP)	Malaysia's Venture Capital Management Berhad was established in 2001 to help nurture infant ICT companies into thriving businesses. Apart from providing financial resources, MAVCAP plays an active role in mentoring their portfolio companies.
Nigeria	YouWIN! SME Growth Fund	The YouWIN! Fund is a commercially focused fund, established by the Federal Ministry of Finance (FMF) of Nigeria and the Nigeria Sovereign Investment Authority (NSIA). Established with a seed capital of N 3.9 billion (approximately $25 million), which is expected to double in size, its objective is to support SMEs in Nigeria. Specifically, YouWIN! focuses on enterprises with the potential to foster innovation, generate attractive returns on investment, create jobs, and promote entrepreneurship and social development in general. The Fund invests between N 25 million to N 45 million per portfolio company in return for an equity share or as secured loans.
Poland	National Capital Fund (NCF)	Poland's National Capital Fund (NCF) was set up as the government's central fund of VC funds. Established in 2005, the NCF provides VC funds with financial support for their investments in innovative SMEs, aiming to help fill the equity gap on the Polish SME market.

Continued

TABLE A11.1 Select Government-Owned and Government-Sponsored Venture Capital Funds in Emerging Markets—cont'd

Country	Fund	Activity
South Africa	Technology Venture Capital Fund	South Africa's Technology Venture Capital Fund was established by the Department of Trade and Industry and is managed by the Industrial Development Corporation. The Fund's objective is to increase the number of productive companies in South Africa, thus contributing to economic growth and international competitiveness through innovation and technological advancement. Focusing especially on the commercialization of innovative products, the Fund provides both seed capital and business support.
Russia	VC Fund (RVC JCS)	Russia's VC Fund (RVC), which is a government fund of funds, is one of Russia's key tools in building its own national innovation system. Established in 2006, the main purpose of RVC JCS is to promote the creation of Russia's VC industry and significantly increase financial resources of VC funds. Since 2015, RVC JCS has also served as a project office for the implementation of the National Technology Initiative (NTI)—the long-term strategy of the country's technological development.
	Tatarstan Investment and Venture Fund (IVF)	At the state level, the Investment and Venture Fund (IVF) of the Republic of Tatarstan was set up in 2004 to focus specifically on the innovation potential of the Republic of Tatarstan itself. The main objective of the IVF is to support entrepreneurial firms and SMEs and create favorable conditions for venture financing. In pursuing this objective, the fund helps implement innovation and investment projects, including those in the early stages of development; provides grants for R&D activities and research; and coinvests in high-tech areas with significant export potential.
Thailand	To be announced	The Government of Thailand decided in late 2014 to set up a VC fund of TBH 25 billion ($750 million) to invest in Thai SMEs. The fund will invest between 5% and 50% of the registered capital of companies in tech companies as well as in startups and SMEs in less tech-intensive sectors.
Turkey	Turkish Growth and Innovation Fund	The Turkish Growth and Innovation Fund aims to support innovative and technology oriented businesses with rapid growth potential. Established in 2016 by various government agencies and the EIF, the fund is Turkey's next generation of fund of funds and succeeds the Istanbul Venture Capital Initiative (IVCI), which was launched in 2007 and made 10 investments, including in some of Turkey's VC and growth capital funds. Although the Turkish Growth and Innovation Fund will continue to commit capital to growth equity funds, with its strong focus on innovation it was formed to provide more firepower for early-stage investments, with its fund size totaling €200 million.

[a]https://mitbrazilventurecapitalstudy.files.wordpress.com/2013/03/mit-brazil-vc-study-2012-2013.pdf.
[b]http://www.ft.com/cms/s/0/73f216c8-9c97-11e4-a730-00144feabdc0.html#axzz4J6IUeczx.
Source: Authors' summaries, based on information provided on governments' websites.

TABLE A11.2 Sovereign Wealth Funds in Emerging Economies (as of April 2017)

Country	Sovereign Wealth Fund	Assets ($B)	Inception
UAE	Abu Dhabi Investment Authority	828	1976
China	China Investment Corporation	814	2007
Kuwait	Kuwait Investment Authority	592	1953
Saudi Arabia	SAMA Foreign Holdings	514	...
China	SAFE Investment Company	441	1997
Qatar	Qatar Investment Authority	335	2005
China	National Social Security Fund	295	2000
UAE	Investment Corporation of Dubai	201	2006
Saudi Arabia	Public Investment Fund	183	2008
UAE	Mubadala Development Company	125	2002
UAE	Abu Dhabi Investment Council	110	2007
Russia	National Welfare Fund	72	2008
Libya	Libyan Investment Authority	66	2006
Kazakhstan	Kazakhstan National Fund	65	2000
Iran	National Development Fund of Iran	62	2011
Kazakhstan	Samruk - Kazyna JSC	61	2008
Malaysia	Khazanah National	35	1993
UAE	Emirates Investment Authority	34	2007
Azerbaijan	State Oil Fund	33	1999
Oman	State General Reserve Fund	18	1980
East Timor	Timor-Leste Petroleum Fund	17	2005
Russia	Reserve Fund	16	2008
Chile	Social and Economic Stabilization Fund	15	2007
Russia	Russia Direct Investment Fund	13	2011
Bahrain	Mumtalkat Holding Company	11	2006
Chile	Pension Reserve Fund	9	2006
Peru	Fiscal Stabilization Fund	8	1999

Continued

TABLE A11.2 Sovereign Wealth Funds in Emerging Economies
(as of April 2017)—cont'd

Country	Sovereign Wealth Fund	Assets ($B)	Inception
Algeria	Revenue Regulation Fund	8	2000
Mexico	Oil Revenues Stabilization Fund	6	2000
Oman	Oman Investment Fund	6	2006
Botswana	Pula Fund	6	1994
Trinidad and Tobago	Heritage and Stabilization Fund	6	2000
China	China–Africa Development Fund	5	2007
Angola	Fundo Soberano de Angola	5	2012
Kazakhstan	National Investment Corporation	2	2012
Nigeria—Bayelsa	Bayelsa Development and Investment Corporation	2	2012
Nigeria	Nigerian Sovereign Investment Authority	1	2012
UAE	RAK Investment Authority	1	2005
Bolivia	FINPRO	1	2012
Senegal	Senegal FONSIS	1	2012
Iraq	Development Fund for Iraq	0.9	2003
Palestine	Palestine Investment Fund	0.8	2003
Venezuela	FEM	0.8	1998
Kiribati	Revenue Equalization Reserve Fund	0.6	1956
Vietnam	State Capital Investment Corporation	0.5	2006
Brazil	Sovereign Fund of Brazil	0.5	2008
Ghana	Ghana Petroleum Funds	0.5	2011
Gabon	Gabon Sovereign Wealth Fund	0.4	1998
Mauritania	National Fund for Hydrocarbon Reserves	0.3	2006
Mongolia	Fiscal Stability Fund	0.3	2011
Equatorial Guinea	Fund for Future Generations	0.1	2002
Total		5029	

Source: Sovereign Wealth Fund Institute; accessed April 30, 2017.

TABLE A11.3 Select Foreign Initiatives of VC Funding in Emerging Economies

Country	Organization	Activity
Germany	Deutsche Investitions- und Entwicklungs- gesellschaft (DEG)	Germany's DEG invests around €1–1.5 billion annually and has an investment portfolio of more than €7 billion, involving both lending and equity operations.[a] DEG takes equity positions directly in small- and medium-sized companies in emerging economies but is also an active fund investor. As an LP, it frequently serves as an anchor investor, aiming to help mobilize other public and private LPs. It is not uncommon for DEG to hold between 20% and 40% of a fund's capital. DEG not only provides capital but also assists GPs in structuring their funds and investments. DEG invests globally, with its portfolio spanning more than 70 countries around the world.
Netherlands	Netherlands Development Finance Company (FMO)	The Netherlands Development Finance Company (FMO) has a portfolio totaling more than €9 billion. Like CDC and DEG, it operates across the entire capital structure of companies in emerging markets. This includes private equity and VC, with FMO serving as one of the most active LPs in emerging-market focused partnerships and investing alongside such funds as a coinvestor. Like CDC and DEG, FMO frequently backs first-time fund managers as an anchor investor in emerging market funds or funds in FMO's focus sectors. Further, FMO s also active as a direct investor, with a sectoral focus on financial institutions and energy companies.
U.K.	CDC Group	CDC pursues a dual strategy of direct and fund investments. Founded in 1948, CDC is the world's oldest DFI, and with an investment portfolio of £3.4 billion, it is also one of the world's largest institutions of its kind. CDC provides capital through the forms of equity, debt, mezzanine, and guarantees. Geographically, CDC's investments now concentrate on Africa and South East Asia, but this concentration is relatively new, and CDC's legacy portfolio still continues a significant amount of assets the institution had invested in under its previous global mandate.
U.S.	Overseas Private Investment Corporation (OPIC)	In contrast to the European DFIs, the OPIC in the United States provides private equity VC exclusively through privately owned and managed investment funds.[b] OPIC is one of the largest private equity and VC fund sponsors in emerging countries and is typically one of the first fund sponsors to enter an unproven market, a characteristic OPIC has in common with most other DFIs. While there is no specific information on OPIC's commitments to VC and growth capital funds as opposed to other strategies (specifically buyouts, distressed debt, and mezzanine), its overall volume of commitments to private equity funds has totaled $4.1 billion since 1987 (as of mid-20 6). In turn, the 62 partnerships in which OPIC has served as an LP have invested $5.6 billion in more than 570 privately owned and managed companies across 65 countries.

[a]This includes investments in DEG's home market, Germany. See DEG (2016).
[b]In addition to private equity and VC fund investments, OPIC is also active in debt financing and political risk insurance.
Source: Authors' collection of information from institutions' websites.

TABLE A11.4 Multilateral Institutions Providing Entrepreneurial Finance

Region	Organization	Activity
Africa	Africa Development Bank (AfDB)	The African Development Bank (AfDB) provides equity capital both through private equity funds including VC funds that back startups in Africa (about 80%) and direct investments (about 20%). The AfDB participates in the Seed Capital Assistance Facility (SCAF), together with the Asian Development Bank (ADB). Implemented through the United Nations Environment Programme, with support from the Global Environment Facility and the United Nations Foundation, this facility aims to increase the availability of investment for early-stage development of low-carbon projects in low-income countries. In pursuing this objective, the SCAF provides conditional grants to VC and private equity funds, helps fund managers source deals, cofinances the development costs of getting seeded projects to full financial close, and offers technical assistance.
Europe (European Union)	European Investment Fund (EIF)	The European Investment Fund, which is part of the European Investment Bank (EIB), is a leading financial institution in the European private equity and VC market. The EIF's portfolio of activities includes both debt and equity operations as well as microfinance. The EIF's mandate for equity investments is to foster innovation and entrepreneurship by helping develop a vibrant European private equity and VC ecosystem. The EIF has made substantial commitments to funds operating across the entire spectrum from seed to later-stage/expansion financings. Of particular interest is the InnovFin Equity initiative, which provides risk capital financing to funds that provide equity and quasi-equity investments focusing on innovative sectors such as ICT, life sciences, clean energy and on societal challenges such as resource efficiency, bioeconomy, health and demographics, climate change. The EIF often backs first-time funds as an anchor investor to serve as a catalyst for commitments from other LPs, especially from the private sector. Geographically, the EIF's mandate is restricted to Europe, investing in entrepreneurial companies in advanced economies in Western Europe as well as emerging markets in central and Eastern Europe. According to its own estimates, 12% of all funds raised by European VC partnerships in 2014 came directly from the EIF.[a] However, its role as a catalyst is estimated to be much larger, with 45% of all capital committed to European VC funds believed to be directly or indirectly associated with the EIF. On the investment side, the EIF has been an equally dominant player, with an estimated share of 41% of the capital received by European startups in 2014.

Europe (European Union)		In November 2016, the EIF and European Commission launched a new Pan-European VC funds-of-funds program to further address Europe's equity gap, the fragmentation of the VC market and to attract additional private funding from institutional investors into the EU VC asset class. Under the program, the EIF provides a maximum of 25% of the total commitments of a fund-of-funds, which in turn invest in funds on the basis of their investment strategy. The maximum size of each investment in a selected fund-of-funds is limited to €300 million. The program is sponsored by the EU and forms part of the Capital Markets Union Action Plan, the Digital Single Market Strategy, and the Open Innovation strand of Horizon 2020.
	European Angels Fund (EAF)	More recently, the EIF has set up the European Angels Fund (EAF). At the end of 2015, the EAF had a volume of €253 million, including €75 million that had already been committed. The EAF acts as a co-investor alongside business angels aiming to support innovative companies in the seed, early, and growth stage. However, instead of granting coinvestments on a deal-by-deal basis, the EAF maintains long-term contractual relationships with business angels. According to the coinvestment framework agreements between the EAF and business angels, the former commits a predefined amount of equity upfront for future investments. As of mid-2016, the EAF was operational only in a handful of European countries, all advanced economies (Austria, Germany, Ireland, the Netherlands, and Spain), but there are plans to extend the fund's geographical focus, including into Central and Eastern Europe.
Europe (Central and Eastern Europe; Former Soviet Union; member countries in adjacent regions)	European Bank For Reconstruction and Development (EBRD)	The mandate of the European Bank for Reconstruction and Development (EBRD) differs in several ways from that of the EIF. While the EIF focuses on fostering innovation and entrepreneurship in Europe through investments in VC funds that back startups in their early phases, the EBRD also commits capital to partnerships that undertake leveraged buyouts, invest in distressed situations or provide mezzanine capital. Geographically, however, the EBRD's portfolio is restricted to investments in eligible member countries in central and Eastern Europe and the former Soviet Union (FSU). Finally, unlike the EIF, the EBRD also undertakes direct investments through its Direct Investment Facility (DIF), focusing on small businesses based in countries at an early stage in their transit on to the market economy.[b]

TABLE A11.4 Multilateral Institutions Providing Entrepreneurial Finance

Region	Organization	Activity
Latin America and the Caribbean	Multilateral Investment Fund (MIF)	The most active regional development institution in Latin America investing in VC is the Multilateral Investment Fund (MIF), which has been set up by the Inter-American Development Bank (IDB) as its innovation lab. Established in 1993, the MIF has invested in a significant number of VC partnerships backing startups at their seed to expansion stages. Through its commitments to these partnerships, the MIF aims to foster the development of a VC ecosystem in the region. Its investment strategy focuses especially on first-time managers, helping them to build a track record and attract additional capital. Serving as a catalyst for private sector participation, its fund commitments are usually contingent on the fund manager raising additional private sector commitments. Thus, the MIF reports a similarly high success rate as the European EIF, with every invested dollar mobilizing four dollars in additional private fund resources.
	Development Bank of Latin America (CAF)	In contrast to the MIF, the Development Bank of Latin America (CAF) has a broader investment mandate. Although CAF invests in VC funds, it also commits capital to private equity partnerships backing SMEs that have already reached a more advanced stage in their life cycle. CAF additionally invests directly in companies through equity and debt transactions.
Multilateral	International Finance Corporation (IFC)	At the global level, public investments in VC are channeled through the International Finance Corporation (IFC), a member of the World Bank Group. The majority of IFC's VC operations focus on direct investments, with some transactions involving businesses in the preseed investment stage. At the same time, the IFC serves as an LP in a significant number of emerging-market VC funds. Through both strategies, it has built a highly diversified portfolio, across geographies and sectors, encompassing startups as varied as Andela, a Nigerian education company; Portea, an Indian healthcare company; Planet Labs, a satellite imagery company; Hepsiburada, a Turkish consumer Internet company; and Souq.com, a Middle Eastern consumer Internet company (as of the middle of 2016).
		Across all sectors, the IFC's investment decisions are intended to promote innovative technologies that can have transformative impact on people's lives, by lowering costs and expanding access to essential goods and services. Consistent with this objective, it favors transactions that help accelerate cross-border technology transfers. Through its recently launched TechEmerge program, the IFC connects tech startups from around the world with larger corporations in emerging markets to conduct local pilot projects and build commercial partnerships.

[a]See Kraemer-Eis et al. (2016).
[b]As of June 2016, eligible countries are Armenia, Azerbaijan, Belarus, Georgia, Kyrgyz Republic, Moldova, Mongolia, Tajikistan, Turkmenistan, and Uzbekistan.
Source: Authors' collection of information from institutions' websites.

REFERENCES

Achleitner, A., Bock, C., Watzinger, M., 2012. The selection effect of taxes: the case of venture capital investment In: European Economic Association & Econometric Society Annual Meeting 2012. Spain, Malaga.

Andonov, A., Hochberg, Y.V., Rauh, J.D., 2016. Pension fund board composition and investment performance: evidence from private equity. Unpublished Working Paper. Hoover Institution Economics. http://www.hoover.org/sites/default/files/research/docs/16104_-_pension_ fund_board_composition_and_investment_performance_-_andonov_hochberg_and_rauh. pdf, Accessed January 30, 2017.

Arrow, K.J., 1962. Economic welfare and the allocation of resources for invention. In: Nelson, R.R. (Ed.), The Rate and Direction of Inventive Activity: Economic and Social Factors. Princeton University Press, Princeton, pp. 609–642.

Babina, T., Quimet, P., Zarutskie, R., 2016. Going entrepreneurial? IPOs and new firm creation. Unpublished Working Paper Federal Reserve Board. https://www.aeaweb.org/conference/2017/ preliminary/paper/BiYBAstD.

Bernstein, S., Lerner, J., Schoar, A., 2013. The investment strategies of sovereign wealth funds. J. Econ. Perspect. 27 (2), 219–238.

Black, B.S., Gilson, R.J., 1998. Venture capital and the structure of capital markets: banks versus stock markets. J. Financ. Econ. 47, 243–277.

Boadway, R., Tremblay, J.-F., 2005. Public economics and start-pp entrepreneurs. In: Keuschnigg, C., Kanniainen, V. (Eds.), Venture Capital, Entrepreneurship, and Public Policy. MIT Press, Cambridge, MA, pp. 181–219.

Borgdorff, W., 2004. Public money is harming the VC industry. Financial Times (February 16).

Bozkaya, A., Kerr, W.R., 2011. Labor regulations and European venture capital. Unpublished Working Paper Harvard Business School. http://www.hbs.edu/faculty/Publication%20Files/08-043.pdf.

Brander, J.A., Du, Q., Hellmann, T., 2015. The effects of government-sponsored venture capital: international evidence. Rev. Financ. 19, 1–48.

Cumming, D.J., Schmidt, D., Walz, U., 2010. Legality and venture capital exits. J. Bus. Ventur. 25, 54–57.

Deutsche Investitions- und Entwicklungsgesellschaft mbH, 2016. Jahresabschluss. Lageberi-cht 2016. DEG, Cologne. https://www.deginvest.de/DEG-Dokumente/Download-Center/ Jahresabschlussbericht_2015_D.pdf..

Fallick, B., Fleischman, C., Rebitzer, J., 2006. Job-hopping in Silicon Valley: some evidence concerning the micro-foundations of a high-technology cluster. Rev. Econ. Stat. 88, 472–481.

Gompers, P., Lerner, J., 1998. What drives venture capital fundraising? Brook. Pap. Econ. Act. 149–192.

Gonzales-Uribe, J., Leatherbee, M., 2016. Business accelerators: evidence from Start-up Chile. https://papers.ssrn.com/sol3/papers.cfm?abstract_id=2651158.

Gonzales-Uribe, J., Paravisini, D., 2016. Howe sensitive is young firm investment to the cost of outside equity? https://workspace.imperial.ac.uk/business-school/Public/research/f_agroup/ Gonzalez-Uribe%20abstract.pdf. Accessed January 30, 2017.

Gordon, R., 1998. Can high personal tax rates encourage entrepreneurial activity? IMF Staff. Pap. 45, 49–80.

Griliches, Z., 1992. The search for R&D spillovers. Scand. J. Econ. 94, 29–47.

Grilli, L., Murtinu, S., 2014. Government, venture capital and the growth of European high-tech entrepreneurial firms. Res. Policy 43, 1523–1543.

Hall, B.H., 2002. The financing of research and development. Oxf. Rev. Econ. Policy 18, 35–51.

Hochberg, Y.V., Rauh, J.D., 2013. Local overweighting and underperformance: evidence from limited partner private equity investments. Rev. Financ. Stud. 26 (2), 403–451.

Jaffe, A., Lerner, J., 2004. Innovation and Its Discontents: How Our Broken Patent System Is Endangering Innovation and Progress, and What to Do About It. Princeton University Press, Princeton.

Jeng, L., Wells, P., 2000. The determinants of venture capital funding: evidence across countries. J. Corp. Finan. 6, 241–289.

Kaplan, S.N., Martel, F., Strömberg, P., 2007. How do legal differences and experience affect financial contracts? J. Financ. Intermed. 16, 273–311.

Keuschnigg, C., Nielsen, S.B., 2004. Start-ups, venture capitalists and the capital gains tax. J. Public Econ. 87, 1011–1042.

Keuschnigg, C., Nielsen, S.B., 2005. Public policy for start-up entrepreneurship with venture capital and bank finance. In: Kanniainen, V., Keuschnigg, C. (Eds.), Venture Capital, Entrepreneurship, and Public Policy. MIT Press, Cambridge, MA, pp. 221–250.

Kraemer-Eis, H., Signore, S., Prencipe, D., 2016. The European venture capital landscape: Volume I: The impact of EIF on the VC ecosystem. EIF Working Paper 2016/34. European Investment Fund, Luxembourg.

Lerner, J., 2009. Boulevard of Broken Dreams. Why Public Efforts to Boost Entrepreneurship and Venture Capital Have Failed–And What to Do About It. Princeton University Press, Princeton.

Lerner, J., Schoar, A., 2005. Does legal enforcement affect financial transactions? The contractional channel in private equity. Q. J. Econ. 120, 223–246.

Lerner, J., Schoar, A., Wongsunwai, W., 2007. Smart institutions, foolish choices: the limited partner performance puzzle. J. Financ. 62, 731–764.

Lerner, J., Tag, J., 2013. Institutions and venture capital. Ind. Corp. Chang. 22 (1), 153–182.

Mazzucato, M., 2015. The Entrepreneurial State: Debunking Private Versus Public Sector Myths. Anthem Press, London.

Michelacci, C., Suarez, J., 2004. Business creation and the stock market. Rev. Econ. Stud. 113, 207–225.

Mollica, M., Zingales, L., 2007. The impact of venture capital on innovation and the creation of new businesses. Unpublished Working Paper. University of Chicago.

National Venture Capital Association, 2016. Yearbook. http://nvca.org/research/stats-studies/.

Organisation of Economic Co-operation and Development, 2016. Pension Markets in Focus. OECD, Paris.

PWC, 2017. China private equity/venture capital 2016 review and 2017 outlook. https://www.pwccn.com/en/private-equity/pe-china-review-feb2017.pdf.

Robb, A.M., Robinson, D.T., 2012. The Capital structure decisions of new firms. Rev. Financ. Stud. 27 (1), 153–179.

Tech Crunch, May 12, 2016. South Korea's government launches its first accelerator program forinternational startups. https://techcrunch.com/2016/05/12/south-koreas-government-launchesits-first-accelerator-program-for-international-startups/.

Wilson, K.E., 2015. Policy lessons from financing innovative firms. OECD Science, Technology and Industry Policy Papers No. 24 OECD, Paris.

World Bank, 2016a. Enterprise surveys. http://www.enterprisesurveys.org/data/exploretopics/finance#--13.

World Bank, 2016b. Doing Business 2017: Equal Opportunity for All. The World Bank, Washington, DC.

Index

Note: Page numbers followed by *f* indicate figures and *t* indicate tables.

A

Accelerators, 227–228
  characteristics, 249–251
  government-sponsored business, 278–280
  successful programs, 251–252
ACRL Framework, 133
Advanced nursing practice, doctoral education
  for, 138
Alibaba Group Holding Ltd., 88
Alibaba's CVC investments, in China, 233*f*
American Nurses Association, 137
American Research and Development
  (ARD), 221
Angel investments, 240–241
Angel investors
  business executives, 246–247
  early-stage funding, 240–243
  financing's impact, 247–249
  investments market size, 244–247
Artificial intelligence (AI), 88, 177–178

B

Baccalaureate education
  locating evidence, 135
  professional nursing practice, 135
Baidu, Alibaba, and Tencent (BAT), 105
Balance-sheet lending, 175–176
  market volume, 178*t*
Bangladesh Rehabilitation Assistance
  Committee (BRAC), 170
Bank lending, 169
Banks, 166–170
Biotechnology, 193–194
  CVC-backed, 231
Bombay Stock Exchange (BSE), 124
Broadband, 122–123
Business environment
  quality of, 7–10
  subpillar, 53
Business sophistication pillar, 62*t*
Business-to-business (B2B) commerce, 20–21

C

Cash-on-delivery (C.O.D) model, 20
China
  equity-based crowdfunding projects,
    253, 258
  innovation ecosystem, 90–93
    emerging multinational, 82
    Tencent's growth, 100
  market and possibilities, 102–104
ChinaAccelerator, 250–251
China science and technology (S&T) policies
  deepening reform phase (1996–2006), 72
  experimental phase (1978–85), 70–71
  latest reforms, 79–80
  long-term plan and policy optimization
    (2006–14), 72–73
  outcomes and analysis
    cultivation of R&D workforce, 77
    innovation results, 74–76
    R&D investment, 73
    science education, 76
  systemic reform phase (1985–95), 71–72
Chinese Internet industry, 105
Chinese Unicorns, 212*t*
Cityelite, 95
Clustering leaders, 42–45
Compound annual growth rate (CAGR), 123,
  123*f*, 209
Confederation of Indian Industry (CII), 120
Corporate venture capital (CVC), 23, 185–186
  corporate venture cycles, 223–226
  emerging markets, 232–236
  intelligence-gathering initiative, 220
  internal investments, 220
  market size, 221–223
  market transformations, 220
  organizational forms, 226–229
  success measurement, 229–232
Country codes, 42–43, 43*f*
Creative outputs pillar, 66*t*
Credit availability, 54
Credit constraints, 166–170

Credit gap, 167*f*, 168
Credit-scoring technology, 177–178
Credit subpillar, 54–55
Crowdfunding, 25, 175
Crowd investing, 25
    business model, 252–256
    investment risk, 255
    market size, 256–259
    role of regulation, 256–259

D

Debt financing, 272
Development financial institutions
    (DFIs), 264
Doctoral education, for advanced nursing
    practice, 138
Driving investments, 230

E

E-commerce, 104, 202–209
Economic development, 3–5
Emergent investments, 229
Employee Retirement Income Security Act
    (ERISA), 223
Enabling investments, 235
Entrepreneurial finance
    accelerators
        characteristics, 249–251
        successful programs, 251–252
    angel investors
        early-stage funding, 240–243
        financing's impact, 247–249
        investments market size, 244–247
    crowd investing
        business model, 252–256
        market size, 256–259
        role of regulation, 256–259
    multilateral institutions, 290*t*
    venture capital, 239
Entrepreneurial start-ups, 219
Entrepreneurship, 7–10, 128
    emerging economies, 165*f*
    and finance, 13–14, 13*f*, 163–166
    funding sources for companies, 15*f*
    income taxes, 271
    public funding
        business accelerators and incubators,
          278–280
        government loans and loan guarantees,
          272–274
        public pension funds and SWFs, 280–282
        as venture capitalist, 274–278

Equity crowdfunding. *See also* Crowd
    investing
    market volume, 257*t*
European VC funds, 276*f*
Evidence-based practice, 133

F

Facebook, advertising revenues for, 98*t*
Fee-based revenue, 99
Financial market development, 268–269
Financial technology (fintech), 163, 258–259
    credit constraints, 166–170
    entrepreneurship, 163–166
    marketplace lending, 173–181
    microcredit, 170–172
    role of banks, 166–170
    venture capital investments, 173*f*
Foreign direct investment (FDI), 47
Freemium revenue model, 108

G

Gaming business, 108
GEM motivational index, 6–7
    entrepreneurial activity *vs.* level of
        prosperity, 7*f*
General partner (GP), 187–188, 264
Global competitiveness report (GCR), 199–200
Global entrepreneurship monitor (GEM), 202
Global Financial Crisis of 2008–2009, 1
Global innovation index (GII), 5, 15–17,
        33–45, 34*f*, 70, 77, 90, 120, 204
    annual ranking of countries, 121
    conceptual framework, 51–57
    GDP per capita, 43*f*
    innovation
        in emerging countries, characteristics of,
          45–47
        and entrepreneurship, 31
        measurement of, 32–33
        policies to developing countries, 47–50
    movement in top 10, 36*f*
    policymakers, 32
Global VC investing, 199*f*
Global venturing, 223*f*
Goods and Services Tax (GST), 129
Google, advertising revenues for, 98*t*
Government-backed guarantee covering
    loans, 274
Government intervention
    active VC market, 267–272
    coinvest facility, 275*f*
    entrepreneurial finance, 264, 282–283

entrepreneurship, public funding of
  business accelerators and incubators,
    278–280
  government loans and loan guarantees,
    272–274
  public pension funds and SWFs, 280–282
  as venture capitalist, 274–278
  market failures, 265–267
  public fund-of-funds structure, 275*f*
Government loans, 272–274
Government-owned VC funds (GOVCs),
  274–275, 284*t*
Government-sponsored venture capital funds
  (GSVCs), 276–277, 284*t*
Government venture capital (GVC), 278
Gross capital formation, 124
Gross domestic expenditure on R&D (GERD),
  55, 77–78, 119
Gross domestic product (GDP), 1, 118, 164,
  188–189
  growth in China, 69–70

H

High net worth individuals (HNWI), 241
High-quality innovation, 39
High-tech start-ups, 267
Human capital and research pillar, 59*t*

I

Income group, 41*f*
  top performers by, 41–42
Incubators, 227–228, 250
  government-sponsored business, 278–280
Independent venture capital (IVC), 23,
  185–186, 219, 225, 278
Indian Unicorns, 212*t*
India's innovation performance
  GII findings and pillars, 119–120
  global innovation index 2015, 117–118
  policy landscape, and research and
    development growth, 118–119
  strengths and weaknesses
    access to higher education, 127
    broadband, 122–123
    gross capital formation, 124
    information technology, 122–123
    IPR, 125–127
    market capitalization, 124
    mobile networks, 122–123
    publication citations, 121
    SMEs, 124–125
    top Indian universities, 121

Industrial Policy Resolution of 1956, 118
Industrial Policy Statement of 1977, 118
Information and communication technologies
  (ICTs), 49–50, 54, 127
Information literacy, for higher education,
  134–135
Information technology (IT), 122–123, 193,
  270–271
  yearly revenue growth, 123*f*
Infrastructure pillar, 60*t*
Initial public offering (IPO), 12, 22, 171, 186,
  223, 269–270
  VC-backed companies, 270
Innovation, 5–7
  ecosystem, 90
  efficiency ratio, 33, 42–43, 52
  in emerging countries, characteristics of,
    45–47
  and entrepreneurship, 31, 118
  input subindex, 33, 52
    business sophistication, 55–56
    creative outputs, 57
    human capital and research, 53–54
    infrastructure, 54
    institutions, 52–53
    knowledge and technology outputs,
      56–57
    market sophistication, 54–55
  leaders, 38*f*
  measurement of, 32–33
  metrics for quality, 40*f*
  output subindex, 33, 41–42, 52, 56–57
  policies to developing countries, 47–50
Innovation achievers, 37, 37*f*, 42–45
  in 2017, 37
Institutions pillar, 58*t*
Intel capital, 234–235*f*
Intellectual property (IP) policies, 48
Intellectual property rights (IPR), 125–129
Internal rate of return (IRR), 224
Internationalization
  M&A investment, 89–90, 91*t*
  patent applications, 89
  WeChat, 89
Internet-based consumer lending, 176–177
Internet-based crowdfunding transactions,
  253–254
Internet Plus action plan, 92–93
Internet-related investments, 194
Internet-related services, 202–209, 207*f*
  VC investing per Internet user, 208*f*
Investment subpillar, 55
IT-enabled services (ITeS), 127

K

Kansas Public Employees Retirement System (KPERS), 281
Knowledge and technology outputs pillar, 64t
Korea's K-Startup Grand Challenge program, 279

L

Limited partners (LP), 187–188, 224, 265
Literacy Competency Standards for Nursing (ILCSN)
  defined, 133
  search strategies, 133
Loan guarantees, 272–274
Loan-to-GDP ratios, 167f

M

Market-based business lending volume, 180
Market-based/P2P lending, 180–181
Market capitalization, 124
Marketplace lending
  crowdfunding, 175
  digital finance, 173
  mobile and digital technologies, 174
Market size, 221–223
Market sophistication pillar, 61t
Master's education, in nursing, 138
M-commerce, 211
Messaging services, 94–95
Microcredit, 170–172
Microfinance institutions (MFIs), 162–163, 170–171
Micro-, small-, and medium-sized enterprises (MSMEs), 166, 168–169
Micro & Small Enterprises Cluster Development Programme (MSE-CDP), 124–125
Mobile networks, 122–123
Mobile phones, 83–84
M-Pesa, 174–175, 211
M-Shwari, 174
Multinational enterprises (MNEs), 49–50

N

National angel markets, 247
National innovation policies, 32, 47
National Manufacturing Competitiveness Programme (NMCP), 125
National Stock Exchange (NSE), 124
National Venture Capital Association, 219
Nondisclosure agreement (NDA), 254
Non-R&D innovative expenditure, 33, 51

Non-U.S. CVC investments, 222f
Nursing education and practice, 133
  baccalaureate education for professional, 137
  doctoral education for advanced, 138
  master's education, 138
  QSEN prelicensure, 137
  research-focused doctoral program, 138–139
  searching skills, 137
  teaching tips, 139–142

O

Online business lending, 177
Online-to-offline (O2O) services, 96
Organization for Economic Cooperation and Development (OECD), 5, 32
Overall GII score, 33, 52
Overseas Private Investment Corporation (OPIC), 264

P

Pacific Century Cyberworks Ltd. (PCCW), 83
Patent laws, 265–266
Peer-to-peer (P2P) business, 163, 176, 253, 258
Pengyou, 95
PICOT framework, 133
Policymakers, 46, 49
Political environment subpillar, 53
Private VC, 277
Professional nursing practice, 137
Project creators, 180
Public funding, 272–282
Public pension funds, 280–282
Purchasing power parity (PPP), 1
  GDP per capita, 42–43
  per-capita income, 1, 2f

Q

QQ messenger, 95
Quality and Safety Education for Nurses (QSEN), 137
Qzone, 95

R

Regression discontinuity design (RDD), 247–248
Regulatory environment subpillar, 53
Research and development (R&D), 5, 69–70, 73, 74–75f, 118–119, 185–186, 195, 219–220, 265
  China, cultivation of, 77

corporate venturing, 226–227
technological product innovation, 32
Research-focused doctoral program, in
    nursing, 138–139

S

Science and technology innovation (STI)
    policy, 48
Science and technology (S&T) policies
    deepening reform phase (1996–2006), 72
    distribution of, 74f
    experimental phase (1978–85), 70–71
    latest reforms, 79–80
    long-term plan and policy optimization
        (2006–14), 72–73
    outcomes and analysis
        cultivation of R&D workforce, 77
        innovation results, 74–76
        R&D investment, 73
        science education, 76
    systemic reform phase (1985–95), 71–72
Science education, 76, 77f
Seed Accelerator Rankings Project, 251
Seed Enterprise Investment Scheme (SEIS),
    271
Self-made entrepreneurs, 10
SKS Microfinance, Ltd., 171–172
Small- and medium-sized enterprises (SMEs),
    123–125, 167f, 168
Small Business Innovation Research (SBIR),
    274
Social networks, 94–95
Sovereign wealth funds (SWFs), 185–186,
    265, 280–282
    in emerging economies, 287t
Start-Up Chile sponsors, 280
Start-ups, 274
Supporting businesses, Tencent
    entertainment platforms, 97
    O2O services, 96
    payment platforms, 96–97
    search engine and email, 96
    software and apps, 96

T

Technological progress, 3–5
Technology Policy Statement of 1983, 118
Tencent
    advertising revenues for, 98t
    Alibaba against Baidu, 106
    Baidu against Alibaba, 105–106
    challenges, 106–109

China's innovation ecosystem, 90–93
Chinese market and possibilities, 102–104
connected universe model, 93–95, 93f
factors contributing to success, 100–102
founders, 101t
future aspects, 109
internationalization, 88–90
leadership (nonfounders), 103t
milestones, 82–88
protected environment, 104–106
revenue sources, breakdown of, 99f
stock performance, 81–82
supporting businesses, 95–97
unique business model, 93–95, 93f, 97–100
venture capital investments from 1999 to
    2017, 110t
Tencent Holdings, Ltd., 81
Theory of Economic Development, 163
Traffic-based revenue, 99
Transaction-based revenue, 99
Transformational entrepreneurs, 5–7, 10–13, 203

U

Underperformers, 42–45
Unicorns, VC-backed, 205t
Unique business model, 93–95, 93f, 97–100
    Tencent's "connection" strategy, 97t, 109
United Nations International Development
    Organization (UNIDO), 124–125
United States (U.S.)
    CVC investments, 221f
    markets, 108–109
    Metropolitan Statistical Areas (MSAs), 252
    public pension funds, 281
    Tech Coast Angels, 248
    VC investments, 192f
        angel investments vs., 244–245f

V

VC-backed companies, 196
VC-backed entrepreneurs, 11
Venture capital (VC), 2–3, 264
    angel investors, 241
    China's innovation ecosystem, 92
    e-commerce, 202–209
    in emerging economies, 289t
    emerging markets by major countries, 200f
    entrepreneurial finance, 186, 239
    existing and emerging unicorns, 209
    fostering innovation, 193–197
    general partner, 187–188
    government as, 274–278

Venture capital (VC) *(Continued)*
   government interventions, 26
   income taxes, 271
   internet roles, 202–209
   investments, 84–88, 85–87*f*
   investment stages, 188
   labor market regulations, 270
   limited partners, 187–188
   macroeconomic stability, 267–268
   minority shareholders, protection of, 269*f*
   new business ownership rate *vs.* VC
      investments/GDP, 203*f*
   next frontier, 209–211
   public equity investments, 273*f*
   seed financing, 189
   syndication process, 190
   U.S. VC investments, 192*f*

W

WeChat (Weixin), 89, 93, 100, 107
World Bank Employment Surveys,
   202–203
World Bank Enterprise Surveys, 162, 168

Printed in the United States
By Bookmasters